Cancún, Cozumel, Yucatán Peninsula

The complete guide, thoroughly up-to-date

Packed with details that will make your trip

The must-see sights, off and on the beaten path

What to see, what to skip

Mix-and-match vacation itineraries

City strolls, countryside adventures

Smart lodging and dining options

Essential local do's and taboos

Transportation tips, distances and directions

Key contacts, savvy travel tips

When to go, what to pack

Clear, accurate, easy-to-use maps

Background essay

Fodor's Travel Publications, Inc.
New York • Toronto • London • Sydney • Auckland
www.fodors.com/

Fodor's Cancún, Cozumel, Yucatán Peninsula

EDITOR: Deborah Field Washburn

Editorial Contributors: Patricia Alisau, Robert Andrews, David Brown, Richard Harris, Christina Knight, Wendy Luft, Dan Millington, Heidi Sarna, Helayne Schiff, M. T. Schwartzman (editor), Dinah A. Spritzer
Editorial Production: Linda K. Schmidt
Maps: David Lindroth, *cartographer*; Steven K. Amsterdam, *map editor*
Design: Fabrizio La Rocca, *creative director*; Guido Caroti, *associate art director*; Jolie Novak, *photo editor*
Cover Photograph: Joan Iaconetti
Production/Manufacturing: Rebecca Zeiler

Copyright

ISBN 0–679–03453–6

Special Sales

Fodor's Travel Publications are available at special discounts for bulk purchases for sales promotions or premiums. Special editions, including personalized covers, excerpts of existing guides, and corporate imprints, can be created in large quantities for special needs. For more information, contact your local bookseller or write to Special Markets, Fodor's Travel Publications, 201 East 50th Street, New York, NY 10022. Inquiries from Canada should be directed to your local Canadian bookseller or sent to Random House of Canada, Ltd., Marketing Department, 1265 Aerowood Drive, Mississauga, Ontario L4W 1B9. Inquiries from the United Kingdom should be sent to Fodor's Travel Publications, 20 Vauxhall Bridge Road, London SW1V 2SA, England.

PRINTED IN THE UNITED STATES OF AMERICA

10 9 8 7 6 5 4 3 2 1

CONTENTS

On the Road with Fodor's   v

About Our Writers *v*
New This Year *v*
How to Use This Book *v*
Please Write to Us *vi*

The Gold Guide   xii

1 Destination: Cancún, Cozumel, Yucatán Peninsula   1

A Place Apart *2*
New and Noteworthy *3*
What's Where *4*
Pleasures and Pastimes *4*
Fodor's Choice *6*
Festivals and Seasonal Events *9*

2 Cancún   11

3 Isla Mujeres   41

4 Cozumel   57

5 Mexico's Caribbean Coast   85

6 Campeche   123

7 Mérida and the State of Yucatán   149

8 Portraits of the Yucatán Peninsula   190

Chronology of the Maya and History of Yucatán *191*
"The Three Faces of the Yucatán," by Richard Harris *196*

Spanish Vocabulary   202

Index   208

Maps

Yucatán Peninsula *viii–ix*
Mexico *x–xi*
Cancún *16*
Cancún Hotel Zone Dining and Lodging *19*
Downtown Cancún Dining and Lodging *23*
Isla Mujeres *45*
Downtown Isla Mujeres Dining and Lodging *48*
Cozumel *62*
Cozumel Hotel Zones Dining and Lodging *67*
San Miguel Dining and Lodging *68*
Mexico's Caribbean Coast *90*
Tulum *106*
State of Campeche *128–129*
Campeche City *130*
State of Yucatán *155*
Mérida *156*
Chichén Itzá *171*
Uxmal *177*

ON THE ROAD WITH FODOR'S

WE'RE ALWAYS THRILLED to get letters from readers, especially one like this:

It took us an hour to decide what book to buy and we now know we picked the best one. Your book was wonderful, easy to follow, very accurate, and good on pointing out eating places, informal as well as formal. When we saw other people using your book, we would look at each other and smile.

Our editors and writers are deeply committed to making every Fodor's guide "the best one"—not only accurate but always charming, brimming with sound recommendations and solid ideas, right on the mark in describing restaurants and hotels, and full of fascinating facts that make you view what you've traveled to see in a rich new light.

About Our Writers

Our success in achieving our goals—and in helping to make your trip the best of all possible vacations—is a credit to the hard work of our extraordinary writers.

Patricia Alisau, who updated the Carribean Coast, Campeche, and Mérida and the State of Yucatán chapters, is a psychologist-turned-journalist and archaeology buff. She was so drawn to the surrealism of Mexico City—"Where in the U.S. can you find pyramids?" she asks—that she moved to the capital; what began as a one-week vacation became a 20-year sojourn. She was restaurant-and-nightclub columnist for the *News,* Mexico's English-language daily, worked as a photo stringer for the Associated Press during the Nicaragua Revolution, and has written for Mexico's *Vogue* magazine.

Richard Harris, who wrote the "Three Faces of Yucatán" essay in our Portraits section, left a law practice in 1981 to study Pre-Columbian Indian ruins. He is the author of two books on the archaeology and ecology of the Yucatán Peninsula. As president of PEN New Mexico, the only English-Spanish bilingual chapter of the writers'-rights group PEN International, he spends much of his time in Mexico as an advocate for imprisoned or threatened Latin American writers.

A freelance writer and photographer based in Laguna Beach, California, **Dan Millington** has traveled extensively in Mexico and is familiar with many regions of the country. This past year he updated the chapters on Cancún, Isla Mujeres, and Cozumel.

We'd also like to thank Burson-Marsteller and Aeromexico for their help with travel arrangements.

This book was originally written by freelance writer and translator **Erica Meltzer,** who first visited the Yucatán in 1967. It was then that she learned the truth of the old Mexican proverb "He who has been touched by the dust of Mexico will never again find peace in any land." She moved to Mexico City for three years, and from her current base in New York gets back to the country as frequently as possible.

New This Year

This year, Fodor's joins Rand McNally, the world's largest commercial mapmaker, to bring you a detailed color map of Cancún, Cozumel, and the Yucatán Peninsula. Just detach it along the perforation and drop it in your tote bag.

On the Web, check out Fodor's site (http://www.fodors.com/) for information on major destinations around the world and travel-savvy interactive features. The Web site also lists the 80-plus stations nationwide that carry the Fodor's Travel Show, a live call-in program that airs every weekend. Tune in to hear guests discuss their wonderful adventures—or call in to get answers for your most pressing travel questions.

How to Use This Book

Organization

Up front is the **Gold Guide,** an easy-to-use section divided alphabetically by topic. Under each listing you'll find tips and information that will help you accomplish what you need to in Cancún, Cozumel, and the Yucatán Peninsula. You'll also find addresses and telephone numbers of organizations and companies that offer destination-related services and detailed information and publications.

The first chapter in the guide, Destination: Cancún, Cozumel, Yucatan Peninsula, helps get you in the mood for your trip. New and Noteworthy cues you in on trends and happenings, What's Where gets you oriented, Pleasures and Pastimes describes the activities and sights that make Cancún, Cozumel, and the Yucatán Peninsula really unique, Fodor's Choice showcases our top picks, and Festivals and Seasonal Events alerts you to special events you'll want to seek out.

Chapters in Fodor's *Cancún, Cozumel, Yucatán Peninsula '98* are arranged geographically, moving clockwise in a rough circle from the peninsula's prime destination, Cancún (Chapter 2). Nearby Isla Mujeres, a popular day trip from Cancún, is covered in Chapter 3, and Cozumel, an easy boat ride from both, is the focus of Chapter 4. We travel down the Caribbean coast in Chapter 5, then hop over to the gulf coast and the state of Campeche in Chapter 6. Directly north, Mérida and the state of Yucatán comprise Chapter 7.

Each island chapter and major city section begins with an Exploring section, followed by a recommended walking or driving tour and a list of sights in alphabetical order. Each regional chapter is divided by geographical area. Within each area, towns are covered in logical geographical order, and within town sections all restaurants and lodgings are grouped together. The A to Z section that ends all chapters covers getting there and getting around. It also provides helpful contacts and resources.

At the end of the book you'll find Portraits, including a chronology of the Maya and the history of Yucatán and "The Three Faces of the Yucatán," a lively, in-depth essay on the region by Richard Harris. Finally, there's also a **Spanish vocabulary** to help you learn a few basics.

Icons and Symbols

★ Our special recommendations
✕ Restaurant
🏠 Lodging establishment
✕🏠 Lodging establishment whose restaurant warrants a special trip
🐤 Good for kids (rubber duckie)

☞ Sends you to another section of the guide for more information
✉ Address
☎ Telephone number
🕐 Opening and closing times
💲 Admission prices (those we give apply to adults; substantially reduced fees are almost always available for children, students, and senior citizens)

Numbers in white and black circles that appear on the maps, in the margins, and within the tours correspond to one another.

The restaurants and lodgings we list are the cream of the crop in each price range. Price charts appear in the Dining and Lodging sections of island chapters, and in the Pleasures and Pastimes section that follows each regional chapter introduction.

Hotel Facilities

We always list the facilities that are available—but we don't specify whether they cost extra: When pricing accommodations, always ask what's included. In addition, assume that all rooms have private baths unless otherwise noted.

Assume that hotels operate on the **European Plan** (EP, with no meals) unless we note that they use the **Continental Plan** (CP, with a Continental breakfast daily), **Modified American Plan** (MAP, with breakfast and dinner daily), or are **all-inclusive** (all meals and most activities).

Restaurant Reservations and Dress Codes

Reservations are always a good idea; we note only when they're essential or when they are not accepted. Book as far ahead as you can, and reconfirm when you get to town. Unless otherwise noted, the restaurants listed are open daily for lunch and dinner. We mention dress only when men are required to wear a jacket or a jacket and tie. Look for an overview of local habits in the Gold Guide and in the Pleasures and Pastimes section that follows each chapter introduction.

Credit Cards

The following abbreviations are used: **AE,** American Express; **DC,** Diners Club; **MC,** MasterCard; and **V,** Visa.

Please Write to Us

You can use this book in the confidence that all prices and opening times are based on information supplied to us at press time; Fodor's cannot accept responsibility for any errors. Time inevitably brings changes, so always confirm information when it matters—especially if you're making a detour to visit a specific place. In addition, when making reservations be sure to mention if you have a disability or are traveling with children, if you prefer a private bath or a certain type of bed, or if you have specific dietary needs or other concerns.

Were the restaurants we recommended as described? Did our hotel picks exceed your expectations? Did you find a museum we recommended a waste of time? If you have complaints, we'll look into them and revise our entries when the facts warrant it. If you've discovered a special place that we haven't included, we'll pass the information along to our correspondents and have them check it out. So send us your feedback, positive *and* negative: email us at editors@fodors.com (specifying the name of the book on the subject line) or write the *Cancún, Cozumel, Yucatán Peninsula* editor at Fodor's, 201 East 50th Street, New York, New York 10022. Have a wonderful trip!

Karen Cure
Editorial Director

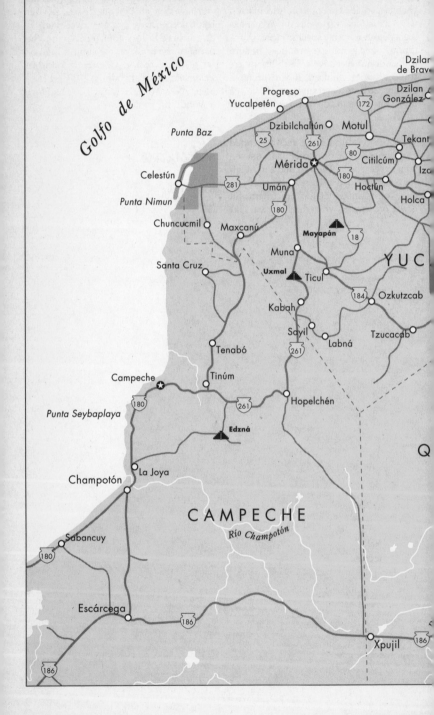

Golfo de México

Dzilam
de Brav

Dzilan
Progreso
Yucalpetén
González

Punta Baz
Dzibilchaltún
Motul

Tekant
172

25
261
Mérida
80
Citilcúm
Iza

Celestún
180
Hoctún

Umán
Holca
Punta Nimun

180
Chuncucmil
Maxcanú
Mayapán
18
YUC

Muna

Santa Cruz
Uxmal
Ticul

Kabah
184
Ozkutzcab

Sayil
Tzucacab
Labná

Tenabó

261
Tinúm

Campeche
Hopelchén

180
261

Punta Seybaplaya
Edzná

La Joya
Champotón

CAMPECHE
Río Champotón

Sabancuy
180

Escárcega
186

186
Xpujil

186

Q

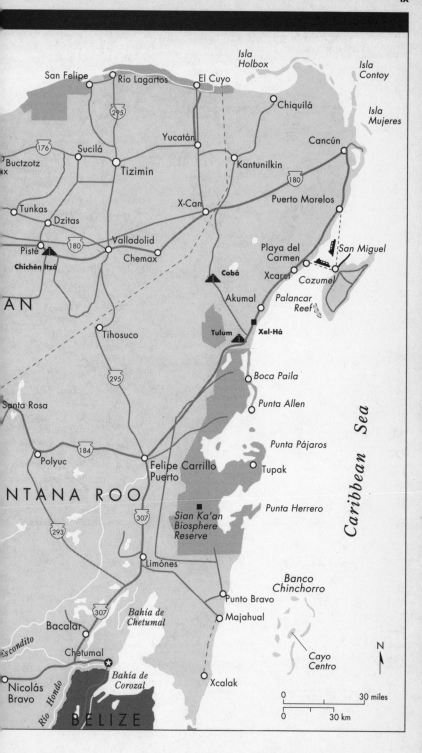

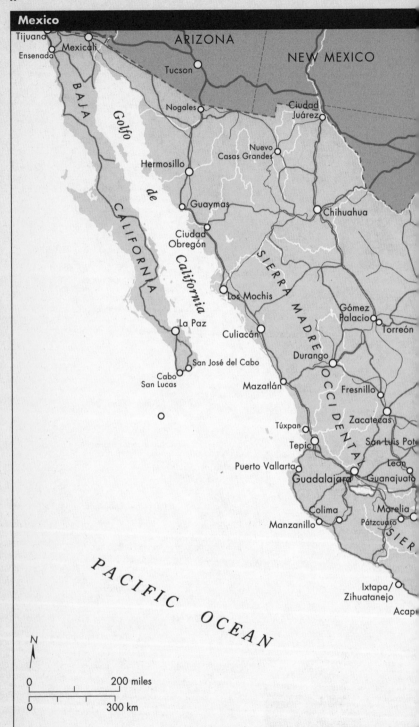

Mexico

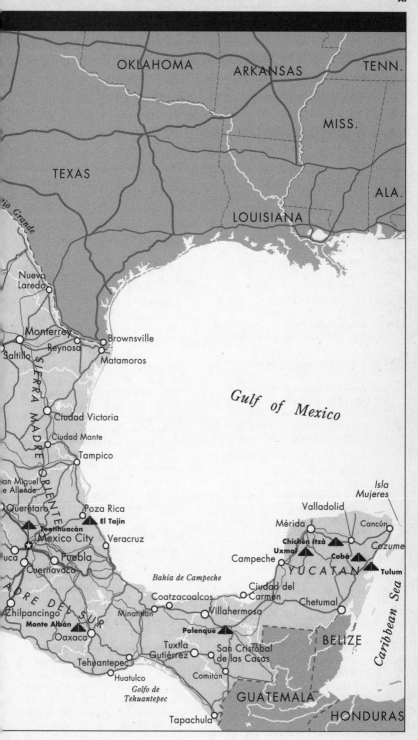

SMART TRAVEL TIPS A TO Z

*Basic Information on Traveling in Cancún,
Savvy Tips to Make Your Trip a Breeze,
and Companies and Organizations to Contact*

A

AIR TRAVEL

MAJOR AIRLINE OR LOW-COST CARRIER?

Most people choose a flight based on price. Yet there are other issues to consider. Major airlines offer the greatest number of departures; smaller or regional carriers—including low-cost and no-frill airlines—usually have a more limited number of flights daily. Major airlines have frequent-flyer partners, which allows you to credit mileage earned on one airline to your account with another. Low-cost airlines offer a definite price advantage and fewer restrictions such as advance-purchase requirements. Safety-wise, low-cost carriers as a group have a good history, but **check the safety record before booking** any low-cost carrier; call the Federal Aviation Administration's Consumer Hotline (☞ Airline Complaints, *below*).

➤ MAJOR AIRLINES: **Aeromexico** (☎ 800/237–6639) to Cancún, Cozumel. **American** (☎ 800/433–7300) to Cancun. **Continental** (☎ 800/231–0856) to Cancún, Cozumel. **Delta** (☎ 800/241–4141) to Cancún. **Mexicana** (☎ 800/531–7921) to Cancún. **Lacsa** (☎ 800/225–2272) to Cancún. **US Airways** ☎ 800/426–4322) to Cancún.

➤ REGIONAL AIRLINES: For air packages from other local charter operators, *see* Tour Operators, *below*.

➤ FROM THE U.K.: **American Airlines** (☎ 0345/789–789) via Miami and Dallas. **British Airways** (☎ 0345/222–111) daily from Gatwick or Heathrow via Mexico City. **Continental** (☎ 0800/776–464) from Gatwick via Newark. **Northwest** (☎ 0990/561–000) via Detroit and Tampa. **TWA** (☎ 0800/222–222) via St. Louis.

➤ WITHIN THE YUCATÁN: **Aerocaribe** (reserve through Mexicana, ☎ 800/531–7921) services Cancún, Cozumel, Mérida, Chichén Itzá, Villahermosa, Palenque, Ciudad del Carmen, and Playa del Carmen. **Aviacsa** (☎ 5/559–1955, in Mexico City, or through your travel agent) services Cancún, Chetumal and Mérida.

GET THE LOWEST FARE

The least-expensive airfares to Cancún are priced for round-trip travel. Major airlines usually require that you **book far in advance and stay at least seven days** and no more than 30 to get the lowest fares. **Ask about "ultrasaver" fares,** which are the cheapest; they must be booked 90 days in advance and are nonrefundable. A little more expensive are "supersaver" fares, which require only a 30-day advance purchase. Remember that penalties for refunds or scheduling changes are stiffer for international tickets, usually about $150. International flights are also sensitive to the season: **plan to fly in the off season** for the cheapest fares. If your destination or home city has more than one gateway, **compare prices to and from different airports.** Also price flights scheduled for off-peak hours, which may be significantly less expensive.

To save money on flights from the United Kingdom and back, **look into an APEX or Super-PEX ticket.** Both sorts should be booked in advance and have certain restrictions, though they can sometimes be purchased right at the airport.

DON'T STOP UNLESS YOU MUST

When you book, **look for nonstop flights** and **remember that "direct" flights stop at least once.** International flights on a country's flag carrier are almost always nonstop; U.S. airlines often fly direct. Try to **avoid connecting flights,** which require a change of plane. Two airlines may jointly operate a connecting flight, so ask if your airline operates every segment—you may find that your preferred carrier flies you only part of the way.

USE AN AGENT

Travel agents, especially those who specialize in finding the lowest fares (☞ Discounts & Deals, *below*), can be especially helpful when booking a plane ticket. When you're quoted a price, **ask your agent if the price is likely to get any lower.** Good agents know the seasonal fluctuations of airfares and can usually anticipate a sale or fare war. However, waiting can be risky: The fare could go *up* as seats become scarce, and you may wait so long that your preferred flight sells out. A wait-and-see strategy works best if your plans are flexible, but if you must arrive and depart on certain dates, don't delay.

CHECK WITH CONSOLIDATORS

Consolidators buy tickets for scheduled flights at reduced rates from the airlines then sell them at prices that beat the best fare available directly from the airlines, usually without advance restrictions. Sometimes you can even get your money back if you need to return the ticket. Carefully **read the fine print** detailing penalties for changes and cancellations, and **confirm your consolidator reservation with the airline.**

➤ CONSOLIDATORS: **United States Air Consolidators Association** (✉ 925 L St., Suite 220, Sacramento, CA 95814, ☎ 916/441–4166, ℻ 916/441–3520).

AVOID GETTING BUMPED

Airlines routinely overbook planes, knowing that not everyone with a ticket will show up, but sometimes everyone does. When that happens, airlines ask for volunteers to give up their seats. In return these volunteers usually get a certificate for a free flight and are rebooked on the next flight out. If there are not enough volunteers the airline must choose who will be denied boarding. The first to get bumped are passengers who checked in late and those flying on discounted tickets, so **get to the gate and check in as early as possible,** especially during peak periods.

Always **bring a photo ID to the airport.** You may be asked to show it before you are allowed to check in.

ENJOY THE FLIGHT

For better service, **fly smaller or regional carriers,** which often have higher passenger-satisfaction ratings. Sometimes you'll find leather seats, more legroom, and better food.

For more legroom, **request an emergency-aisle seat;** don't however, sit in the row in front of the emergency aisle or in front of a bulkhead, where seats may not recline.

If you don't like airline food, **ask for special meals when booking.** These can be vegetarian, low-cholesterol, or kosher, for example.

Some carriers have prohibited smoking throughout their systems; others allow smoking only on certain routes or even certain departures from that route, so **contact your carrier regarding its smoking policy.**

COMPLAIN IF NECESSARY

If your baggage goes astray or your flight goes awry, **complain right away.** Most carriers require that you file a claim immediately.

➤ AIRLINE COMPLAINTS: **U.S. Department of Transportation Aviation Consumer Protection Division** (✉ C-75, Washington, DC 20590, ☎ 202/366–2220). **Federal Aviation Administration (FAA) Consumer Hotline** (☎ 800/322–7873).

AIRPORTS & TRANSFERS

The major gateways to the Cancún area are **Cancún Airport** and **Cozumel Airport.** Mérida, Campeche, Chetumal, and Playa del Carmen have smaller airports served primarily by domestic carriers. Some ruins have airstrips that can handle small planes.

Cancún is 3½ hours from New York and from Chicago, 4½ hours from Los Angeles. Flights to Cozumel and Mérida are comparable in length.

➤ AIRPORT INFORMATION: **Cancún Airport** (☎ 011–52–981/42239). **Cozumel Airport** (☎ 011–52–987/20485).

B

BUS TRAVEL

Bus travel in Yucatán, as throughout Mexico, is inexpensive by U.S. standards, with rates averaging about $3 per hour. Buses run the gamut from comfortable air-conditioned coaches with bathrooms, televisions, and hostess service (*especial,* deluxe, and first-class) to dilapidated "vintage" buses (second- and third-class) on which pigs and chickens travel and stops are made in the middle of nowhere. While a lower-class bus ride can be interesting if you are not in a hurry and want to see the sights and experience the local culture, these fares are only about 10% to 20% lower than those in the premium categories. Therefore, travelers planning a long-distance haul are well advised to **buy the first-class or *especial* tickets** when traveling by bus within Mexico; unlike tickets for the other classes, these can be reserved in advance. ADO (Autobuses del Oriente) is the principal first-class bus company serving the Yucatán peninsula.

The Mexican bus network is extensive, far more so than the railroads. Buses go where trains do not, service is more frequent, tickets can be purchased on the spot (except during holidays and on long weekends, when advance purchase is crucial), and first-class buses are faster and much more comfortable than trains. **Bring something to eat on all overnight bus rides** in case you don't like the restaurant where the bus stops, and **bring toilet tissue,** as rest rooms vary in cleanliness. Smoking is prohibited on a growing number of Mexican buses, though the rule is occasionally ignored.

BUSINESS HOURS

Most businesses are open weekdays 9–2 and 4–7. Banks are open weekdays 9–5. Some banks open on Saturday mornings.

C

CAMERAS, CAMCORDERS, & COMPUTERS

Always **keep your film, tape, or computer disks out of the sun.** Carry an extra supply of batteries, and **be prepared to turn on your camera, camcorder, or laptop** to prove to security personnel that the device is real. Always **ask for hand inspection of film,** which becomes clouded after successive exposure to airport x-ray machines, and **keep videotapes and computer disks away from metal detectors.**

➤ PHOTO HELP: Kodak Information Center (☎ 800/242–2424). *Kodak Guide to Shooting Great Travel Pictures,* available in bookstores or from Fodor's Travel Publications (☎ 800/533–6478; $16.50 plus $4 shipping).

CUSTOMS

Before departing, **register your foreign-made camera or laptop with U.S. Customs** (☞ Customs & Duties, *below*). If your equipment is U.S.-made, call the consulate of the country you'll be visiting to find out whether the device should be registered with local customs upon arrival.

CAR RENTAL

Rates in Cancun begin at $35 a day and $189 a week for an economy car with air conditioning, a manual transmission, and unlimited mileage. This does not include tax on car rentals, which is 10%.

➤ MAJOR AGENCIES: Alamo (☎ 800/327–9633, 800/879–2847 in Canada). Budget (☎ 800/527–0700, 0800/181181 in the U.K.). Hertz (☎ 800/654–3001, 800/263–0600 in Canada, 0345/555888 in the U.K.). National InterRent (☎ 800/227–3876; 0345/222525 in the U.K., where it is known as Europcar InterRent).

CUT COSTS

To get the best deal, **book through a travel agent who is willing to shop around.**

Also **ask your travel agent about a company's customer-service record.** How has it responded to late plane arrivals and vehicle mishaps? Are there often lines at the rental counter, and, if you're traveling during a holiday period, does a confirmed reservation guarantee you a car?

Be sure to **look into wholesalers,** companies that do not own fleets but rent in bulk from those that do and often offer better rates than traditional car-rental operations. Prices are best during off-peak periods. Rentals booked through wholesalers must be paid for before you leave the United States.

➤ RENTAL WHOLESALERS: Auto Europe (☎ 207/828–2525 or 800/223–

5555). The **Kemwel Group** (☎ 914/835–5555 or 800/678–0678).

NEED INSURANCE?

Regardless of any coverage afforded you by your credit-card company, **you must have Mexican auto-liability insurance.** This is usually provided by car-rental agencies and included in the cost of the car. Be sure that you have been provided with proof of such insurance: If you drive without it, you are not only liable for damages, but are breaking the law. For about $14 a day, rental companies sell insurance, known as a collision damage waiver (CDW), that eliminates your liability for damage to the car; it's always optional and should never be automatically added to your bill. Before you rent, **see what coverage you already have** under the terms of your personal auto-insurance policy and credit cards.

BEWARE SURCHARGES

Before you pick up a car in one city and leave it in another, **ask about drop-off charges or one-way service fees,** which can be substantial. Note, too, that some rental agencies charge extra if you return the car before the time specified on your contract. To avoid a hefty refueling fee, **fill the tank just before you turn in the car,** but be aware that gas stations near the rental outlet may overcharge.

MEET THE REQUIREMENTS

In Cancún your own driver's license is acceptable. An International Driver's Permit is a good idea; it's available from the American or Canadian automobile association, or, in the United Kingdom, from the Automobile Association or Royal Automobile Club.

CHILDREN IN CANCÚN

All children, including infants, must have proof of citizenship for travel to Mexico. Children traveling with a single parent must also have a notarized letter from the other parent stating that the child has his or her permission to leave the home country. In addition, parents must fill out a tourist card for each child over 10 years of age traveling with them.

The advisability of traveling with children in the Yucatán will depend on the age and maturity of your child. Infants may be bothered by the heat, and finding pure water or fresh milk in remote areas may be a problem. Because children are especially prone to diarrhea, special care must be taken with regard to food. If they enjoy travel in general, children will do well in the Yucatán, where, as in the rest of Mexico, children are welcome almost everywhere.

Be sure to plan ahead and **involve your youngsters** as you outline your trip. When packing, include things to keep them busy en route. On sightseeing days try to schedule activities of special interest to your children. If you are renting a car don't forget to **arrange for a car seat** when you reserve.

HOTELS

Most hotels in Cancún allow children under a certain age to stay in their parents' room at no extra charge, but others charge them as extra adults; be sure to **ask about the cutoff age for children's discounts.**

➤ BEST CHOICES: Several hotel chains provide services that make it easier to travel with children. The **Fiesta Americana Coral Beach Cancún** and **Condesa** (☎ 800/343–7821) offer free activities for children and teenagers in high season. The **Cancún Sheraton Resort & Towers** (☎ 800/334–8484) provides connecting "family rooms" at regular rates. **Camino Real** (☎ 800/7–CAMINO) **Westin Regina** (☎ 800/228–3000) and the **Presidente Inter-Continental** (☎ 800/327-1200) offer children's "clubs" during school vacations.

FLYING

As a general rule, infants under two not occupying a seat fly at greatly reduced fares and occasionally for free. If your children are two or older **ask about children's airfares.**

In general the adult baggage allowance applies to children paying half or more of the adult fare. When booking, **ask about carry-on allowances for those traveling with infants.** In general, for babies charged 10% of the adult fare you are allowed one carry-on bag and a collapsible stroller, which may have to be checked; you may be limited to less if the flight is full.

According to the FAA it's a good idea to use safety seats aloft for children weighing less than 40 pounds. Airlines, however, can set their own policies: U.S. carriers allow FAA-approved models but usually require that you buy a ticket, even if your child would otherwise ride free, since the seats must be strapped into regular seats. Airline rules vary regarding their use, so it's important to **check your airline's policy about using safety seats during takeoff and landing.** Safety seats cannot obstruct any of the other passengers in the row, so get an appropriate seat assignment as early as possible.

When making your reservation, **request children's meals or a free-standing bassinet** if you need them; the latter are available only to those seated at the bulkhead, where there's enough legroom. Remember, however, that bulkhead seats may not have their own overhead bins, and there's no storage space in front of you—a major inconvenience.

GROUP TRAVEL

If you're planning to take your kids on a tour, **look for companies that specialize in family travel.**

➤ FAMILY-FRIENDLY TOUR OPERATORS: **Rascals in Paradise** (✉ 650 5th St., Suite 505, San Francisco, CA 94107, ☎ 415/978–9800 or 800/872–7225).

Whenever possible, **pay with a major credit card** so you can cancel payment if there's a problem, provided that you can provide documentation. This is a good practice whether you're buying travel arrangements before your trip or shopping at your destination.

If you're doing business with a particular company for the first time, **contact your local Better Business Bureau and the attorney general's offices** in your state and the company's home state, as well. Have any complaints been filed?

Finally, if you're buying a package or tour, always **consider travel insurance** that includes default coverage (☞ Insurance, *below*).

➤ LOCAL BBBs: **Council of Better Business Bureaus** (✉ 4200 Wilson Blvd., Suite 800, Arlington, VA 22203, ☎ 703/276–0100, FAX 703/525–8277).

Cozumel and Playa del Carmen have become increasingly popular ports for Caribbean cruises. Cruise lines that depart from Miami include **Caribbean** (☎ 800/327–6700), **Dolphin** (☎ 800/222–1003), **Fantasy/Celebrity** (☎ 800/423–2100), **Majesty** (☎ 800/532–7788), and **Norwegian** (☎ 800/327–7030). Lines with Caribbean cruises stopping in the Yucatán from other Florida ports (principally Fort Lauderdale, Port Manatee, and Tampa) include **Cunard** (☎ 800/221–4770), **Norwegian** (☎ 800/327–7030), **Princess** (☎ 800/421–0522), **Regal** (☎ 800/270–SAIL), and **Royal** (☎ 800/227–4534). From New Orleans: **Commodore** (☎ 800/237–5361) and **Holland America** (☎ 800/426–0327); and from Galveston, TX: **Sun** (☎ 800/872–6400).

DISCOUNT CRUISES

Usually, the best deals on cruise bookings can be found by consulting a cruise-only travel agency. Contact the **National Association of Cruise Only Travel Agencies (NACOA)** (✉ 3191 Coral Way, Suite 622, Miami, FL 33145, ☎ 305/446–7732, FAX 305/446–9732) for a listing of such agencies in your area.

When shopping, **keep receipts** for all of your purchases. Upon reentering the country, **be ready to show customs officials what you've bought.** If you feel a duty is incorrect, appeal the assessment. If you object to the way your clearance was handled, get the inspector's badge number. In either case, first ask to see a supervisor, then write to the port director at the address listed on your receipt. Send a copy of the receipt and other appropriate documentation. If you still don't get satisfaction you can take your case to customs headquarters in Washington.

ENTERING CANCÚN

Entering Mexico, you may bring in (1) 400 cigarettes or 50 cigars or 250 grams of tobacco, (2) one photographic camera and one nonprofessional film or video camera and 12 rolls of film for each, and (3) gift items not exceeding a combined value of $300. You are not allowed to bring meat, vegetables, plants, fruit, or flowers into the country.

ENTERING THE U.S.

You may bring home $400 worth of foreign goods duty-free if you've been out of the country for at least 48 hours and haven't already used the $400 allowance or any part of it in the past 30 days.

Travelers 21 and older may bring back 1 liter of alcohol duty-free. In addition, regardless of your age, you are allowed 200 cigarettes and 100 non-Cuban cigars. Antiques, which the U.S. Customs Service defines as objects more than 100 years old, enter duty-free, as do original works of art done entirely by hand, including paintings, drawings, and sculptures.

You may also send packages home duty-free: up to $200 worth of goods for personal use, with a limit of one parcel per addressee per day (and no alcohol or tobacco products or perfume worth more than $5); label the package PERSONAL USE, and attach a list of its contents and their retail value. Do not label the package UNSOLICITED GIFT, or your duty-free exemption will drop to $100. Mailed items do not affect your duty-free allowance on your return.

➤ INFORMATION: **U.S. Customs Service** (Inquiries, ✉ Box 7407, Washington, DC 20044, ☎ 202/927–6724; complaints, ✉ Commissioner's Office, 1301 Constitution Ave. NW, Washington, DC 20229; registration of equipment, ✉ Resource Management, 1301 Constitution Ave. NW, Washington DC, 20229, ☎ 202/927–0540).

ENTERING CANADA

If you've been out of Canada for at least seven days you may bring in C$500 worth of goods duty-free. If you've been away for fewer than seven days but more than 48 hours, the duty-free allowance drops to C$200; if your trip lasts 24–48 hours, the allowance is C$50. You may not pool allowances with family members. Goods claimed under the C$500 exemption may follow you by mail; those claimed under the lesser exemptions must accompany you.

Alcohol and tobacco products may be included in the seven-day and 48-hour exemptions but not in the 24-hour exemption. If you meet the age requirements of the province or territory through which you reenter Canada you may bring in, duty-free, 1.14 liters (40 imperial ounces) of wine or liquor or 24 12-ounce cans or bottles of beer or ale. If you are 16 or older you may bring in, duty-free, 200 cigarettes and 50 cigars; these items must accompany you.

You may send an unlimited number of gifts worth up to C$60 each duty-free to Canada. Label the package UNSO-LICITED GIFT—VALUE UNDER $60. Alcohol and tobacco are excluded.

➤ INFORMATION: **Revenue Canada** (✉ 2265 St. Laurent Blvd. S, Ottawa, Ontario K1G 4K3, ☎ 613/993–0534, 800/461–9999 in Canada).

ENTERING THE U.K.

From countries outside the EU, including Mexico, you may import, duty-free, 200 cigarettes or 50 cigars; 1 liter of spirits or 2 liters of fortified or sparkling wine or liqueurs; 2 liters of still table wine; 60 milliliters of perfume; 250 milliliters of toilet water; plus £136 worth of other goods, including gifts and souvenirs.

➤ INFORMATION: **HM Customs and Excise** (✉ Dorset House, Stamford St., London SE1 9NG, ☎ 0171/202–4227).

D

DINING

Eating breakfast or having cocktails in other hotels is a good way of getting to know different properties. For lunch and dinner, however, in such areas as Cancún, it is generally best to **stay away from restaurants in the large chain hotels** because prices there tend to be exorbitant. (That said, some of the best restaurants may be located in such hotels; they are reviewed when that's the case.) Also, when buying fish from beachside and roadside palapas, **make sure the facilities are sanitary** so you don't get food poisoning. Be especially careful with shellfish and anything to which mayonnaise may have been added.

Restaurants in the Yucatán, including those in hotels, are for the most part very casual. The exceptions will be noted within reviews. Most restaurants are open daily for lunch and dinner during high season (Dec.–Apr.), but opening hours tend to be more erratic during the rest of the year. It's always a good idea to **phone ahead.**

ACCESS IN CANCÚN

For people with disabilities, traveling in the Yucatán can be both challenging and rewarding. Travelers with mobility impairments used to venturing out on their own in the United States should not be surprised if locals try to prevent them from doing things. This is mainly out of concern; most Mexican families take complete care of relatives who use wheelchairs, so the general public is not accustomed to interacting with them. Additionally, very few places in the Yucatán have handrails, let alone special facilities and means of access. Not even Cancún offers wheelchair-accessible transportation. Knowing how to ask for assistance is extremely important. If you are not fluent in Spanish, be sure to **take along a pocket dictionary.** Travelers with vision impairments who have no knowledge of Spanish will probably need a translator; people with hearing impairments who are comfortable using body language usually get along very well.

TIPS AND HINTS

When discussing accessibility with an operator or reservationist, **ask hard questions.** Are there any stairs, inside *or* out? Are there grab bars next to the toilet *and* in the shower/tub? How wide is the doorway to the room? To the bathroom? For the most extensive facilities meeting the latest legal specifications, **opt for newer accommodations in the larger hotel chains,** which are more likely to have been designed with access in mind. Older buildings or ships may offer more limited facilities. Be sure to **discuss your needs before booking.**

➤ COMPLAINTS: Disability Rights Section (✉ U.S. Department of Justice, Box 66738, Washington, DC 20035–6738, ☎ 202/514–0301 or 800/514–0301, FAX 202/307–1198, TTY 202/514–0383 or 800/514–0383) for general complaints. **Aviation Consumer Protection Division** (☞ Air Travel, *above*) for airline-related problems. **Civil Rights Office** (✉ U.S. Department of Transportation, Departmental Office of Civil Rights, S-30, 400 7th St. SW, Room 10215, Washington, DC, 20590, ☎ 202/366–4648) for problems with surface transportation.

TRAVEL AGENCIES & TOUR OPERATORS

The Americans with Disabilities Act requires that travel firms serve the needs of all travelers. That said, you should note that some agencies and operators specialize in making travel arrangements for individuals and groups with disabilities.

➤ TRAVELERS WITH MOBILITY PROBLEMS: **Access Adventures** (✉ 206 Chestnut Ridge Rd., Rochester, NY 14624, ☎ 716/889–9096), run by a former physical-rehabilitation counselor. **Accessible Journeys** (✉ 35 W. Sellers Ave., Ridley Park, PA 19078, ☎ 610/521–0339 or 800/846–4537, FAX 610/521–6959), for escorted tours exclusively for travelers with mobility impairments. **CareVacations** (✉ 5019 49th Ave., Suite 102, Leduc, Alberta T9E 6T5, ☎ 403/986–6404, 800/648–1116 in Canada) for group tours and cruise vacations. **Hinsdale Travel Service** (✉ 201 E. Ogden Ave., Suite 100, Hinsdale, IL 60521, ☎ 630/325–1335), a travel agency that benefits from the advice of wheelchair traveler Janice Perkins. **Wheelchair Journeys** (✉ 16979 Redmond Way, Redmond, WA 98052, ☎ 206/885–2210 or 800/313–4751), for general travel arrangements.

Be a smart shopper and **compare all your options before making a choice.** A plane ticket bought with a promotional coupon may not be cheaper than the least expensive fare from a discount ticket agency. For high-price travel purchases, such as packages or tours, keep in mind that what you get is just as important as what you save. Just because something is cheap doesn't mean it's a bargain.

LOOK IN YOUR WALLET

When you use your credit card to make travel purchases you may get free travel-accident insurance, collision-damage insurance, and medical or legal assistance, depending on the card and the bank that issued it. American Express, MasterCard, and Visa provide one or more of these services, so **get a copy of your credit card's travel-benefits policy.** If you are a member of the American Automobile Association (AAA) or an oil-company-sponsored road-assistance plan, always **ask hotel or car-rental reservationists about auto-club discounts.** Some clubs offer additional discounts on tours, cruises, or admission to attractions. And don't forget that auto-club membership entitles you to free maps and trip-planning services.

DIAL FOR DOLLARS

To save money, **look into "1-800" discount reservations services,** which use their buying power to get a better price on hotels, airline tickets, even car rentals. When booking a room, always **call the hotel's local toll-free number** (if one is available) rather than the central reservations number—you'll often get a better price. Always ask about special packages or corporate rates.

When shopping for the best deal on hotels and car rentals **look for guaranteed exchange rates,** which protect you against a falling dollar. With your rate locked in you won't pay more even if the price goes up in the local currency.

➤ AIRLINE TICKETS: ☎ 800/FLY-4-LESS. ☎ 800/FLY-ASAP.

➤ HOTEL ROOMS: Room Finders USA (☎ 800/473-7829).

SAVE ON COMBOS

Packages and guided tours can both save you money, but don't confuse the two. When you buy a package your travel remains independent, just as though you had planned and booked the trip yourself. Fly/drive packages, which combine airfare and car rental, are often a good deal.

JOIN A CLUB?

Many companies sell discounts in the form of travel clubs and coupon books, but these cost money. You must use participating advertisers to get a deal, and only after you recoup the initial membership cost or book

price do you begin to save. If you plan to use the club or coupons frequently you may save considerably. Before signing up, **find out what discounts you get for free.**

➤ DISCOUNT CLUBS: Entertainment Travel Editions (✉ Box 1068, Trumbull, CT 06611, ☎ 800/445-4137; $28-$53, depending on destination). **Great American Traveler** (✉ Box 27965, Salt Lake City, UT 84127, ☎ 800/548-2812; $49.95 per year). **Moment's Notice Discount Travel Club** (✉ 7301 New Utrecht Ave., Brooklyn, NY 11204, ☎ 718/234-6295; $25 per year, single or family). **Privilege Card International** (✉ 201 E. Commerce St., Suite 198, Youngstown, OH 44503, ☎ 330/746-5211 or 800/236-9732; $74.95 per year). **Sears's Mature Outlook** (✉ Box 9390, Des Moines, IA 50306, ☎ 800/336-6330; $14.95 per year). **Travelers Advantage** (✉ CUC Travel Service, 3033 S. Parker Rd., Suite 1000, Aurora, CO 80014, ☎ 800/548-1116 or 800/648-4037; $49 per year, single or family). **Worldwide Discount Travel Club** (✉ 1674 Meridian Ave., Miami Beach, FL 33139, ☎ 305/534-2082; $50 per year family, $40 single).

DRIVING

The road system in the Yucatán Peninsula is extensive and generally in good repair. **Route 307** parallels most of the Caribbean coast from Punta Sam, north of Cancún, to Tulum; there it turns inward for a while before returning to the coast at Chetumal and the Belize border. **Route 180** runs west from Cancún to Valladolid, Chichén Itzá, and Mérida, then turns southwest to Campeche, Isla del Carmen, and on to Villahermosa. From Mérida, there is also the windier, more scenic **Route 261,** which provides good access to some of the more off-the-beaten track archaeological sites on the way south to Campeche and Francisco Escárcega, where it joins **Route 186** going east to Chetumal. These highways are two-lane roads. **Route 295** (from the north coast to Valladolid and Felipe Carrillo Puerto) is also a good two-lane road.

The *autopista,* or *carretera de cuota,* an eight-lane toll highway between Cancún and Mérida, was completed in 1993. It runs roughly parallel to Route 180 and cuts driving time between Cancún and Mérida—formerly around 4½ hours—by about one hour. Tolls between Mérida and Cancún can run as high as $30, and there are long stretches between highway exits.

Once off the main highways, motorists will find the roads in varying conditions. Some roads are unmarked, which makes it confusing to reach a given destination. Many are unpaved and full of potholes. If you must take one of the smaller roads, the best course is to **allow plenty of daylight hours and never travel at night.** Always slow down when approaching towns and villages—which you are forced to do by the ubiquitous *topes* (speed bumps)—because you will find small children and animals in abundance. Children selling oranges, nuts, or candies will almost certainly approach your car. Some people feel that it is best not to buy from them, reasoning that if they can make money this way, they will not go to school. Others choose to buy from them on the theory that they would probably go to school if they could afford it, and need the meager profits to survive. Judge for yourself.

Always park your car in a parking lot, or at least in a populated area. Never leave anything of value in an unattended car.

Make sure there is proof of Mexican liability insurance in your rental car; if you're driving your own car, be sure to purchase Mexican insurance at the border. Do not rely on credit-card companies' assurances that you do not have to purchase auto insurance in Mexico unless you are ready to fork over large sums and be reimbursed later. If you are involved in an accident and don't have liability insurance, Mexican authorities will demand that damage be paid for on the spot, in cash; you might also land in jail.

SPEED LIMITS

Mileage and speed limits are given in kilometers. One kilometer is approximately ⁶⁄₁₀ mile. In small towns, observe the posted speed limits, which can be as low as 20 kph (12 mph).

FUEL AVAILABILITY AND COSTS

PEMEX, Mexico's government-owned petroleum monopoly, franchises all gas stations, so prices throughout the Yucatán will be the same. Gas prices tend to be slightly higher than those in the United States; some stations in Mexico now accept American credit cards and dollars. Fuel quality is not up to United States standards—fuel injected engines are likely to have problems after a while. Unleaded fuel, known as *Magna Premio* and *Magna Sin* (lower octane), is available at most PEMEX stations. When filling your tank, ask for a specific peso amount of gas rather than for a number of liters. **Keep the tank full,** because gas stations are not plentiful.

NATIONAL ROAD-EMERGENCY SERVICES

The Mexican Tourism Ministry operates a fleet of some 280 pickup trucks, known as *Los Angeles Verdes,* or the Green Angels, to render assistance to motorists on the major highways. The bilingual drivers provide mechanical help, first aid, radio-telephone communication, basic supplies and small parts, towing, and tourist information. Services are free, and spare parts, fuel, and lubricants are provided at cost. Tips are always appreciated.

The Green Angels patrol fixed sections of the major highways twice daily 8–8, later on holiday weekends. If your car breaks down, **pull as far as possible off the road,** lift the hood, hail a passing vehicle, and ask the driver to **notify the patrol.** Most bus and truck drivers will be quite helpful. If you witness an accident, do not stop to help, but instead find the nearest official.

➤ GREEN ANGELS: ☎ in Mexico City, 5/250–8221.

➤ AUTO CLUBS: In the U.S., **American Automobile Association** (☎ 800/564–6222). In the U.K., **Automobile Association** (AA, ☎ 0990/500600), **Royal Automobile Club** (RAC, membership ☎ 0990/722722 for membership inquiries, 0345/121345 for insurance).

E

ELECTRICITY

Electrical converters are not necessary because the country operates on the 60-cycle, 120-volt system; however, many Mexican outlets have not been updated to accommodate three-prong and polarized plugs (those with one larger prong), so **bring an adapter.**

F
FERRY TRAVEL

The Yucatán is served by a number of ferries and boats, ranging from the spiffy, usually efficient hydrofoils (motorized catamarans) between Playa del Carmen and Cozumel to the more modest launches plying the waters from Puerto Juárez and Cancún to Isla Mujeres, and the tiny craft and catamarans heading out to the smaller offshore islands (Isla Holbox, Isla del Carmen, the Alacranes Reef).

Schedules are approximate and often vary with the weather and the number of passengers. Prices are generally quite reasonable.

G
GAY & LESBIAN TRAVEL

➤ Tour Operators: **R.S.V.P. Travel Productions** (✉ 2800 University Ave. SE, Minneapolis, MN 55414, ☎ 612/379–4697 or 800/328–7787), for cruises and resort vacations for gays. **Olivia** (✉ 4400 Market St., Oakland, CA 94608, ☎ 510/655–0364 or 800/631–6277), for cruises and resort vacations for lesbians. **Atlantis Events** (✉ 9060 Santa Monica Blvd., Suite 310, West Hollywood, CA 90069, ☎ 310/281–5450 or 800/628–5268), for mixed gay and lesbian travel. **Toto Tours** (✉ 1326 W. Albion Ave., Suite 3W, Chicago, IL 60626, ☎ 773/274–8686 or 800/565–1241, FAX 773/274–8695), for groups.

➤ Gay- and Lesbian-Friendly Travel Agencies: **Advance Damron** (✉ 1 Greenway Plaza, Suite 800, Houston, TX 77046, ☎ 713/682–2002 or 800/695–0880, FAX 713/888–1010). **Club Travel** (✉ 8739 Santa Monica Blvd., West Hollywood, CA 90069, ☎ 310/358–2200 or 800/429–8747). **Islanders/Kennedy Travel** (✉ 183 W. 10th St., New York, NY 10014, ☎ 212/242–3222 or 800/988–1181). **Now Voyager** (✉ 4406 18th St., San Francisco, CA 94114, ☎ 415/626–1169 or 800/255–6951). **Yellowbrick Road** (✉ 1500 W. Balmoral Ave., Chicago, IL 60640, ☎ 773/561–1800 or 800/642–2488). **Skylink Women's**

Travel (✉ 3577 Moorland Ave., Santa Rosa, CA 95407, ☎ 707/585–8355 or 800/225–5759), serving lesbian travelers.

H
HEALTH

STAYING WELL

In the Yucatán, the major health risk is posed by the contamination of drinking water, fresh fruit and vegetables by fecal matter, which causes the intestinal ailment known as *turista*, or traveler's diarrhea. Bad shellfish can also be a culprit. To prevent such an unpleasant interruption to your vacation, **watch what you eat.** Stay away from ice, uncooked food, seafood that may not have been refrigerated, and unpasteurized milk and milk products, and **drink only bottled water or water that has been boiled** for at least 20 minutes. When ordering cold drinks at untouristed establishments, skip the ice—ask for your beverage *"sin hielo."* (You can usually identify ice made commercially from purified water by its uniform shape and the hole in the center.) Hotels with water-purification systems will post signs to that effect in the rooms. If these measures fail, try paregoric, a good antidiarrheal agent that dulls or eliminates abdominal cramps—it requires a doctor's prescription in Mexico—or Imodium (loperamide), which can be purchased over the counter. In mild cases, try Pepto-Bismol. Drink plenty of purified water or tea; chamomile tea (known as *te de manzanilla,* and readily available in restaurants throughout Mexico) is a good folk remedy for diarrhea. In severe cases, rehydrate yourself with a salt-sugar solution (½ tsp. salt and 4 tbsp. sugar per quart/liter of water).

According to the Centers for Disease Control (CDC), there is a limited risk of malaria and dengue fever in certain rural areas of the Yucatán Peninsula, especially the states of Campeche and Quintana Roo. Travelers in most urban or easily accessible areas need not worry. However, if you plan to visit remote regions or stay for more than six weeks, **check with the CDC's International Travelers Hotline** (☎ 404/332–4559). In areas with malaria and dengue fever, which are both carried by mosquitoes, take mosquito nets, wear clothing that covers the body, apply repellent containing DEET, and use a spray against flying insects in living and sleeping areas. The hot line recommends chloroquine (analen) as an antimalarial agent; no vaccine exists against dengue fever.

MEDICAL PLANS

No one plans to get sick while traveling, but it happens, so **consider signing up with a medical-assistance company.** Members get doctor referrals, emergency evacuation or repatriation, 24-hour telephone hot lines for medical consultation, cash for emergencies, and other personal and legal assistance. Coverage varies by plan, so **review the benefits carefully.**

➤ MEDICAL-ASSISTANCE COMPANIES: **International SOS Assistance** (✉ Box 11568, Philadelphia, PA 19116, ☎ 215/244–1500 or 800/523–8930; ✉ Box 466, pl. Bonaventure, Montréal, Québec H5A 1C1, ☎ 514/874–7674 or 800/363–0263; ✉ 7 Old Lodge Pl., St. Margarets, Twickenham TW1 1RQ, England, ☎ 0181/744–0033). **MEDEX Assistance Corporation** (✉ Box 5375, Timonium, MD 21094, ☎ 410/453–6300 or 800/537–2029). **Traveler's Emergency Network** (✉ 3100 Tower Blvd., Suite 1000B, Durham, NC 27707, ☎ 919/490–6055 or 800/275–4836, FAX 919/493–8262). **TravMed** (✉ Box 5375, Timonium, MD 21094, ☎ 410/453–6380 or 800/732–5309). **Worldwide Assistance Services** (✉ 1133 15th St. NW, Suite 400, Washington, DC 20005, ☎ 202/331–1609 or 800/821–2828, FAX 202/828–5896).

DIVERS' ALERT

Do not fly within 24 hours of scuba diving.

HOLIDAYS

Banks, government offices, and many businesses close on these days, so plan your trip accordingly: January 1, New Year's Day; February 5, Constitution Day; January 6, the Feast of the Epiphany and the celebration of the founding of Mérida; March 21, Benito Juárez's birthday; May 1, Labor Day; September 16, Independence Day; November 20, Revolution Day; and December 25, Christmas Day.

Banks and government offices close during Holy Week, especially the Thursday and Friday before Easter; on May 5, anniversary of the Battle of Puebla; May 10, Mother's Day; September 1, opening of Congress; October 12, Día de la Raza; November 1 and 2, Day of the Dead; December 12, Feast of the Virgin of Guadalupe; and December 25–January 2, Christmas week.

I

INSURANCE

Travel insurance is the best way to protect yourself against financial loss. The most useful policies are trip-cancellation-and-interruption, default, medical, and comprehensive insurance.

Without insurance you will lose all or most of your money if you cancel your trip, regardless of the reason. It's essential that you **buy trip-cancellation-and-interruption insurance,** particularly if your airline ticket, cruise, or package tour is nonrefundable and cannot be changed. When considering how much coverage you need, look for a policy that will cover the cost of your trip plus the nondiscounted price of a one-way airline ticket, should you need to return home early. Also **consider default or bankruptcy insurance,** which protects you against a supplier's failure to deliver.

Medicare generally does not cover health-care costs outside the United States, nor do many privately issued policies. If your own policy does not cover you outside the United States, **consider buying supplemental medical coverage.** Remember that travel health insurance is different from a medical-assistance plan (☞ Health, *above*).

Citizens of the United Kingdom can buy an annual travel-insurance policy valid for most vacations during the year in which it's purchased. If you are pregnant or have a preexisting medical condition, make sure you're covered.

If you have purchased an expensive vacation, particularly one that involves travel abroad, comprehensive insurance is a must. **Look for comprehensive policies that include trip-delay insurance,** which will protect you in the event that weather problems cause you to miss your flight, tour, or cruise. A few insurers sell waivers for preexisting medical conditions. Companies that offer both features include Access America, Carefree Travel, Travel Insured International, and Travel Guard (☞ *below*).

Always **buy travel insurance directly from the insurance company**; if you buy it from a travel agency or tour operator that goes out of business you probably will not be covered for the agency or operator's default, a major risk. Before you make any purchase, **review your existing health and home-owner's policies** to find out whether they cover expenses incurred while traveling.

➤ TRAVEL INSURERS: In the U.S., **Access America** (⊠ 6600 W. Broad St., Richmond, VA 23230, ☎ 804/285–3300 or 800/284–8300), **Carefree Travel Insurance** (⊠ Box 9366, 100 Garden City Plaza, Garden City, NY 11530, ☎ 516/294–0220 or 800/323–3149), **Near Travel Services** (⊠ Box 1339, Calumet City, IL 60409, ☎ 708/868–6700 or 800/654–6700), **Travel Guard International** (⊠ 1145 Clark St., Stevens Point, WI 54481, ☎ 715/345–0505 or 800/826–1300), **Travel Insured International** (⊠ Box 280568, East Hartford, CT 06128–0568, ☎ 860/528–7663 or 800/243–3174), **Travelex Insurance Services** (⊠ 11717 Burt St., Suite 202, Omaha, NE 68154-1500, ☎ 402/445–8637 or 800/228–9792, FAX 402/491–0016), **Wallach & Company** (⊠ 107 W. Federal St., Box 480, Middleburg, VA 20118, ☎ 540/687–3166 or 800/237–6615). In Canada, **Mutual of Omaha** (⊠ Travel Division, 500 University Ave., Toronto, Ontario M5G 1V8, ☎ 416/598–4083, 800/268–8825 in Canada). In the U.K., **Association of British Insurers** (⊠ 51 Gresham St., London EC2V 7HQ, ☎ 0171/600–3333).

L

LANGUAGE

Spanish is the official language of Mexico, although Indian languages are spoken by approximately 20% of the population, many of whom speak no Spanish at all. This is the case in Mérida and much of the state of Yucatán, where a number of modern languages derived from Maya are spoken. In the beach resorts of Cancún and Cozumel, English is understood by most people employed in tourism; at the very least, shopkeepers will know the numbers for bargaining purposes. Mexicans welcome even the most halting attempts to use their language, and if you are in Mérida, you may even be introduced to a few Maya words and phrases. For a rudimentary vocabulary of terms that travelers are likely to encounter in the Yucatán, **review the Spanish Vocabulary at the end of this book.**

The Spanish that most U.S. and Canadian citizens learn in high school is based on Castilian Spanish, which is different from Latin American Spanish. In terms of grammar, Mexican Spanish ignores the *vosotros* form of the second person plural, using the more formal *ustedes* in its place. As for pronunciation, the lisped Castilian "c" or "z" is dismissed in Mexico as a sign of affectation. The most obvious differences are in vocabulary: Mexican Spanish has thousands of indigenous words, and the use of *¿mande?* instead of *¿cómo?* (excuse me?) is a dead giveaway that one's Spanish was acquired in Mexico. Words or phrases that are harmless or commonplace in one Spanish-speaking country can take on salacious or otherwise offensive meanings in another. Unless you are lucky enough to be briefed on these nuances by a native coach, the only way to learn is by trial and error. Some recommended language schools in Mérida are listed in Chapter 7.

LODGING

If you plan to stay in Cancún or Cozumel, you'll have a variety of accommodations to choose from. There are luxurious and expensive internationally affiliated properties with numerous food and beverage outlets, the latest room amenities, boutiques, and sports facilities. These beach resorts also have more modest hostelries—usually a short walk or a shuttle ride from the water. As you get into the less-populated and less-visited areas of the Yucatán, particularly the cities, accommodations tend to be simpler and more "typically Mexican." The hotels discussed in this book all meet a minimum standard of cleanliness, and most have a certain rustic charm. Inexpensive bungalows, campsites, and places to hang a hammock along many of the beaches are other options.

APARTMENT AND VILLA RENTALS

If you want a home base that's roomy enough for a family and comes with cooking facilities, **consider a furnished rental.** These can save you money; however, some rentals are luxury properties, economical only when your party is large. Home-exchange directories list rentals (often second homes owned by prospective house swappers), and some services search for a house or apartment for you (even a castle if that's your fancy) and handle the paperwork. Some send an illustrated catalog; others send photographs only of specific properties, sometimes at a charge. Up-front registration fees may apply.

➤ RENTAL AGENTS: **At Home Abroad** (⊠ 405 E. 56th St., Suite 6H, New York, NY 10022, ☎ 212/421–9165, FAX 212/752–1591). **Europa-Let/ Tropical Inn-Let** (⊠ 92 N. Main St., Ashland, OR 97520, ☎ 541/482– 5806 or 800/462–4486, FAX 541/482– 0660). **Property Rentals International** (⊠ 1008 Mansfield Crossing Rd., Richmond, VA 23236, ☎ 804/378– 6054 or 800/220–3332, FAX 804/379– 2073). **Rent-a-Home International** (⊠ 7200 34th Ave. NW, Seattle, WA 98117, ☎ 206/789–9377 or 800/ 488–7368, FAX 206/789–9379). **Vacation Home Rentals Worldwide** (⊠ 235 Kensington Ave., Norwood, NJ 07648, ☎ 201/767–9393 or 800/633–3284, FAX 201/767–5510). **Villas International** (⊠ 605 Market St., Suite 510, San Francisco, CA 94105, ☎ 415/281–0910 or 800/ 221–2260, FAX 415/281–0919). **Hideaways International** (⊠ 767 Islington St., Portsmouth, NH 03801, ☎ 603/430–4433 or 800/843–4433, FAX 603/430–4444) is a travel club whose members arrange rentals among themselves; yearly membership is $99.

HOME EXCHANGES

If you would like to exchange your home for someone else's, **join a home-exchange organization,** which will send you its updated listings of available exchanges for a year and will include your own listing in at least one of them. Making the arrangements is up to you.

➤ EXCHANGE CLUBS: **HomeLink International** (⊠ Box 650, Key West, FL 33041, ☎ 305/294–7766 or 800/ 638–3841, FAX 305/294–1148) charges $78 per year.

M

MAIL

It costs 2.70 pesos to mail a postcard or letter weighing less than 20 grams to the United States or Canada. The cost to Great Britain is 3.40 pesos.

RECEIVING MAIL

Mail can be sent either to your hotel, to the post office, or, if you are an American Express card member, to the local branch of American Express. American Express offices in the Yucatán are located in Campeche City, Mérida, Cancún, and Cozumel. Another option is the Mexican postal service's *lista de correos* (poste restante) service. To use this service, you must first register with the local post office in which you wish to receive your mail. Mail should be addressed to: your name; a/c Lista de Correos; town name; state; postal code; Mexico. Mail is held at post offices for 10 days, and a list of recipients is posted daily. Postal codes for the main Yucatán destinations are as follows: Cancún, 77500; Isla Mujeres, 77400; Cozumel, 77600; Campeche, 24000; Mérida, 97000. Be forewarned, however, that mail service to and within Mexico is notoriously slow and can take anywhere from 10 days to three weeks. **Never send anything of value to Mexico through the mail.**

MONEY

At press time (April 1997), the peso was still "floating" after the devaluation enacted by the Zedillo administration in late 1994. While exchange rates were as favorable as one U.S. dollar to 7.9 Mexican pesos, one Canadian dollar to 5.75 pesos, and a pound sterling to 12.86 pesos, the market and prices are likely to continue to adjust. **Check with your bank or the financial pages of your local newspaper for current exchange rates.**

Mexican currency comes in denominations of 10, 20, 50, 100, 200 and 500 peso bills. Coins come in denominations of 20, 10, and 5 pesos and 50, 20, 10, and 5 centavos. Some denominations of bills and coins are very similar, so check carefully. To avoid fraud, it's wise to **make sure that "pesos" is clearly marked on all credit-card receipts.**

Dollar bills, but not coins, are widely accepted in many parts of the Yucatán, particularly in Cancún and Cozumel. Many tourist shops and market vendors, as well as virtually all hotel service personnel, take them, too.

Traveler's checks and all major U.S. credit cards are accepted in most tourist areas of Mexico. The large hotels, restaurants, and department stores accept cards readily. Most of the smaller, less expensive restaurants and shops, however, will only take cash. Credit cards are generally not accepted in small towns and villages, except in tourist-oriented hotels. When shopping, you can usually get better prices if you **pay with cash.**

ATMS

Before leaving home, **make sure that your credit cards have been programmed for ATM use in Mexico.** Note that Discover is accepted mostly in the United States. Local bank cards often do not work overseas; **ask your bank about a MasterCard/Cirrus or Visa debit card,** which works like a bank card but can be used at any ATM displaying a MasterCard/Cirrus or Visa logo.

➤ ATM LOCATIONS: **Cirrus** (☎ 800/424–7787). A list of **Plus** locations is available at your local bank.

COSTS

Mexico has a reputation for being inexpensive, particularly compared with other North American vacation spots such as the Caribbean. Cancún, however, is probably the most expensive destination in Mexico. In Mérida and the other cities in the Yucatán, where fewer American tourists visit, you will find the best value for your money. For obvious reasons, if you stay at international chain hotels and eat at restaurants geared to tourists (especially hotel restaurants), you may not find the Yucatán such a bargain.

Rates in the Yucatán decrease in the off-season by as much as 30%. Speaking Spanish is helpful in bargaining and when asking for dining recommendations. As a general rule, the less English spoken in a region, the cheaper things will be (☞ Language, *above*).

Sample costs are as follows: cup of coffee, 6–12 pesos; bottle of beer, 10–35 pesos; plate of tacos with trimmings, 10–30 pesos; grilled fish platter at a tourist restaurant, 25–55 pesos; 2-kilometer taxi ride, 15 pesos.

Off-season, Cancún hotels cost one-third to one-half what they cost during peak season. Cozumel is a bit less costly than Cancún, and Isla Mujeres is slightly less expensive than Cozumel.

CURRENCY EXCHANGE

For the most favorable rates, **change money at banks.** Although fees charged for ATM transactions may be higher abroad than at home, Cirrus and Plus exchange rates are excellent, because they are based on wholesale rates offered only by major banks. You won't do as well at exchange booths in airports or rail and bus stations, in hotels, in restaurants, or in stores, although you may find their hours more convenient. To avoid lines at airport exchange booths, **get a small amount of local currency before you leave home.**

➤ EXCHANGE SERVICES: **Ruesch International** (☎ 800/424–2923 for locations). **Thomas Cook Currency Services** (☎ 800/287–7362 for locations).

TRAVELER'S CHECKS

Whether or not to buy traveler's checks depends on where you are headed. Take cash if your trip includes rural areas and small towns, traveler's checks to cities. If your checks are lost or stolen, they can usually be replaced within 24 hours. To ensure a speedy refund, **buy your checks yourself** (don't ask someone else to make the purchase). When making a claim for stolen or lost checks, the person who bought the checks should make the call.

P

PACKING FOR CANCÚN

Pack light, because you may want to save space for purchases: the Yucatán is filled with bargains on clothing, leather goods, jewelry, pottery, and other crafts.

Resort wear is all you will need for the Caribbean beach towns: Bring lightweight sports clothes, sundresses, bathing suits, sun visors, and cover-ups for the beach and a jacket or sweater to wear in the chilly, air-conditioned restaurants, or to tide you over a storm or an unusual cool spell. If you plan to visit any ruins, **bring comfortable walking shoes** with rubber soles. Light-weight rain gear is a good idea during the rainy season. Cancún is the dressiest spot on the peninsula, but even fancy restaurants don't require men to wear jackets. Women may wear shorts at the ruins, on the beaches, and in the beach towns but should not do so in cities such as Mérida.

Insect repellent, sunscreen, sunglasses, and umbrellas are musts for the Yucatán. Other handy items—especially if you will be traveling on your own or camping—include toilet paper, facial tissues, a plastic water bottle, and a flashlight (for occasional power outages or use at campsites). Snorkelers should consider bringing their own equipment unless traveling light is a priority; shoes with rubber soles for rocky underwater surfaces are also advised. For long-term stays in remote rural areas, *see* Health, *above.*

Bring an extra pair of eyeglasses or contact lenses in your carry-on luggage, and if you have a health problem, **pack enough medication** to last the entire trip or have your doctor write you a prescription using the drug's generic name, because brand names vary from country to country. It's important that you **don't put prescription drugs or valuables in luggage to be checked**: it might go astray. To avoid problems with customs officials, carry medications in the original packaging. Also, don't forget the addresses of offices that handle refunds of lost traveler's checks.

LUGGAGE

In general, you are entitled to check two bags on flights within the United States and on international flights leaving the United States. A third piece may be brought on board, but it must fit easily under the seat in front of you or in the overhead compartment.

If you are flying between two foreign destinations, note that baggage allowances may be determined not by piece but by weight—generally 88 pounds (40 kilograms) in first class, 66 pounds (30 kilograms) in business class, and 44 pounds (20 kilograms) in economy. If your flight between two cities abroad *connects* with your transatlantic or transpacific flight, the piece method still applies.

Airline liability for baggage is limited to $1,250 per person on flights within the United States. On international flights it amounts to $9.07 per pound or $20 per kilogram for checked baggage (roughly $640 per 70-pound bag) and $400 per passenger for unchecked baggage. Insurance for losses exceeding these amounts can be bought from the airline at check-in for about $10 per $1,000 of coverage; note that this coverage excludes a rather extensive list of items, which is shown on your airline ticket.

Before departure, **itemize your bags' contents** and their worth, and label the bags with your name, address, and phone number. (If you use your home address, cover it so that potential thieves can't see it readily.) Inside each bag, **pack a copy of your itinerary.** At check-in, **make sure that each bag is correctly tagged** with the destination airport's three-letter code. If your bags arrive damaged or fail to arrive at all, file a written report with the airline before leaving the airport.

PASSPORTS & VISAS

Once your travel plans are confirmed, **get a passport even if you don't need one to enter Cancún**—it's always the best form of I.D. It's also a good idea to **make photocopies of the data page**; leave one copy with someone at home and keep another with you, separated from your passport. If you lose your passport, promptly call the nearest embassy or consulate and the local police; having a copy of the data page can speed replacement.

U.S. CITIZENS

For stays of up to 180 days , any proof of citizenship is sufficient for entry into Mexico. Minors traveling with one parent need notarized permission from the absent parent. All U.S. citizens, even infants, need a valid passport to enter Mexico for stays of more than 180 days.

➤ INFORMATION: **Office of Passport Services** (☎ 202/647–0518).

CANADIANS

You need only proof of citizenship to enter Mexico for stays of up to 180 days.

U.K. CITIZENS

Citizens of the United Kingdom need only a valid passport to enter Mexico for stays of up to 180 days.

➤ INFORMATION: **London Passport Office** (☎ 0990/21010) for fees and documentation requirements and to request an emergency passport.

S

SAFETY

When visiting the Yucatán, even in such resort areas as Cancún and Cozumel, **use common sense.** Wear a money belt, make use of hotel safes when available, and carry your own baggage whenever possible. Reporting a crime to the police is often a frustrating experience unless you speak excellent Spanish and have a great deal of patience.

Women traveling alone are likely to be subjected to catcalls, although this is less true in the Yucatán than in other parts of Mexico. Avoid direct eye contact with men on the streets—it invites further acquaintance. Don't wear tight clothes if you don't want to call attention to yourself. Also be aware that clothing that seems innocuous to you, such as sleeveless shirts or Bermuda shorts, may be inappropriate in more conservative rural areas. If you speak Spanish and are being harassed, pretend you don't understand and ignore would-be suitors or say "no" to whatever they say. Don't enter street bars or cantinas alone.

SENIOR-CITIZEN TRAVEL

To qualify for age-related discounts, **mention your senior-citizen status up front** when booking hotel reservations (not when checking out) and before you're seated in restaurants (not when paying the bill). Note that discounts may be limited to certain menus, days, or hours. When renting a car, **ask about promotional car-rental discounts,** which can be cheaper than senior-citizen rates.

➤ EDUCATIONAL TRAVEL PROGRAMS: **Elderhostel** (✉ 75 Federal St., 3rd floor, Boston, MA 02110, ☎ 617/426–7788). **Interhostel** (✉ University of New Hampshire, 6 Garrison Ave., Durham, NH 03824, ☎ 603/862–1147 or 800/733–9753).

SHOPPING

Shopping is convenient in such resort areas as Cancún and Cozumel, but often you'll be paying top peso for items that you can find in smaller towns for less money. As for bargaining, it is widely accepted in the markets, but you should understand that in many small towns the locals earn their livelihoods from the tourist trade, and not all will start out with outrageous prices. If you feel the price quoted is too high, start off by offering no more than half the asking price and then slowly go up, usually to about 70% of the original price. Bargaining is not accepted in most shops, except when you are paying cash.

STUDENTS

To save money, **look into deals available through student-oriented travel agencies.** To qualify you'll need a bona fide student ID card. Members of international student groups are also eligible.

➤ STUDENT IDS AND SERVICES: **Council on International Educational Exchange** (✉ CIEE, 205 E. 42nd St., 14th floor, New York, NY 10017, ☎ 212/822–2600, FAX 212/822–2699), for mail orders only, in the United States. **Travel Cuts** (✉ 187 College St., Toronto, Ontario M5T 1P7, ☎ 416/979–2406 or 800/667–2887) in Canada.

➤ HOSTELING: **Hostelling International—American Youth Hostels** (✉ 733 15th St. NW, Suite 840,

Washington, DC 20005, ☎ 202/783–6161, FAX 202/783–6171).
Hostelling International—Canada (✉ 400–205 Catherine St., Ottawa, Ontario K2P 1C3, ☎ 613/237–7884, FAX 613/237–7868). **Youth Hostel Association of England and Wales** (✉ Trevelyan House, 8 St. Stephen's Hill, St. Albans, Hertfordshire AL1 2DY, ☎ 01727/855215 or 01727/845047). Membership in the U.S., $25; in Canada, C$26.75; in the U.K., £9.30).

➤ STUDENT TOURS: **Contiki Holidays** (✉ 300 Plaza Alicante, Suite 900, Garden Grove, CA 92640, ☎ 714/740–0808 or 800/266–8454).

T

TAXES

➤ AIRPORT: An air departure tax of US$13.37 or the peso equivalent must be paid in cash at the airport for international flights from Mexico, and there is a domestic air departure tax of around US$10. Traveler's checks and credit cards are not accepted as payment for these taxes.

➤ HOTEL: Hotels in the state of Quintana Roo are now charging a 2% lodging tax, the income from which is to be used for tourism promotion.

➤ VAT: Mexico has a value-added tax, or I.V.A. (*impuesto de valor agregado*), of 15% (10% along the Cancún–Tulum corridor). Many establishments already include the I.V.A. tax in the quoted price. Occasionally (and illegally) it will be waived for cash purchases.

TELEPHONES

The country code for Mexico is 52.

LONG-DISTANCE

International phone calls can be made from many hotels, but excessive taxes and surcharges—on the order of 60% to 70%—usually apply. Cancún, Cozumel, and Mérida are putting up more and more "LADATEL" phone booths on streets and in some hotel lobbies; these phones accept pre-paid electronic cards (sold at pharmacies and grocery stores), which are inserted into the phone and debited for the cost of the call. LADATEL phones also allow you to make collect and calling-card calls to the United States. Throughout Mexico, **dial 09 to place an international call; 02 for long-distance calls; and 04 for information.** When calling the United States or Canada, dial 001 before the area code and phone number. When calling Europe, Latin America, of Japan, dial 00 before the country and city codes.

Before you go, **find out the local access codes** for your destinations. AT&T, MCI, and Sprint long-distance services make calling home relatively convenient, but you may find the local access number blocked in many hotel rooms. First ask the hotel operator to connect you. If the hotel operator balks, ask for an international operator, or dial the international operator yourself. One way to improve your odds of getting connected to your long-distance carrier is to travel with more than one company's calling card (a hotel may block Sprint, for example, but not MCI). If all else fails, call your phone company collect in the United States or call from a pay phone in the hotel lobby.

➤ TO OBTAIN ACCESS CODES: **AT&T** USADirect (☎ 800/874–4000). **MCI** Call USA (☎ 800/444–4444). **Sprint** Express (☎ 800/793–1153).

TIPPING

At restaurants it's customary to leave a 10%–15% tip (make sure, however, that a service charge has not already been added). Bellhops and porters should be given $1 to $2; hotel maids, $1 per day, per room. Tour guides warrant about $1 per person for a half-day tour, $2 for a full day, and $10 per person for a week. Tour-bus drivers should receive 5–8 pesos per person per day. Car watchers and windshield wipers (usually young boys), as well as gas station attendants and theater ushers, should be satisfied with 2–5 pesos. Taxi drivers (unless extraordinarily helpful) and shoe shiners do not expect tips.

TOUR OPERATORS

Buying a prepackaged tour or independent vacation can make your trip to Cancún less expensive and more hassle-free. Because everything is prearranged you'll spend less time planning.

Operators that handle several hundred thousand travelers per year can use their purchasing power to give you a good price. Their high volume may also indicate financial stability. But some small companies provide more personalized service; because they tend to specialize, they may also be more knowledgeable about a given area.

A GOOD DEAL?

The more your package or tour includes, the better you can predict the ultimate cost of your vacation. Make sure you know exactly what is covered, and **beware of hidden costs.** Are taxes, tips, and service charges included? Transfers and baggage handling? Entertainment and excursions? These can add up.

If the package or tour you are considering is priced lower than in your wildest dreams, **be skeptical.** Also, **make sure your travel agent knows the accommodations** and other services. Ask about the hotel's location, room size, beds, and whether it has a pool, room service, or programs for children, if you care about these. Has your agent been there in person or sent others you can contact?

BUYER BEWARE

Each year consumers are stranded or lose their money when tour operators—even very large ones with excellent reputations—go out of business. So **check out the operator.** Find out how long the company has been in business, and ask several agents about its reputation. **Don't book unless the firm has a consumer-protection program.**

Members of the National Tour Association and United States Tour Operators Association are required to set aside funds to cover your payments and travel arrangements in case the company defaults. Nonmembers may carry insurance instead. Look for the details, and for the name of an underwriter with a solid reputation, in the operator's brochure. Note: When it comes to tour operators, **don't trust escrow accounts.** Although there are laws governing charter-flight operators, no governmental body prevents tour operators from raiding the till. For more information, *see* Consumer Protection, *above.*

➤ Tour-Operator Recommendations: **National Tour Association** (✉ NTA, 546 E. Main St., Lexington, KY 40508, ☎ 606/226–4444 or 800/755–8687). **United States Tour Operators Association** (✉ USTOA, 342 Madison Ave., New York, NY 10173, ☎ 212/599–6599).

USING AN AGENT

Travel agents are excellent resources. When shopping for an agent, however, you should **collect brochures from several sources**; some agents' suggestions may be skewed by promotional relationships with tour and package firms that reward them for volume sales. If you have a special interest, **find an agent with expertise in that area** (☞ Travel Agents, *below*). Don't rely solely on your agent, who may be unaware of small-niche operators. Note that some special-interest travel companies only sell directly to the public and that some large operators only accept bookings made through travel agents.

SINGLE TRAVELERS

Prices for packages and tours are usually quoted per person, based on two sharing a room. If traveling solo, you may be required to pay the full double-occupancy rate. Some operators eliminate this surcharge if you agree to be matched with a roommate of the same sex, even if one is not found by departure time.

PACKAGES

Like group tours, independent vacation packages are available from major tour operators and airlines. The companies listed below offer vacation packages in a broad price range.

➤ Air/Hotel: **American Airlines Fly AAway Vacations** (☎ 800/321–2121). **Certified Vacations** (✉ 110 E. Broward Blvd., Fort Lauderdale, FL 33302, ☎ 954/522–1440 or 800/233–7260). **Continental Vacations** (☎ 800/634–5555). **Delta Dream Vacations** (☎ 800/872–7786, FAX 954/357–4687). **USAirways Vacations** (☎ 800/455–0123).

➤ From the U.K.: In the United Kingdom contact **Club Med** (✉ 106–10 Brompton Rd., London SW3 1JJ, ☎ 0171/581–1161, FAX 0171/581–4769), **Kuoni Travel** (✉ Kuoni House, Dorking, Surrey RH5 4AZ, ☎ 01306/742–222, FAX 01306/744–222), and **Sunset Travel** (✉ 4 Abbeyville Mews,

88 Clapham Park Rd., London SW4 7BX, ☎ 0171/498–9922, FAX 0171/978–1337).

THEME TRIPS

➤ ADVENTURE: **Trek America** (⊠ Box 189, Rockaway, NJ 07866, ☎ 201/983–1144 or 800/221–0596, FAX 201/983–8551).

➤ ART AND ARCHAEOLOGY IN THE YUCATÁN: **Far Horizons Archaeological & Cultural Trips** (⊠ Box 91900, Albuquerque, NM 87199-1900, ☎ 505/343–9400 or 800/552–4575, FAX 505/343–8076). **Maya-Carib Travel** (⊠ 7 Davenport Ave., #3F, New Rochelle, NY 10805, ☎ 914/354–9824 or 800/223–4084, FAX 914/353–7539). **M.I.L.A.** (⊠ 100 S. Greenleaf Ave., Gurnee, IL 60031-3378, ☎ 847/249–2111 or 800/367–7378, FAX 847/249–2772). **Sanborn Tours** (⊠ 2015 S. 10th St., McAllen, TX 78505, ☎ 210/682–9872). From the U.K.: **Journey Latin America** (⊠ 14–16 Devonshire Rd., Chiswick, London W4 2HD, ☎ 0181/747–8315, FAX 0181/742–1312). **Mexican Tours** (⊠ Unit 215, 211–216 Chalk Farm Rd., Camden Town, London NW1 8AF, ☎ 0171/284–2550, FAX 0171/267–2004). **Steamond International** (⊠ 23 Eccleston St., London SW1W 9LX, ☎ 0171/730–8640).

➤ BICYCLING: **Backroads** (⊠ 801 Cedar St., Berkeley, CA 94710-1800, ☎ 510/527–1555 or 800/462–2848, FAX 510/527–1444).

➤ FISHING: **Anglers Travel** (⊠ 3100 Mill St., #206, Reno, NV 89502, ☎ FAX 702/853–9132). **Cutting Loose Expeditions** (⊠ Box 447, Winter Park, FL 32790, ☎ 407/629–4700 or 800/533–4746). **Fishing International** (⊠ Box 2132, Santa Rosa, CA 95405, ☎ 707/539–3366 or 800/950–4242, FAX 707/539–1320). **Mexico Sportsman** (⊠ 100-115 Travis St., San Antonio, TX 78205, ☎ 210/212–4566 or 800/633–3085, FAX 210/212–4568). **Rod and Reel Adventures** (⊠ 3507 Tully Rd., #B6, Modesto, CA 95356-1052, ☎ 209/524–7775 or 800/356–6982, FAX 209/524–1220).

➤ SPAS: **Spa-Finders** (⊠ 91 5th Ave., Ste. 301, New York, NY 10003-3039, ☎ 212/924–6800 or 800/255–7727).

➤ VILLA RENTALS: Contact **Villas International** (⊠ 605 Market St., San Francisco, CA 94105, ☎ 415/281–0910 or 800/221–2260, FAX 415/281–0919).

TRAVEL AGENCIES

A good travel agent puts your needs first. **Look for an agency that specializes in your destination, has been in business at least five years, and emphasizes customer service.** If you're looking for an agency-organized package or tour, your best bet is to choose an agency that's a member of the National Tour Association or the United States Tour Operator's Association (☞ Payments *and* Tour Operators, *above*).

➤ LOCAL AGENT REFERRALS: **American Society of Travel Agents** (⊠ ASTA, 1101 King St., Suite 200, Alexandria, VA 22314, ☎ 703/739–2782). **Alliance of Canadian Travel Associations** (⊠ Suite 201, 1729 Bank St., Ottawa, Ontario K1V 7Z5, ☎ 613/521–0474, FAX 613/521–0805). **Association of British Travel Agents** (⊠ 55–57 Newman St., London W1P 4AH, ☎ 0171/637–2444, FAX 0171/637–0713).

TRAVEL GEAR

Travel catalogs specialize in useful items, such as compact alarm clocks and travel irons, that can save space when packing. They also offer dual-voltage appliances, currency converters, and foreign-language phrase books.

➤ MAIL-ORDER CATALOGS: **Magellan's** (☎ 800/962–4943, FAX 805/568–5406). **Orvis Travel** (☎ 800/541–3541, FAX 540/343–7053). **TravelSmith** (☎ 800/950–1600, FAX 415/455–0329).

U

U.S. GOVERNMENT

The U.S. government can be an excellent source of inexpensive travel information. When planning your trip, **find out what government materials are available.**

➤ ADVISORIES: **U.S. Department of State American Citizens Services Office** (⊠ Room 4811, Washington, DC 20520); enclose a self-addresses, stamped envelope. Interactive hot line

(☎ 202/647–5225, FAX 202/647–3000). Computer bulletin board (☎ 202/647–9225).

➤ PAMPHLETS: **Consumer Information Center** (✉ Consumer Information Catalogue, Pueblo, CO 81009, ☎ 719/948–3334) for a free catalog that includes travel titles.

V

VISITOR INFORMATION

For general information contact the government tourist office nearest you.

➤ MEXICAN GOVERNMENT TOURIST OFFICES (MGTO): U.S. Nationwide: (☎ 800/446–3942). New York City: (✉ 405 Park Ave., Suite 1402, New York, NY 10022, ☎ 212/838–2949 or 212/421–6655, FAX 212/753–2874). Chicago: (✉ 70 E. Lake St., Suite 1413, Chicago, IL 60601, ☎ 312/606–9252, FAX 312/606–9012). Los Angeles: (✉ 1801 Century Pk. E., Ste 1080, Los Angeles, CA 90067, ☎ 310/203–8191, FAX 310/203–8316). Houston: (✉ 5075 Westheimer, Ste 975W, Houston, TX 77056, ☎ 713/629–1611, FAX 713/629–1837). Coral Gables: (✉ 2333 Ponce de Leon Blvd., Ste. 710, Coral Gables, FL 33134, ☎ 305/443–9160, FAX 305/443–1186). Canada: (✉ 1 Place Ville Marie, Suite 1626, Montréal, Québec H3B 2B5, ☎ 514/871–1052, FAX 514/871–3825; ✉ 2 Bloor St. W, Suite 1801, Toronto, Ontario M4W 3E2, ☎ 416/925–0704, FAX 416/925–6061; ✉ 999 W. Hastings St., Suite 1610, Vancouver, British Columbia V6C 2WC, ☎ 604/669–2845, FAX 604/669–3498). U.K.: 60 Trafalgar Sq., London WC2N 5DS, ☎ 0171/734–1058, FAX 0171/930–9202).

W

WHEN TO GO

High season along the Mexican Caribbean runs from mid-December through Easter week. Seasonal price changes are less pronounced in Mérida and other inland regions than at the beach resorts, but it still may be difficult to find a room during Christmas and Easter, as well as the last week of July and the first three weeks of August, when most Mexicans take their vacations.

CLIMATE

Spring and summer are usually pleasant along the coast, although you may experience some afternoon rain and evening breezes; in autumn, storms are common. The steamiest time of year inland is late spring, just before the May–October rainy season. What follows are the average daily maximum and minimum temperatures for Cancún; the rest of the Yucatán follows the same general pattern.

Climate in Cancún

Jan.	84F	29C	May	91F	33C	Sept.	89F	32C
	66	19		73	23		75	24
Feb.	85F	29C	June	92F	33C	Oct.	87F	31C
	66	19		75	24		73	23
Mar.	88F	31C	July	91F	33C	Nov.	86F	30C
	69	21		73	23		71	22
Apr.	89F	32C	Aug.	91F	33C	Dec.	84F	29C
	71	22		73	23		68	20

➤ FORECASTS: **Weather Channel Connection** (☎ 900/932–8437), 95¢ per minute from a Touch-Tone phone.

1 Destination: Cancún, Cozumel, Yucatán Peninsula

A PLACE APART

THE YUCATÁN PENINSULA has captivated travelers since the early Spanish explorations. "A place of white towers, whose glint could be seen from the ships. . . temples rising tier on tier, with sculptured cornices" is how the expeditions' chroniclers described the peninsula, then thought to be an island. Rumors of a mainland 10 days west of Cuba were known to Columbus, who obstinately hoped to find "a very populated land," and one that was richer than any he had yet discovered. Subsequent explorers and conquistadors met with more resistance there than in almost any other part of the New World, and this rebelliousness continued for centuries.

Largely because of their geographic isolation, Yucatecans tend to preserve ancient traditions more than many other indigenous groups in the country. This can be seen in such areas as housing (the use of the ancient Maya thatched hut, or *na*); dress (*huipiles* have been made and worn by Maya women for centuries); occupation (most modern-day Maya are farmers, just as their ancestors were); language (while the Maya language has evolved considerably, basically it is very similar to that spoken at least 500 years ago); and religion (ancient deities persist, particularly in the form of gods associated with agriculture, such as the *chacs,* or rain gods, and festivals to honor the seasons and benefactor spirits maintain the traditions of old).

This vast peninsula encompasses 113,000 square km (43,630 square mi) of a flat limestone table covered with sparse topsoil and scrubby jungle growth. Geographically, it comprises the states of Yucatán, Campeche, and Quintana Roo, as well as Belize and a part of Guatemala (these two countries are not discussed in this book). Long isolated from the rest of Mexico and still one of the least Hispanicized (or Mexicanized) regions of the country, Yucatán catapulted into the tourist's vocabulary with the creation of its most precious manmade asset, Cancún.

Mexico's most popular resort destination owes its success to its location on the superb eastern coastline of Yucatán, which is washed by the exquisitely colored and translucent waters of the Caribbean and endowed with a semitropical climate, unbroken stretches of beach, and the world's fifth-longest barrier reef, which separates the mainland from Cozumel. Cancún, along with Cozumel and to a lesser extent Isla Mujeres, incarnates the success formula for sun-and-sand tourism: luxury hotels, sandy beaches, water sports, nightlife, and restaurants that specialize in international fare.

Although Cancún is no longer less expensive than its Caribbean neighbors, it can be reached via more nonstop flights and it offers a far richer culture. With the advent of Cancún, the peninsula's Maya ruins—long a mecca for archaeology enthusiasts—have become virtual satellites of that glittering star. The proximity of such compelling sites as Chichén Itzá, Uxmal, and Tulum allows Cancún's visitors to explore the vestiges of one of the most brilliant civilizations in the ancient world without having to journey too far from their base.

Yucatán offers a breathtaking diversity of other charms, too. The waters of the Mexican Caribbean are clearer and more turquoise than those of the Pacific; many of the beaches are unrivaled. Scuba diving (in natural sinkholes and along the barrier reefs), snorkeling, deep-sea fishing, and other water sports attract growing numbers of tourists. They can also go birding, camp, spelunk, and shop for Yucatán's splendid handicrafts. There is a broad spectrum of settings and accommodations to choose from: the high-rise, pricey strip of hotels along Cancún's Paseo Kukulcán; the less showy properties on Cozumel, beloved by partying college-age scuba divers; and the relaxed ambience of Isla Mujeres, where most lodgings consist of rustic bungalows with ceiling fans and hammocks.

There are also the cities of Yucatán. Foremost is Mérida, wonderfully unaltered by time, where Moorish-inspired, colonnaded colonial architecture blends handsomely with turn-of-the-century pomposity. In Mérida, café life remains an art, and the Maya still live proudly as Maya. Campeche, one of the few walled cities in North America, possesses an eccentric charm; it is slightly out of step with the rest of the country and not the least bothered by the fact. Down on the border with Belize stands Chetumal, a ramshackle place of wood-frame houses that is pervaded by the hybrid culture of coastal Central America and the pungent smell of the sea. Progreso, at the other end of the peninsula on the Gulf of Mexico, is Chetumal's northern counterpart, an overgrown fishing village turned commercial port. Hotels in these towns, while for the most part not as luxurious as the beach resort properties, range from the respectable if plain 1970s commercial buildings to the undated fleabags so popular with detective novelists (one thinks especially of Raymond Chandler) and filmmakers.

Wildlife is another of Yucatán's riches. Iguanas, lizards, tapirs, deer, armadillos, and wild boars thrive on this alternately parched and densely foliated plain. Flamingos and herons, manatees and sea turtles, their once-dwindling numbers now rising in response to Mexico's newly awakened ecological consciousness, find idyllic watery habitats in and above the coastline's mangrove swamps, lagoons, and sandbars, acres of which have been made into national parks. Both Río Lagartos and the coast's Sian Ka'an Biosphere Reserve sparkle with Yucatán's natural beauty. Orchids, bougainvillea, and poinciana are ubiquitous; dazzling reds and pinks and oranges and whites spill into countless courtyards—effortless hothouses. And while immense palm groves and forests of precious hardwood trees slowly succumb to fire and disease, the region's edible tropical flora—coconuts, papaya, bananas, and oranges—remains a succulent ancillary to the celebrated Yucatecan cuisine.

But perhaps it is the colors of Yucatán that are most remarkable. From the stark white, sun-bleached sand, the sea stretches out like some immense canvas painted in bands of celadon greens, pale aquas, and deep dusty blues. At dusk the sea and the horizon meld in the sumptuous glow of a lavender sunset, the sky just barely tinged with periwinkle and violet. Inland, the beige, gray, and amber stones of ruined temples are set off by riotous greenery. The colors of newer structures are equally intoxicating: Tawny, gray-brown thatched roofs sit atop white oval huts. Colonial mansions favor creamy pastels of bisque, salmon, and coral tones, again highlighted by elegant white: white arches, white balustrades, white rococo porticos. Brilliant colors glimmer in carved hardwood doors, variegated tile floors, brown and green pottery and rugs affixed to walls, and snatches of bougainvillea rushing down the sides of buildings.

YUCATÁN'S COLOR extends beyond the physical to the historical. From the conquistadors' first landfall off Cape Catoche in 1517 to the bloody skirmishes that wiped out most of the Indians to the razing of Maya temples and burning of their sacred books, the peninsula was a battlefield. Pirates wreaked havoc off the coast of Campeche for centuries. Half the Indian population was killed during the 19th-century uprising known as the War of the Castes, when the enslaved indigenous population rose up and massacred thousands of Europeans; Yucatán was attempting to secede from Mexico, and dictator Porfirio Díaz sent in his troops. These events, like the towering Maya civilization, have left their mark throughout the peninsula: in its archaeological museums, its colonial monuments, and the opulent mansions of the hacienda owners who enslaved the natives to cultivate their henequen.

But despite the past's violent conflicts with foreigners, the people of Yucatán treat today's visitors with genuine hospitality and friendliness, especially outside the beach resorts. If you learn a few words of Spanish, you will be rewarded with an even warmer welcome.

— Erica Meltzer

NEW AND NOTEWORTHY

The crisis triggered by the late-1994 peso devaluation was tempered by a U.S.-led bailout of Mexico's economy, but the recovery is tenuous at best. Travelers should be aware of the financial desperation of many Mexicans and avoid wearing expensive jewelry or displaying large sums of cash. While creating hardship for residents, the devaluation has resulted in increased purchasing power for visitors (though prices of chain hotels, calculated in dollars in resort areas like Cancún, have remained stable). However, many projects in progress during the early 1990s—including tourist developments—are on hold until the dust from the economic bombshell settles.

At the same time, new types of tourism ventures are being developed. The opening of the first of several planned environmentally friendly jungle lodges in the Xpujil area of the state of Campeche (☞ Chapter 6) has made possible extended visits to the ruins at Bécan, Xpujil, Hormiguero, Río Bec, and Calakmul, all of which are undergoing restoration. And in addition to the hotels, shopping malls, and golf courses that *have* been completed in the '90s, a new marina, San Buenaventura, is under construction in Cancún.

WHAT'S WHERE

Cancún

The jewel of Mexico's Caribbean coast, Cancún is for those who want dazzle for their dollar: The hotel zone is lined with high-rise lodgings, glitzy discos, air-conditioned malls, and gorgeous beaches. For a taste of the real Mexico, go downtown, where Yucatecan specialties are served at casual eateries.

Isla Mujeres

Only 8 km (5 mi) across the bay from Cancún, Isla Mujeres is an ocean away in attitude, as sleepy and unassuming as its neighbor is outgoing. Snorkeling and lazing under a *palapa* (thatched roof) are about as energetic as it gets here, though there are some interesting remnants of the island's pirate past to explore.

Cozumel

A morning's boat ride from Cancún and Isla Mujeres, Cozumel strikes a balance between the two in tone. Mexico's largest cruise ship port, the island is at once commercial and laid back. Along with day trippers, Cozumel draws sport-fishing enthusiasts and divers who come to explore some of the world's best reefs.

The Caribbean Coast

Although the eastern shore of the Yucatán is no longer as pristine as it was in the past—what's been termed the Cancún–Tulum corridor is getting increasingly developed—it still offers plenty of secluded beaches to escape to. Visit the Sian Ka'an Biosphere Reserve to see the area's abundant wildlife, including crocodiles, jaguars, and wild boars, as well as more than 300 species of birds.

Campeche

Ruins of the fortifications built to fend off the pirates who ravaged Yucatán's gulf coast make the walled city of Campeche well worth exploring. Among the remnants of Maya settlements that dot the rest of this little-explored state, Edzná is the best known and most interesting.

Mérida and the Yucatán Peninsula

Long a favorite of archaeologists, the state of Yucatán hosts the two most spectacular Maya ruins, Chichén Itzá and Uxmal. Many travelers are also coming to appreciate the charms of Mérida, with its excellent restaurants and markets and its unique mix of Spanish, Maya, and French architectural styles.

PLEASURES AND PASTIMES

Beaches

Cancún and the rest of Yucatán offer a wonderful variety of beaches: There are white sands, rocky coves and promontories, curvaceous bays, and murky lagoons. Those who thrive on the resort atmosphere will probably enjoy Playa Chac Mool and Playa Tortugas on the bay side of Cancún, which is calmer if less beautiful than the windward side. On the north end of Isla Mujeres, Playa Cocoteros and Playa Norte offer handsome sunset vistas. Beaches on the east coast of Cozumel—once frequented by buccaneers—are rocky, and the swimming is treacherous, but they offer privacy. On the relatively sheltered leeward side are the widest and best sand beaches.

The Caribbean coast abounds with hidden and not-so-hidden beaches (at Xcaret, Paamul, Chemuyil, Xcacel, Punta Bete, south of Tulum, and along the Boca Paila peninsula). There are also long stretches of white sand, usually filled with sunbathers, at Puerto Morelos, Playa del Carmen, and especially Akumal.

Travelers to Campeche and Progreso will find the waters of the Gulf of Mexico deep green, shallow, and tranquil. Such beaches as Payucán, Sabancuy, Isla del Carmen, and Yucalpetén are less visited by North Americans; facilities are minimal, but some prefer it that way.

Bird-Watching

The Yucatán Peninsula is one of the finest areas for birding in Mexico. Habitats range from wildlife and bird sanctuaries to unmarked lagoons, estuaries, and mangrove swamps. Frigates, tanagers, warblers, and macaws inhabit Isla Contoy (off Isla Mujeres) and the Laguna Colombia on Cozumel; an even greater variety of species are to be found in the Sian Ka'an Biosphere Reserve on the Boca Paila peninsula south of Tulum. Along the north and west coasts of Yucatán—at Río Lagartos, Laguna Rosada, and Celestún—flamingos, herons, ibis, cormorants, pelicans, and peregrine falcons thrive.

Dining

The mystique of Yucatecan cooking has a lot to do with the generous doses of local spices and herbs, although generally the food tends not to be too spicy. Among the specialties are *cochinita píbil* and *pollo píbil* (succulent chicken baked in banana leaves with a spicy, pumpkin-seed-and-chili sauce); *poc chuc* (Yucatecan pork marinated in a sour-orange sauce with pickled onions); *tikinchic* (fried fish prepared with sour orange); *panuchos* (fried tortillas filled with black beans and topped with turkey, chicken, or pork, pickled onions, and avocado); *papadzules* (tortillas piled high with hard-boiled eggs and drenched in a sauce of pumpkin seed and fried tomato); and *codzitos* (rolled tortillas in pumpkin-seed sauce). *Achiote* (annatto), cilantro (coriander), and the fiery *chile habanero* are highly favored condiments.

Yucatecans are renowned for—among other things—their love of idiosyncratic beverages. *Yztabentún,* a liqueur made of fermented honey and anise, dates back to the ancient Maya; like straight tequila, it's best drunk in small sips between bites of fresh lime. Local brews, such as the dark bock León Negra and the light Montejo, are excellent but hard to find in peninsular restaurants. On the healthier side, *chaya* is the bright-green juice of a local plant resembling spinach. Yucatecan *horchata,* a favorite all over Mexico, is made from milled rice and water flavored with vanilla. Also try the *licuados,* either milk- or water-based smoothies, made from the tropical fruits of the region (but avoid outdoor stands, because they often use unpasteurized milk and unpurified water).

Fishing

Sport fishing is popular in Cozumel and throughout the Caribbean coast. The rich waters of the Caribbean and the Gulf of Mexico support hundreds of species of tropical fish, making the Yucatán coastline and the outlying islands a paradise for deep-sea fishing, fly-fishing, and bone-fishing. Particularly between the months of April and July, the waters off Cancún, Cozumel, and Isla Mujeres teem with sailfish, marlin, red snapper, tuna, barracuda, and wahoo, among other denizens of the deep. Bill fishing is so rich around Cozumel and Puerto Aventuras that each holds an annual tournament.

Farther south, along the Boca Paila peninsula, banana fish, bonefish, mojarra, shad, permit, and sea bass provide great sport for flat fishing and fly-fishing, while oysters, shrimp, and conch lie on the bottom of the Gulf of Mexico near Campeche and Isla del Carmen. At Progreso, on the north coast, sport fishing for grouper, dogfish, and pompano is quite popular.

Hunting

Hunting, although increasingly frowned upon as a result of Mexico's heightened ecological awareness, is good along the northwestern side of the peninsula and around Mérida and Campeche. Game includes waterfowl, quail, and wild boar. Inquire at your local Mexican consulate about mandatory permits.

Ruins

Amateur archaeologists will find heaven in the Yucatán, where the ancient Maya most abundantly left their mark. Pick your period and your preference, whether for well-excavated sites or overgrown, out-of-the-way ruins barely touched by a scholar's shovel. The major Maya sites are Cobá and Tulum (☞ Chapter 5) and Chichén Itzá and Uxmal (☞ Chapter 7), but smaller ruins scattered throughout the peninsula are often equally fascinating.

Oxkintok, just off the main road between Mérida and Campeche, is one of the more rewarding unrestored Maya sites in the Yucatán. Only a few structures have been excavated at this rarely visited spot, but the magnitude of overgrown ruins is impressive, and the presence of sculptures, pottery shards, and other on-site artifacts lets adventurous sightseers experience a more direct link with the ancient past.

Scuba Diving and Snorkeling

Underwater enthusiasts come to Cozumel, Akumal, Xcalak, Xel-Há, and other parts of Mexico's Caribbean coast for the clear turquoise waters, the colorful and assorted tropical fish, and the exquisite coral formations along the Belize reef system. Currents allow for drift diving, and both reefs and offshore wrecks lend themselves to dives, many of which are safe enough for neophytes. The peninsula's cenotes, or natural sinkholes, provide an unusual dive experience. Individual chapters will direct you to the dive sites that will best suit you.

Water Sports

All manner of water sports—jet skiing, catamaran sailing, sailboarding, waterskiing, sailing, and parasailing—are practiced in Cancún, Cozumel, and along the Caribbean coast, where you'll find well-equipped water-sports centers.

FODOR'S CHOICE

Archaeological Sites

★ **Chichén Itzá.** The best-known Maya ruin, Chichén Itzá was the most important city in the Yucatán from the 11th to the 13th centuries. Its eclectic architecture is evidence of a complex intermingling of ancient cultures.

★ **Cobá.** Once a central city-state in the Maya domain, this site has long languished in a lush, tropical setting. Only about 5% of its more than 6,000 structures have been excavated.

★ **Edzná.** Archaeologists consider this remote and little explored ruin crucial for its transitional role among several Maya architectural styles. This ruin is remarkably intact.

★ **Tulum.** The spectacular backdrop of the Caribbean and proximity to Cancún explain why Tulum is the most visited archaeological site in the Yucatán.

★ **Uxmal.** Arguably the most beautiful of Mexico's ruins, Uxmal represents Maya style at its purest, including ornate stone friezes, intricate cornices, and soaring arches.

Beaches

★ **Akumal.** Long stretches of this popular section of the Caribbean coast are filled with shells, crabs, and migrant birds. Protected coves with tranquil water are ideal for swimming or snorkeling.

★ **Playa Norte.** A white sand beach on the northern tip of Isla Mujeres, Playa Norte—sometimes called Cocoteros or Cocos—is both scenic and social.

★ **Punta Celerain.** The lighthouse at the southern end of Cozumel affords wonderful views of pounding waves, swamps, and jungle.

★ **Xcalak peninsula.** One of the Caribbean coast's still-remote spots, this peninsula is lush with mangrove swamps, tropical flowers, and wildlife.

Nature Reserves and Natural Beauty

★ **Isla Contoy.** An unspoiled island preserve off the coast of Isla Mujeres, Isla Contoy is especially notable for its birds; more than 70 species pass through in the fall.

★ **Laguna de Bacalar.** The second largest lake in Mexico is known as "The Lake of Seven Colors" because of the stunning hues that a mix of seawater, freshwater, and seaweed produce.

★ **Loltún Caves.** This largest of the many limestone caverns that honeycomb the central Yucatán Peninsula has colorful rock formations as well as pictographs left by the Maya, who lived here for thousands of years.

⭐ **Parque Natural del Flamenco Mexicano.** One of the biggest colonies of flamingos in North America rests here from September through April; deer and armadillo roam this huge wildlife preserve, too.

⭐ **Río Lagartos National Park.** Another beautiful place in the Yucatán to view flamingos, Río Lagartos also attracts green turtles, who lay their eggs on the beach at night.

⭐ **Sian Ka'an Biosphere Reserve.** At this 1.3-million-acre preserve, you can see half-submerged Maya ruins in mangrove canals or bird-watch for exotic species in the jungle.

Shopping

⭐ **Mercado de Artisanís "García Rejón," Mérida.** Come to this handicraft market for hammocks, Panama hats, baskets, and other Yucatán souvenirs.

⭐ **Los Cinco Soles, Cozumel.** Cruise ship passengers with limited time to shop can find a large array of well-priced clothing and crafts here.

⭐ **Mercado Municipal, Mérida.** The best general market in the Yucatán sells everything from live birds and food to intricate local crafts.

Dining

⭐ **La Dolce Vita, Cancún.** Terrific Italian food and a romantic atmosphere draw beach lovers to this restaurant, recently relocated to Laguna Nichupte in the hotel zone. $$$

⭐ **Casa Cenote, Mexico's Caribbean coast.** This unique restaurant near the ruins of Tulum allows diners to plunge into a large natural pool before enjoying tasty American and Mexican fare. $$

⭐ **La Bella Epoca, Mérida.** At this gracious converted mansion, diners indulge in platters of Middle Eastern specialties along with well-prepared versions of French and Yucatecan dishes. $$

⭐ **La Choza, Cozumel.** The super-fresh Mexican entrées at this friendly, family-run place include chicken mole and grilled lobster; tortillas are baked on the premises. $$

⭐ **Marganzo, Campeche.** The food at this popular, low-key place typifies the distinctive seafood dishes known as *estilo campechano* (Campeche-style) all over Mexico. $

⭐ **Velazquez, Isla Mujeres.** This quintessential palapa-style eatery is right on the beach. Don't be misled by the simple, rustic ambience; here you'll find the best seafood on the island. $

Lodging

⭐ **Casa Turquesa, Cancún.** This small luxury hotel offers the ultimate in taste, culture, and personal attention. Also on the property is the internationally known restaurant **Celebrity.** $$$$

⭐ **Presidente Inter-Continental Cozumel.** A great water-sports center, a fine beach for snorkeling, and bright, contemporary-style rooms make this the luxury-class choice on Cozumel. $$$$

⭐ **Ritz-Carlton Cancún.** The Cancún link of this international chain adds class to the beachfront hotel zone. Its facilities and restaurants are superb. $$$$

⭐ **Na Balam, Isla Mujeres.** The rooms here are attractive in a simple, folk-art fashion, and their proximity to sea and sand is hard to beat. $$$

⭐ **Gran Hotel, Mérida.** The oldest hotel in Mérida combines character—an Art Nouveau courtyard, high-ceiling, balconied rooms—with reasonable prices. $$

⭐ **Ramada Ecovillage Resort, Campeche.** Comfort and even a bit of luxury can be found at this jungle lodge on the fringe of the Calakmul rain forest and near a little-explored archaeological zone. $$

⭐ **Villa Arqueólogica Cobá, Mexico's Caribbean coast.** Enjoy sleeping among the ruins at this Club Med, about 10 minutes away from Cobá. The lakeside setting is lovely, and the food is the best in the area. $$

Nightlife

⭐ **Azucar, Cancún.** Locals and visitors of all ages gather at this hot nightspot for the best live salsa in Cancún.

⭐ **Dady'O, Cancún.** Though it's been around for a while, this is still *the* place to come if you need a cure for Saturday Night Fever.

★ **Joe's Lobster House, Cozumel.** Beginning about 9 PM, live rollicking reggae and hot salsa spice up the music menu here. This quaint nightspot, popular with locals, hops into the wee hours.

★ **YaYa's, Isla Mujeres.** Live rock and Texas-style chili dogs have proved a winning combination here.

FESTIVALS AND SEASONAL EVENTS

Traditional religious and patriotic festivals rank among Yucatán's most memorable activities. Towns throughout the region host a number of additional annual fairs, shows, and local celebrations.

Hotel rooms may be hard to get in some places during festival times; be sure to book far in advance, for example, if you want to be near Chichén Itzá around the equinoxes or in Mérida in early January, when the city's founding is commemorated.

WINTER

JAN. 1➤ **New Year's Day** is celebrated throughout the region.

JAN. 6➤ **El Día de Los Reyes** (Feast of the Epiphany, or Three Kings Day) coincides with the anniversary of the founding of Mérida (1542). In that city, the traditional day of gift-giving is also one of parades, fireworks, and outdoor parties.

FEB.–MAR.➤ **Carnaval** (Mardi Gras) festivities take place the week before Lent, with parades, floats, outdoor dancing, music, and fireworks; they are especially spirited in Mérida, Cozumel, Isla Mujeres, Campeche, and Chetumal.

SPRING

MAR. 21 AND SEPT. 21➤ At the **Equinoxes,** Kukulcán, the plumed serpent deity, appears to emerge from his temple atop El Castillo Pyramid at Chichén Itzá and slithers down to earth.

LATE APR.➤ The **Sol a Sol International Regatta,** launched from St. Petersburg, Florida, arrives in Isla Mujeres, sparking regional dances and a general air of festivity.

LATE APR.–JUNE➤ **Billfish Tournaments** take place in Cozumel, Puerto Aventuras, and Cancún.

APR. 28–MAY 3➤ **Holy Cross Fiestas** in Chumayel, Celestún, Hopelchén—all in Yucatán state—include cockfights, dances, and fireworks.

EARLY MAY➤ **Regatta al Sol** brings a fleet of sailboats from Pensacola, Florida, to Isla Mujeres.

MAY 20–27➤ **Hammock Festival,** hailing the furnishing that originated here, is held in Tecoh, on the southern outskirts of Mérida.

MEMORIAL DAY WEEKEND➤ The **Cancún Jazz Festival,** an annual event as of 1991, has featured such top musicians as Wynton Marsalis and Gato Barbieri.

AUTUMN

SEPT. 14➤ *Vaquerías* (traditional cattle-branding feasts) attract aficionados to rural towns for bullfights, fireworks, and music.

SEPT. 14–28➤ **Fiesta of San Román** attracts 50,000 people to Campeche to view the procession carrying the Black Christ of San Román—the city's most sacred patron saint—through the streets.

SEPT. 15–16➤ **Independence Day,** the commemoration of a historic speech, known as the *grito* (shout), by Independence leader Padre Miguel Hidalgo, is celebrated throughout Mexico with fireworks and parties.

SEPT. 27➤ **Fiesta of Our Lord of the Blisters** (Cristo de las Ampollas) begins two weeks or more of religious events and processions in Mérida; dances, bullfights, and fireworks take place in Ticul and other small villages.

OCT. 18–25➤ **Fiesta of the Christ of Sitilpech** in Izamal, an hour from Mérida, heralds a week of daily processions in which the image of Christ is carried from Sitilpech village to Izamal; dances and fireworks accompany the walks.

NOV. 1–2➤ On the **Day of the Dead,** or All Saints' Day, Mexicans all over the country visit cemeteries to construct marigold-strewn altars on the graves of loved ones and ancestors, and to symbolically share a meal with them by leaving offerings and having graveside picnics. Bakers herald the annual return of the departed from the spirit world with pastry skulls and candy.

NOV. 29–DEC. 8➤ **Fiesta of Isla Mujeres** honors the island's patron saint, as members of various guilds stage processions, dances, and bullfights.

NOV. 30–DEC. 8➤ **Fiesta of the Virgin of the Conception** is held each year in Champotón, Campeche.

EARLY DEC.➤ **Cancún Fair** serves as a nostalgia trip for provincials who now live along the Caribbean shore but still remember the small-town fiestas back home.

DEC. 3–9➤ **Day of the Immaculate Conception** is observed for six days in the village of Kantunilkin, Quintana Roo, with processions, folkloric dances, fireworks, and bullfights.

DEC. 8–12➤ The **Aquatic Procession** highlights festivities at the fishing village of Celestún, west of Mérida.

DEC. 16–25➤ **Christmas** is celebrated in the Yucatán villages of Espita and Temax with processions culminating in the breaking of candy-filled piñatas.

2 Cancún

The jewel of Mexico's Caribbean coast, Cancún is for those who want dazzle for their dollar: The hotel zone is lined with high-rise lodgings, glitzy discos, air-conditioned malls, and gorgeous beaches. For a taste of the real Mexico, go downtown, where Yucatecan specialties are served at casual eateries.

FLYING INTO CANCÚN, Mexico's most popular destination, you see nothing but green treetops for miles.
It's clear from the air that this resort was literally carved
out of the jungle. When development began here in 1974, the beaches
were deserted except for their iguana inhabitants. Now, luxury hotels
line the oceanfront, and nearly 2 million visitors a year come for the
white sand beaches and crystalline Caribbean waters. They also come
for the sizzling nightlife and, in some cases, for proximity to the Yucatán ruins. Although the resort is too glitzy and tourist-oriented for
many, it draws thousands of repeat visitors.

Updated by
Dan Millington

Cancún City is on the mainland, but the hotel zone is on a 22½-km
(14-mi) barrier island off the Yucatán Peninsula. The resort is designed to please American tastes; most people speak English, and devotees of cable TV and Pizza Hut will not be disappointed. Beach lovers
can bask in Cancún's year-round tropical warmth and sunny skies. The
sun shines an average of 240 days a year, reputedly more than at almost any other Caribbean spot. Temperatures linger appealingly at about
80°F. You can sample Yucatecan foods and watch folkloric dance
demonstrations as well as knock back tequila slammers at the myriad
nightspots.

But there can be more to the resort than plopping down under a *palapa*
(thatched roof). For divers and snorkelers, the reefs off Cancún, nearby
Cozumel, and Isla Mujeres are among the best in the world. Cancún
also provides a relaxing home base for visiting the stupendous ruins
of Chichén Itzá, Tulum, and Cobá on the mainland—remnants of the
area's rich Maya heritage—as well as the Yucatán coast and its lagoons.

The most important buildings in Cancún, however, are modern hotels.
The resort has gone through the life cycle typical of any tourist destination. At its inception, the resort drew the jet set; lately, it has attracted
increasing numbers of less affluent tourists, primarily package-tour tak-
ers and college students, particularly during spring break when hordes
of flawless, tanned young bodies people the beaches and restaurants.

As for the island's history, not much was written about it before its
birth as a resort. The island does not appear on the early navigators'
maps, and little is known about the Maya who lived here; apparently
Cancún's marshy terrain discouraged development. It is recorded that
Maya settled the area during the pre-classical era, in about AD 200,
and remained until about the 14th or 15th century. In the mid-19th
century minor Maya ruins were sighted; however, they were not studied by archaeologists until the 1950s. In 1970 then-president Luis
Echeverría first visited the site that had been chosen to retrieve the state
of Quintana Roo from obscurity and abject poverty.

Cancún's natural environment has paid a price. Its lagoons and mangrove swamps have become polluted, and a number of species, like conch
and lobster, are dwindling. Although the beaches still appear pristine
for the most part, an increased effort will have to be made in order to
preserve the physical beauty that is the resort's prime appeal.

Pleasures and Pastimes

Archaeological Sites

Would-be archaeologists can start their exploration of the Maya world
in Cancún, which is dotted with the vestiges of an AD 900–AD 1520
settlement. The resort also serves as a gateway for the magnificent Maya
site at Tulum, an easy day-trip away.

Beaches

Although the Mexican government designed the resort, nature provided its most striking features—its cool, white, porous limestone sand and clear blue waters. Except for the tip of Punta Cancún, Cancún Island is one long beach. The beaches along the island's windward side—those fringing the Bahía des Mujeres—have the calmest water and are ideal for water sports and swimmers of all levels of proficiency. On the eastern coast, facing the open Caribbean, things pick up a bit—waves are bigger and the pounding surf can sometimes surprise the unwary with currents and riptides. Beaches are federal property in Mexico and anyone with stamina can walk for miles, either along the more popular beaches, like Playa Chac Mool and Playa Tortugas, which have restaurants, bars, and sports facilities, or along the less trafficked eastern strand, where Playa Delfines offers spectacular views near the tip of the island.

Dining

One of the most appealing aspects of Cancún's dining options is their diversity. Many restaurants offer a hybrid cuisine that combines fresh fish from local waters, elements of Yucatecan and Mexican cuisines, and a fusion of French, Italian, and American influences. Fiesta dinners are a weekly staple at many hotels, so you can sample a variety of Mexican favorites without venturing out. Those who enjoy high drama at dinner will find places where the waiters artistically prepare meals table-side or where cocktails are served flaming.

Visitors with a taste for a more local dining experience can find Cancún menus that emphasize seafood. Fish caught from the waters around the island, then grilled and seasoned with lime juice, is a sure bet. Other favorites of Yucatecan regional cuisine are *sopa de lima* (chicken broth spiked with lime juice); grilled pork and chicken prepared with spices used in Maya cooking, such as *achiote*; pork or chicken *píbil* (baked in banana leaves with a tangy sour-orange sauce); and *papadzules* (tortillas piled high with hard-boiled egg in a pumpkin-seed and tomato sauce).

Lodging

Cancún's hotels presently number more than 110. The resort's architecture, especially in the hotel zone, tends to be a cross between Mediterranean and Maya. In many cases the combination yields an appealing, if sometimes kitschy, style. Typical Mediterranean structures—low, solid, rectangular, with flat, red-tile roofs, Moorish arches, and white stucco walls covered with exuberantly pink bougainvillea—acquire palapas and such ornamental devices as colonnettes, latticework, and beveled cornices. Inside, you'll find bland contemporary-style furniture and lots of pastel hues.

Set back from the principal boulevard, Paseo Kukulcán, in nicely landscaped tropical settings highlighted by palm trees, waterfalls, or tiered pools, the hotels pride themselves on offering endless opportunities for fun—water sports, marinas, golf, tennis, kids' clubs, fitness centers, spas, shopping, entertainment, excursions, several dining options—all infused with inimitable Mexican friendliness and attentive service. To keep costs down, choose more modest digs downtown, where local color far outweighs resort facilities.

Nightlife

Cancún is the place for party animals, especially during spring break, when the ultramodern discos and nightclubs pound from late night to early dawn. Entertainment centers like Planet Hollywood and the Hard Rock Cafe are also magnets for a younger crowd. A less frenetic nighttime sport is barhopping in the big resort hotels; some lobby bars offer 2-for-1 drinks at happy hour, and most provide live music—everything from classic guitar or flute to mariachi, salsa, reggae, jazz, and rock. You can admire the architecturally diverse hotel interiors as you bar-hop. For a taste of old Mexico, spend an evening at the folkloric ballet dinner show at the convention center. And for a waterborne night out, take a dinner cruise on the *Cancún Queen* or *Columbus*, featuring dancing under the stars.

Water Sports

Cancún is one of the water sports capitals of the world, and the athletically minded can make optimum use of the Caribbean and the still waters of Laguna Nichupté. Visitors can go fishing, sailing, swimming, jet skiing, windsurfing—the list seems endless. Snorkeling or diving among the host of tropical fish and colorful marine creatures that live along the coral reefs hugging Mexico's Caribbean coast is an incomparable experience. If you want to view the mysterious underwater world but don't want to get your feet wet, a glass-bottom boat or "submarine" is the ticket.

EXPLORING CANCÚN

The island of Cancún, which is shaped roughly like the numeral seven, is divided into two zones, with the hotel zone the much larger of the two. Picture the horizontal leg as extending east from the mainland into the Caribbean; Punta Cancún is where the vertical leg takes over, going north–south. Hotel development began at the north end (close to the mainland), headed east toward Punta Cancún, and is moving south to Punta Nizuc, where the tip of the seven almost joins up again with the mainland. The other zone—Cancún City or downtown Cancún, known as *el centro*—is actually 4 km (2½ mi) west of the hotel zone on the mainland. The seven is separated from the mainland by a system of lagoons: Nichupté, the largest (about 29 square km, or 18 square mi), containing both fresh and salt water; Bojórquez, at the juncture of the two legs of the seven; and Río Inglés to the south. North of the horizontal leg lies Bahía de Mujeres, the 9-km- (5½-mi-) wide bay that separates Cancún from Isla Mujeres. Regularly placed kilometer markers on the roadside help indicate where you are; they go from Km 1 on the mainland, near downtown, to Km 20 at Punta Nizuc.

Paseo Kukulcán is the main drag in the hotel zone, and because most of the seven is less than 1 km wide, both the Caribbean and the lagoons can be seen from either side of it. The hotel zone consists entirely of hotels, restaurants and shopping complexes, marinas, and time-share condominiums; there are no residential areas as such. It's not the sort of place you can get to know by walking. Paseo Kukulcán is punctuated by driveways with steep inclines turning into the hotels, most of which are set at least 100 yards from the road. The lagoon side of the boulevard consists of scrubby stretches of land, many of them covered with construction cranes, alternating with marinas, shopping centers, and restaurants. What is most scenic about Cancún is the dramatic contrast between the vivid turquoise-and-violet sea and the blinding alabaster-white sands. Because there are so few sights, no orientation tours of Cancún are offered: Simply ride the local bus circuit to get a feel for the island's layout.

When you first visit Cancún City (downtown), you may be confused by the layout. There are four principal avenues: Tulum and Yaxchilán, which run north–south; and Uxmal and Cobá, which go east–west. Streets bounded by those avenues and running perpendicular to them are actually horseshoe-shaped, so you will find two parallel streets named

Tulipanes, for instance. However, street numbers or even street names are not of much use in Cancún; the proximity to landmarks, such as specific hotels, is the preferred way of giving directions.

Numbers in the text correspond to numbers in the margin and on the Cancún map.

A Good Tour

Cancún's scenery consists mostly of its beautiful beaches and crystal-clear waters, but there are also a few intriguing historical sites tucked away among the modern hotels. In addition to the attractions listed below, two modest vestiges of the ancient Maya civilization are worth a visit, but only for dedicated archaeology buffs. Neither is identified by name. On the 12th hole of Pok-Ta-Pok golf course (⊠ Paseo Kukulcán, between Km 6 and Km 7), whose Maya name means "ball game," stands a ruin consisting of two platforms and the remains of other buildings. And the ruin of a tiny Maya shrine is cleverly incorporated into the architecture of the Hotel Camino Real (on the beach at Punta Cancún).

You don't need a car in Cancún, but if you've rented one to make extended trips, it might be worth starting in the southern hotel zone at **Ruinas del Rey** ① and **San Miguelito** ②, driving north to **Yamil Lu'um** ③ and then stopping in at the **convention center** ④ before heading west to **downtown** ⑤.

Sights to See

❹ **Cancún Convention Center.** This strikingly modern venue for cultural events is the jumping off point for a ½-mi-long string of shopping malls that extends west to the Presidente Inter-Continental Cancún. In the convention center complex itself, **Inter Plaza** contains 15 restaurants, 21 boutiques, a bank, and several airline offices. At press time, a 525-ft observation tower was still under construction. Originally scheduled for completion in late 1994, and now set for 1997, it will feature the highest viewing platform in Latin America. ⊠ *Paseo Kukulcán, Km 9,* ☎ *98/830199.*

The **National Institute of Anthropology and History,** the small museum on the ground floor of the convention center, traces Maya culture by showcasing a fascinating collection of 1,000- to 1,500-year-old artifacts collected throughout Quintana Roo. ☎ *98/830305.* ⚒ *About $3, free Sun.* ☉ *Tues.–Sun. 9–7. Guided tour in English, French, German, and Spanish.*

❺ **Downtown Cancún.** The main thoroughfare is **Avenida Tulum,** which begins at the spot where Paseo Kukulcán turns into Avenida Cobá. Many restaurants and shops are located along here, as is Ki Huic, the largest crafts market in Cancún. Life-size reproductions of ancient Mexican art, including the Aztec calendar stone, a giant Olmec head, the Atlantids of Tula, and the Maya *chac mool* (reclining rain god), line the grassy strip dividing Tulum's northbound and southbound lanes. Visitors looking for shopping bargains, however, generally find better prices on the parallel **Avenida Yaxchilán.**

❶ **Ruinas del Rey.** Located on the lagoon side at Cancún Island, roughly opposite El Pueblito and Playa de Oro hotels, these small ruins have been incorporated into the Caesar Park Beach & Golf Resort complex; large signs point out the site. First mentioned in a 16th-century travelogue and then in 1842 when they were sighted by American explorer John Lloyd Stephens and his draftsman, Frederick Catherwood, the ruins were finally explored by archaeologists in 1910, though excavations did not begin until 1954. In 1975 archaeologists, along with the Mexican government, began the restoration of Ruinas del Rey and San Miguelito (☞ *below*), a nearby ruin that is now inaccessible.

Cancún

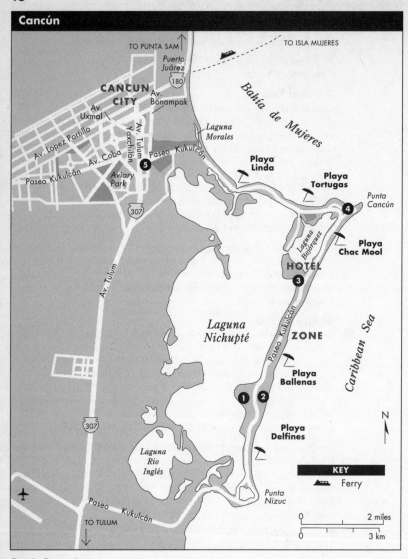

TO PUNTA SAM

TO ISLA MUJERES

Puerto
Juárez

Bahía de Mujeres

**CANCÚN
CITY**

Av.
Bonampak

Av
Uxmal

Av. Lopez Portillo

Av. Tulum
Yaxchilán

*Laguna
Morales*

**Playa
Linda**

**Playa
Tortugas**

*Punta
Cancún*

Av. Coba

Paseo Kukulcán

④

Paseo Kukulcán

*Aviary
Park*

⑤

307

**Playa
Chac Mool**

*Laguna
Bojórquez*

HOTEL

③

*Laguna
Nichupté*

ZONE

Av. Tulum

Paseo Kukulcán

Caribbean Sea

**Playa
Ballenas**

① ②

**Playa
Delfines**

*Laguna
Rio
Inglés*

N

307

KEY

🚢 Ferry

✈

Paseo Kukulcán

*Punta
Nizuc*

0 ———— 2 miles
0 ———— 3 km

TO TULUM

Cancún Convention
Center, **4**
Downtown Cancún, **5**
Ruinas del Rey, **1**
San Miguelito, **2**
Yamil Lu'um, **3**

Del Rey may not be particularly impressive when compared to major archaeological sites such as Tulum or Chichén Itzá, but it is the largest ruin in Cancún and definitely worth a look. It's notable for its unusual architecture: two main plazas bounded by two streets. Most of the other Maya cities, which were not in any sense planned but had developed over centuries, contained one plaza with a number of ceremonial satellites and few streets. The pyramid here is topped by a platform, and inside its vault are stucco paintings. Skeletons found buried both at the apex and at the base indicate that the site may have been a royal burial ground. Originally named Kin Ich Ahau Bonil, Maya for "King of the Solar Countenance," the 2nd- to 3rd-century BC site was linked to astronomical practices in the ancient Maya culture.

Depending on your attitude toward reptiles, one aspect of these ruins can be considered either a drawback or a draw: They're home to hundreds of large iguanas. One reader reported that, when he and his fellow tourists stood still, they were approached by about a dozen of the lizards, who begged food like squirrels, and that two of them licked his shoes. ⊠ *Paseo Kukulcán, Km 17, no phone.* ▣ *About $3, free Sun.* ☉ *Daily 8–5.*

② **San Miguelito.** On the east side of Paseo Kukulcán is a very small stone building (about the size of a shack) with a number of columns about 4 ft high. At press time, this modest Maya site was fenced off and not accessible to the public, but this may change after archaeologists have fully examined the ruins. ⊠ *Paseo Kukulcán, Km 16.5, no phone.*

③ **Yamil Lu'um.** A small sign at the Sheraton will direct you to the dirt path leading to this site, which stands on the highest point of Cancún, adjoining the hotel—the name Yamil Lu'um means "hilly land." Although it comprises two structures—one probably a temple, the other probably a lighthouse—this is the smallest of Cancún's ruins. Discovered in 1842 by John Lloyd Stephens, the remains date from the late 13th or early 14th century. ⊠ *Paseo Kukulcán, Km 12, no phone.*

BEACHES

Cancún Island is one long, continuous beach. By law, the entire coast of Mexico is federal property and open to the public; in practice, however, hotel security guards keep peddlers off the beaches, and hotel guests are easily identified by the color of the towels they place on their beach lounge chairs. Most hotel beaches have lifeguards, but, as with all ocean swimming, use common sense—even the calmest-looking waters can have currents and riptides. Overall, the beaches on the windward stretch of the island—those closest to the city, facing the Bahía de Mujeres—are best for swimming; farther out, the undertow can be tricky. It's best not to swim when the red danger flags fly; yellow flags indicate that you should proceed with caution; green or blue means waters are calm. On shore, be sure to protect yourself from the searing tropical sun, an obvious precaution once you feel the heat or see the scorched bodies here. Avoid prolonged exposure during peak sunlight hours (11–3) and always use sunscreen or sunblock.

Two popular areas, **Playa Tortugas** (Km 7) and **Chac Mool** (Km 10), have restaurants and changing areas, making them especially appealing for vacationers who are staying at the beachless downtown hotels. Be careful of strong waves at Chac Mool, where it's tempting to walk far out into the shallow water. South of Chac Mool are the usually deserted beaches of **Playa Ballenas** (between Km 15 and Km 16) and **Playa Delfines** (between Km 20 and Km 21), noted for its expansive views.

Swimming can be treacherous in the rough surf of Ballenas and Delfines, but they offer a breezy, restful venue for solitary sunbathing.

DINING

At last count, there were more than 1,200 restaurants in Cancún, but—according to one successful restaurateur—only about 100 are worth their salt, so to speak. Finding the right restaurant in Cancún is not easy. The downtown restaurants that line the noisy Avenida Tulum often have tables spilling onto pedestrian-laden sidewalks; however, gas fumes and gawking tourists tend to detract from the romantic outdoor-café ambience. Many of the hotel-zone restaurants, on the other hand, cater to what they assume is a tourist preference for bland, not-too-foreign-tasting food.

One key to good dining in Cancún is to find the haunts—mostly in the downtown area—where locals go for Yucatán-style food prepared by the experts. A cheap and filling trend in Cancún's dining scene is the sumptuous buffet breakfasts offered by an increasing number of restaurants and hotels on the island. These are especially pleasant when served at palapa restaurants on the beach. At about $15, the brunches are a good value—eat on the late side and you won't be hungry until dinner.

When reviewing Cancún's restaurants, we looked for places where you will get the best values and enjoy your meal the most. Only the truly exceptional hotel restaurants are listed, allowing for more comprehensive coverage of independently operated cafés. Unless otherwise stated, restaurants serve lunch and dinner daily.

What to Wear
Generally speaking, dress is casual here, but many restaurants will not admit diners with bare feet, short shorts, or no shirts.

CATEGORY	COST*
$$$$	over $35
$$$	$25–$35
$$	$15–$25
$	under $15

per person, excluding drinks and service

Hotel Zone

$$$$ ✕ **Blue Bayou.** Seven levels of snug dining areas, decorated in wood, rattan, bamboo, and flourishing greens, create the atmosphere for a memorable evening. Sounds from the cascading waterfall and waiters dressed in black pants, white shirts with colorful arm bands, and straw boaters heighten a sophisticated New Orleans riverboat tone, set off by jazz that drifts in from the adjoining bar. Blackened meat, fish, and lobster—Cajun and Creole style—are featured on the menu, which is nicely balanced by a number of Mexican specialties. ✉ *Hyatt Cancún Caribe, Paseo Kukulcán,* ☎ *98/830044. AE, DC, MC, V. No lunch.*

$$$$ ✕ **Bogart's.** Whether you consider it amusingly elaborate or merely pretentious, it's hard to be neutral about Bogart's, probably the most expensive and talked-about restaurant in town. Taking off from the film *Casablanca,* the place is decorated with Persian rugs, fans, velvet-cushioned banquettes, and fountains; waiters wear fezzes and white suits. A menu as eclectic as the patrons of Rick's Cafe features many seafood and Mediterranean dishes. The food is okay, but don't expect large portions; servings are nouvelle style. ✉ *Paseo Kukulcán, Hotel Krystal,* ☎ *98/831133. Reservations essential. AE, DC, MC, V. No lunch.*

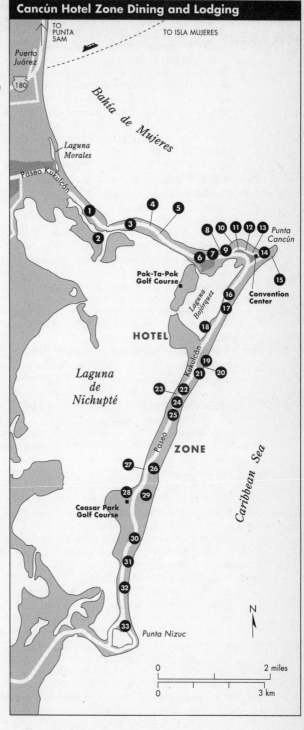

Cancún Hotel Zone Dining and Lodging

Dining

Augustus Caesar, **11**
Blue Bayou, **17**
Bogart's, **15**
Captain's Cove, **3, 28**
Carlos 'n Charlie's, **5**
Casa Rolandi, **12**
Celebrity Restaurant, **20**
Club Grill, **21**
El Mexicano, **11**
Hacienda
El Mortero, **15**
Jalapeños, **6**
La Dolce Vita, **23**
La Fisheria, **12**
Lorenzillos, **18**
Mikado, **22**
100% Natural, **10, 19**
Savio's, **12**
Shooter's Waterfront
Café, U.S.A., **27**
Splash, **19**

Lodging

Caesar Park Beach &
Golf Resort, **29**
Calinda Viva
Cancún, **8**
Casa Turquesa, **20**
Club Las Velas, **2**
El Pueblito
Beach Hotel, **30**
Fiesta Americana
Cancún, **9**
Fiesta Americana
Condesa, **25**
Fiesta Americana Coral
Beach Cancún, **13**
Hyatt Cancún Caribe
Villas & Resort, **17**
Hyatt Regency
Cancún, **14**
Krystal Cancún, **15**
Marriott
CasaMagna, **22**
Meliá Cancún, **24**
Omni Cancún, **26**
Presidente Inter-
Continental Cancún, **7**
Ritz-Carlton
Cancún, **21**
Royal Solaris
Caribe, **31**
Sierra Cancún, **16**
Sun Palace, **32**
Villa Deportiva
Juvenil Cancún, **1**
Villas Tacul, **4**
Westin Regina
Resort Cancún, **33**

$$$$ ✕ **Celebrity Restaurant.** One of Cancún's best restaurants can be found
★ in the Casa Turquesa, a small luxury hotel that does indeed cater to many
celebrities. The nautically themed dining room has both a street and
hotel lobby entrance. Subtly lit, with a soaring palapa roof, swirling ceiling fans, potted palms, rattan furniture, and an elegantly polished dark
wood floor, it scores high on the romance scale. Live classic and Spanish guitar music add to the ambience. The creative cuisine accents local
seafood: Try the red snapper filet with smoked salmon served on spinach
or tuna medallions with red wine sauce. There's also an interesting selection of meat and poultry dishes and a good choice of wines. The Mexican coffee, with vanilla ice cream, orange peel, and sugar, flambéed
table-side with Xtabentum, an anise-based liqueur, is excellent. ⊠ *Paseo
Kukulcán, Casa Turquesa,* ☎ 98/852924. *AE, MC, V. No lunch.*

$$$$ ✕ **Club Grill.** Cancún's hands-down favorite for gourmet dining and
★ a prime choice for that romantic, special occasion dinner, the **Ritz-
Carlton's** fine dining room is divided into intimate chambers; one of
them has a dance floor and a small stage for live music in the evening.
Walls are trimmed with rich wood, fresh flower arrangements abound,
and tall windows look out onto a bubbling courtyard fountain and the
Caribbean beyond. European grill is the house specialty; rich sauces
and decorative touches give a distinctly Mexican spin to the grilled chops,
steaks, chicken, and seafood. White bean soup, lobster ravioli, and blackened rib eye steak with Yucatecan spices are popular menu choices.
Try the *chipotle* (a smoked pepper) duck in honey tequila sauce. Service is attentive and discreet. ⊠ *Paseo Kukulcán (Retorno del Rey 36),*
☎ 98/850808. *AE, DC, MC, V.*

$$$ ✕ **Hacienda El Mortero.** Pampering waiters, strolling mariachis, lush
hanging plants, fig trees, and candlelight make this reproduction plan-
tation home a popular spot to dine. The menu offers a selection of coun-
try cooking, and the chicken fajitas and rib steaks are first class. ⊠
Paseo Kukulcán, Hotel Krystal, ☎ 98/831133. *Reservations essential.
AE, DC, MC, V. No lunch.*

$$$ ✕ **La Dolce Vita.** Over the past decade, this appealing restaurant de-
★ veloped a strong and well-deserved local following at its original down-
town location on Avenida Cobá. In its new (1996) incarnation in the
hotel zone, across from the Marriott CasaMagna and overlooking Laguna Nichupté, La Dolce Vita has maintained its romantic atmosphere, with lots of hanging plants and candle-lighted tables with lace
cloths. Its space has almost doubled, however. Favorites from the excellent Northern Italian and Continental menu include seafood antipasto,
boquinete dolce vita (a local white fish stuffed with shrimp and mushrooms and baked in puff pastry), and creamy *tiramisù.* ⊠ *Paseo Kukulcán, Km 14.5,* ☎ 98/850150 or 98/850161. *AE, MC, V.*

$$$ ✕ **La Fisheria.** George Savio did such a booming business with his Ital-
ian place on the opposite side of the mall (☞ Savio's, *below*) that he
decided to branch out and try a seafood restaurant. Not wanting to
forsake a proven formula, he offers his popular wood-oven pizzas in
addition to seafood standards such as New England clam chowder,
steamed mussels, smoked salmon, and, of course, lobster. The setting
is ultramodern, with polished stone floors, galvanized steel stairs, and
glass walls. There is often live entertainment in the evenings. ⊠ *Plaza
Caracol,* ☎ 98/831395. *AE, MC, V.*

$$$ ✕ **Lorenzillos.** Perched on its own peninsula in the lagoon, this nauti-
cal spot provides a pleasant place to watch the sun set, sip a drink on
the outdoor patio, or sample excellent seafood. Specialties include
grilled or broiled lobster (you can pick your own) and whole fish
Veracruz-style. The seafaring theme extends to the names of the dishes
(like Jean Lafitte beef) and the restaurant itself (Lorenzillo was a 17th-
century pirate). ⊠ *Paseo Kukulcán, Km 10.5,* ☎ 98/831254. *MC, V.*

$$$ ✕ **Mikado.** Sit around the grill and watch the utensils fly as the chef prepares steaks, seafood, vegetables, and rice *teppanyaki*-style. As is true of Japanese steak houses everywhere, the showy preparation makes the meal. The sushi here is surprisingly good, especially an interesting concoction of rice and grilled eel rolled in avocado. ✉ *Marriott CasaMagna, Paseo Kukulcán,* ☎ *98/852000. AE, DC, MC, V.*

$$ ✕ **Augustus Caesar.** In spite of the shopping-center location and the constant stream of shoppers passing by, this restaurant produces classic Italian specialties with an emphasis on seafood in a sophisticated, impressive setting. The gray, pink, and white color scheme, enhanced by white stucco columns, potted palms, tile floors, and soft jazz, creates a romantic ambience at night. ✉ *La Mansión–Costa Blanca Shopping Center,* ☎ *98/833384. AE, MC, V.*

$$ ✕ **Captain's Cove.** Both waterfront locations serve breakfast buffets under palapa roofs. The decor is decidedly nautical, with rigging draped on the walls and chandeliers in the shape of ships' steering wheels. The restaurant near the Casa Maya Hotel overlooks the Caribbean toward Isla Mujeres; the other is beside the Nichupté Lagoon. Both offer lunch and dinner menus filled with seafood dishes and charbroiled steak and chicken. Parents appreciate the lower-priced children's menu, an unusual feature in Cancún. ✉ *Paseo Kukulcán, Km 16.5, lagoon-side across from Royal Mayan Hotel,* ☎ *98/850016; beach-side next to Casa Maya Hotel,* ☎ *98/830669. Reservations not accepted. AE, MC, V.*

$$ ✕ **Carlos 'n Charlie's.** A lively atmosphere, a terrific view of the lagoon, and good food make this newly remodeled restaurant—part of the popular Anderson chain—Cancún's best-known hot spot. You'll never run out of bric-a-brac to look at: The walls are catchalls, with tons of photos; sombreros, bird cages, and wooden birds and animals hang from the ceilings. For dinner you may be tempted by the barbecued ribs sizzling on the open grill, or one of the steak or seafood specials. After your meal, dance off the calories under the stars at the restaurant's **Pier Dance Club.** ✉ *Paseo Kukulcán, Km 5.5,* ☎ *98/830846. Reservations not accepted. AE, MC, V.*

$$ ✕ **Casa Rolandi.** Authentic northern Italian and Swiss dishes are skill-
★ fully prepared by the Italian owner-chef, who grew up near the Swiss border. If it's on the menu, start with the lobster-stuffed black ravioli, and go on to grilled seafood garnished with a zesty olive oil. Alternatively, try the homemade lasagna, baked in the large stucco oven; accompanied by a lavish antipasto bar, it makes for a satisfying dinner. Many fish and beef dishes are also on the menu. Service is friendly and efficient, and prices surprisingly reasonable for this level of cuisine. The decor is appropriately Mediterranean—white walls, lots of plants, and copper plates decorating the tables—and the back room offers a view of the beach. ✉ *Plaza Caracol,* ☎ *98/831817. AE, MC, V.*

$$ ✕ **El Mexicano.** This restaurant seats 300 for a folkloric dinner show in a room resembling the patio of a hacienda. Details such as elaborately hand-carved chairs created by Indians from central Mexico and numerous regional Mexican dishes convey a feeling of authenticity. Be forewarned, however: Though indisputably popular, this is a touristy spot, and the dancing-girl show is not a window into Yucatecan culture. Granted that, try the *empanxonostle* (steamed lobster, shrimp, fish, and herbs); it's as extravagant as El Mexicano's surroundings. ✉ *La Mansión–Costa Blanca Shopping Center,* ☎ *98/832220 or 98/832220.* ☉ *Folkloric ballet at 8. AE, MC, V.*

$$ ✕ **Jalapeños.** Folks crowd this place in the morning for its inexpensive breakfast buffet and in the evening for the dinner party package, which includes Mexican carnival games, an open bar, a Mexican buffet dinner, and dancing under the stars to Caribbean, marimba, and mariachi music. Six TV screens broadcast major sports events, while bartenders whip up tropical fruit drinks and margaritas to go along with jalapeños stuffed with shrimp or grouper prepared with wine, cilantro, and garlic. ⊠ *Paseo Kukulcán, Km 7,* ☎ *98/832704. Reservations not accepted. AE, MC, V.*

$$ ✕ **Savio's.** The sea-green, white, and peach decor, a central staircase, floor-to-ceiling windows, and a sleek design with lots of greenery make this mall restaurant a fresh, lively spot for lunch. For dinner, candlelight and guitar and flute music create a romantic setting. The menu's focus is homemade pastas and seafood. ⊠ *Plaza Caracol,* ☎ *98/832085. Reservations not accepted. AE, MC, V.*

$$ ✕ **Splash.** Art Deco furnishings, lots of purple and aqua, and neon lights
★ add to the sleek atmosphere of this restaurant. During high season, the outside terrace with its peek-a-boo view of the lagoon is usually full. Never mind—the inside bar area and dining room are cooler. The downstairs area offers the most intimate dining experience. You can't go wrong with any of the homemade pastas or the charcoal-grilled grouper Bora Bora–style (in a rich sauce of peaches and clarified butter). Splash has great happy hour specials and all-you-can-eat breakfast, lunch, and dinner deals. ⊠ *Paseo Kukulcán at Kukulcán Plaza,* ☎ *98/853011. Reservations not accepted. AE, MC, V.*

$ ✕ **100% Natural.** Looking for something light? Head to one of the three
★ locations of this cheery open-air eatery, all done up in colorful tropical colors and featuring the green neon 100% Natural sign. Two are in the hotel zone, one at Kukulcán Plaza and the other in the Plaza Terramar across from the Fiesta Americana; the latter location is open 24 hours. The newest location is downtown, across the street from the Caribe Internacional Hotel. Identical menus at all three restaurants appeal to vegetarians, with a broad array of soups, fruit and veggie salads, fresh fruit drinks (39 at last count), and other nonmeat menu items. Egg dishes, sandwiches, grilled chicken and fish, and Mexican and Italian fare are available as well. The three- and four-course breakfast, lunch, and dinner specials are a bargain. ⊠ *Paseo Kukulcán at Kukulcán Plaza,* ☎ *98/852904;* ⊠ *Plaza Terramar,* ☎ *98/831180;* ⊠ *Av. Sunyaxche 62,* ☎ *98/843617. Reservations not accepted. AE, MC, V.*

$ ✕ **Shooters Waterfront Cafe, U.S.A.** Popular with tourists year-round for its reasonably priced breakfast, lunch, and dinner specials, this casual restaurant overflows during spring break with college-age revelers who come here as much for the good food as for the frosty margaritas and raucous atmosphere. The decor of the spacious thatched-roof dining room is functional, with dark wood furnishings; most prominent are the three TVs playing the day's sports events. There is a deck overlooking Lagoon Nichupté, an outdoor bar with informal white plastic café tables, and a pool where diners can have a quick swim before eating. This is not the place to come if you're offended by bikini contests. Shooters is across Paseo Kukulcán from the Omni Hotel. ⊠ *Paseo Kukulcán, Km 16.5.* ☎ *98/850267. AE, DC, MC, V.*

Downtown

$$$ ✕ **Bucanero.** Quiet dining in a candle-lit marine atmosphere is the drawing card for this seafood restaurant, built to resemble the interior of a Spanish galleon, and the seafood—particularly the lobster specialties—is tops. Start the meal with lobster bisque or black bean soup, and round it out with the seafood combination, which includes lobster in garlic sauce, shrimp brochette, and fish fillet. Heaping servings are enough to feed two (which puts this in the $$ price range if you don't mind sharing your meal). Piano music played throughout the evening and waiters dressed as pirates add character to the place. ⊠ *Av. Cobá 88,* ☎ *98/842280. AE, MC, V. No lunch.*

Dining

Bucanero, **1**

Carrillo's, **7**

El Pescador, **9**

El Tacolote, **3**

La Habichuela, **13**

La Parrilla, **16**

Perico's, **10**

Pizzeria
Rolandi's, **2**

Rosa Mexicano, **4**

Lodging

Antillano, **5**

Caribe
Internacional, **14**

Holiday Inn
Centro Cancún, **17**

Margarita
Cancún, **15**

María del
Lourdes, **6**

Plaza Carrillo's, **8**

Posada Lucy, **12**

Tropical Inn, **11**

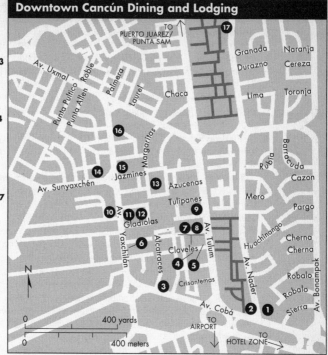

Downtown Cancún Dining and Lodging

$$$ ✕ **La Habichuela.** This charmer—once an elegant home—is perfect for hand-holding romantics or anyone looking for a relaxed, private atmosphere. Located next to La Palapa Park, this candle-lighted garden, with white, wrought-iron chairs, pebbled ground, and thick, tropical greenery, exudes peacefulness while a statue of Pakal, the Maya god of astronomy and culture, surveys the scene. Try the *cocobichuela* (lobster and shrimp in a light Indian sauce served on a bed of rice inside a coconut), a specialty of the house. ⌂ *Margaritas 25,* ☎ *98/843158. AE, MC, V.*

$$ ✕ **Carrillo's.** This cheerful restaurant, with a sweeping veranda and pink-and-purple palm trees, specializes in lobster—brochettes, thermidor, and Mexican-style. Other house favorites include broiled red snapper smothered with ham, cheese, bacon, shrimp, and a red sauce; a seafood platter massive enough to feed two; and strong Spanish coffee. Carrillo's also provides entertainment and festivities, including a musical trio that plays nightly. ⌂ *Claveles 33,* ☎ *98/841227. AE, MC, V.*

$$ ✕ **El Pescador.** It's first-come, first-served, with long lines, especially
★ during high season. But people still flood into this rustic Mexican-style restaurant with nautical touches; the open-air patio is especially popular. Heavy hitters on the menu include red snapper broiled with garlic and freshly caught lobster specials. For dessert, consider sharing the cake filled with ice cream and covered with peaches and strawberry marmalade. **La Mesa Del Pescador,** a newer offshoot in Plaza Kukulcán (☎ 98/850505), is not usually as crowded as this place. ⌂ *Tulipanes 28,* ☎ *98/842673. Reservations not accepted. AE, MC, V.*

$$ ✕ **La Parrilla.** If you're looking for the place where local Mexicans—young and old—hang out, you've found it in this popular downtown spot, a classic by Cancún standards (it opened in 1975). Everything from the food to the bougainvillea and palapa roof is authentic. Popular dishes include the grilled beef with garlic sauce and the tacos *al*

pastor (with pork, pineapple, coriander, onion, and salsa). ⊠ *Av. Yaxchilán 51,* ☎ *98/845398. Reservations not accepted. AE, MC, V.*

$$ ✕ **Perico's.** Find the antique car perched atop the palapa roof and you've spotted this zany, eclectic restaurant and bar. Saddles top bar stools, caricature busts of political figures from Castro to Queen Elizabeth line the walls, and waiters dressed as *zapatas* (revolutionaries) serve flaming desserts. The Mexican menu, including Pancho Villa (grilled beef with Mexican side dishes), is reliable, but the real reason to come here is the party atmosphere that begins nightly at 7 when the mariachi and marimba bands play. ⊠ *Av. Yaxchilán 61,* ☎ *98/843152. AE, MC, V.*

$$ ✕ **Pizzeria Rolandi's.** Bright red-and-yellow decor, plants, wood beams, ceiling fans, and visible wood-burning ovens have turned this otherwise simple sidewalk pizza place into a quick-dining treat. Ten homemade pasta dishes and 15 different pizzas—some with chicken or fish—make up a large part of the huge wooden menu that's slid across the floor from table to table. ⊠ *Av. Cobá 12,* ☎ *98/844047. Reservations not accepted. MC, V.*

$$ ✕ **Rosa Mexicano.** One of Cancún's prettiest Mexican colonial-style
★ restaurants presents waiters dressed as *charros* (Mexican cowboys), pottery and embroidered wall hangings, floor tiles with floral designs, and a cozy, softly lighted atmosphere. For extra romance, make a reservation for the candle-lit patio. Savory appetizers include *nopalitos* (cactus strips sautéed with corn, cilantro, and cheese). Specialties are *filete* Rosa (beef and onions in a tequila-orange sauce) and *camarones al ajillo* (shrimp sautéed in olive oil and garlic, with chili peppers). ⊠ *Calle Claveles 4,* ☎ *98/846313. AE, MC, V. No lunch.*

$ ✕ **El Tacolote.** A lively neighborhood *taquería* (taco stand), El Tacolote has successfully expanded on its original tacos offerings and now serves fajitas, grilled kebabs, and other traditional Mexican favorites. You get three tacos with a standard order. Mix and match fillings, and don't overlook the filet mignon taco. Bowls of sliced limes and salsa come with your order, in keeping with the very casual tone of this brightly tiled and comfortable place. ⊠ *Av. Cobá 19,* ☎ *98/873045. Reservations not accepted. MC, V.*

LODGING

Choosing from the variety of hotels in Cancún can be bewildering, because in brochures most sound—and look—alike.

If proximity to downtown is a priority, then staying at one of the hotel zone properties at the island's northern end is advantageous; many of the malls are within walking distance, and taxis to downtown and to the ferries at Puerto Juárez cost less than from hotels farther south. If, however, you seek something more secluded, there is less development at the southern end.

For the most part, the downtown hotels don't offer anything near the luxury or amenities of the hotel zone properties. They do, however, afford visitors the opportunity to stay in a popular resort without paying resort prices, and many offer free shuttle service to the beach. In addition, a downtown location has the advantage of proximity to Cancún's craft market (Ki Huic) and restaurants that are more authentic—and less costly—than those you'll find in the hotel zone.

Expect mini-bars, satellite TV, laundry and room service, private safes (check to see if there is an extra charge for safe use), and bathroom hair dryers in hotels in the $$$$ category; in addition, almost every major hotel has suites, rooms for people with disabilities, and no-smoking rooms, an in-house travel agency and/or a car-rental concession, guest parking, water-sports facilities, and a daily schedule of planned games and activities for guests. Unless otherwise noted, all hotels have air-conditioning and private baths.

All Cancún hotels are within the 77500 postal code. Price categories are based on non-discounted rates in the peak winter season, December–early May. For more information, but *not* for reservations, contact the **Cancún Hotel Association** (✉ Av. Ign. García de la Torre, SM 1, Lote 6, Cancún, QR 77500, ☎ 98/842853 or 98/845895, ℻ 98/847115).

CATEGORY	COST*
$$$$	over $175
$$$	$120–$175
$$	$50–$120
$	under $50

All prices are for a standard double room, excluding 12% tax.

Hotel Zone

$$$$ 🏨 **Caesar Park Beach & Golf Resort.** Liberal use of Mérida marble, Mexican tile murals, and colorful oil paintings give this appealing Westin property, one of Cancún's newest luxury resorts, a distinctly Mexican flavor. Rooms, too, carry out the theme, with terra-cotta tile floors, rattan furniture, woven fiber headboards, and local artwork; some have a private balcony with a view of the ocean, and a few let you see the resort's championship 18-hole golf course across Paseo Kukulcán. Lavish interconnecting pools (*seven* of them) and streams wind through palm-dotted lawns; a terraced fountain in the cavernous central atrium brings the dancing water into the hotel's interior. The Royal Beach Club section comprises 80 oceanfront villas with extra-spacious rooms. ✉ *Paseo Kukulcán, Km 17 (Box 1810),* ☎ *98/818000 or 800/228–3000,* ℻ *98/818080. 426 rooms. 3 restaurants, 3 bars, lobby lounge, 7 pools, beauty salon, 2 hot tubs, 2 saunas, 18-hole golf course, 2 tennis courts, aerobics, exercise room, shops, children's programs. AE, DC, MC, V.*

$$$$ 🏨 **Casa Turquesa.** The tranquil atmosphere of this small, elegant re-
★ treat belies its central location next to the bustling Plaza Kukulcán. The hotel's entrance is unassuming, but the public rooms are palatial, with high ceilings, stone bas-reliefs, marble floors, and oversize sofas. The 31 spacious suites are decorated individually in pastel tones, with modern furnishings; all have ocean-view private balconies with whirlpool baths. The Royal Suite, with a full kitchen and its own beach, and the duplex Presidential Suite, are the priciest accommodations. The privacy and discreet service afforded at this intimate retreat have made it the choice for celebrities such as Ivana Trump and the Planet Hollywood crew. For dinner, the **Celebrity Restaurant** (☞ Dining, *above*) offers imaginatively prepared seafood. ✉ *Paseo Kukulcán, Km 13.5,* ☎ *98/852924,* ℻ *98/852922. 31 suites. 2 restaurants, 2 bars, pool, beauty salon, sauna, tennis court, exercise room. AE, MC, V.*

$$$$ 🏨 **Fiesta Americana Cancún.** The first of three Fiestas in Cancún, this intimate-feeling hotel is a perennial favorite among Europeans and Mexicans as well as Americans. A warm atmosphere and colorful design—painted villas in rose, yellow, and sand—make it a standout. The lobby, with its potted plants, ceiling fans, and rattan furniture, is a lovely, eclectic mix of Mexican, South Seas, and Mediterranean designs. Eat lunch at the poolside Bikini Bar or slumber by the calm northern waters of Bahía de Mujeres on this palapa-dotted beach. Rooms, which all have balconies, are spacious; they're brightly furnished with rattan and white wood furnishings complemented by white, cobalt-blue, and sea-foam green hues. ✉ *Paseo Kukulcán, Km 9.5 (Box 696),* ☎

98/831400 or 800/343–7821, ⓕⓐⓧ 98/832502. *281 rooms. 3 restaurants, 3 bars, pool. AE, DC, MC, V.*

$$$$ 🏨 **Fiesta Americana Condesa.** This sprawling, friendly hotel offers the same casual elegance and luxurious amenities as its older sister, the Fiesta Americana Cancún. Situated toward the southern end of the hotel zone, the Condesa has a Mediterranean-style facade featuring balconies, rounded arches, and alternating ocher, salmon, and sand-colored walls. But it's the huge palapa fronting the structure that makes it hard to miss. An attractive and spacious lobby bar has Tiffany-style stained-glass awnings, tall palms, and ceiling fans. Three 7-story towers overlook a tranquil inner courtyard with hanging plants and falling water. The rooms, highlighted by dusty-pink stucco walls and Mexican tile floors, offer the same tranquillity. Balconies are shared by three standard rooms; the costlier accommodations have their own. Oceanfront suites have a private hot tub on the terrace. ✉ *Paseo Kukulcán, Km 16.5 (Box 5478),* ☎ *98/851000 or 800/343–7821,* ⓕⓐⓧ *98/851650. 502 rooms. 5 restaurants, 2 bars, pool, beauty salon, 3 tennis courts, health club, shops. AE, DC, MC, V.*

$$$$ 🏨 **Fiesta Americana Coral Beach Cancún.** The newest of the Cancún Fiesta properties, this all-suite hotel lies just in front of the convention center and shopping malls at the rotary opposite the Hyatt Regency. The large salmon-colored structure—built in Mediterranean style with blue wrought-iron balconies—houses a lobby with marble-tile floors, potted palms, and a stained-glass skylight. All rooms are ample in size, with oceanfront balconies and marble floors; slate-blue, lavender, and beige tones create a soothing, pleasant mood. The hotel's **La Joya** restaurant, serving nouvelle-style Mexican fare, is a fine spot for dinner. As for outdoor activities, choose between the 1,000-ft beach and the 660-ft pool. This is Cancún's largest convention hotel; expect the clientele and occasional slow service to match. ✉ *Paseo Kukulcán, Lote 6 (Box 14),* ☎ *98/832900 or 800/343–7821,* ⓕⓐⓧ *98/833173. 602 suites. 3 restaurants, 3 bars, pool, 3 tennis courts, health club, shops. AE, DC, MC, V.*

$$$$ 🏨 **Hyatt Cancún Caribe Villas & Resort.** Intimate yet endowed with modern conveniences, this semicircular property was one of the first hotels in Cancún, but it was remodeled after suffering damage from Hurricane Gilbert. An attractive, contemporary room decor with Mexican accents now predominates: colorful stenciled borders on the walls near the ceilings, tile floors, curtains and bedspreads in dusty pinks and pale green prints, and light wood furniture. Beach-level rooms have gardens, and all rooms in the main tower offer ocean views. ✉ *Paseo Kukulcán (Box 353),* ☎ *98/830044 or 800/223–1234,* ⓕⓐⓧ *98/831514. 201 rooms, including 26 beachfront villas. 3 restaurants, 2 bars, 3 pools, beauty salon, 3 hot tubs, 3 tennis courts, jogging, dock, shop. AE, DC, MC, V.*

$$$$ 🏨 **Marriott CasaMagna.** The 6-story Marriott is rather eclectically designed: In the lobby modern furnishings are set in an atrium with Mediterranean-style arches, crystal chandeliers, and hanging vines. Three restaurants overlook the handsome pool area and the ocean. The rooms, decorated in contemporary Mexican style, have tile floors and ceiling fans and follow a soft rose, mauve, and earth-tone color scheme. You can learn to prepare Mexican dishes if you attend cooking lessons (one of many guest activities), or you can sit back and watch the chef do the work at **Mikado** (☞ Dining, *above*), the hotel's fine Japanese steak house. ✉ *Paseo Kukulcán (Retorno Chac L-41),* ☎ *98/852000 or 800/228–9290,* ⓕⓐⓧ *98/851385. 414 rooms, 36 suites. 3 restaurants, bar, beauty salon, 2 hot tubs, sauna, 2 tennis courts, health club, dock, shops. AE, DC, MC, V.*

$$$$ 🏨 **Meliá Cancún.** The Meliá Cancún is a boldly modern version of a Maya temple, fronted by a sheer black marble wall and a sleek waterfall. The spacious, airy atrium, filled with lush tropical flora, is dappled with sunlight flooding in from corner windows and from the steel-and-glass pyramid skylight overhead. Public spaces exude elegance; the boutiques could not be more chic. Ivory, dusty-pink, and light-blue hues softly brighten rooms (all with private balcony or terrace); ivory-lacquered furniture and wall-to-wall carpeting create a luxurious ambience. An upscale spa, with modern cardiovascular and strength training equipment and an array of pampering and rejuvenating body treatments, was added in early 1995. To the chagrin of some guests, the hotel strictly enforces a policy against bringing in outside food or beverages (except bottled water). The **Meliá Turquesa**, a 408-room sister property across the street from Flamingo Plaza, is not as glitzy, but has a more intimate, friendlier atmosphere. ⊠ *Paseo Kukulcán, Km 16,* ☎ *98/851160 or 800/336–3542,* FAX *98/851263. 450 rooms. 5 restaurants, 3 bars, 2 pools, spa, 18-hole golf course, 3 tennis courts, health club, paddle tennis, shops. AE, DC, MC, V.*

$$$$ 🏨 **Omni Cancún.** This 10-story pink hotel, topped off by a Spanish-style orange tile roof, offers an all-inclusive option, though European plan rates are still available if you don't care to take all your meals at the hotel. The small lobby conveys the same elegant but comfortable feel as the guest rooms, which feature marble floors, sea-green and pink color schemes, and tasteful wood furniture. Some rooms have balconies; all have either ocean or lagoon views (the former are more expensive). Ranking as a primary attraction is the three-level pool, divided by a bar. ⊠ *Paseo Kukulcán, Lote 48 (Box 127),* ☎ *98/850226 or 800/843–6664,* FAX *98/850059. 331 rooms and 15 villas. 3 restaurants, 2 bars, pool, 2 tennis courts, exercise room, dock, shops. AE, DC, MC, V.*

$$$$ 🏨 **Presidente Inter-Continental Cancún.** It's hard to miss the striking Mexican-yellow entryway of this hotel, five minutes from Plaza Caracol. One of the first to open in Cancún, but extensively remodeled in 1988, it boasts a quiet beach and a waterfall in the shape of a Maya pyramid by the pool. Well-appointed, larger-than-average rooms are done in royal blue or beige and have light wicker furniture and area rugs on Yucatecan *conchuela* stone floors. Even larger suites offer contemporary furnishings, in-room video equipment, and spacious balconies. ⊠ *Paseo Kukulcán, Km 7.5,* ☎ *98/830200 or 800/327–0200,* FAX *98/832602 or 98/832515. 298 rooms. 2 restaurants, bar, 2 pools, beauty salon, 6 hot tubs, tennis court, exercise room, shops. AE, DC, MC, V.*

$$$$ 🏨 **Ritz-Carlton Cancún.** This ultra-posh, peach-colored property with
★ a Spanish-tile roof, wrought-iron railings, and splashing fountains in open courtyards opened in 1993, setting new standards for luxury and service in Cancún. The air-conditioned lobby and public areas are richly appointed with fine European and American antiques, thick carpets, and marble floors; the fourth-floor atrium is topped by a massive stained-glass dome. Stylish rooms, done in comfortable shades of blue, beige, and peach, offer all the amenities—wall-to-wall carpeting, travertine marble bathrooms with telephones, separate tub and shower, plush terry robes, and large balconies overlooking the Caribbean. The hotel's elegant restaurants, especially the **Club Grill** (☞ Dining, *above*) and the recently opened **Fantino** (serving Northern Italian dinners), are standouts. ⊠ *Paseo Kukulcán, Retorno del Rey 36,* ☎ *98/850808 or 800/241–3333,* FAX *98/851015. 369 rooms. 3 restaurants, 2 bars, 3 pools, beauty salon, hot tub, spa, 3 tennis courts, health club, pro shop, shops. AE, DC, MC, V.*

$$$$ 🏨 **Sierra Cancún.** Formerly the Maeva, this pleasant, all inclusive resort hotel has the advantage of being closer to town than the hotels on the southern end, while still seeming to be away from it all. Rooms are decorated in tropical colors, with light-wood furnishings and tile floors; all have a sunken lanai or private balcony. The poolside palapa restaurant is a serene spot for lunch. The hotel management strictly prohibits guests from bringing onto the premises any food or beverage purchased outside. The hotel has a resident doctor. ⊠ *Paseo Kukulcán, Km 10,* ☎ *98/832444 or 800/544–4686,* ℻ *98/833486. 261 rooms. 2 restaurants, bar, 2 pools, beauty salon, tennis court, dock, shop. AE, DC, MC, V.*

$$$$ 🏨 **Sun Palace.** The water pressure in the showerheads is fantastic, and in case you have trouble figuring out how to turn on the whirlpool, it's the little white button behind you in the bathtub. The resort's marble-floored suites, delicate desert pastel appointments, and spare, cool furnishings are a virtual massage to the senses. Every suite overlooks the Caribbean's sparkling, aquamarine water, and windows open to the sea breeze. All-inclusive means convenience: There are unlimited food and beverages, day-and-night entertainment and activities—including use of an above-ground diving tank and a variety of nonmotorized water sports equipment and tours to Maya ruins and to Isla Mujeres—but meals are a disappointment. There's a three-night minimum stay. ⊠ *Paseo Kukulcán, Km 20,* ☎ *98/851555 or 800/346–8225. 227 rooms. 3 restaurants, indoor and outdoor pools, outdoor hot tub, tennis court, exercise room, Ping-Pong, billiards, recreation room. AE, MC, V.*

$$$$ 🏨 **Villas Tacul.** The accommodations in this large complex (23 villas on 5 acres), set on its own stretch of beach en route to downtown, are appointed with red-tile floors and authentic Mexican colonial–style furniture, wagon-wheel chandeliers, and tin-work mirrors. Each villa has a kitchen and from two to five bedrooms, making this a good place for families and couples traveling together. An individual housekeeper keeps each unit spotless and serves private breakfasts for an extra charge. There are a few modestly priced studio rooms without kitchen facilities. The grounds are beautifully landscaped, with well-trimmed lawns and islands of palm trees in the pool. ⊠ *Paseo Kukulcán, Km 5.5,* ☎ *98/830000, 98/830080, or 800/842–0193,* ℻ *98/830349. 23 villas. Restaurant, bar, pool, 2 tennis courts, basketball. AE, DC, MC, V.*

$$$$ 🏨 **Westin Regina Resort Cancún.** Opened in 1991, this luxury property stands at the southern end of the island, on Punta Nizuc. It is one of the few hotels with direct access to both a 1,600-ft beach and Laguna Nichupté. The low-rise, postmodern-style hotel was designed and decorated by one of Latin America's leading architects. In the public areas, stark white stucco walls contrast with brilliant pink or blue recessed areas framing an array of sculptures and other artwork; from the lobby, you can look down on a stylish restaurant with stunning ocean views. In the spacious guest rooms, handsome rustic furnishings and colorful Mexican folk art stand out against white walls and pale marble floors. Concierge tower rooms are available. ⊠ *Paseo Kukulcán, Km 20 (Box 1808),* ☎ *98/850086, 98/850537, or 800/228–3000,* ℻ *98/850074. 385 rooms. 4 restaurants, 3 bars, 5 pools, hot tub, 5 outdoor hot tubs, 2 tennis courts, exercise room, children's programs. AE, DC, MC, V.*

$$$
★ 🏨 **Club Las Velas.** Once you go past the wrought-iron gates of this all-inclusive property, you'll be in a delightfully private enclave. The complex is a replica of a Mexican village, complete with central plaza, fountains, a natural aquarium, and lush gardens. Winding stone pathways connect the Mexican colonial–style attached villas and four five-story towers with the Laguna Nichupté beachfront, palapa restaurant, and pools. Nonmotorized water sports, children's programs, and a water taxi to a nearby ocean beach are part of the package. Rooms are light and airy, with white stucco walls, tropical print bedspreads, and rattan furniture. Tower rooms from the second floor up all have balconies. The duplex villas are especially suited to families, as adjoining bedrooms can easily form two or three bedroom suites. The food—served buf-

fet style at breakfast, and buffet style or à la carte at dinner—is plentiful and good. Nightly theme parties with live entertainment fill the plaza after dinner. ⊠ *Paseo Kukulcán and Galeon,* ☎ *98/832222 or 800/707–8815,* FAX *98/832118. 226 rooms, 59 villas. 2 restaurants, 2 bars, snack bar, 2 pools, 2 tennis courts, aerobics, exercise room, shops, children's programs. AE, MC, V.*

$$$ ⊡ **Hyatt Regency Cancún.** A cylindrical 14-story tower with the Hyatt trademark—a striking central atrium filled with tropical greenery and topped by a sky-lighted dome—affords a 360° view of the sea and the lagoon. Plants spill over the inner core of the cylinder, at the base of which is a bar. Soothing blue, green, and beige tones prevail in the rooms, which also feature contemporary Mexican furniture and striking green or rose-colored marble vanities. This hotel, much larger and livelier than its sister property, has an enormous two-level pool with a waterfall. **Cilantro,** the hotel's pretty waterfront dining room, offers a good breakfast buffet. The Punta Cancún location is convenient to the convention center and several shopping malls. ⊠ *Paseo Kukulcán (Box 1201),* ☎ *98/830966, 98/831234, or 800/233–1234,* FAX *98/831438. 300 rooms. 2 restaurants, 3 bars, pool, health club, recreation room. AE, MC, V.*

$$$ ⊡ **Krystal Cancún.** Its lobby tends to be hectic, but the location of this hotel, part of a Mexican chain, can't be beat. At the tip of Punta Cancún, within walking distance of three major shopping malls and across the street from the convention center, the Krystal affords spectacular views of the entire ocean coast of the island, the lagoon, and parts of downtown. A 1994 renovation perked up rooms with window planter boxes, rattan furniture, and pastels, but the hotel also went time-share at the time, and guests may be exposed to the sales push. The property hosts **Bogart's** and **Hacienda El Mortero,** two of the best-known restaurants in town (☞ Dining, *above*), as well as the popular **Christine** disco (☞ Nightlife, *below*). ⊠ *Paseo Kukulcán, Lote 9,* ☎ *988/31133 or 800/231–9860. 322 rooms. 4 restaurants, 4 bars, pool, hot tub, sauna, 2 tennis courts, exercise room, shops. AE, DC, MC, V.*

$$$ ⊡ **Royal Solaris Caribe.** This all-inclusive property comprises two separate hotel buildings; the grounds between them are covered with lush tropical foliage. A number of the units are time-share apartment suites, with large living rooms, kitchenettes, and bathtubs (as opposed to the shower stalls in the smallish standard rooms). Studio rooms, which also have kitchenettes, offer twice the space of "superior" rooms. The hotel bills its swimming pool as the largest in Cancún. ⊠ *Paseo Kukulcán, Km 20,* ☎ *98/850600, 98/850100, or 800/221–5333,* FAX *98/850354. 488 rooms. 7 restaurants, 5 bars, pool, 2 hot tubs, tennis court, basketball, exercise room, shops, dance club, children's programs. AE, DC, MC, V.*

$$ ⊡ **Calinda Viva Cancún.** This beige stucco 8-story building—part of the Quality hotel chain—is not one of the most attractive in town, but it makes a reliable standby and is in a good location, on the north beach near many malls. Redecorated in late 1994, the functional, moderate-size rooms have marble floors and contemporary pastel decor; half have private balconies and ocean views. The property also has a small garden, a beach, and a Mexican restaurant. ⊠ *Paseo Kukulcán, Km 8.5 (Box 673),* ☎ *98/830800 or 100/221–2222. 216 rooms. Restaurant, bar, pool, 2 tennis courts, dock, shops. AE, DC, MC, V.*

$$ ⊡ **El Pueblito Beach Hotel.** El Pueblito, meaning little town, is an apt
★   name for this all-inclusive property, which consists of clusters of guest rooms in tri-level units with arches, terraces, balconies, and other architectural details that invoke Old Mexico. Interconnecting pathways lined with tropical foliage lead to intriguing terrace pools with waterfalls and stone archways; there's even a long water slide for kids.

Rooms, which are large for the price, have marble floors and simple rattan furnishings; a few have kitchenettes. ⊠ *Paseo Kukulcán, Km 17.5,* ☎ *98/850422,* FAX *98/850731. 239 rooms. 3 restaurants, bar, 5 pools, tennis court, shops, travel services. AE, MC, V.*

$ 🏨 **Villa Deportiva Juvenil Cancún.** This government-run youth hostel on the beach has glass walls, a cable TV room, a pool, and dormitory beds (separate rooms for men and women). A lounge lends itself to the sort of congenial mingling one expects of a youth hostel. There is also an area for camping. ⊠ *Paseo Kukulcán, Km 3,* ☎ *98/831337. 33 rooms (300 beds) with shared baths. Basketball, Ping-Pong, volleyball. No credit cards.*

Downtown

$$$ 🏨 **Holiday Inn Centro Cancún.** The place to stay if you want to be down-
★   town and have all the amenities, this is the newest (built in 1990) and most upscale hotel in the area. It's less expensive than similar properties in the hotel zone and provides free transportation to the beach of the Crown Princess Club. The attractive pink 4-story structure, with a Spanish tile roof, affords easy access to restaurants and shops. Although rooms are generic motel modern, with mauve and blue color schemes, they have appealing Mexican touches. ⊠ *Av. Nader 1, SM 2,* ☎ *98/84455 or 800/465–4329,* FAX *98/847954. 246 rooms. 2 restaurants, 2 bars, pool, beauty salon, tennis court, exercise room, nightclub, coin laundry, travel services, car rental. AE, DC, MC, V.*

$$ 🏨 **Antillano.** This old but prettily appointed property features wood fur-
★   nishings, a cozy little lobby bar, and a tiny pool. Extras such as tiled bathroom sinks and air-conditioning in the halls and rooms make this hotel stand out from the others in its league. ⊠ *Av. Tulum at Calle Claveles,* ☎ *98/841532 or 98/841132,* FAX *98/841878. 48 rooms. Pool, shops. AE, DC, MC, V.*

$$ 🏨 **Caribe Internacional.** Located on a major traffic circle downtown, this relatively modern hotel can be somewhat noisy. The concrete exterior is covered by stucco and the rooms—although on the small side and sparsely furnished—are pleasant enough and have pastel-colored walls. The small pool in a garden at the back adds a bit to this otherwise average property, and the free beach shuttle is a plus. ⊠ *Yaxchilán 36, at Sunyaxchén,* ☎ *98/843999,* FAX *98/841993. 55 rooms, 25 suites. Restaurant, cafeteria, pool, travel services. AE, MC, V.*

$$ 🏨 **Margarita Cancún.** This 5-story hotel, just across from the Caribe Internacional, is Mission-style white stucco with yellow-tile trim. Rooms, done in monochromatic tones of blue or beige, have tile floors; ask for one with a view of the pool. ⊠ *Av. Yaxchilán 41, SM 22,* ☎ *98/849333,* FAX *98/841324. 100 rooms. Restaurant, lobby lounge, snack bar, pool, travel services. AE, MC, V.*

$$ 🏨 **María del Lourdes.** The María del Lourdes has some nice touches throughout, such as the colonial-style restaurant with rust-and-white stucco walls and the garden surrounding a small pool in the back. The rooms are uninspired, however, with dark brown furnishings and small windows. ⊠ *Av. Yaxchilán 80,* ☎ *98/844744,* FAX *98/841242. 81 rooms. Restaurant, bar, pool, coin laundry. AE, MC, V.*

$$ 🏨 **Plaza Carrillo's.** One of the first hotels to be built in Cancún City,
★   this one is conveniently located in the heart of the downtown area next to the Plaza Carrillo shopping arcade and **Carrillo's** restaurant (☞ Dining, *above*), which are under the same ownership. The hotel corridors are exceptionally clean and well maintained. Rooms are bright, with simple functional decor. ⊠ *Calle Claveles 35,* ☎ *98/841227,* FAX *98/842371. 43 rooms. Restaurant, pool. AE, MC, V.*

$$ 🏨 **Tropical Inn.** This 3-story Spanish colonial–style hotel, a block south of the Margarita Cancún, reopened in 1995 after a floor-to-ceiling ren-

ovation. Long popular with students, Europeans, and Canadians, it has rooms done in tasteful tones of brown. A pretty courtyard entrance leads to the reception desk. ⊠ *Av. Yaxchilán 31,*☎ *98/843078 or 98/843–3690,* FAX *98/849209. 81 rooms. Restaurant, bar, pool. AE, DC, MC, V.*

$ 🏨 **Posada Lucy.** This place isn't much to look at outside, but its location, on a quiet side street, is good. The rather seedy pink-and-beige rooms in the main building are small, with no views, but some include kitchenettes. Another 12 rooms, in an adjacent building behind Restaurant Pericos, are available for monthly rental. Expansion in 1995 added eight third-floor rooms and a Mexican restaurant to the property. ⊠ *Gladiolas 8, SM 22,* ☎ *98/844165. 33 rooms. Restaurant. AE.*

NIGHTLIFE AND THE ARTS

The Arts

Festivals

Cancún's **Jazz Festival** premiered in 1991 and featured Wynton Marsalis and Gato Barbieri. It's an annual event that takes place in late May; at press time, the 1998 schedule was not yet available. The Cancún Hotel Association (⊠ Av. Ign. García de la Torre, SM 1, Lote 6, Cancún, QR 77500, ☎ 98/842853) can provide information about this popular gathering.

Film

Local movie theaters showing American and Mexican films include **Telecines Kukulcán** (⊠ Plaza Kukulcán, ☎ 98/853021) and **Tulum Plus** (⊠ Av. Tulum, SM 2, ☎ 98/843451).

Performances

The **ballet folklórico** dinner show (⊠ Hotel Continental Villas Plaza, Paseo Kukulcán, Km 11, ☎ 98/831095) consists of stylized performances of regional Mexican dances including the hat dance and *la bamba.* By comparison with the renowned Ballet Nacional Folklórico of Mexico City, this troupe suffers, but if it's all you'll get to see of the brilliant Mexican dance traditions, which blend pre-Hispanic and Iberian motifs, then go for it. An admission price of about $50 includes the buffet—a sampling of regional Mexican cooking—the show, and one drink. Performances are held Monday through Saturday; dinner is at 7, the show at 8:30.

The **convention center** hosts a popular ballet folklórico dinner show nightly (⊠ Paseo Kukulcán, Km 9, ☎ 98/830199). Cocktails are at 6:30; dinner, a typical Mexican buffet, is at 7; and the dance production goes on at 8.

Mexican fiesta dinner shows are held once a week at the **Westin Regina** (☎ 98/850086, ext. 193/194) and the **Meliá Turquesa** (☎ 98/832544). Both include folkloric ballet, mariachi music, and a Mexican buffet, and drinks. Call for dates, prices, and reservations.

A Mexican *charreada,* or rodeo show (⊠ El Corral de JF, Km 6, Prolongación Av. Lopez Portillo, no phone), is performed Monday–Saturday at 7 PM. In addition to the show you get dinner and domestic drinks. You can book reservations through your hotel.

Nightlife

The multistory **Party Center** (⊠ Paseo Kukulcán, Km 9, ☎ 98/830351), next to the convention center, is an entertainment complex that hosts several clubs, a sports bar, and two discos (**Tequila Rock** and **Baja Beach**

Club), as well as numerous restaurants, specialty boutiques, and a money exchange. Live folkloric bands perform nightly in the central courtyard that provides access to the clubs, bars, discos, and restaurants.

Dinner Cruises

A dinner cruise on board the 62-ft vessel **Columbus** (☎ 98/831488 or 98/833268) includes a full lobster or steak spread, open bar, and dancing for $70; the boat departs the Royal Mayan Yacht Club Monday–Saturday and sails at 4 and 7:30. The **Cancún Queen** (☎ 98/852288), a paddle wheeler departing from the AquaWorld Marina (⊠ Paseo Kukulcán, Km 15.2), runs a similar excursion for $65. **Aqua Tours Adventures** (⊠ Paseo Kukulcán, Km 6.25, ☎ 98/830400) offers a pleasantly romantic lobster dinner and sunset cruise to Isla Mujeres that includes dancing under the stars and an open bar. Departures are at 6 PM on Monday, Tuesday, Thursday, and Saturday. On evening cruises with **Asterix Party Fishing** (⊠ Paseo Kukulcán, Km 5.5 at Carlos 'n Charlies, ☎ 98/864847) you catch the fish and the crew prepares it for you. The price is $50, including an open bar and fishing gear; boats depart weekdays at 6 PM and return at midnight. **Pirates Night,** departing from Playa Langosta Dock (⊠ Paseo Kukulcán, ☎ 98/831488), offers a three-course buffet dinner with trips to Treasure Island. Kids under 12 sail at half price and those under 5 sail free. Cruises are Tuesday and Thursday, leaving at 6:30 PM and returning at 11:30. It's wise to be at the dock 30 minutes before departure time.

Discos

Cancún wouldn't be Cancún without its glittering discos, which generally start jumping about 10:30. **Azucar** (⊠ Hotel Camino Real, ☎ 98/830100) sizzles to a salsa beat nightly; the beautiful people don't turn up here until *really* late. **Dady'O** (⊠ Paseo Kukulcán, Km 9.5, ☎ 98/833333) has been around for a while but is still a very "in" place, especially with the younger set. The **Dady Rock** (⊠ Paseo Kukulcán, Km 9.5, ☎ 98/831626) bar and grill, next door to Dady'O, opens at 6 PM, and draws a high energy clientele with live music, a giant screen, contests, and food specials. **Christine** (⊠ Krystal Cancún hotel, ☎ 98/831133) attracts a slightly older, elegantly attired crowd and puts on an incredible light show. **La Boom** (⊠ Paseo Kukulcán, Km 3.5, ☎ 98/831152) includes a video bar with a light show and is not always crowded, although it can squeeze in 1,200 people.

Music

Batacha (⊠ Hotel Miramar Misión, ☎ 98/831755), a small Caribbean nightclub, is a low-key spot to enjoy some Latin sounds. Visit the **Hard Rock Cafe** (⊠ Plaza Lagunas, Paseo Kukulcán, ☎ 98/832024) for live rock bands (generally six nights a week) and molto music nostalgia. You can hear Caribbean beat dance music (marimba, mariachi, reggae, etc.) at **Jalapeños** (⊠ Paseo Kukulcán, Km 7, ☎ 98/832896) nightly from 8. The place to go for hot live reggae is **Mango Tango** (⊠ Paseo Kukulcán, Km 14.2, ☎ 98/850303), which sits lagoonside across the street from the Ritz-Carlton. **Planet Hollywood** (⊠ Flamingo Plaza, Paseo Kukulcán, Km 11.5, ☎ 98/850723) is currently the top ticket in town; crowds push their way in for the Hollywood memorabilia—and hope to catch a glimpse of such stars as Demi Moore and Arnold Schwarzenegger, who occasionally check in on their investment.

OUTDOOR ACTIVITIES AND SPORTS

Bullfighting

The Cancún **bullring,** a block south of the Pemex station, hosts year-round bullfights. A matador, *charos* (Mexican cowboys), a mariachi band, and flamenco dancers entertain during the hour preceding the bullfight (from 2:30 PM). ⊠ *Paseo Kukulcán and Av. Bonampak,* ☎ *98/845465 or 98/848248.* ☜ *About $40.* ☉ *Fights Wed. at 3:30.*

Golf

The main course is at **Pok-Ta-Pok** (⊠ Paseo Kukulcán between Km 6 and Km 7, ☎ 98/830871), a club with fine views of both sea and lagoon, whose 18 holes were designed by Robert Trent Jones, Sr. The club also has a practice green, a swimming pool, tennis courts, and a restaurant. The greens fees are $70 ($55 after 2 PM); electric cart, $25; clubs, $15; caddies, $20; and golf clinics, $25 per hour. Playing hours are 6 AM–6 PM (last tee-off is at 4 PM). There is a new 18-hole championship golf course at the **Caesar Park Beach and Golf Resort** (⊠ Paseo Kukulcán, Km 17, ☎ 98/818000); greens fees are $95 ($75 for hotel guests), carts are included, and club rentals run from $20 to $30. The 18-hole executive course (par 53) at the **Hotel Meliá Cancún** (⊠ Paseo Kukulcán, Km 12, ☎ 98/851160) forms a semi-circle around the property and shares its beautiful ocean views. The greens fee is about $20.

Health Clubs

Most of the deluxe hotels have their own health clubs, although few of them are very large. There are, however, two gyms in Cancún: Both **Gold's Gym** (⊠ Av. Ixcun, SM 32, ☎ 98/846948 or 98/847092) and **Star's Gym** (⊠ Av. Sayil 22, in the Holiday Inn, ☎ 98/874455) have modern equipment and exercise facilities.

Jogging

Although to some people the idea of jogging in the intense heat of Cancún sounds like a form of masochism, fanatics should know that there is a 14-km (9-mi) track extending along half the island, running parallel to Paseo Kukulcán from the Punta Cancún area into Cancún City.

Water Sports

There are myriad ways you can get your adrenalin going while getting wet in Cancún. The most popular ones are detailed below. In addition, you'll also be able to find places to go parasailing (about $35 for eight minutes); waterskiing ($70 per hour); or jet skiing ($70 per hour, or $60 for Wave Runners, double-seated Jet Skis). Paddle boats, kayaks, catamarans, and banana boats are also readily available. **Aqua Tours** (⊠ Paseo Kukulcán, Km 6.25, ☎ 98/830400, FAX 98/830403) and **AquaWorld** (⊠ Paseo Kukulcán, Km 15.2, ☎ 98/852288, FAX 98/852299) maintain large fleets of water toys.

Fishing

Some 500 species of tropical fish, including sailfish, bluefin, marlin, barracuda, and red snapper, live in the waters adjacent to Cancún. Deep-sea fishing boats and other gear may be chartered from outfitters for about $350 for four hours, $450 for six hours, and $550 for eight hours. Charters generally include a captain, a first mate, gear, bait, and beverages. **Aqua Tours, AquaWorld,** and the **Royal Yacht Club** (⊠ Paseo Kukulcán, Km 16.5, ☎ 98/852930) are just a few of the companies

t operate large fishing fleets. **Pelican Pier Fishing Excursions,** (⊠ Paseo
ukulcán, Km 5.5—across from the Casa Maya Hotel, ☎ 98/830315)
fers 6 hours on their 6-person charter boats for $99 per person. Price
cludes soft drinks, bait, and fishing gear. Also available are deep-sea
harters starting at $318 for 4 hours.

Marinas

A new marina, **San Buenaventura,** between Bahía de Mujeres and Laguna Nichupté, was scheduled for completion in late 1995, but the facility was only approaching completion in early 1997. Other marinas
include **Aqua Tours Adventures** (☎ 98/830400, FAX 98/830403), **Aqua-
World** (☎ 98/852288, FAX 98/852299), **Blue Bay Club & Marina** (☎ 98/
801070), **Club Lagoon** (☎ 98/833109), and **Scuba Cancún** (☎ 98/831011).

Sailboarding

Although some people sailboard on the ocean side in the summer, activity is limited primarily to the bay between Cancún and Isla Mujeres.
If you visit the island in July, don't miss the National Windsurfing Tournament (☎ 98/843212). The **International Windsurfer Sailing School**
(☎ 98/842023), at Playa Tortugas, rents equipment and gives lessons;
the **Windsurf Association of Quintana Roo** (☎ 98/871771) can provide
information about the tournament. Sailboards are available for about
$50 an hour; classes go for about $35 an hour.

Snorkeling and Scuba Diving

Snorkeling is best at Punta Nizuc, Punta Cancún, and Playa Tortugas,
although you should be especially careful of the strong currents at the
last; gear can be rented for $10 per day. Some charter-fishing compa-
nies offer a two-tank scuba dive for about $100. As the name implies,
Scuba Cancún (☎ 98/831011) specializes in diving trips and offers
NAUI, CMAS, and PADI instruction. **Aqua Tours Adventures** (☎
98/830400 or 98/830227) offers scuba tours and a resort course, as well
as snorkeling trips. **AquaWorld Adventures** (☎ 98/852288) runs 2½-
hour daily jungle tours through dense mangroves. A guide leads the way
as you drive your own Aqua Ray motor boat on Laguna Nichupté. The
$40 price includes snorkeling and light refreshments. Trips leave daily
at 8, 9, and 11 AM, noon, and 2 and 3 PM. If you've brought your own
snorkeling gear and want to save money, just take a city bus down to
Club Med and walk along the resort's beach for less than 1 km until
you get to Punta Nizuc. **Blue Peace Diving** (⊠ Paseo Kukulcán, Km 16.2,
☎ 98/851447) offers 2-tank dives for $85 with Naui, SSI, and Padi in-
struction. The areas explored are Cozumel, Akumal, Xpu-ha, and Isla
Mujeres. Extended 3-day diving trips are available for about $280.

SHOPPING

Resort wear and handicrafts are the most popular purchases in Cancún, but the prices are high and the selection standard. "Caveat emp-
tor" applies as much to Cancún as it does to the "bargain" electronics
stores on 5th Avenue in New York City or in Hong Kong. If you're
traveling elsewhere in Mexico, it's best to postpone your shopping spree
until you reach another town. Still, you can find a respectable variety
of Mexican handicrafts ranging from blown glass and hand-woven textiles to leather goods and jewelry made from local coral and tortoiseshell. (Don't be tempted by the tortoiseshell products: The turtles they
come from are endangered species, and it is illegal to bring tortoiseshell into the United States and several other countries.)

Throughout Mexico you will often get better prices by paying with cash
(pesos or dollars) or traveler's checks. This is because Mexican merchants are averse to the commissions charged by credit-card compa-

nies, and frequently tack that commission—6% or more—onto your bill. If you can do without the plastic, you may even get the 12% sales tax lopped off.

Bargaining is expected in Cancún, but mostly in the market. Suggest half the asking price and slowly come up, but do not pay more than 70% of the quoted price. Shopping around is a good idea, too, because the crafts market is very competitive. But closely examine the merchandise you are purchasing: Some "authentic" items—particularly jewelry—may actually be shoddy imitations.

In Cancún, shopping hours are generally weekdays 10–1 and 4–7, although more and more stores are staying open throughout the day rather than closing for siesta between 1 and 4 PM. Many shops keep Saturday morning hours, and some are now open on Sunday until 1 PM. Shops in the malls tend to be open weekdays from 9 or 10 AM to 8 or 10 PM.

Shopping Districts, Streets, and Malls

Shopping can be roughly categorized by location: In the malls and in-house boutiques in the hotel zone, prices are generally—but not always—higher than in the shops and markets downtown. However, at the markets you'll have to sift through lots of overpriced junk and haggle a bit in order to land some good deals in silver or handicrafts.

Downtown

The wide variety of shops downtown along Avenida Tulum (⊠ between Avs. Cobá and Uxmal) includes **Fama** (⊠ Av. Tulum 105, ☎ 98/846586), a department store offering clothing, English reading matter, sports gear, toiletries, liquor, and *latería* (crafts made of tin). Also on Tulum is the oldest and largest of Cancún's crafts markets, **Ki Huic** (⊠ Av. Tulum 17, between Bancomer and Banco Atlantico, ☎ 98/843347), which is open daily from 9 AM to 10 PM and houses about 100 vendors.

Hotel Zone

Fully air-conditioned malls (known as *centros comerciales*), as stream-lined and well kept as any in the United States or Canada, sell everything from fashion clothing, beachwear, and sportswear to jewelry, household items, video games, and leather goods.

The newest mall on the scene is **Kukulcán Plaza** (⊠ Paseo Kukulcán, Km 13), with around 130 shops (including Izod, Benetton, and Harley Davidson boutiques), 12 restaurants, a bar, a liquor store, a bank, a cinema, bowling lanes, and a video arcade.

Flamingo Plaza (⊠ Paseo Kukulcán, Km 11.5, across from the Hotel Flamingo) includes an exchange booth, some designer emporiums and duty-free stores, several sportswear shops, two boutiques selling Guatemalan imports, a drug store, and a Planet Hollywood boutique. At the food court, in addition to the usual McDonald's, Domino's Pizza, and fried chicken concessions, you'll find Checándole, offering what might be the only fast-food mole enchiladas around.

Just across from the convention center site, **Plaza Caracol** (⊠ Paseo Kukulcán, Km 8.5) is the largest and most contemporary mall in Cancún, with about 200 shops and boutiques, including two pharmacies, art galleries, a currency exchange, and folk art and jewelry shops, as well as cafés and restaurants. Fashion boutiques include Benetton, Bally, Gucci, and Ralph Lauren; in all these stores, prices are lower than in their U.S. counterparts. Weary shoppers can rest their feet at the café tables near the first-floor frozen yogurt stand or the fast-food court nearby.

To the back of—and virtually indistinguishable from—Plaza Caracol are two outdoor shopping complexes. The pink stucco **La Mansión–Costa Blanca** specializes in designer clothing and has several restaurants, art galleries, a bank, and a liquor store. **Plaza Lagunas** is the home of the Hard Rock Cafe; some fast food places (KFC, Subway, Dunkin' Donuts); sportswear shops, such as Ellesse; and a number of souvenir stands. Also near Plaza Caracol, **Plaza Terramar** (opposite the Hotel Fiesta Americana) sells beachwear, souvenirs, and folk art, and has a restaurant and a pharmacy.

Specialty Shops

Galleries

Orbe (⊠ Plaza Caracol, ☎ 98/831571) specializes in sculptures and paintings by contemporary Mexican artists. **Mordo's** (⊠ La Mansión–Costa Blanca mall, ☎ 98/830838) is the local outlet for a small Mexico City chain that sells handcrafted leather jackets, belts, and boots, and can customize your purchase with decorative patches, needlework, or metallic trim. **Mayart** (⊠ La Mansión–Costa Blanca mall, ☎ 98/841272 or 98/841569) displays replicas of Maya art, temple rubbings, and contemporary painting and sculpture. Those interested in contemporary art should stop by the **Xamanek Gallery** (⊠ Plaza Caracol, no phone) to see the work of Sergio Bustamante, one of the most popular Mexican artists today.

Grocery Stores

Major supermarkets include **Comercial Mexicana** (⊠ Av. Lopez Portillo at Libramiento Kabah, ☎ 98/871303); **San Francisco de Asís** (⊠ Av. Tulum 18, ☎ 98/841155); **Super Deli** (⊠ Av. Tulum at Xcaret, ☎ 98/841122, ext. 149; Plaza Nautilus, ☎ 98/831903); **Comercial Mexicana de la Glorieta** (⊠ Av. Tulum at Av. Uxmal, ☎ 98/843330 or 98/844258); and the newest and largest, **Chadraul** (⊠ Av. Tulum 58–59 at Av. Cobá, ☎ 98/841036).

CANCÚN A TO Z

Arriving and Departing

By Bus

The bus terminal (⊠ Av. Tulum and Av. Uxmal, ☎ 98/841378 or 98/843948) downtown serves first-class buses making the trip from Mexico City and first- and second-class buses arriving in Cancún from Puerto Morelos, Playa del Carmen, Tulum, Chetumal, Cobá, Valladolid, Chichén Itzá, and Mérida. Public buses (Rte. 8) make the trip out to Puerto Juárez and Punta Sam for the ferries to Isla Mujeres, and taxis will take you from the bus station to Puerto Juárez for about two dollars.

By Car

Cancún is at the end of Route 180, which goes from Matamoros on the Texas border to Campeche, Mérida, and Valladolid. The road trip from Texas to Cancún can take up to three days. Cancún can also be reached from the south via Route 307, which passes through Chetumal and Belize. There are few gas stations on these roads, so try to keep your tank filled. Route 307 has a Pemex station between Cancún and Playa Del Carmen. Construction is ongoing, changing this route from two to four lanes.

By Plane

Cancún International Airport is 16 km (9 mi) southwest of the heart of Cancún City, 10 km (6 mi) from the southernmost point of the hotel zone. **Aeromexico** (☎ 98/841097 or 98/843571) flies nonstop from

Houston, Miami, and New York. **American** (☎ 98/860086) has non-stop service from Dallas and Miami. **Continental** (☎ 98/860040) offers daily direct service from Houston. **Mexicana** (☎ 98/874444 or 98/860120) nonstops depart from Los Angeles, Miami, and New York. In Cancún, Mexicana subsidiaries **Aerocaribe** (downtown, ☎ 98/842000; airport, ☎ 98/860083) and **Aerocozumel** (downtown, ☎ 98/842000; airport, ☎ 98/860162) offer flights to Cozumel, the ruins at Chichén Itzá, Mérida, and other Mexican destinations.

BETWEEN THE AIRPORT AND HOTELS

A counter at the airport exit sells tickets for vans (called *colectivos*) and for taxis; prices for the latter range from $15 to $25, depending on the exact destination. Buses, which cost about $8, are air-conditioned and sell soft drinks and beer on board, but may be slow if they're carrying a lot of passengers and need to stop at many hotels. Approximate taxi fares: from the airport to the hotel zone, $22; from the hotel zone to the airport, $10.

Getting Around

Motorized transportation of some sort is necessary, as the island is somewhat spread out. Public bus service is good, and taxis are relatively inexpensive.

By Bus

Public buses operate between the hotel zone and downtown from 6 AM to midnight; the cost is about 3 pesos. There are designated bus stops, but drivers can also be flagged down along Paseo Kukulcán. The service is a bit erratic, but buses run frequently and can save you considerable money on taxis, especially if you're staying at the southern end of the hotel zone.

By Car and Moped

Renting a car for your stay in Cancún is probably an unnecessary expense, entailing tips for valet parking, as well as gasoline and rather costly rental rates (on a par with those in any major resort area around the world). What's more, driving here can be harrowing when you don't know your way around. Downtown streets, being cobblestoned to give the area an "Old Mexico" look, are frequently clogged with traffic. However, if you plan to do some exploring, using Cancún as a base, the roads are excellent within a 100-km (62-mi) radius.

By Ship

Boats leave Puerto Juárez and Punta Sam—both north of Cancún City—for Isla Mujeres every half hour or so (☞ Chapter 3).

By Taxi

Taxis to the ferries at Punta Sam or Puerto Juárez cost $15–$20 or more; between the hotel zone and downtown, $8 and up; and within the hotel zone, $5–$7. All prices depend on the distance, your negotiating skills, and whether you pick up the taxi in front of the hotel or go onto the avenue to hail a green city cab (the latter will be cheaper). Since taxi rates fluctuate according to gasoline taxes and the drivers' whims, check with your hotel. Most list rates at the door; confirm the price with your driver before you set out. If you lose something in a taxi or have questions or a complaint, call the **Sindicato de Taxistas** (☎ 98/886985).

Contacts and Resources

Banks

Generally, banks in Cancún are open weekdays 9–5, with money-exchange desks open 9–1:30. To exchange or wire money, try **Banamex** (⊠ Av. Tulum 19, next to City Hall, ☎ 98/845411). Other centrally located banks downtown include **Banco del Atlantico** (⊠ Av. Tulum 15, ☎ 98/841095) and **Bancomer** (⊠ Av. Tulum 20, ☎ 98/844400).

Car and Moped Rentals

Rental cars are available at the airport or from any of a dozen agencies in town, and most are standard-shift subcompacts and Jeeps; air-conditioned cars with automatic transmissions should be reserved in advance. Rental agencies include **Avis** (airport, ☎ 98/860222; ⊠ Hotel Calinda Viva, ☎ 98/830800; ⊠ Mayfair Plaza, ☎ 98/830803); **Budget** (8 locations: airport ☎ 98/860026; ⊠ Av. Tulum 231, ☎ 98/840204); **Econo-Rent** (airport, ☎ 98/876487; ⊠ Av. Bonampak, ☎ 98/860171); **National** (airport, ☎ 98/860153); or **Hertz** (9 locations: airport, ☎ 98/860150; ⊠ Reno 35, ☎ 98/876644). The **Car Rental Association** (☎ 98/842039) can help you arrange a rental as well. Rates average around $45 per day.

Mopeds and scooters are also available throughout the island. While fun, they are risky, and there is no insurance available for the driver or the vehicle. The accident rate is high, especially downtown, which is considered too congested for novice moped users. Rates start at around $25 per day.

Consulates

U.S. Consulate (⊠ Av. Nader 40, SM 2A, Edificio Marruecos 31, ☎ 98/830272) is open Monday–Friday, 9–1.

Canadian Consulate (⊠ Plaza Mexico Local 312, upper floor, ☎ 98/846716) is open daily 11 AM–1 PM. For emergencies outside office hours, call the Canadian Embassy in Mexico City (☎ 5/254-3288).

Doctors and Dentists

Hospital Americano (⊠ Calle Viento 15, ☎ 98/846133) and **Total Assist** (⊠ Claveles 5, ☎ 98/841092 or 98/848116), both with English-speakers on staff, provide emergency medical care.

Emergencies

Police (☎ 98/841913). **Red Cross** (⊠ Av. Xcaret and Labná, SM 21, ☎ 98/841616). **Highway Patrol** (☎ 98/841107).

English-Language Bookstores

Fama (⊠ Av. Tulum 105, ☎ 98/846586) specializes in books on the Yucatán Peninsula and offers a large selection of English-language magazines. **La Surtidora** (⊠ Av. Tulum 17, ☎ 98/841103) sells a variety of English- and Spanish-language books.

Guided Tours

AIR TOURS

Trans Caribe (☎ 98/871599 or 98/871692) sea planes offer panoramic tours of Cancún that depart daily from Laguna Nichupté. Prices vary according to the length of the ride, starting at about $35 for 20 minutes. Trans Caribe also will take you island-hopping to Isla Mujeres or Cozumel for diving, and sightseeing to the archaeological sites at Tulum and Chichén Itzá.

Aerolatino (⊠ Plaza México, Av. Tulum 200, ☎ 98/871353 or 98/843938), a small Guatemalan carrier, flies between Cancún and Guatemala City, continuing on to Flores and the ruins at Tikal, for $290 round-trip.

DAY CRUISES

Day cruises to Isla Mujeres are popular; they include sno ... Garrafón, time for shopping downtown, as well as Conti...... ...... fast, open-bar buffet lunch, and music. **Aqua Tours Adventures** (⊠ Paseo Kukulcán, Km 6.25, ☎ 98/830400) books the "Isla Mujeres Adventure," which is particularly popular with locals; it departs at 10 AM from the pier in front of Fat Tuesday's, returns at 5 PM, and costs about $55. The **Tropical Cruiser** (⊠ Playa Langosta, ☎ 98/831488) runs an excursion cruise to Isla Mujeres Monday through Saturday, departing from Playa Langosta.

Dolphin Discovery (⊠ Playa Langosta, ☎ 98/830779 or 98/830780) sails daily from Playa Langosta and Playa Tortugas to the company's dock on Isla Mujeres. The day's program includes an instruction video, a 30-minute swim session with the dolphins, and time to explore the island. The excursion costs about $69.

SUBMARINE CRUISES

Nautibus (☎ 98/833552 or 98/832119), or the "floating submarine," has a 1½-hour Caribbean-reef cruise that departs the Playa Linda marina four times daily. The $30 price includes music and drinks. Tours aboard one of the **Sub See Explorer** (☎ 98/852288) "yellow submarines" depart from AquaWorld in the central hotel zone and can be combined with snorkeling for a full day's outing; the cost with snorkeling is about $40, $35 without. Latest to join the underwater ranks is **Atlantis** (☎ 98/833021), Cancún's first true submarine (the others float on the surface and have window seats below). Tours, available every hour from 10 to 3, include an hour-long cruise from Playa Linda to and from the submarine site, and 50 minutes dive time in the sub. The basic price is $80; add $10 and more time if you want to include lunch (not advised if you're prone to motion sickness).

Late-Night Pharmacies

Farmacia Turística (⊠ Plaza Caracol, ☎ 98/831894) and **Farmacia Extra** (⊠ Plaza Caracol, ☎ 98/832827) deliver to hotels 9 AM–10 PM, and **Farmacia Paris** (⊠ Av. Yaxchilán, Marrufo Bldg., ☎ 98/840164) also fills prescriptions.

Mail

The **post office** (⊠ Av. Sunyaxchén at Xel-há, ☎ 98/841418) is open weekdays 8–5, Saturday 9–1; there's also a **Western Union** office (☎ 98/841529) in the building. Mail can be received here if marked "Lista de Correos, Cancún, QR 77500, México." Bear in mind, however, that postal service to and from Mexico is extremely slow and may take two weeks or more. If you have an American Express card, you can have mail sent to you at the **American Express Cancún Office** (⊠ Av. Tulum 208, at Agua, ☎ 98/844554 or 98/841999), open weekdays 9–6, Saturday 9–1.

Publications

At the state tourism office, at the airport, and at many hotels, you can pick up a copy of **Cancún Tips,** a free pocket-size guide to hotels, restaurants, shopping, and recreation that usually contains a discount card for use at various establishments. Although it's loaded with advertising, the booklet, published four times a year in English and Spanish editions, has useful maps and up-to-date information. The magazine staff also runs information centers around town, including one at Plaza Caracol (☎ 98/832745) that is open daily 10–10. Several similar publications, among them *Cancún Nights, Cancún Restaurants,* and *Passport Cancún,* are also available at the airport, as well as at malls and hotels around town.

Telephones

Phones set up by Mexico's long-distance service, Ladatel, which enable you to pay for calls by credit card, are in many hotels and on downtown streets. From these phones, you can also dial 01 and reach an AT&T operator in the states, allowing you to charge calls to an AT&T card or call collect. The operator can connect you to any 800 number, a useful service if you must report lost or stolen credit cards. Direct-dial international calls can be made through AT&T operators from most of the hotels on Paseo Kukulcán, but the hotels also charge $3–$5 per call extra for this service. Bypassing the Mexican phone system is worthwhile, however, even if it means calling collect, because of the 60% tax on overseas calls. Be sure to always go through an AT&T operator or you may find your call to the U.S. costing up to $15 per minute.

Travel Agencies and Tour Operators

American Express (✉ Av. Tulum at Agua, ☎ 98/841999); **Intermar Caribe** (✉ Av. Bonampak at Calle Careza, ☎ 98/844266); **Turismo Aviomar** (✉ Calle Venado 30, ☎ 98/846433).

Visitor Information

Cancún Tips (✉ Av. Tulum 29, Suites 1–5, ☎ 98/841458), open daily 9–9.

The Mexican Ministry of Tourism has established a 24-hour English-language help line for tourists: ☎ 800/90392.

3 Isla Mujeres

Only 8 kilometers across the bay from Cancún, Isla Mujeres is an ocean away in attitude, as sleepy and unassuming as its neighbor is outgoing. Snorkeling and lazing under a palapa *(thatched roof) are about as energetic as it gets here, though there are some interesting remnants of the island's pirate past to explore.*

ATINY, FISH-SHAPE ISLAND 8 km (5 mi) off Cancún, Isla Mujeres (*ees*-lah moo-*hair*-ayce) is a tranquil alternative to its bustling western neighbor. Only about 8 km (5 mi) long by 1 km (½ mi) wide, Isla has flat sandy beaches on its northern end and steep rocky bluffs to the south. Because of its proximity to Cancún, it has turned into a small-scale tourist destination, but it is still a peaceful island retreat with a rich history and culture centered on the sea.

Updated by
Dan Millington

Part of that history is blessed by the presence of Isla's first known inhabitants, the ancient Maya. Their legacy lies in the names, features, and language of their descendants here, but not, unfortunately, in the observatory they built on the southern tip—Hurricane Gilbert obliterated the well-preserved ruin in '88 (restoration efforts are ongoing).

The Spanish conquistadors followed: After setting sail from Cuba in 1517, Hernández de Córdoba's ship blew here accidentally in a storm. Credited with "discovering" the island, he and his crew dubbed their find "Isle of Women." One explanation of the name's origins is that Córdoba and company came upon wooden idols of Maya goddesses. Another theory claims the Spaniards found only women when they arrived—the men were out fishing.

For the next several centuries, Isla, like many Caribbean islands, became a haven for pirates and smugglers, then settled into life as a quiet fishing village. In this century, it started out as a vacation destination for Mexicans; the '60s witnessed a hippie influx; and since the late '70s, day-trippers from Cancún increasingly disembark here, bringing Isla's hotel, restaurant, and shop owners more business than ever.

Most important, the laid-back island life attracts a crowd that prefers beach pleasures to nightlife—scuba diving, snorkeling, and relaxation to the cable TV and rollicking discos of Cancún. Thanks to concerned locals like Ramon Bravo, a renowned expert on sharks, underwater filmmaker, and author, isleños themselves are working to preserve the island's ecology and tranquillity so that those arriving here for the first time will still find an unusually peaceful, authentically Mexican retreat.

As part of this effort, plans are currently afoot to have the Mexican government declare Isla Mujeres a national park. A fee would be levied on tourists who visit the island—money that would be used, it is argued, to keep the island's fragile ecology intact and to provide better services for visitors without damaging the site's unique character. As of early 1997 this plan has not been realized, and arriving tourists are not charged a fee.

Pleasures and Pastimes

Beaches

The island's finest and most popular beach is **Playa Norte**, where you can wade far out in the placid waters or relax at congenial palapa bars for drinks and snacks. The view at sunset is truly spectacular. **Playa Paraíso** and **Playa Lancheros** on the western shore are both pleasant spots for beachcombing.

Bird-Watching

About 45 minutes north of Isla Mujeres is **Isla Contoy** (Isle of Birds), a national wildlife park and bird sanctuary. The tiny island—a place of sand dunes, mangroves, and coconuts—is a beautiful and unspoiled spot. Birders come to see the more than 70 species of bird life.

Dining

Dining on Isla Mujeres offers what you would expect on a small island: plenty of fresh-grilled seafood—lobster, shrimp, conch, and fish. You can also try Mexican and Yucatecan specialties like *carne asada* (broiled beef), mole *poblano* (a spicy sauce of chili, chocolate, sesame, and almonds), *pollo píbil* (chicken baked in banana leaves in a tangy sour orange sauce), and *poc chuc* (pork marinated in sour orange sauce with pickled onions). Those who crave more familiar fare can opt for pizza, steak, or shish kebab.

Fishing

Billfish are a popular catch in spring and early summer; the rest of the year, you can fish for barracuda and tuna, as well as for shad, sailfish, grouper, red snapper, and Spanish mackerel.

Lodging

The island's 25 or so hotels offer a surprisingly broad range of options. Most expensive are the charming beachfront hotels that provide a perfect island getaway complete with modern comforts. Budget accommodations, in the heart of the town, are clean and simple.

Snorkeling and Scuba Diving

Even though there is widespread concern over loss of reef, ocean lovers will still be impressed by the underwater spectacle here. From the surface and below, plenty of fascinating sea life can be observed. During the summer months, fish are attracted to the mild temperatures and calm waters that prevail between 8 AM and 3 PM. However, the decrease of minute algae in the slightly cooler water in winter produces better visibility.

EXPLORING ISLA MUJERES

For orientation purposes, think of Isla Mujeres as an elongated fish: The southern tip is the head and the northern prong the tail. The minute you step off the boat, it's clear how small Isla is. Street names and addresses don't matter much here (islanders have been known to look up their own addresses, and signs are virtually nonexistent). One main paved road, Avenida Rueda Medina, runs the length of the island.

The island's only town, known simply as *el pueblo,* extends the full width of Isla's northern "tail." The village is sandwiched between sand and sea to the north, south, and east; no high rises block the view. Activity centers around the waterfront piers, where the ferries from Puerto Juárez arrive, and on the coastal main drag, Avenida Rueda Medina. Two blocks inland, past the commercial T-shirt and souvenir shops, you'll find the other spot where everyone gathers—the main square (bounded by avenidas Morelos, Bravo, Guerrero, and Hidalgo). Also called (*la placita* or *el parque),* the main square is the ideal place to take in the daily life of the town—basketball games on the permanent courts, children running around the playground, and locals gathered to chat in front of the Government Palace. On holidays and weekends the square gets set up for dances, concerts, and fiestas.

From town, you can easily walk to the island's northwest beaches and to the historical cemetery, but you'll have to rent a moped or hire a taxi to see the rest of Isla's sights.

Numbers in the text correspond to numbers in the margin and on the Isla Mujeres map.

A Good Tour

Start out in the island's little town and walk north on Avenida Lopez Mateos to reach Isla's historical **cemetery** ①. To explore the rest of the island, you'll need to take a moped or taxi south along Avenida Rueda Medina, which leads out of town. The first landmark you'll pass after the piers is the Mexican naval base. It's off-limits to tourists, but from the road you can see the modest flag-raising and -lowering ceremonies at sunrise and sunset (no photo-taking permitted). Continue south and you'll see the **Laguna Makax** ② on your right.

At the end of the lagoon, a dirt road to the left leads to the remains of the **Hacienda Mundaca** ③. About a block southeast of the hacienda, turn right off the main road at the sign that says SAC BAJO to a smaller, unmarked side road, which loops back north. Approximately ½ km (¼ mi) farther on the left is the entrance to the **Tortuga Marina Turtle Farm** ④. When you return to the main Avenida Rueda Medina and go south past Playa Lancheros, you'll soon see **El Garrafón National Park** ⑤. Slightly more than ½ km (¼ mi) along the same road, on the windward side of the tip of Isla Mujeres, is a small **Maya ruin** ⑥, which stood for centuries but was destroyed by Hurricane Gilbert in 1988. You've now come to one of the island's most scenic patches of coastline. Follow the paved perimeter road north into town; it's a beautiful drive, with a few rocky pull-off areas along the way, perfect for a secluded picnic since this road sees little traffic.

Sights to See

① **Cemetery.** You'll find Isla's unnamed cemetery, with its hundred-year-old gravestones, on Lopez Mateos, the road parallel to Playa Norte. Among the lovingly decorated tombs, many in memory of children, is that of Fermín Mundaca (☞ Hacienda Mundaca, *below*). A notorious 19th-century slave trader (often billed more glamorously as a pirate), Mundaca is said to have carved his own tombstone with a skull and crossbones. On one side of the tomb an inscription reads in Spanish AS YOU ARE, I ONCE WAS; the other side warns, AS I AM, SO SHALL YOU BE. Mundaca's grave is empty, however; his remains lie in Mérida where he died. The monument is not easy to find—ask a local to point out the unidentified marker.

⑤ **El Garrafón National Park.** The snorkeling mecca for day-trippers from Cancún is still lovely, but Garrafón—which lies at the bottom of a bluff—was once almost magical in its beauty. Now, as a result of the hands and fins of eager divers, Hurricane Gilbert, and anchors cast from the fleets of tourist boats continually arriving from Cancún, the coral reef here is virtually dead. There has been talk of closing the park to give the coral time to grow back (it's estimated that coral grows at the rate of about 1 centimeter every 40 years), but too many locals make their living from the park for this solution to be feasible. Still, nearly 25,000 visitors each year are impressed by the scenery—parrotfish, angelfish, and the rich blue-green water. Arrive early if you want to avoid the crowds, which start to form about 10 AM. There are food stands and souvenir shops galore, as well as palapas, lockers, equipment rental, rest rooms, and a small aquarium. ☒ *Av. Rueda Medina, 2½ km (1½ mi) south of Playa Lancheros, no phone.* ☎ *Less than $2.* ☉ *Daily 9–4.*

③ **Hacienda Mundaca.** A dirt drive and stone archway mark the entrance to the remains of the mansion built by Fermín Mundaca de Marechaja, the 19th-century slave trader-cum-pirate. When the British navy began cracking down on slavers, he settled on the island and built an ambitious estate with resplendent tropical gardens. The story goes that he

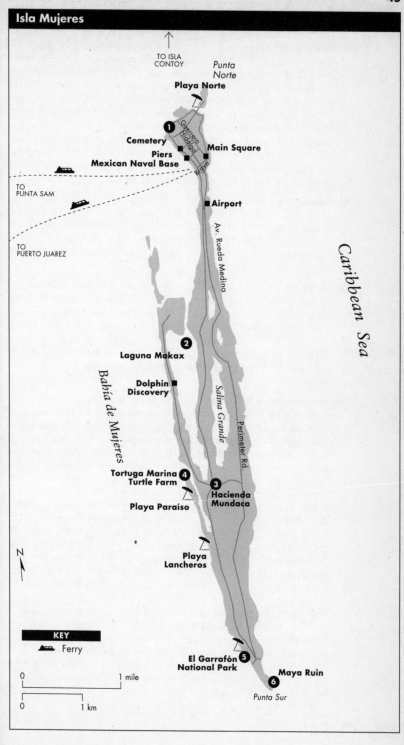

Isla Mujeres

TO ISLA
CONTOY

Punta Norte

Playa Norte

1

Guerrero
Hidalgo

Cemetery

Piers

Mexican Naval Base

Bravo

Main Square

TO
PUNTA SAM

TO
PUERTO JUAREZ

Airport

Av. Rueda Medina

Caribbean Sea

2

Laguna Makax

Dolphin Discovery

Bahía de Mujeres

Salina Grande

Perimeter Rd.

Tortuga Marina Turtle Farm **4**

3

Hacienda Mundaca

Playa Paraíso

N

Playa Lancheros

KEY

🚤 Ferry

0 _____ 1 mile

0 _____ 1 km

El Garrafón National Park **5**

Maya Ruin **6**

Punta Sur

constructed it to woo a certain island maiden who, in the end, chose another man.

What little remained of the hacienda has mysteriously vanished, except for a sorry excuse of a guardhouse, an arch, a pediment, and a well. Locals say that the government tore down the mansion, or at least neglected its upkeep. If you push your way through the jungle—the mosquitoes are fierce—you'll eventually come to the ruined stone archway and triangular pediment, carved with the following inscription: *Huerta de la Hacienda de Vista Alegre MDCCCLXXVI* (Orchard of the Happy View Hacienda, 1876). To get here, continue south from town along the main road until you come to the "S" curve at the end of Laguna Makax (☞ *below*). You'll see the dirt road to your left. ⊠ *East off Av. Rueda Meina, no phone.* ☜ *Free.*

❷ **Laguna Makax.** Heading south from town along Avenida Rueda Medina, you'll pass a Mexican naval base and see some *salinas* (salt marshes) on your left; across the road is this lagoon, where pirates are said to have anchored their ships as they lay in wait for the hapless vessels plying the Spanish Main (the geographical area in which Spanish treasure ships trafficked).

❻ **Maya ruin.** The sad vestiges of a temple once dedicated to Ixchel, the goddess of fertility, are about 1 km (½ mi) below El Garrafón National Park, at the southern tip of Isla. Though Hurricane Gilbert walloped the ruin and succeeded in blowing most of it away, restoration efforts are under way. The adjacent **lighthouse** still stands, and the keeper sometimes allows visitors to ascend it. The island's most scenic patches of coastline lie along the perimeter road between the lighthouse and town.

❹ **Tortuga Marina Turtle Farm.** Run by an outfit called Eco Caribe, this facility is devoted to the study and preservation of sea turtles. During working hours, visitors can examine tanks that contain hundreds of hatchlings and young turtles of various species. The farm's budget is small, but because the turtle population of the Mexican Caribbean continues to dwindle toward extinction, these dedicated ecologists have devoted themselves to care for the hatchlings until they are large enough to be let out to sea; they release about 6,000 infant turtles each month during the hatching season (May through September). Within the confines of the turtle farm are various fenced-in beachfront areas where turtles can be viewed swimming and feeding in the ocean. To get here, follow the main road until, about a block southeast of Hacienda Mundaca, it forks. Follow the right-hand fork, the smaller road that loops back north. About ½ km (¼ mi) to the left you'll see the entrance to the turtle farm. *No phone.* ☜ *$2.* ☉ *Daily 9–5.*

NEED A BREAK?	Walk north from the Turtle Farm along the lovely beach past the Cristalmar Hotel to reach **Hacienda Gomar** (☎ 987/70541), a good Mexican restaurant featuring a buffet lunch and marimba music. If you'd rather not put your shoes back on, try the excellent barbecued grouper, snapper, or barracuda at **Blacky's** (⊠ Playa Paraíso; no phone) open grill on the beach. Also in the area you'll find handicraft and souvenir shops, a beach bar, and small palapas for shade.

BEACHES

The island's finest and most popular beach is on the northwest part of the island: Follow any of the north–south streets in town to **Playa Norte** (sometimes called Playa Cocoteros, or Cocos). You can wade far out in the placid waters. Hurricane Gilbert's only good deed, according to isleños, was to widen this and other leeward-side beaches by blowing sand over from Cancún. You can sit at congenial palapa bars for drinks and snacks; recommended is **Rutilio's y Chimbo's,** twin palapa restaurant-bars right on the beach, where locals come to drink beer, play dice, and chat. There are lots of stands on the beach where you can rent snorkel gear, Jet Skis, floats, sailboards, and sometimes parasails. A glorious setting at the end of the day, Playa Norte is a great place to talk to isleños, who are clearly happy to share the beauty of this place.

At the northernmost end of Playa Norte, you'll find **Punta Norte** and come upon an abandoned hotel on its own private islet. A wood-planked bridge leads to the property, which has changed hands several times and for a long time was supposed to open as an all-inclusive resort called the Costa Club; those plans have been dropped indefinitely. The other building you'll see jutting out on a rocky point is a private home.

On the western side of Isla, you'll find **Playa Paraíso** and **Playa Lancheros,** tranquil spots where you can have lunch or shop for handicrafts, souvenirs, and T-shirts at the small stands. Also housed at Playa Lancheros, in a sea pen, are some pet sea turtles and harmless *tiburónes gatos* (nurse sharks). On the ocean side live the carnivorous *tintorera* (female sharks), which have seven rows of teeth and weigh as much as 500 kilograms (1,100 pounds).

DINING

As in the rest of Mexico, locals eat their main meal during siesta hours, between 1 and 4, and have a light dinner in the evening. Unless otherwise stated, restaurants are open daily for lunch and dinner.

What to Wear

Generally, restaurants on the island are informal, though shirts and shoes are required at most indoor dining rooms. Some, but not all, outdoor terraces or palapas request that swimsuits and feet be covered.

CATEGORY	COST*
$$$	$15–$20
$$	$8–$15
$	under $8

per person, excluding drinks and service

$$$ ✕ **Chez Magaly.** A pleasant establishment on the grounds of the Nautibeach Condo-Hotel, this poolside restaurant is eclectically decorated with wood floors, plants, plastic chairs, Chinese blinds, and traditional cloth place settings. The menu is hybrid, too, with elements of French, Caribbean, and Mexican fare. Seafood grills, lobster quiche, jambalaya (Caribbean seafood and rice), and tequila-flambéed mangos are among the specialties. ⊠ *Av. Rueda Medina, Playa Norte,* ☎ *987/70259 or 987/70436. MC, V. Closed Mon. and 2 wks in June.*

$$$ ✕ **Maria's Kan Kin.** Near El Garrafón, at the southern end of the island, this appealing beach restaurant has a choice location and attractive decor: Wrought-iron tables are set with peach linens on three levels of flagstone terraces. Handprinted on straw place mats, the menu itself is a work of art, illustrated with lovely, colorful drawings. Choose a live lobster or try one of the specialties, such as lobster bisque and coconut mousse, which tend to be prepared with a French twist. It's the perfect spot for a long lunch that extends to sunset. ⊠ *Main road to Garrafón,* ☎ *987/70015. AE, MC, V.*

48

Dining
Bucanero, **10**
Cafécito, **8**
Chez Magaly, **5**
Lonchería
La Lomita, **18**
Maria's Kan
Kin, **16**
Mirtita's, **14**
Pizza Rolandi, **8**
Red Eye Café, **7**
Velazquez, **12**
Villa del Mar, **13**
Zazil-Ha, **1**

Lodging
Belmar, **11**
Cabañas María
del Mar, **2**
Cristalmar, **15**
Mesón del
Bucanero, **9**
Na Balam, **1**
Perla del
Caribe, **4**
Poc-Na, **3**
Posada del
Mar, **6**
Private
Bungalows, **17**

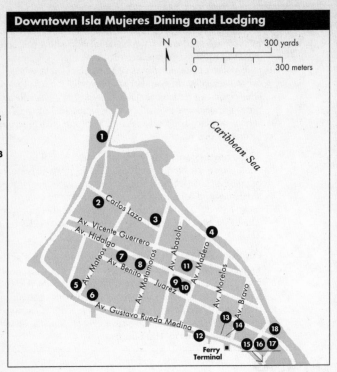

Downtown Isla Mujeres Dining and Lodging

$$$ ✕ **Zazil-Ha.** This fine restaurant, on the grounds of the **Hotel Na Balam** at Playa Norte, offers well-prepared regional specialties as well as interesting vegetarian dishes. The service is friendly and the setting is relaxing; you can eat indoors in the cozy palapa dining room or outdoors on a shady terrace. Light wood furnishings, Mexican tile floors, and walls decorated with pottery create a charmingly rustic ambience. Try the shrimp ceviche for the first course, followed by the seafood special of the day—maybe fresh lobster meat sautéed in butter with lots of garlic. *Chaya* (Maya spinach) with pasta is a house specialty. At breakfast, the restaurant features homemade bread, tropical fruits, and good coffee, plus a full array of egg dishes. Seating on the second level offers good views of the azure waters of Playa Norte. ⊠ *Hotel Na Balam,* ☎ *987/70279. AE, MC, V.*

$$ ✕ **Bucanero.** With a prime location, on one of the main pedestrian drags near the main square, this appealing restaurant has attractive wood tables with blue-and-white inset tiles and terra-cotta floors. For breakfast, the *huevos motuleños* (fried eggs served on a corn tortilla heaped with beans, ham, cheese, peas, marinated red onions, all drenched in tomato sauce) are excellent and cheap; lunch and dinner specialties include avocado stuffed with shrimp and *mar y cielo* (fish fillet and chicken breast with french fries and onions). Simple pastas and pizza are also available. The palapa-roofed section is a good choice for quiet conversation away from the busy street-front. ⊠ *Av. Hidalgo 11,* ☎ *987/70210. Reservations not accepted. MC, V.*

$$ ✕ **Cafécito.** This airy café is a popular hangout for locals and Europeans who come for coffee, ice cream, crepes, and waffles. Artfully decorated with glass-topped turquoise wood tables, shells, and mobiles, Cafécito serves full dinners during high season. ⊠ *Avs. Juárez and Matamoros,* ☎ *987/70438. Reservations not accepted. No credit cards. Closed Thurs. No lunch Fri.–Wed.*

$$ ✕ **Pizza Rolandi.** Red tables, yellow director's chairs, and green walls
★ and window trim set an upbeat tone at this very "in" chain restaurant.
Select from a broad variety of Italian food: lobster pizzas, calzones,
and pastas. Grilled fresh fish and shrimp are highly recommended, and
salads are excellent. Or just stop in for a drink at one of the outside
tables; the margaritas, cappuccino, and espresso are the best in town.
⊠ *Av. Hidalgo between Avs. Madero and Abasolo,* ☎ *987/70430. Reservations not accepted. AE, MC, V.*

$ ✕ **Lonchería La Lomita.** With a bright aqua interior and plastic table-
★ cloths, this simple, homestyle diner isn't much to look at, but you'll
find hearty servings of chicken, steak, and seafood cooked to order
(grilled, fried, or sautéed) here. The octopus sautéed in butter and gar-
lic is particularly tasty. Amazingly low-priced lunch and dinner set menus
include beans, rice, and tortillas or bread; breakfast is also available.
On Avenida Juárez between Avenidas Madero and Morelos is La
Lomita II, like its sister establishment a no-frills eatery that offers
daily specials featuring generous servings and good value. ⊠ *Av. Juárez
25-B, past Av. Allende, no phone. Reservations not accepted. No credit
cards.*

$ ✕ **Mirtita's** and **Villa del Mar.** Next to each other on Avenida Rueda
Medina across from the ferry dock, these are favorite local hangouts.
Both serve fresh seafood and Yucatecan specialties. ⊠ *Av. Rueda Me-
dina, no phone. No credit cards.*

$ ✕ **Red Eye Café.** A bright red awning marks this open-air cafe where
Gus and Inga serve hearty American-style breakfasts with German flair.
Fresh German sausage, made by a German sausage maker in Cancún,
accompanies the egg dishes. ⊠ *Av. Hidalgo, no phone. No credit
cards. Closed Tues.*

$ ✕ **Velazquez.** This family-owned palapa-style restaurant on the beach
★ serves the best seafood on the island. Don't forget to duck your head
before entering. *No credit cards.*

LODGING

The approximately 25 hotels (about 600 rooms) on Isla Mujeres gen-
erally fall into one of two categories: The older, more modest places
are situated right in town, and the newer, more costly properties tend
to have beachfront locations around Punta Norte and, increasingly, on
the peninsula near the lagoon. Most hotels have ceiling fans; some have
air-conditioning, but few offer TVs or phones. Luxurious, self-contained
time-share condominiums are another option, which you can learn more
about from the tourist office (☎ 987/70316). All hotels share the
77400 postal code.

CATEGORY	COST*
$$$	$60–$90
$$	$25–$60
$	under $25

All prices are for a standard double room, excluding 12% tax.

$$$ 🏨 **Cristalmar.** Although the location of this condo-hotel (a five-minute
drive from town) is inconvenient for those without their own trans-
portation, the property—situated on a peninsula by the lagoon on lovely
Playa Paraíso—boasts a stunning sea view. Spacious one-, two-, and
three-bedroom suites open to the courtyard, which has a pool and a
palapa bar. Local artwork adorns the walls and dark brown or white
wicker furnishings and glass-top tables decorate the rooms. ⊠ *Paraíso
Laguna Mar, Lot 16,* ☎ *987/70007 or 800/552–4550. 38 suites.
Restaurant, bar, air-conditioning, kitchenettes, pool, beach, dive shop.
AE, MC, V.*

$$$ ▥ **Na Balam.** This intimate, informal hostelry set on Playa Norte will
★   fulfill all your tropical-paradise fantasies. Three corner suites with
balconies affording outstanding views of sea and sand are well worth
the price (approximately $85). The simple, attractive rooms have
turquoise-tile floors, carved wood furniture, dining areas, and patios
facing the beach; photos of Mexico in its bygone days and Mexican
carvings grace the walls. A swimming pool and eight more rooms
were added in 1995. Breakfast at the hotel's **Zazil Ha** restaurant (☞
Dining, *above*) is a delightful way to kick off the day. ✉ *Calle Zazil
Ha 118,* ☎ *987/70279 or 800/552–4550,* ℻ *987/70446. 31 rooms.
Restaurant, bar, air-conditioning, pool, beach. AE, MC, V.*

$$$ ▥ **Perla del Caribe.** On the eastern edge of town facing the new sea
wall and promenade, the 3-story Perla has rooms that look out either
on the open sea or town, priced accordingly. All rooms have balconies
and are comfortable and functional but not palatial. You can listen to
music in the restaurant/bar most evenings. ✉ *Av. Madero 2,* ☎ *987/
70444 or 800/258–6454,* ℻ *987/70011. 91 rooms. Restaurant, bar,
air-conditioning, pool. AE, MC, V.*

$$ ▥ **Belmar.** Right in the heart of town, above Pizza Rolandi, this small
hotel shares a charming plant-filled inner courtyard with the restau-
rant, which means it can occasionally be noisy here until 11 PM. Stan-
dard rooms are pretty, with tiled baths and light-wood furniture. One
enormous suite features a private whirlpool bath on a patio, a tiled
kitchenette, and a sitting area. All rooms have phones, satellite TV, and
air-conditioning. ✉ *Av. Hidalgo 110, between Avs. Madero and Aba-
solo,* ☎ *987/70430,* ℻ *987/70429. 11 rooms. AE, MC, V.*

$$ ▥ **Cabañas María del Mar.** A rather mind-boggling assortment of
★   rooms is available in this friendly beachfront hotel, but all have a great
deal of character, and the place as a whole has a unique Mexican atmosphere. Some of the rooms are rather spare, but those in the slightly
more expensive "castle" section have hand-carved wood furnishings by
local artisans in a combination of Spanish and Maya styles, folk art,
tiled baths, and hand-painted sinks. The hotel has a prime location on
Playa Norte, next to Na-Balam, and its reasonable room rates include
Continental breakfast. ✉ *Av. Carlos Lazos 1,* ☎ *987/70179 or 800/
552–4550,* ℻ *987/70213. 41 rooms, 14 cabañas. Restaurant, bar, air-
conditioning, pool, motor bikes, travel services. MC, V.*

$$ ▥ **Mesón del Bucanero.** This Spanish colonial–style hotel features at-
tractive contemporary wood furnishings in bright rooms. Reasonably
priced suites have small sitting areas and balconies, and large closets.
Standard rooms are unusually diminutive but functional. ✉ *Av. Hi-
dalgo 11,* ☎ *987/70210,* ℻ *987/70126. 6 rooms. Restaurant. MC, V.*

$$ ▥ **Posada del Mar.** This hotel's assets include its prime location between town and Playa Norte and its reasonable prices. Rooms have
balconies overlooking a main road and beyond to the waterfront. The
simple wood furnishings appear somewhat worse for wear, although
baths are clean, with cheerful colored tiles. Private bungalows in the
$ price category are also available. A recently added bar next to the
pool is as popular as the street-front palapa-roof restaurant. ✉ *Av. Rueda
Medina 15A,* ☎ *987/70300 or 987/70044 or 800/552–4550,* ℻ *987/
70266. 40 rooms. Restaurant, bar, pool. AE, MC, V.*

$ ▥ **Poc-Na.** The island's youth hostel at the eastern end of town rents
bunks or hammocks (which cost less) in dormitory-style rooms with
showers and lockers that sleep eight. The management requires guests
to leave their passports as a deposit for the length of their stay. Proximity to the beach is a bonus. ✉ *Av. Matamoros 15,* ☎ *987/70090 or
987/70059. Dining room. No credit cards.*

Private Bungalows

Several pretty, small bungalows near Garrafón are rented for the long term by the owner, Tino. Inquire at **Mexico Divers** (☎ 987/70131).

NIGHTLIFE AND THE ARTS

The Arts

Festivals and cultural events are held on many weekends, with live entertainment on the outdoor stage in the main square. The whole island celebrates the spring regattas and the Caribbean music festivals. **Casa de la Cultura,** near the youth hostel, offers folkloric dance classes year-round. The center also operates a small public library and book exchange. ⊠ *Av. Guerrero,* ☎ *987/70639.* ۞ *Mon.–Sat. 9–1 and 4–8.*

Nightlife

Most restaurant bars feature a happy hour, offering two drinks for the price of one, from 5 to 7; the palapa bars at Playa Norte are an excellent place to watch the sun set. The current hot spot is **YaYa's** (⊠ Av. Rueda Medina 42, near the lighthouse and Playa Norte, no phone), run by some good ol' boys from Dallas who serve up huge Texas steaks, chili dogs, and shrimp etouffé along with live jazz, rock, and reggae jam sessions until 2 or 3 AM. The bar at the **Posada del Mar** (⊠ Av. Rueda Medina 15A, ☎ 987/70300) can be subdued or hopping, depending on what's going on in town. **Buho's,** the bar/restaurant at Cabañas María del Mar (⊠ Av. Carlos Lazo 1, ☎ 987/70179), serves food and is a good choice for a relaxing drink at sunset or later at night. **Restaurante La Peña** (⊠ Av. Guerrero 5, ☎ 987/70309) has music and dancing on its open-air terrace overlooking the sea. **Palapa Disco** (⊠ Playa Norte off Av. Rueda Medina) has music and dancing from midnight until 4 AM.

OUTDOOR ACTIVITIES AND SPORTS

For any water sport, beaches on the north and west sides are the calmest.

Fishing

Bahía Dive Shop (⊠ Av. Rueda Medina 166, across from pier, ☎ FAX 987/70340) charges $250 for a day of deep-sea fishing, $200 a day for cast fishing (tarpon, snook, and bonefish), and $20 an hour for offshore fishing (barracuda, snapper, and smaller fish).

Snorkeling and Scuba Diving

The famous coral reefs at **El Garrafón** have suffered tremendously from negligent tourists, the effects of Hurricane Gilbert, and the constant dropping of anchors, now outlawed. Though still a beautiful sight (you can spot parrotfish, angelfish, and schools of sergeant majors), the reef is far from its past splendor. Get there early; Cancún day-trippers start churning up the waters at around 10. Good snorkeling continues near Playa Norte on the north end. Underneath the waters near the **lighthouse** (*el farolito*) is a partially buried but still visible statue of the Virgin.

Offshore, there's excellent diving and snorkeling at **Xlaches** (pronounced *ees*-lah-chay) reef, due north on the way to Isla Contoy (☞ Side Trip to Isla Contoy, *below*). Another one of the island's most alluring diving attractions is the **Cave of the Sleeping Sharks,** east of the northern tip. The caves were discovered by an island fisherman known as Vulvula and extensively explored by Ramon Bravo, a local diver, cinematographer, and Mexico's foremost expert on sharks. *National Geographic* and Jacques Cousteau have also studied the curious phenomena of the snoozing black tip, bull, and lemon sharks—it's a fascinating site for experienced divers.

At the extreme southern end of the island on the leeward side lies **Los Manchones.** At 30–40 ft deep and 3,300 ft off the southwestern coast, this coral reef makes a good dive site. During the summer of 1994, an ecology group hoping to divert divers and snorkelers from El Garrafón commissioned and sunk a statue called the Cruz de la Bahía (Cross of the Bay) near the southern end of Los Manchones. **Los Cuevones,** to the southwest near La Bandera, reaches a depth of 45 ft. On the windward side of the islet north of Mujeres is an unnamed site complete with two shipwrecked galleons. Dive shops will be able to direct you to this spot and others. They're also described in detail in *Dive Mexico,* a colorful magazine readily available in local shops.

Bahía Dive Shop (⊠ Av. Rueda Medina 166, across from the pier, ☎ FAX 987/70340) rents snorkeling and scuba equipment and runs three-hour boat and dive trips to the reefs and the Cave of the Sleeping Sharks. Snorkel gear goes for $5 a day; tanks, $45–$60, depending on the length of the dive. **Mexico Divers** (⊠ Av. Rueda Medina and Av. Medaro, 1 block from ferry, ☎ 987/70131), also called **Buzos de México,** runs three-hour snorkeling tours for $15; two-tank scuba trips start at $55 for a reef dive and $75 for the shark-cave dive. Rental gear is available. Dive master Carlos Gutiérrez also gives a resort course for $80 and open-water PADI certification for $350 (his prices are generally negotiable).

Swimming with Dolphins

If you're fascinated by Flipper and his ilk, **Dolphin Discovery** (☎ 987/70742) will give you the chance to sport in the water with them in a small, supervised group. There are four swims daily, at 9 and 11 AM and 1 and 3 PM. Each session is one hour, consisting first of a half hour instruction video, and then 30 minutes in the water; the cost is $79.

SHOPPING

Shopping on Isla Mujeres used to be limited to basic resort wear, suntan lotions, and groceries. Now more Mexican crafts shops offering good deals on silver, fabric bags, and handcrafted objects are opening here. Even the smaller shops often accept credit cards. Shopping hours are generally daily 10–1 and 4–7, although many stores now stay open through siesta.

Crafts

Casa del Arte Mexica (⊠ Av. Hidalgo 6, ☎ 987/70459) has a good choice of clay reproductions, silver jewelry, batiks, rubbings, wood carvings, leather, and hammocks.

La Sirena (⊠ Av. Morelos, 1 block from the ferry dock through the pine arch marking the way to the island's shopping area, ☎ 987/70223) is set apart from neighoring shops by its extensive array of handcrafted goods. The owners of this small store have collected masks, textiles, and other fine Mexican crafts—including unusual clothing, pottery, and jewelry. While the prices are not low, they are fair for the quality of items offered.

Van Cleef & Arpels (⊠ Aves. Juárez and Morelos, ☎ 987/70299), was opened in 1991 with an impressive jewelry selection in a large corner shop.

Tienda Paulita (⊠ Avs. Morelos and Hidalgo, ☎ 987/70014) features a standard selection of folk art and handmade clothing in a fairly large space.

Grocery Stores

There are two fair-size groceries: **Super Betino** (⊠ Av. Morelos 3) and **Super Mirtita** (⊠ Avs. Juárez and Bravo). Food, including fresh fruit, can also be purchased in the municipal market on Avenida Guerrero Norte.

SIDE TRIP TO ISLA CONTOY

About 30 km (19 mi) north of Isla Mujeres, Isla Contoy (Isle of Birds) is a national wildlife park and bird sanctuary and a perfect getaway, even from Isla Mujeres. Birders, snorkelers, and fishing aficionados come here to enjoy the setting and the numerous varieties of animal life. This lovely spot enjoys protected sanctuary status, and the number of visitors is carefully regulated. The island, which is only 6½ km (4 mi) long and less than 1 km (about ½ mi) wide, is officially open from 9 to 5:30; overnight visits are not allowed.

In order to land on Contoy, it is necessary to purchase an authorization ticket ($5) in Isla Mujeres; this is included in the cost of guided tours. If landing on Contoy is important to you, be sure to specify this when booking a day trip. Many operators simply cruise around Contoy to view the wildlife and land on other islands for lunch. However, government officials may at some point stop all landings on the island in order to protect the fragile environmental balance.

Some 70 species of bird life—including gulls, pelicans, petrels, cormorants, cranes, ducks, flamingos, herons, frigates, sea swallows, doves, quail, spoonbills, and hawks—fly this way in late fall, some of them to breed and make their nests. Although the number of species is diminishing, Contoy is still a rare treat for bird-watchers.

Anyone with an interest in nature will be fascinated by the sea life around this nearly deserted island. For snorkelers, the coral and fish are dazzling. Immense rays, occasionally visible in the shallows, average about 5 ft across and can sometimes be seen jumping out of the water. The island's waters also abound with mackerel, barracuda, flying fish, trumpet fish, and shrimp; in December, lobsters pass through in great (though diminishing) numbers as their southerly migration route takes them past.

Black rocks and coral reefs fringe the island's east coast, which drops off abruptly 15 ft into the sea; at the west are sand, shrubs, and coconut palms. At the north and the south you find nothing but trees and small pools of water. The sand dunes inland on the east coast rise as high as 70 ft above sea level. Other than the birds and the dozen or so park rangers who make their home on Contoy, the island's only denizens are iguanas, lizards, turtles, hermit crabs, and boa constrictors.

Visit the outdoor museum, which displays about 50 photographs depicting the island, with captions in English, French, and Spanish. An observation tower offers a superb view of the surroundings.

See Tour Operators, *below,* for details on getting to Contoy from Isla Mujeres. From Cancún, **Asterix** (☎ 98/864270) offers Isla Contoy cruises that depart from the Playa Caracol dock next to the Coral Beach Hotel Monday through Saturday at 9 AM and return at 5 PM. The package, which costs $70, includes Continental breakfast, swimming or snorkeling (equipment rental $5, or bring your own), and an open-bar lunch.

You can ask about the island at the Isla Mujeres tourist office (☞ Visitor Information *in* Isla Mujeres A to Z, *below*). **SEDESOL** (Cancún, ☎ 98/845955), the national ecology and urban-development ministry, can also provide information about Isla Contoy.

ISLA MUJERES A TO Z

Arriving and Departing

By Boat

TO ISLA MUJERES

The **Caribbean Express** and the **Caribbean Miss** (☎ 987/70254 or 987/70253), both air-conditioned cruisers with bar service, make several 30-minute crossings daily. They leave Puerto Juárez on the mainland for the main ferry dock in Isla Mujeres from 6:30 AM to 8 PM at approximately 20-minute intervals; the fare is under $3 per person.

There are three slower **passenger ferries** that leave every hour 7:30–7:30 and at 10 AM; the schedule varies depending on the season, so check the times posted at the dock. The one-way fare is only about $1.50 and the trip takes 45 minutes, but delays and crowding are frequent.

A convenient, more expensive service, the **Shuttle** (Cancún, ☎ 98/83448) runs directly from the Playa Tortugas dock in Cancún's hotel zone at least four times a day and costs about $15 round-trip.

Cars are unnecessary on Isla, unless you want to explore the far reaches of the island, but **municipal ferries** that accommodate vehicles as well as passengers leave from Punta Sam and take about 45 minutes. Check departure times posted at the pier, but you can count on the schedule running from about 7 AM to 9 PM. The fare is under $2 per person and $10 per vehicle. In addition, a number of tour companies offer day trips to Isla Mujeres from Cancún (☞ Chapter 2).

FROM ISLA MUJERES

The **Caribbean Express** and the **Caribbean Miss** (☎ 987/70254 or 987/70253) make the trip from Isla Mujeres to Puerto Juárez between 7 AM and 8 PM at approximately 30-minute intervals; the fare is under $3 per person. The slower **passenger ferry** departs from the main dock at Isla Mujeres to Puerto Juárez at approximately 5, 6, 6:30, 7:30, 8:15, 8:45, 9:30, 10:30, and 11:30 AM, and at 12:30, 1:30, 2:30, 3:30, 4:30, 5, 5:30, 6:30, and 7:30 PM. The first **car ferry** from Isla Mujeres to Punta Sam leaves at about 6 AM and the last departs at about 7:15 PM. Again, schedules change often, so you should call ahead or check the boat schedule posted at the pier.

Getting Around

By Bicycle

Bicycles are available for hardy cyclists, but don't underestimate the hot sun and the tricky road conditions. Watch for the many speed bumps, which can give you an unexpected jolt, and avoid riding at night; some roads have no street lights. **Rent Me Sport Bike** (✉ Avs. Juárez and Morelos, 1 block from main pier, no phone) offers five-speed cycles starting at less than $2 for an hour; a full day costs about $5. You can leave your driver's license in lieu of a deposit; the place is open daily 8–6.

By Bus

Municipal buses (☎ 987/70529 or 987/74173) run at 20- to 30-minute intervals daily between 6 AM and 10 PM (generally following the ferry schedule) from the Posada del Mar hotel on Avenida Rueda Medina out to Colonia Salinas on the windward side. There is also service from the dock to Playa Lancheros on the leeward side, toward the south end of the island. As you might expect, however, the service is slow, because the buses make frequent stops.

By Car

There is little reason for tourists to bring cars to Isla Mujeres, because there are plenty of other forms of transportation that cost far less than renting and transporting a private vehicle. Moreover, though the main road is paved, speed bumps abound, and some areas are poorly lighted.

By Golf Cart

The newest way for tourists to explore Isla is by golf cart. **P'pe's Rentadora** (⊠ Av. Hidalgo 19, ☎ 987/70019) and almost all of the moped rental shops listed below, as well as some hotels, rent them for about $10 an hour.

By Moped

The island is full of moped rental shops. **Motorent Kankin** (⊠ Av. Abasolo 15, no phone) will provide a two-seater, three-speed Honda for about $5 per hour or $20 per day ($40 for 24 hours); a $20 deposit—or a credit card or passport left behind—is required. **P'pe's Rentadora** (⊠ Av. Hidalgo 19, ☎ 987/70019) offers two-seater, fully automatic Honda Aeros, starting at $5 per hour, for a minimum of two hours; it's under $35 for 24 hours. **Ciro's Motorent** (⊠ Av. Guerrero Norte 11 at Av. Matamoros, ☎ 987/70578) has two-seater Honda Tact 50 mopeds.

By Taxi

If your time is limited you can hire a **taxi** (⊠ Av. Rueda Medina, ☎ 987/70066) for a private island tour at about $15 an hour. Fares will run about $1 from the ferry or downtown to the hotels on the north end, at Playa Norte. Taxis line up right by the ferry dock around the clock.

Contacts and Resources

Banks

Banco del Atlántico (⊠ Av. Rueda Medina 3, ☎ 987/70104 or 987/70005), the only bank on the island, is open from 9–1:30 and exchanges money from 10–noon.

Emergencies

Medical Service (☎ 987/70195 or 987/70607). **Hospital** (☎ 987/70017). **Police** (☎ 987/70082). **Red Cross** (☎ 987/70282).

Guided Tours

BOAT TOURS

Cooperativa Lanchera (waterfront, near the dock, no phone) offers four-hour launch trips to the Virgin near Playa Norte, the lighthouse, the turtles at Playa Lancheros, the coral reefs at Los Manchones, and El Garrafón for about $10 without meals, $12 with meals. **Cooperativa Isla Mujeres** (⊠ Av. Rueda Medina, ☎ 987/70274), next to Mexico Divers, rents out boats at $120 for a maximum of four hours and six people, and $15 per person for an island tour with lunch (minimum six people).

At least two of Isla Mujeres's boating cooperatives sell day tours to Isla Contoy (☞ Side Trip to Isla Contoy, *above*). **Sociedad Cooperativa "Isla**

Mujeres" (⊠ pier, ☎ 987/70274) and **La Isleña** (⊠ ½ block from the pier, corner of Avs. Morelos and Juárez, ☎ 987/70036) launch boats daily at 8:30 AM; they return at 4 PM. Tour operators provide a fruit breakfast on the boat and stop at Xlaches reef on the way to the island for snorkeling (gear is included). The tour of Contoy's leeward side includes views from the water of Bird Beach and Puerto Viejo Lagoon. Along the way, your crew trolls for the lunch they'll cook on the beach at the Contoy National Park Station—you may be in for anything from barracuda to snapper (unlimited beer and soda are also included). While they barbecue the catch, you'll have time to explore the island, snorkel some more, check out the small museum and biological station, or just laze under a palapa. The size of the group depends on the boat, but it's usually a minimum of six and a maximum of 12. The trip from Isla Mujeres to Isla Contoy takes about 45 minutes, again depending on the boat, and the day tours run about $30 to $40.

TOUR OPERATORS
Club de Yates de Isla Mujeres (⊠ Av. Rueda Medina, ☎ 987/70211 or 987/70086), open daily 9–noon.

Late-Night Pharmacies
Farmacia Isla Mujeres (⊠ Av. Juárez, next to the Caribbean Tropic Boutique, ☎ 987/70178) and **Farmacia Lily** (⊠ Avs. Madero and Hidalgo, ☎ 987/70164) are open Monday–Saturday 8:30 AM–9:30 PM and Sunday 8:30 AM–3 PM.

Mail
The **post office** (⊠ Av. Guerrero, ½ block from the market, ☎ 987/70085) is open weekdays 8–7 and Saturday 9–1.

Publications
At the tourist office (☞ Visitor Information, *below*) or at your hotel, you can pick up a copy of the monthly **Islander** magazine, which has a wealth of tourist information.

Telephones
Ladatel phones allow you to reach an AT&T operator in the United States by dialing 01 or to charge calls using major credit cards. They may be found at various places around the island, including Avenida Rueda Medina, across from the ferry; outside Bucanero's restaurant (☞ Dining, *above*); across from the taxi stand; and outside the post office. In addition, long-distance phone service is available in the lobby of the **Hotel María José** (⊠ Av. Madero 21) or at **Club de Yates** (☞ *above*).

Visitor Information
Tourist office (⊠ Plaza Isla Mujeres, north end of main shopping street, ☎ 987/70316), open weekdays 9–2 and 7–9.

4 Cozumel

Mexico's largest cruise ship port, Cozumel is at once commercial and laid back. Along with day-trippers, the island draws sport-fishing enthusiasts and divers who come to explore some of the world's best reefs.

COZUMEL PROVIDES A BALANCE between Cancún and Isla Mujeres: Though attuned to North American tourism, the island has managed to keep development to a minimum. Its expansive beaches, superb coral reefs, and copious wildlife—in the sea, on the land, and in the air—attract an active, athletic crowd. Rated one of the top destinations in the world among underwater enthusiasts, Cozumel is encircled by a garland of reefs entrancing divers and snorkelers alike. Despite the inevitable effects of docking cruise ships (shops and restaurants actively recruit customers on an increasingly populous main drag), the island's earthy charm and tranquillity remain intact. The relaxing atmosphere here is typically Mexican—friendly and unpretentious. Cozumel's rich Maya heritage is reflected in the faces of 60,000 or so isleños; you'll see people who look like ancient statues come to life, and occasionally hear the Maya language spoken.

Updated by
Dan Millington

A 490-square-km (189-square-mi) island 19 km (12 mi) to the east of Yucatán, Cozumel is mostly flat, its interior covered by parched scrub, dense jungle, and marshy lagoons. White sandy beaches with calm waters line the island's leeward (western) side, which is fringed by a spectacular reef system, while the powerful surf and rocky strands on the windward (eastern) side, facing the Caribbean, are broken up here and there by calm bays and hidden coves. Most of Cozumel is undeveloped, with a good deal of the land and the shores set aside as national parks; a few Maya ruins provide what limited sightseeing there is aside from the island's glorious natural attractions. San Miguel is the only established town.

Although the island was first inhabited by distant cousins of the Maya, it was the Maya who transformed it into a key center of trade and navigation as well as the destination for pilgrimages honoring Ixchel, the goddess of fertility, childbirth, and the moon; it is said that every Maya woman was required to visit the site at least once in her lifetime. The Maya called the island *Ah-Cuzamil-Peten* (Place of the Swallows).

In 1518, Spanish explorer Juan de Grijalva arrived on Cozumel in search of slaves. His tales of gold and other treasures inspired Hernán Cortés, Mexico's most famous Spanish explorer, to visit the island the following year and, shortly thereafter, to settle two missionaries there to convert the Indians. Although the Spaniards never succeeded in colonizing Cozumel, disease eventually wiped out much of the native population that had not already been massacred. By 1600 the island was abandoned.

During the 17th and 18th centuries Cozumel became a hideout for pirates and buccaneers, including Jean Laffite and Henry Morgan, who found the catacombs and tunnels dug by the Indians useful for burying their treasure. These corsairs also laid siege to numerous cargo ships, many of which still lie at the bottom of the surrounding waters. In the 19th century Cozumel was primarily a fishing village and supply port for shipping routes to Central America.

At the start of this century, the island began to capitalize on its abundant supply of *zapote* (sapodilla) trees, which produce chicle, prized by the chewing-gum industry. Forays into the jungle in search of chicle led to interest in the archaeological remains. Many of the ruins still stand, but Cozumel's importance as a seaport and a chicle-producing region diminished with the advent of the airplane and the invention of synthetic chewing gum.

For some decades Cozumel was just another backwater, where locals hunted alligators and iguanas and worked on coconut plantations to produce copra (dried kernels from which coconut oil is extracted). Cozumeleños subsisted largely on the fruits of the sea, including lobster, conch, sea turtles, and fish, which remain staples of the economy. In the 1950s the island eked out an existence as a health resort for wealthy Yucatecans. It was not until the 1960s and the arrival of oceanographic explorer Jacques Cousteau, who had learned of its magnificent diving opportunities, that Cozumel began its climb out of oblivion.

Pleasures and Pastimes

Beaches

Inviting, sandy beaches line the leeward side of the island. The most popular, **Playa San Francisco**, a 5-km (3-mi) expanse, has restaurants, a bar, and water sports equipment for rent. On the windward side, where the rough surf of the Caribbean pounds, are mostly rocky coves and narrow beaches. It's fine for sun worshipers, but usually too rough for swimming along here.

Dining

Cozumel's restaurants offer Yucatecan specialties with an emphasis on seafood, fine cuisine with a Mediterranean accent—and everything in between. Regional dishes employing savory lobster, king crab, grouper, and red snapper fillets are highlights.

Fishing

The waters off Cozumel swarm with more than 230 species of fish, the numbers upholding the island's reputation as one of the world's best locations for trolling, deep-sea fishing, and bottom fishing. Beaky jawed billfish—including swordfish, blue marlin, white marlin, and sailfish—are plentiful here from late April through June, their migration season. World records for catches are frequently set on the island in these months.

Deep-sea fishing for tuna, barracuda, wahoo, and kingfish is productive year-round. Aficionados also enjoy Cozumel's bottom fishing (grouper, yellowtail, and snapper) on the shallow sand flats at the northern end of the island, which also harbor bonefish, tarpon, snook, cubera, and small sharks. The best times to fish are sunrise and sunset, just before a full moon.

Lodging

The selection of appealing options includes modern beachfront resorts with sybaritic creature comforts and all-inclusive properties with the barefoot ambience of a secret island hideaway. Those with tighter budgets can stay in town, where homey atmosphere and modest facilities prevail.

Scuba Diving

Because of the diversity of coral formations and the dramatic underwater peaks and valleys, divers rank Cozumel's **Palancar reef** among the top five in the world. With more than 30 charted reefs whose average depths range 50–80 ft and a water temperature that hits about 75°F–80°F during peak diving season (June–August, when hotel rates are coincidentally at their lowest), Cozumel is far and away Mexico's number-one diving destination. Sixty thousand divers come here each year to explore the underwater coral formations, caves, sponges, sea fans, and tropical fish.

Shopping

Shopping is an even bigger industry for Cozumel than diving, principally because of the lucrative trade with cruise-ship passengers (Cozumel is Mexico's largest cruise-ship port). Thousands disembark each year in San Miguel, and consequently prices are relatively high compared to, say, Mérida. The variety of folk art ranges from downright schlocky curios to some excellent silver jewelry, pottery, painted balsa-wood animals, blown glass, and *huipiles* (embroidered cotton dresses).

Snorkeling

Snorkeling ranks just after diving among the island's popular sports. There is good snorkeling in the morning off the piers at the Presidente Inter-Continental and La Ceiba hotels, where fish are fed. The shallow reefs in Chankanaab Bay, Playa San Francisco, and the northern beach at the Club Cozumel Caribe also provide clear views of brilliantly colored fish and sea creatures, among them fingerlings, parrot fish, sergeant majors, angelfish, and squirrel fish, along with elk coral, conch, and sand dollars.

EXPLORING COZUMEL

Cozumel is about 53 km (33 mi) long and 15 km (9 mi) wide, but only a small percentage of its roads—primarily those in the southern half—are paved. Dirt roads can be explored, with care, in a four-wheel-drive vehicle. Beware of flash flooding during the rainy season: A number of the dirt roads can become difficult to navigate in minutes.

Aside from the 3% of the island that has been developed, Cozumel is made up of expanses of sandy or rocky beaches, quiet little coves, palm groves, scrubby jungles, lagoons and swamps, and a few low hills (the maximum elevation is 45 ft). Brilliantly feathered tropical birds, lizards, armadillos, coati, deer, and small foxes populate the undergrowth and the marshes. In addition to the sites detailed in the Sights to See section, *below,* several minor **Maya ruins** dot the eastern coast of the island. One of them, **Tumba del Caracol,** may have served as a lighthouse. There are also a couple of minuscule ruins, **El Mirador** and the **Throne,** identified by roadside markers.

San Miguel, Cozumel's hub, is simply laid out in characteristically Mexican grid fashion. **Avenida Benito Juárez** stretches east from the pier for 16 km (10 mi) across the island, dividing north from south. Running perpendicular is **Avenida Rafael Melgar,** the coastal road on the island's leeward side (the walkway across the street, on the ocean side, is known as the *malecón*). Avenues, which are labeled "norte" or "sur" depending on where they fall in relation to Juárez, parallel Melgar and are numbered in multiples of five. This means that the avenue after Avenida 5a Sur is Avenida 10a Sur, but if you were to cross Juárez on Avenida 5a Sur it would turn into Avenida 5a Norte. The side streets are even-numbered north of Avenida Juárez (2, 4, 6, etc.) and odd south of the avenue (3, 5, 7, etc.). This is less confusing than it sounds; it will be clear once you've walked around town.

The main strip of shops and restaurants is Avenida Rafael Melgar, along the waterfront. The **Plaza del Sol** is the main square, most often simply called *la plaza* or *el parque*. Directly across from the docks, it's hard to miss. A number of government buildings are here, including the large and modern convention center (used more for local functions than for formal conferences) and the state tourist office. The square is the heart of the town, where everyone congregates in the evenings. Heading inland (east) from the malecón takes you away from the touristy zone and toward the residential sections.

The commercial district is concentrated in the 10 blocks between Calle 10 Norte and Calle 7 Sur. North of that point, you find almost no development until you reach the stretch of hotels beyond the airport; south of town, development continues almost uninterrupted to **La Ceiba,** one of a second cluster of hotels and shops and adjacent to the international passenger terminal for cruise ships.

Numbers in the text correspond to numbers in the margin and on the Cozumel map.

A Good Tour

It's worth renting a Jeep to explore Cozumel, which has more sights than either Cancún or Isla Mujeres. If you head south from Cozumel's principal town, **San Miguel** ①, in about 10 minutes you'll come to **Chankanaab Nature Park** ②. Continue past Chankanaab and past Playa Corona, Playa San Francisco, and Playa del Sol; at Km 17.5 a turnoff leads about 3 km (2 mi) inland to the village and ruins of **El Cedral** ③ (take this detour only if you have a four-wheel-drive vehicle). Backtrack to the coast and go south past Playa de Palancar (the famous reef lies offshore) to the island's southern tip, where you'll find a dirt trail to **Laguna Colombia** ④.

If you head east on the paved road, you'll come to the eastern Caribbean coast. Make a right turn onto a dirt road and follow it for 4 km (3 mi) south to get to the **Punta Celerain Lighthouse** ⑤. When you return to the paved road and head north, you will first pass the Tumba del Caracol, another Maya ruin that may have served as a lighthouse; a bit farther on are the minuscule ruins of El Mirador and the Throne. Beyond Punta Chiqueros, Playa Bonita, Playa Chen Río, and Punta Morena you'll see Playa Oriente, where the cross-island road meets the east coast; you can take the cross-island road west toward town or continue north. If you choose the latter route, you'll need a four-wheel-drive vehicle to travel on a rough dirt road that dead-ends past Punta Molas; eventually you'll have to turn around. A sign at this junction warns that drivers proceed at their own risk. This pothole-ridden road is the preferred sunbathing spot of boa constrictors, crocodiles, and other jungle denizens.

If you're headed toward town, it's worth making a detour inland to view the ruins of **San Gervasio** ⑥; take the cross-island road west to the army airfield and turn right; follow this road north for 7 km (4 mi). The road to the ruins is a good one, but a nearly unmaneuverable dirt road leads northeast of San Gervasio back to the unpaved coast road. At the junction is a marvelously deserted beach where you can camp. Heading north along this beach, you'll come to **Castillo Real** ⑦, another Maya site. A number of other minor ruins are spread across the northern tip of Cozumel, which terminates at the **Punta Molas Lighthouse** ⑧.

Sights to See

❼ **Castillo Real.** A Maya site on the eastern coast, near the northern tip of the island, the *castillo* (castle) comprises a lookout tower, the base of a pyramid, and a temple with two chambers capped by a false arch. The waters here harbor several shipwrecks, remnants from the days when buccaneers lay in wait for richly cargoed galleons en route to Europe. It's a fine spot for snorkeling because there are few visitors to disturb the fish.

❷ **Chankanaab Nature Park.** Chankanaab (the name means "small sea"), a 10-minute drive south of San Miguel, is a lovely saltwater lagoon that the government has made into a wildlife sanctuary, botanical garden, and archaeological park. The treasures from the Cozumel Archaeological Park—Toltec, Mexican, and Maya statues and stone carvings—have re-

Cozumel

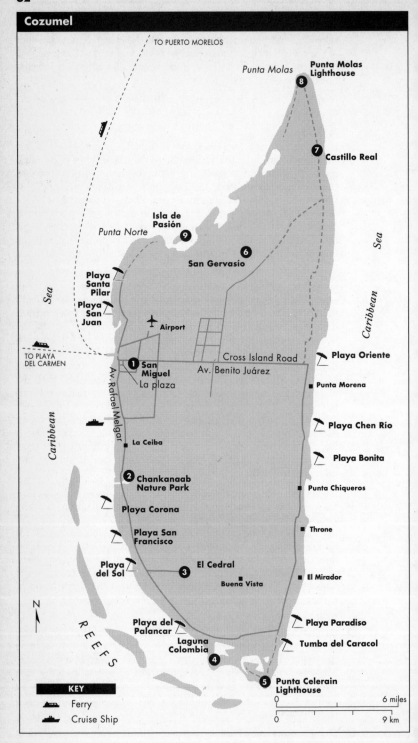

TO PUERTO MORELOS

Punta Molas

Punta Molas Lighthouse

8

7 **Castillo Real**

Sea

Punta Norte

Isla de Pasión

9

6

San Gervasio

Playa Santa Pilar

Playa San Juan

Sea

✈ **Airport**

Caribbean

TO PLAYA DEL CARMEN

1 **San Miguel**

La plaza

Cross Island Road

➤ **Playa Oriente**

Av. Benito Juárez

■ **Punta Morena**

Av. Rafael Melgar

■ **La Ceiba**

➤ **Playa Chen Río**

➤ **Playa Bonita**

2 **Chankanaab Nature Park**

■ **Punta Chiqueros**

➤ **Playa Corona**

➤ **Playa San Francisco**

■ **Throne**

Playa del Sol ➤

3 **El Cedral**

■ **Buena Vista**

■ **El Mirador**

Caribbean

N ➤

R E E F S

Playa del Palancar ➤

➤ **Playa Paradiso**

Laguna Colombia

➤ **Tumba del Caracol**

4

5 **Punta Celerain Lighthouse**

0 —————— 6 miles

0 —————— 9 km

KEY

⛴ Ferry

🚢 Cruise Ship

cently found a new home here. Underwater caves, offshore reefs, a protected bay, and a sunken ship attract droves of snorkelers and scuba divers. The botanical garden boasts about 350 varieties of plant life from more than 20 countries; scattered throughout are reproductions of Maya ruins and typical living quarters. (If mosquitoes are particularly attracted to you, consider buying insect repellent at one of the park's shops before you venture on the nature walk into the jungle.) Some 60-odd species of marine life, including fish, coral, turtles, and various crustaceans, reside in the lagoon; however, a major scientific study is currently under way, so swimming through the underwater tunnels from the lagoon to the bay or walking through the shallow lagoon is no longer permitted. Still, there's plenty to see in the bay, which hides crusty old cannons and anchors as well as statues of Jesus Christ and Chac Mool. Because the reef's ecological system is extremely fragile, it is forbidden to wear tanning lotion, feed the fish, or touch any of the underwater specimens. An interactive educational museum, four dive shops, two restaurants, two gift shops, a snack stand, and a dressing room with lockers and showers are on the premises. ⊠ *Carretera Sur, Km 9, no phone.* ☎ *$7.* ☉ *Daily 6–5:30.*

❸ El Cedral. Once the tiny village and ruins comprised the largest Maya site on Cozumel; this was the temple sighted by the original Spanish explorers in 1518, and the first Mass in Mexico was reportedly celebrated here. These days, there's little archaeological evidence of El Cedral's past glory. Much of the temple was torn down by the conquistadors; at the turn of this century the site was uninhabited, and the ruined temple was used as a jail. The U.S. Army Corps of Engineers destroyed most of the rest of the ruin during World War II to make way for the island's first airport, and now all that remains is a small structure capped by jungle growth; its Maya arch, best viewed from inside, is covered by faint traces of paint and stucco. Numerous small ruins are hidden in the heavy growth of the surrounding area, but you'll need a guide (there are usually one or two hanging around the main ruin) to find them. Every May a fair, with dancing, music, and a cattle show, is held here. After exploring the ruins, you can take a rest nearby in a small green-and-white cinder-block church, typical of rural Mexico. Inside, a number of crosses are shrouded in embroidered lace; during religious festivals, the simple room is adorned with folk art. ⊠ *Turn at Km 17.5 of main island road, then drive 3 km (2 mi) inland to site, no phone.*

❾ Isla de Pasión. Beyond Punta Norte, in the middle of Abrigo Bay, this tiny island is now part of a state reserve. Fishing is permitted and the beaches are secluded, but there are no facilities on the island, and since so few people go, there are no scheduled tours. You'll have to bargain with a local boat owner for transportation if you want to visit.

❹ Laguna Colombia. A prime site for jungle aficionados, this lagoon lies at the island's southern tip and is most commonly reached by boat, although there is a trail. Fish migrate here to lay their eggs, and barracuda, baby fish, and birds show up in great numbers in season. Popular diving and snorkeling spots can be found offshore in the reefs of Tunich, Colombia, and Maracaibo.

❺ Punta Celerain Lighthouse. Located on the southernmost tip of the island, the lighthouse is surrounded by sand dunes at the narrowest point of land. It affords a misty, mesmerizing view of pounding waves, swamps, and scraggly jungle. Alligators were once hunted nearby; nowadays you may spot a soldier or two from the adjacent army post catching an iguana. The point comes to life at midday when the lighthouse keeper serves fried fish and beer, and locals and tourists gather to chat; Sundays are particularly popular. The lighthouse is at the end of a 4-km-long (2½-mi-long) dirt road—a four-wheel-drive vehicle is strongly recommended if you plan to visit.

❽ Punta Molas Lighthouse. If you are going to attempt to reach the northernmost tip of the island, be sure you have plenty of time and a reliable four-wheel-drive vehicle: The pothole-ridden road is the preferred sunbathing spot of boa constrictors, crocodiles, and other jungle denizens. The lighthouse is an excellent spot for sunbathing, birding, and camping. Although this entire area is accessible only by four-wheel-drive vehicles or by boat, the jagged shoreline and the open sea offer magnificent views, making it well worth the trip.

❻ San Gervasio. These ruins of the largest existing Maya and Toltec site on Cozumel are worth visiting. San Gervasio was once the island's capital and probably its ceremonial center, dedicated to the fertility goddess Ixchel. The classical- and postclassical-style site was continuously occupied from AD 300 to AD 1500. Typical architectural features from the era include limestone plazas and masonry superstructures atop stepped platforms, as well as stelae, bas-reliefs, and frescoes. What remains today are several small mounds scattered around a plaza and several broken columns and lintels that were once part of the main building or observatory. Each of the ruins is clearly identified and explained on three-language plaques (Maya, Spanish, and English) and placed in context with individual maps. There are a snack bar and some gift shops at the entrance. To get here, take the cross-island road (Av. Juárez) to the San Gervasio access road; follow this road north for 7 km (4 mi). ✉ *Access to road $1, to ruins $3.50.* ☉ *Daily 8–5.*

❶ San Miguel. Cozumel's only town retains the laid-back tenor of a Mexican village, although its streets are dotted with an interesting variety of shops and restaurants. Avenida Rafael Melgar, San Miguel's waterfront boulevard, has a wide cement walkway, called the malecón. The malecón separates Avenida Rafael Melgar from the town's narrow sandy beach. As in most Mexican towns, the main square, here called the **Plaza del Sol**, is where townspeople and visitors hang out, particularly on Sunday nights when mariachi bands join the nightly assortment of food and souvenir vendors.

♻ Museo de la Isla de Cozumel is housed on two floors of what was once the island's first luxury hotel. Four permanent exhibit halls of dioramas, sculptures, and charts, explain the island's history and ecosystem. Well laid-out and labeled displays cover pre-Hispanic, colonial, and modern times and detail the local geology, flora, and fauna. A charming reproduction of a Maya house is a highlight. The museum also presents temporary exhibits, guided tours, and workshops. ✉ *Av. Rafael Melgar between Calles 4 and 6 Norte,* ☎ *987/21475.* ✉ *$3.* ☉ *Daily 10–6.*

| NEED A BREAK? | On the terrace off the second floor of the Cozumel museum, the **Restaurante del Museo** (☎ 987/20838) offers breakfast, drinks, or a full meal of fajitas or grilled red snapper, all enhanced by a great waterfront view. |

BEACHES

Cozumel's beaches vary from long, treeless, sandy stretches to isolated coves and rocky shores. Virtually all development remains on the leeward (western) side, where the coast is relatively sheltered by the proximity of the mainland 19 km (12 mi) to the west. Reaching beaches on the windward (eastern) side is more difficult and requires transportation, but you'll be rewarded if you are looking for solitude.

Leeward Beaches

The best sand beaches lie along the southern half of Cozumel's leeward side, some 5 km (3 mi) long.

Just south of Chankanaab Nature Park (☞ *above*), **Playa Corona,** which shares access to the Yucab reef, offers the same brilliant marine life as the park. Snorkeling equipment is available for rent, and the restaurant here serves conch and shrimp ceviche, fajitas, and more. The crowds that visit Chankanaab haven't yet discovered this tranquil neighbor.

South of Playa Corona lies **Playa San Francisco,** an inviting 5-km (3-mi) stretch of sandy beach that's considered one of the longest and finest on Cozumel. Comprising the beaches known as Playa Maya and Santa Rosa, San Francisco gets especially crowded during high season, on weekends (with cruise-ship passengers), and on Sunday (when locals come to eat fresh fish and hear live music). Environmental concerns have halted plans to build five new luxury hotels here. In the meantime, however, the beach has everything beach-goers need (though costs run higher here than on other, less frequented beaches): two outdoor restaurants, a bar, dressing rooms, gift shops, volleyball nets, beach chairs, and a variety of water sports equipment for rent. Divers also use this beach as their jumping-off point for dives to the San Francisco reef and the Santa Rosa wall. An abundance of turtle grass in the water makes swimming less popular.

Just south of San Francisco, **Playa del Sol** has complete facilities, including a restaurant-bar, shops, and snorkeling and Jet Ski equipment; you can also rent horses and trot down the beach. One drawback, however, is Playa del Sol's popularity with cruise-ship passengers.

The beach at **Palancar,** with a gently sloping shore enlivened by palm trees, is far more deserted than San Francisco to the north. Offshore lies the famous Palancar Reef (☞ Outdoor Activities and Sports, *below*), which is practically Cozumel's raison d'être. There is a water sports center and a bar-café on the beach here.

Among Cozumel's most lovely and marvelously secluded beaches are those beaches around **Punta Celerain,** near the lighthouse at the island's southern point.

Santa Pilar and **San Juan** beaches, which run along the northern hotel strip, sell soft drinks and rent water-sports equipment. Playa San Juan culminates in Punta Norte.

Windward Beaches

The east coast of Cozumel presents a splendid succession of mostly deserted rocky coves and narrow, powdery beaches—sadly garbage-strewn in spots—posed dramatically against astoundingly turquoise water. Swimming can be treacherous here if you go too far out or if a southwestern wind is blowing, but there is nothing to prevent solitary sunbathing on any of the several beaches.

The southernmost of the windward beaches, which lies near the small Maya ruin known as Tumba del Caracol, **Playa Paradiso** hosts the **Paradise Café,** a good place for a snack, some cold beer, and reggae tunes.

To the north of Playa Paradiso, **Punta Chiqueros** is a moon-shape cove sheltered from the sea by an offshore reef. Part of a longer stretch of beach that most locals call Playa Bonita—it's also known as Playa San Martin or Tortuga Desnuda (Naked Turtle)—it boasts fine sand, clear water, and moderate waves. You can swim and camp here, watch the sun set and the moon rise, and dine at the **Playa Bonita** restaurant-bar, which has fine fresh fish.

A little less than 5 km (3 mi) north of Punta Chiqueros is **Playa Chen Río,** another good spot for camping or exploring, where the waters are clear and the surf is not too strong.

Nearly 1 km (½ mi) north of Chen Río along the main road is **Punta Morena,** where waves crash on the rocky beach and, on June nights when the moon is full, turtles come to lay their eggs. If you're on the beach then, you may be stopped by soldiers who are stationed here to control poaching. This is also the site of the eastern coast's only hotel, also called Punta Morena, which has a small restaurant and bar.

The cross-island road meets the east coast at the **Mezcalito Café** on **Playa Oriente,** a typical windward side beach with pounding surf. The café is a pleasant place for light meals and drinks. If you want to continue farther north, make sure you have a sturdy vehicle; this is where the paved road ends.

There is a string of nameless beaches on the dirt road leading to **Punta Molas** (☞ Punta Molas Lighthouse *in* Exploring Cozumel, *above*), at the island's northern tip. The point itself is a lovely, unspoiled spot for sunbathing and nature viewing, reachable only by boat or four-wheel-drive vehicle.

DINING

Dining options on Cozumel reflect the nature of the place as a whole, with some harmless pretension at times but mainly the insouciant, natural style of the tropical island. More than 80 restaurants in the downtown area alone offer a broad choice, from air-conditioned fast-food outlets—Dairy Queen, Domino's, KFC, Pizza Hut, and Subway—and Americanized places serving Continental fare and seafood in semiformal "nautical" settings to simple outdoor eateries that specialize in fish. For the most part, the more established restaurants accept credit cards, while the café-type places accept only cash. Resort hotels offering buffet breakfasts and dinners are good values for bottomless appetites.

Reservations and What to Wear

Casual dress and no reservations are the rule in most $$ and $ Cozumel restaurants. In $$$ restaurants you would not be out of place if you dressed up, and reservations are advised.

CATEGORY	COST*
$$$	$25–$35
$$	$15–25
$	under $15

per person, excluding drinks and service

$$$ ✕ **Arrecife.** A well-trained staff and impeccably prepared seafood and
★   Mediterranean fare put this hotel restaurant in a class by itself. Tall windows and excellent views of the sea complement the stylish decor—potted palms, white wicker furniture, pink walls—while musicians, who play regularly, further enhance the romantic mood. You might find Arrecife's doors unlocked on the weekends if the hotel is hopping during low season, but the restaurant is officially open from November through Labor Day weekend. ✉ *Presidente Inter-Continental Cozumel hotel,* ☎ *987/20322. AE, DC, MC, V. Closed Sept. and Oct.*

$$$ ✕ **La Cabaña del Pescador.** To get to this rustic palapa-covered hut, you've got to cross a gangplank, but it's worth it if you're looking for well-prepared fresh lobster. The crustaceans are sold by weight, and

Dining
Arrecife, **8**
La Cabaña del
Pescador, **2**

Lodging
Casa del Mar, **6**
Crown Princess Sol
Caribe Cozumel, **7**
Diamond Hotel &
Resort, **10**
Fiesta Americana
Cozumel Reef, **9**
Fiesta Inn, **5**
Galápago Inn, **4**
Meliá Mayan
Peradisus, **1**
Plaza Las Glorias, **3**
Presidente
Inter-Continental
Cozumel, **8**

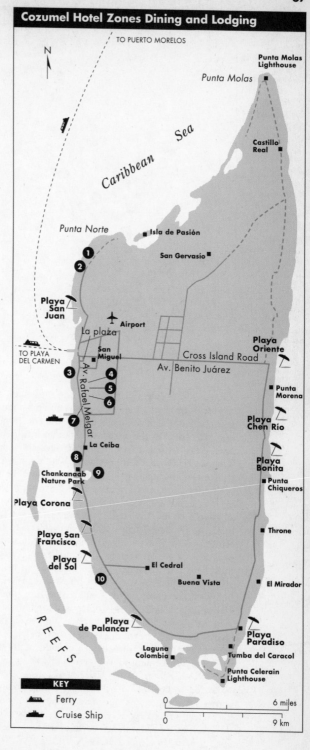

Cozumel Hotel Zones Dining and Lodging

Dining
Café Caribe, **23**
Carlos 'n' Charlie's, **3**
Diamond Café, **12**
El Capi Navegante, **21**
El Foco, **17**
El Moro, **7**
La Choza, **18**
Las Palmeras, **8**
Morgan's, **6**
Pancho's Backyard, **2**
Pepe's Grill, **13**
Pizza Rolandi, **1**
Plaza Leza, **9**
Prima Pasta & Prima Deli, **15**
Santiago's Grill, **19**
Sports Page, **4**
Tony Rome's, **20**

Lodging
Bahía, **16**
Bazar Colonial, **11**
Bed & Breakfast Caribo, **24**
Mary Carmen, **10**
Mesón San Miguel, **5**
Suites Elizabeth, **14**
Villas Las Anclas, **22**

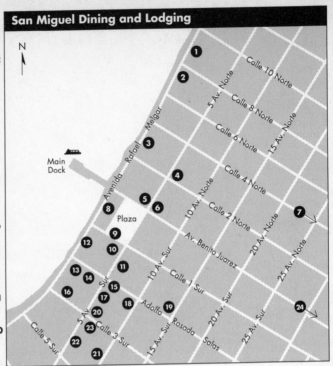

San Miguel Dining and Lodging

the rest—including a delicious eggnog-type drink served at the end of the meal—is on the house. Seashells and nets hang from the walls of this small, dimly lit room; geese stroll outside, hoping to be fed by diners seated next to the windows. Another local seafood favorite, king crab, is the feature at La Cabaña's sister establishment, **El Guacamayo King Crab House**, right next door. With the less-expensive king crab the focus of the menu, El Guacamayo falls into the $$ category. ⊠ *Carretera San Juan, Km 4, across from Playa Azul Hotel north of town, no phone. No credit cards. No lunch.*

$$$ ✕ **Pepe's Grill.** This large, bustling restaurant follows the nautical mode, from the model ships and ship wheels to the wind vanes covering the walls. Tall windows provide exceptional views of the malecón. You can choose between the quiet setting upstairs and the livelier atmosphere in the dining room downstairs. This restaurant caters to the cruise-ship clientele, so most North Americans will feel right at home, but with the comforts of home come long lines and high prices. Caribbean seafood dishes—lobster, shrimp flambée, shellfish grill, and king crab—are featured as specials, but the steaks—particularly the chateaubriand in béarnaise sauce, from the state of Chihuahua—are superb. The grouper fish is fresh and good, as are the Caesar salad and the salad bar. Live music is played daily. ⊠ *Av. Rafael Melgar Sur at Calle Rosada Salas,* ☎ *987/20213. AE, MC, V. No lunch.*

$$ ✕ **Carlos 'n' Charlie's.** Rock 'n' roll, a Ping-Pong table, and drinking contests are the status quo here. American-style ribs, chicken, and beef selections taste good, but the drinks are better. You can recognize this place by the red wall just north of the ferry pier. ⊠ *Av. Rafael Melgar 11, between Calles 2 and 4 Norte,* ☎ *987/20191. AE, MC, V.*

$$ ✕ **El Capi Navegante.** Locals say you'll find the best seafood in town here: The captain's motto is "The fish we serve today slept in the sea last night." Specialties like whole red snapper and stuffed squid are skill-

fully prepared and sometimes flambéed at your table. Highly recommended dishes include conch ceviche and deep-fried whole snapper. Nautical blue-and-white decor, accented by the life preservers on the walls, adds personality to this place. ⊠ *Av. 10a Sur 312, at Calle 3,* ☎ *987/21730. MC, V.*

$$ ✕ **La Choza.** Home-cooked Mexican food—primarily from the capi-
★ tal and among the best in town—is the order of the day at this family-run establishment. A complimentary bowl of guacamole and chips are brought out with the menu. Start off your meal with soup (onion and mushroom are the best) and fresh tortillas. Dona Elisa Espinosa's specialties include chicken mole, red snapper in sweet mustard sauce, and grilled lobster. To finish, you might try frozen avocado pie—cool, dense, and refreshing. The informal palapa-covered patio is furnished with simple wood tables and chairs, oilcloth table coverings, and hand-painted pottery dishes. ⊠ *Calle Rosada Salas 198, at Av. 10a Sur,* ☎ *987/20958. AE, MC, V.*

$$ ✕ **Las Palmeras.** The redbrick patios with the requisite potted palms and ceiling fans set the mood at this unpretentious waterfront restaurant, where breakfast is a bargain. For lunch and dinner expect seafood specialties and some Mexican dishes. The restaurant also sells margaritas and piña coladas to go. ⊠ *Av. Rafael Melgar, across from pier,* ☎ *987/20532. AE, MC, V.*

$$ ✕ **Morgan's.** No longer the big night out it used to be, this restaurant has managed to maintain impeccable service, a quiet atmosphere with candlelight, and an international cuisine. Located in the former customs house and done up in honor of its namesake—the seafaring pirate Henry Morgan, who once plied these waters—the restaurant is decorated with ship paneling, portholes, and compasses. The menu offers such appetizers as avocado cocktail and ham with melon, in addition to a selection of steak and fish entrées. ⊠ *Av. Benito Juárez and Calle 5a, north side of plaza,* ☎ *987/20584. AE, MC, V.*

$$ ✕ **Pancho's Backyard.** A jungle of greenery, trickling fountains, ceil-
★ ing fans, and leather chairs set the tone at this inviting restaurant, located on the cool patio of Los Cincos Soles shopping center. The menu highlights local standards such as black bean soup, *camarones al carbon* (grilled prawns), and fajitas. Round out your meal with coconut ice cream in Kahlua. ⊠ *Av. Rafael Melgar Norte 27, at Calle 8 Norte,* ☎ *987/22141. AE, MC, V. Closed Sun. No lunch Sat.*

$$ ✕ **Santiago's Grill.** Beautiful American cuts of meat, including T-bones and sirloins, as well as beef brochettes and fresh shrimp, draw long lines nightly. Because this small outdoor restaurant, with only 10 tables, is included on a list given to cruise-ship passengers, it is particularly popular with these tourists. ⊠ *Calle Rosada Salas 299, at Av. 15a Sur,* ☎ *987/22137. MC, V. No lunch.*

$$ ✕ **Tony Rome's.** Finger-licking, Texas-style barbecued ribs and Las
★ Vegas–style crooning (courtesy of owner Tony Rome) are the drawing cards of this open-air eatery wrapped around a palapa-covered dance floor. In addition to the ribs and the live entertainment, you'll find chicken, lobster, Kansas City steaks, and great happy hour specials. ⊠ *Av. 5 Sur 21, between Av. Rosado Salas and Calle 3 Sur,* ☎ *987/20131. MC, V.*

$ ✕ **Café Caribe.** Coffee junkies and folks with a serious sweet tooth flock to the little L-shaped Café Caribe for the mouth-watering selection of coffees (Cuban, Irish, espresso, cappuccino), along with Belgian waffles, yogurt, ice cream, and freshly baked cakes, pies, and muffins. Cheerfully decorated with colorful art posters, this little café is open only in the morning and evening. It is the perfect spot for both breakfast and after-dinner coffee and dessert. ⊠ *10 Av. Sur 215,* ☎ *987/23621. No credit cards. Closed Sun. No lunch.*

$ ✕ **Diamond Café.** A discreet signboard at the pink terra-cotta store-
★ front of the elegant Diamond Creations jewelry shop advertises this
airy retreat, located in the back of the store. There's a separate entrance as well on Avenida Rafael Melgar. Artfully decorated like a typical Mexican patio, with a central fountain, hanging plants, and
terraced seating at wrought-iron tables, the café specializes in home-
baked pastries to accompany the espresso and cappuccino brewed on
the premises. The café is open all day, serving breakfast, lunch, and
light snacks until 10 PM. ⊠ *Av. Rafael Melgar 131,* ☎ *987/23869.*
No credit cards. Closed Sun.

$ ✕ **El Foco.** A *taquería* (taco stand) serving soft tacos stuffed with pork,
chorizo (spicy Mexican sausage), and cheese, this eatery also does ribs
and steak. Graffitied walls and plain wood tables make it a casual, fun
spot to grab a bite and a *cerveza* (beer). ⊠ *Av. 5 Sur 13-B, between
Calle Rosado Salas and Calle 3, no phone. No credit cards.*

$ ✕ **El Moro.** This family-run restaurant on the eastern edge of town spe-
cializes in low-priced local cuisine—seafood, chicken, and meat. Inside, the decor follows the regional theme, beginning with Yucatecan
baskets hanging on the walls. Divers flock to this place, so you know
portions are hearty and the food is delicious. Take a taxi; El Moro is
too far to walk to, and difficult to find. ⊠ *Calle 75 Norte between
Calles 2 and 4,* ☎ *987/23029. MC, V. Closed Thurs.*

$ ✕ **Pizza Rolandi.** This trendy chain restaurant is a good choice for ca-
sual Italian fare. Top sellers from the signboard menus carried by the
wait staff include lasagna, Four Seasons pizza (with ham, zucchini, mushrooms, and black olives), and pitchers of homemade sangria. Tables
in the dining room on the main waterfront drive tend to be noisy; select one beneath the trees on the stucco-walled patio out back. ⊠ *Av.
Rafael Melgar 23,* ☎ *987/20946. AE. No lunch Sun.*

$ ✕ **Plaza Leza.** If you're craving the low-key, unpretentious atmosphere
of a Mexican sidewalk café, stop here, where you can dawdle for
hours over a cup of coffee or a beer. Choose a table on the plaza, or
for more privacy, go indoors to the somewhat secluded, cozy inner patio.
Plaza Leza serves everything from *poc chuc* (pork chops grilled Yucatán
style), enchiladas, and lime soup to chicken sandwiches and coconut
ice cream. ⊠ *South side of main plaza,* ☎ *987/21041. AE, MC, V.*

$ ✕ **Prima Pasta & Prima Deli.** Since Texan Albert Silmai opened this
Northern Italian diner just off the plaza in 1992, he's attracted a
strong following of patrons who come for hearty, inexpensive pizzas,
calzone, sandwiches, and pastas. To this winning formula the chef has
added whole king crab and catch-of-the-day seafood dishes. The breezy
dining area on the second floor terrace above the kitchen smells heav-
enly and has a charming Mediterranean mural painted on two walls.
Business has been so good that Silmai branched out in 1994, opening
Prima Deli, a tiny sandwich shop, just a few doors down (at Calle Rosado
Salas 113). ⊠ *Calle Rosado Salas 109,* ☎ *987/24242. AE, MC, V.*

$ ✕ **Sports Page Video Bar and Restaurant.** Signed team T-shirts and pen-
nants line the walls and ceilings of this popular restaurant and water-
ing hole. The main attraction is the sports coverage—large TVs
simultaneously broadcast at least four athletic events—but the food's
good, too. Cheeseburgers are juicy and served with generous portions
of crispy fries. Mexican specialties as well as seafood and steak dinners are offered. The place is open from 9 AM for breakfast, so you can
have your eggs with ESPN. ⊠ *Av. 5a Norte and Calle 2 Norte,* ☎
987/21199. MC, V.

LODGING

Cozumel's hotels are located in three main areas, all on the island's western, or leeward, side: in town, and north and south of town. Because of the proximity of the reefs, divers and snorkelers tend to congregate at the southern properties. Sailors and anglers, on the other hand, prefer the hotels to the north, where the beaches are better. Most budget hotels are in town.

Cozumel offers about 3,200 hotel rooms in more than 60 properties. Before booking you should call around, because you will find many bargains in the form of air, hotel, and dive packages, especially off-season; some packages combine Cozumel and Cancún stays, with free airfare between the two. Christmas reservations must be made at least three months ahead of time. The majority of the resort hotels (north and south of town) are affiliated with international chains and offer all the usual amenities; they also generally rent water-sports equipment and can arrange excursions. All hotels have air-conditioning unless otherwise noted. The more costly properties generally offer no-smoking rooms and on-site travel agencies and transportation rentals, and include in-room hair dryers, safes, minibars, satellite TV, and telephones as part of their amenities. All hotels share the 77600 postal code.

The **Cozumel Island Hotel Association** (✉ Box 228, Cozumel, QR 77600, or 15a Calle 2 Norte, ☎ 987/23132, FAX 987/22809), with 15 member properties, functions unofficially as the island's tourist information bureau.

CATEGORY	COST*
$$$$	over $160
$$$	$90–$160
$$	$40–$90
$	under $40

All prices are for a standard double room, excluding service charges and the 12% tax.

$$$$ ⛨ **Diamond Hotel & Resort.** Completed in early 1993, this large, all-inclusive resort is the southernmost of the island's properties. The hotel is far from town and there is no shuttle service, but lots of water-based activities—the Diamond's beach is close to Palancar and other reefs—as well as nightly entertainment keep guests occupied on the premises. Accommodations, set in bi-level palapa-roof units spread across the grounds, are furnished in light wood and tropical pastels. Standard rooms are not very large (those on the second floor feel larger because of the high palapa ceiling), but duplex suites easily accommodate three or four people. Pack your bug spray to keep the nightly mosquitos from nearby swamps at bay. The buffet meals are fairly institutional, but two à la carte restaurants offer decent Italian and Mexican fare. ✉ *San Francisco Palancar, Km 16.5,* ☎ *987/23554 or 800/858–2258,* FAX *987/24508. 300 rooms. 2 restaurants, 3 bars, 2 pools, 4 tennis courts, aerobics, basketball, shuffleboard, volleyball, snorkeling, bicycles, motorbikes, shops, children's programs, car rentals. AE, MC, V.*

$$$$ ⛨ **Meliá Mayan Peradisus.** Lush tropical foliage and spectacular sunsets over the beach combine with modern architecture and amenities to make this property north of town a memorable place to stay. Large windows in the light, cheerful lobby look out onto a pool and swim-up palapa snack bar. Standard rooms, some with small patios opening out onto the lawn, are attractively decorated with colorful tropical print bedspreads and light-wood furniture; superior rooms are larger and have balconies overlooking the water. This resort turned all-inclusive in late 1994, bringing on an international staff of entertainers and ac-

tivity coordinators to keep guests happily busy. A disco, a kids program and playground, horseback trails, a health club with steam room and fitness equipment, and an array of nonmotorized water-sports equipment were added during the expansion. ⊠ *Box 9, Carretera a Sta. Pilar 6,* ☎ *987/20411 or 800/336–3542,* FAX *987/21599. 200 rooms. 3 restaurants, 5 bars, 2 pools, hot tub, miniature golf, 2 tennis courts, horseback riding, dive shop, bicycles, shops. AE, DC, MC, V.*

$$$$ 🏨 **Plaza Las Glorias.** A Mediterranean atmosphere prevails inside and out: This large, salmon-colored building has Mexican tiles, marble floors, and wrought-iron details in its public areas. The modern all-suites property, within walking distance of town, has private terraces and ocean views from each of its light, spacious units. You can enjoy live music in the lobby bar several nights a week. One caveat: There is a strong time-share contingent here, and hotel guests are often pestered to sit through the sales pitch. ⊠ *Av. Rafael Melgar, Km 1.5,* ☎ *987/22000 or 800/342–AMIGO,* FAX *987/21937. 170 suites. 2 restaurants, 2 bars, pool, dive shop, shops. AE, MC, V.*

$$$$ 🏨 **Presidente Inter-Continental Cozumel.** This hotel exudes luxury,
★   from the courteous, prompt, and efficient service to the tastefully decorated interior. The Presidente is famed not only for possessing one of the best restaurants on the island, **Arrecife** (☞ *Dining, above*), but also for its respectable and professional water-sports center. Located on its own broad, white beach south of the town of San Miguel, the property ranks among the best on the island for snorkeling; barracuda, angelfish, octopus, and more are visible in the waters a few feet off the beach. All rooms are done in bright, contemporary colors with white cedar furnishings; deluxe rooms, with their own private terraces fronting the beach or gardens, are huge. Complimentary coffee is delivered to your room at the time of your wake-up call. In high season, there are weekly theme parties. ⊠ *Carretera a Chankanaab, Km 6.5,* ☎ *987/20322 or 800/327–0200,* FAX *987/21360. 253 rooms. 2 restaurants, 3 bars, coffee shop, pool, hot tub, 2 tennis courts, dive shop, motorbikes, children's program, shops, car rental. AE, DC, MC, V.*

$$$ 🏨 **Crown Princess Sol Caribe Cozumel.** Just across the street from its own small beach (accessible by underground footpath), the hotel, the largest in Cozumel, consists of a 10-story main building with a dramatically designed, wood-beamed, palapa-roofed lobby and an adjoining tower. Rooms in the tower, all with balconies and considered deluxe, are slightly more expensive, but those in the main building—reached by a glass-encased elevator—are the same size (sans balcony) and furnished in a lighter, more cheerful fashion. Nicely landscaped grounds and a large pool with a swim-up bar are among the hotel's pluses. ⊠ *Box 259, Playa Paraíso, Km 3.5,* ☎ *987/20700,* FAX *987/21301. 321 rooms. 3 restaurants, 3 bars, pool, beauty salon, 3 tennis courts, dive shop, dock, motorbikes, shops, travel services, car rental. AE, MC, V.*

$$$ 🏨 **Fiesta Americana Cozumel Reef.** Opened in the summer of 1991 on the less-developed southern end of the island, this property is ideally situated for snorkeling and scuba diving. The hotel's beach, although fairly narrow for sunbathing, offers easy access to spectacular underwater scenery. The hotel building itself is across the road from the beach and the restaurant that overlooks the water; guests either have to cross the road at street level (traffic is usually sparse) or use the walkway over the road to reach them. The high-ceilinged lobby, with its polished marble floors, hosts a glitzy silver shop with some unusual pieces. Standard rooms are large, with sea-green headboards and well-made light-wood furnishings; all have balconies looking out on the ocean. A semicircular cluster of villas with 56 rooms facing the hotel's main entrance was opened in 1996. Reasonable prices and a good location have made the Fiesta Americana one of the most popular hotels on the island. ⊠ *Carretera a Chankanaab,*

Km 7.5, ☎ 987/22622 or 800/343–7821, ℻ 987/22666. 228 rooms. 3 restaurants, 3 bars, 2 pools, 2 tennis courts, dive shop, motorbikes, car rentals, travel services. AE, MC, V.

$$$ ⊞ **Fiesta Inn.** This 3-story Spanish-roofed structure, south of town and across the street from the beach, has all the trademarks of the Fiesta brand name: a comfortable lobby with a fountain and garden, brightly decorated modern rooms with Moorish archways, a large pool, and an international dining facility. Fully carpeted rooms are painted light blue, with cream-color wicker furniture and private balconies; many have safes. Request a room on the 3rd floor (the rate is the same) for an ocean view. The sing-along **Laser-Karaoke Bar** draws exhibitionists from all over town. ✉ *Carretera a Chankanaab, Km 1.7, ☎ 987/22900 or 800/343–7821, ℻ 987/80100. 180 rooms. Restaurant, 2 bars, pool, hot tub, tennis court, dive shop, bicycles, motorbikes. AE, MC, V.*

$$$ ⊞ **Galápago Inn.** This pretty white stucco hotel just south of town primarily accommodates divers; the simply furnished, brightly tiled rooms are not sold by the night but exclusively as part of dive packages—booked through the 800 number or your travel agent—that take full advantage of the hotel's expert diving staff and advanced certification diving school. The central garden, with tiled benches and a small fountain, contributes to the inn's Mediterranean feel. The staff here are cheerful and accommodating. ✉ *Carretera a Chankanaab, Km 1.5, ☎ 987/20663 or 800/847–5708. 58 rooms. 2 restaurants, bar, pool. MC, V.*

$$ ⊞ **Bahía.** The lobby here is small but the hallways are pleasant enough, with white walls and red tile floors. The large accommodations, decorated with the standard stucco, wood, and tile, come with sofa beds and kitchenettes. Ask for a room with a sea view; the balconies overlook the malecón and go for the same price as those facing town. Two penthouse suites are available. ✉ *Av. Rafael Melgar and Calle 3 Sur, ☎ 987/20209, ℻ 987/21387. 27 rooms. Restaurant, bar, kitchenettes. AE, MC, V.*

$$ ⊞ **Casa del Mar.** Located south of town near several boutiques, sports
★ shops, and restaurants, this 3-story hotel is frequented by divers. An unpretentious but tasteful lobby, which has natural wood banisters and overlooks a small garden, exemplifies the overall simplicity of the place. Cheerful rooms feature yellow-tiled headboards, nightstands, and sinks; Mexican artwork; and small balconies with views of the pool just outside or the sea across the road. The bi-level cabañas, which sleep three or four, are a very good buy at $115. ✉ *Box 129, Carretera a Chankanaab, Km 4, ☎ 987/21944 or 800/877–4383, ℻ 987/21855. 98 rooms, 8 cabañas. 2 restaurants, 2 bars, pool, hot tub, dive shop, travel services, car rental. AE, MC, V.*

$$ ⊞ **Villas Las Anclas.** Conveniently located parallel to the malecón, these
★ villas are actually furnished apartments for rent by the day, week, or month. The duplexes include a downstairs sitting room, dining area, and kitchenette, which is fully stocked with dishes, refrigerator, and hot plate; a spiral staircase leads up to a small bedroom with a large desk (but no phone or TV) and inset shelves over the double bed. Rooms are extremely attractive, with tastefully bright patterns set off against white walls; they all overlook a quiet courtyard garden. This property is owned and operated by brother and sister Claus and Eva Reinking, who also roast the best coffee on the island. Each apartment is stocked with fresh coffee and a coffeemaker. If you run out, you can buy fresh-ground at the front desk. ✉ *Box 25, Av. 5a Sur 325, between Calles 3 and 5 Sur, ☎ 987/21403, ℻ 987/21955. 7 units. Kitchenettes. No credit cards.*

$ ⊞ **Bazar Colonial.** This attractive, modern 3-story hotel, located over a small cluster of shops, has pretty red tile floors and bougainvillea, which add splashes of color. Natural wood furniture, TVs (a recent addition), kitchenettes, bookshelves, sofa beds, and an elevator make up for the lack of other amenities, such as a restaurant and a pool. ⊠ *Av. 5a Sur 9, near Calle 3 Sur,* ☎ *987/20506,* 🖷 *987/20542 or 987/20211. 28 rooms. Kitchenettes, shops. AE, MC, V.*

$ 🖸 **Bed & Breakfast Caribo.** Operated in the friendly and comfortable tradition of B&B inns, this recent (1994) Cozumel arrival was formerly a doctor's residence. It was totally renovated and restored by a family from Michigan, and the nine air-conditioned rooms are spacious and well furnished, featuring white wicker, blue floral upholstered chairs, and matching serape bedspreads. All rooms have private baths. There's cable TV for guests in the first floor sitting room. A full (meatless) breakfast buffet, served in the glass-enclosed porch, is included in the price. Weekly and monthly rates are available. One caveat: Avenida Juárez is a main thoroughfare and traffic sounds are audible in the front bedrooms. ⊠ *Av. Juárez 799,* ☎ *987/23195 or 800/830–5558. 7 rooms, 2 apartments. MC, V.*

$ 🖸 **Mary Carmen.** Functional and clean, this hotel rents rooms on the ground floor with both air-conditioning and ceiling fans (but no phones or TVs); on the first floor, only air-conditioning is offered. Although the furniture and rugs are rather worn, the double bed and two chairs are adequate for the night. Drawbacks include an antiseptic smell throughout the place. ⊠ *Av. 5a Sur 4,* ☎ *987/20581. 27 rooms. MC, V.*

$ 🖸 **Mesón San Miguel.** Situated right on the square, this hotel sees a
★ lot of action because of the accessibility of its large public bar and outdoor café, which are often filled with locals. The architecturally eclectic San Miguel, with four stories and an elevator, has a burgundy-and-white–tiled lobby floor and a contemporary-style game room with a pool table. The remodeled rooms are clean and functional, with air-conditioning, satellite TV, phones, and balconies overlooking the plaza—amenities unusual in a budget hotel, making this a good bet for your money. Sip a drink in the evenings at **Video Bar Aladino,** the hotel's bar on the square. ⊠ *Av. Juárez 2 Bis,* ☎ *987/20323 or 987/20233,* 🖷 *987/21820. 60 rooms. Bar, café, pool, recreation room. AE, MC, V.*

$ 🖸 **Suites Elizabeth.** This basic hotel offers rooms with fans or with air-conditioning. The latter include large balconies with a view of the rooftops, and many rooms come with refrigerators and hot plates (but no phones or TVs). The vintage '70s furnishings, including light-orange chenille bedspreads, look dated but are still functional. ⊠ *Box 70, Calle Rosada Salas 44,* ☎ *987/20330. 19 rooms. No credit cards.*

NIGHTLIFE AND THE ARTS

The Arts

Although Cozumel doesn't have much in the way of highbrow performing arts per se, it does offer the visitor an opportunity to attend performances that reflect the island's heritage, including Fiesta Mexicana nights at the **Fiesta Americana Hotel** (☎ 987/22622). The shows, offered Thursday and Sunday from 6–9 PM during high season, feature folkloric dancers, mariachis, a cock fight, an open-bar buffet dinner, and tequila shots; the cost is about $70.

Movies
Cine Cozumel (⊠ Av. Rafael Melgar, between Calles 2 and 4 Norte, ☎ 987/20766) and **Cine Cecillo Borge** (⊠ Av. Benito Juárez, between Avs. 30 and 35, ☎ 987/20402) both show films in English (generally with subtitles) and Spanish nightly at 9.

Nightlife

Cozumel offers enough daytime activities to make you want to retire early, but the young set keeps the island hopping late into the night. There is plenty of nightlife, but a word to the wise: Avoid the temptation to buy or use drugs here. A foreigner involved with drugs will have a particularly difficult time with the Mexican authorities.

Bars

For a quiet drink and good people-watching, try **Video Bar Aladino** at the Mesón San Miguel, at the northern end of the plaza. Serious barhoppers like **Carlos 'n' Charlie's** (⊠ Av. Rafael Melgar 11, between Calles 2 and 4 Norte, ☎ 987/20191) for hang-off-the-rafters, raucous fun; don't come here if you're the retiring type. Folks are always spilling out over the outdoor patio (sometimes literally) at **Sharkey's** (⊠ Av. Rafael Melgar near Av. Benito Juárez, ☎ 987/21832), where a papier-mâché Marilyn Monroe in a *Some Like It Hot* pose surveys a rowdy crowd. The **Hard Rock Cafe** (⊠ Av. Rafael Melgar 2A, near Av. Benito Juárez, ☎ 987/25271) includes all the nostalgic music memorabilia that characterizes the international chain. You and your friends provide the entertainment at the sing-along **Laser-Karaoke Bar** (⊠ Fiesta Inn, ☎ 987/22811). The Terminator and Rambo have done it again with a new **Planet Hollywood** (⊠ Rafael Melgar 161, ☎ 987/25795). Jock types can play video games or check football scores at the **Sports Page Video Bar and Restaurant** (⊠ Corner 5 Av. Norte and Calle 2 Norte, ☎ 987/21199).

Discos

Scaramouche (⊠ Av. Rafael Melgar at Calle Rosada Salas, ☎ 987/20791) features a fantastic laser show and a large dance area. **Neptuno** (⊠ Av. Rafael Melgar at Calle 11 Sur, ☎ 987/21537), preferred by the teenage set and locals, can be loud and fun. However, both of these discos are often empty except on weekends.

Live Music

Sunday evenings bring locals to the **zócalo** (plaza) to hear mariachis and island musicians playing tropical tunes. The piano bar in **La Gaviota** (⊠ Crown Princess Sol Caribe Cozumel, ☎ 987/20700, ext. 251) is well attended, and trios and mariachis perform nightly in the lobby bar from 5 to 11 during high season. For romantic piano or guitar serenades, try the dining room of **Arrecife** (⊠ Presidente Inter-Continental Cozumel hotel, ☎ 987/20322; high season only). If Frank Sinatra–style entertainment turns you on, check out **Tony Rome's** (⊠ Av. 5 Sur 21, between Av. Rosado Salas and Calle 3 Sur, ☎ 987/20131), where the owner holds forth at the microphone. In addition to tasty lobster dishes, **Joe's Lobster House** (⊠ Av. 10 Sur 229, between Calle Rosada Salas and Calle 3 Sur, ☎ 987/23275) serves up lively reggae and salsa every night at 10:30; this is *the* hot spot for live entertainment.

OUTDOOR ACTIVITIES AND SPORTS

Most people come to Cozumel to take advantage of the island's water-related sports—scuba diving, snorkeling, and fishing are particularly big, but jet skiing, sailboarding, waterskiing, and sailing remain popular as well. You will find services and rentals throughout the island, especially through major hotels and water-sports centers such as **Del Mar Aquatics** (⊠ Carretera a Chankanaab, Km 4, ☎ 987/21665 or 800/877-4383, ℻ 987/21833) and **Aqua Safari** (⊠ Av. Rafael Melgar 429, between Calles 5 and 10 Sur, ☎ 987/20101).

Fishing

For the past 22 years, the annual **International Billfish Tournament,** held the last week in April or the first week in May, has drawn anglers from around the world to Cozumel; for more information, contact the International Billfish Tournament (⊠ Box 442, Cozumel 77600, ☎ 800/253–2701, ⅁AX 987/20999).

Please obey regulations forbidding commercial fishing, sportfishing, spear fishing, and the collection of any marine life between the shore and El Cantil Reef and between the cruise-ship dock and Punta Celerain. As part of a growing conservation movement, it's forbidden to kill certain species, including billfish, so be prepared to return prize catches to the sea. (Regular participants in the annual billfish tournament have seen some of the same fish—notched by successful anglers—caught over and over again.) U.S. Customs allows you to bring up to 30 pounds of fish back into the country.

Charters

High-speed fishing boats can be chartered for $300 for a half day or $350 for a full day, for a maximum of six people, from the **Club Naútico de Cozumel** (⊠ Puerto de Abrigo, Av. Rafael Melgar, Box 341, ☎ 987/20118 or 800/253–2701, ⅁AX 987/21135), the island's headquarters for game fishing. Full-day rates include the boat and crew, tackle and bait, and lunch with beer and soda (lunch isn't included on half days). You can also book three- and four-day trips from the United States at discounted rates. Daily charters are easily arranged from the dock or at your hotel, but you might also try **Aquarius Fishing and Tours** (⊠ Calle 3 Sur, ☎ 987/21092) or **Dive Cozumel** (⊠ Av. Rosado Salas 72, at Av. 5 Sur, ☎ 987/24110, ⅁AX 987/21842). The latter's general manager, Mariano Miguel Mendoza, is a font of knowledge about fishing and diving on the island. All rates vary with the season.

Scuba Diving

The diversity of options for divers in Cozumel includes deep dives, drift dives, shore dives, wall dives, and night dives, as well as theme dives focusing on ecology, archaeology, sunken ships, and photography. With all the shops to choose from, divers, especially those with less experience or who don't bring their own equipment, should look for high safety standards and documented credentials. Make sure your instructor has PADI certification (or FMAS, the Mexican equivalent) and is affiliated with the **SSS recompression chamber** (⊠ Calle 5 Sur 21B, between Av. Rafael Melgar and Av. 5a Sur, next to Discover Cozumel, ☎ 987/22387 or 987/21848) or the recompression chamber at the **Hospital Civil** (⊠ Av. 11 Sur, between Calles 10 and 15, ☎ 987/20140 or 987/20525). These chambers, which boast a 35-minute response time from reef to chamber, treat decompression sickness, commonly known as "the bends"; it occurs when divers surface too quickly and nitrogen is absorbed into the bloodstream. Other injuries treated here include nitrogen narcosis, collapsed lungs, and overexposure to the cold. Most of the dive shops in town offer complete dive accident coverage for just $1 per day.

Diving requires that you be reasonably fit. It should also go without saying that—particularly if you are new to diving—you should find a qualified instructor. Another caveat: Always stay at least 3 ft above the reef, not just because the coral can sting or cut you, but also because coral is easily damaged and grows very slowly: It has taken 2,000 years for it to reach its present size.

Dive Shops and Tour Operators

Most dive shops can provide you with all the incidentals you'll need, as well as with guides and transportation. You can choose from a variety of two-tank boat trips and specialty dives ranging from $45 to $60; two-hour resort courses cost about $50–$60, and 1½-hour night dives, $30–$35. Basic certification courses, such as PADI's Discover Scuba or Naui's introductory course, are available for about $350, while advanced certification courses cost as much as $700. Equipment rental is relatively inexpensive, ranging from $6 for tanks or a lamp to about $8–$10 for a regulator and B.C. vest; underwater camera rentals can cost as much as $35, video camera rentals run about $75, and professionally shot and edited videos of your own dive are priced at about $160.

Because dive shops tend to be competitive, it is well worth your while to shop around when choosing a dive operator. In addition to the dive shops in town, many hotels have their own operations and offer dive and hotel packages starting at about $350 for three nights, double occupancy, and two days of diving. You can also pick up a copy of the *Chart of the Reefs of Cozumel* in any dive shop. Before choosing a shop among the many choices, check credentials, look over the boats and equipment, and consult experienced divers who are familiar with the operators here. Here's a list to get you started on your search: **Aqua Safari** (⊠ Av. Rafael Melgar 429, between Calles 5 and 10 Sur, ☎ 987/20101); **Blue Angel** (⊠ Av. Rafael Melgar, next to Hotel Villablanca, ☎ 987/21631), for PADI certification; **Blue Bubble** (⊠ Av. 5a Sur at Calle 3 Sur, ☎ 987/21865), for PADI instruction; **Chino's Scuba** (⊠ Av. Adolfo Rosado Salas 16A, ☎ 987/24487); **Dive Cozumel** (⊠ Av. Rosado Salas 72, at Av. 5 Sur, ☎ 987/24110, ☎ FAX 987/21842); **Dive Paradise** (⊠ Av. Rafael Melgar 601, ☎ FAX 987/21007); **Michelle's Dive Shop** (⊠ Av. 5 Sur 201, at Calle Adolfo Rosado Salas, ☎ 987/20947); **Ramone Zapata Divers** (⊠ Chankanaab Nature Park, ☎ 987/20502); **Scuba Du** (⊠ Presidente Inter-Continental Cozumel hotel, ☎ 987/20322 or 987/21379, FAX 987/24130); **Studio Blue** (⊠ Calle Rosado Salas 121, between Calles 5 and 10, ☎ FAX 987/24330); **Tico's Dive Center** (⊠ Av. 5 Norte 121, between Calles 2 and 4, ☎ FAX 987/20276).

Reef Dives

The reefs stretch for 32 km (20 mi), beginning at the international pier and continuing on to Punta Celerain at the southernmost tip of the island. The following is a rundown of Cozumel's main dive destinations.

CHANKANAAB REEF

This inviting reef lies just south of Chankanaab Nature Park, about 350 yards offshore. Crabs, lobster, tang, and angels inhabit the coral formations at about 55 ft. Drift a bit farther south to see the **Balones de Chankanaab,** balloon-shaped coral heads at 70 ft.

COLOMBIA REEF

This reef, reaching 82–98 ft, is excellent for experienced divers who want to take some deep dives. Its underwater structures are as labyrinthine and varied as those of Palancar (☞ *below*); large groupers, jacks, eagle rays, and even an occasional sea turtle cluster at the mouths of caves and near the overhangs.

MARACAIBO REEF

Generally considered the most difficult of all the Cozumel reefs for divers, this one—located off the southern end of the island—lends itself to drift dives because of its length. You don't even see the ledge of the reef until you go 121 ft below the surface. Although there are shallow areas, only advanced divers who can cope with the current should attempt Maracaibo.

PALANCAR REEF

This reef system, situated nearly 2 km (1 mi) offshore, offers about 40 dive locations. Black and red coral and huge elephant-ear sponges and barrel sponges are among the attractions at the bottom. The reef, which begins at about 15 ft below the surface, is particularly suitable for drift dives. A favorite of divers is the section called **Horseshoe**, comprising several coral heads at the top of the drop-off. Towering coral columns and deep caves, tunnels, and canyons make for some of the most sensational dives in the Caribbean.

PARAÍSO REEF

Just north of the cruise-ship pier, about 328 ft offshore and up to 30 ft deep, Paraíso provides a practice spot for divers before they head to deeper drop-offs. Also a wonderful site for night diving, this reef is inhabited by star coral, brain coral, sea fans and other gorgonians, and sponges, as well as sea eels and yellow rays. From Paraíso you can swim out to the drop-offs called **La Ceiba** and **Villa Blanca.**

PASEO EL CEDRAL

Also known as Cedar Pass, this seldom-dived reef, just northeast of Palancar Reef, contains a spectacular series of small caverns full of fish. At depths ranging 35–55 ft, you're likely to see sea turtles, moray eels, eagle rays, and groupers among the larger specimens.

PLANE WRECK

During a 1977 Mexican motion picture production, this airplane was sunk about about 300 ft away from the La Ceiba pier. Because of its reassuring proximity to the shore and because the average depth of the water is only 9–30 ft, it has been a favorite training ground for neophyte divers ever since. Enormous coral structures and colorful sponges surround the reef, while an underwater trail guides divers by the marine life.

SAN FRANCISCO REEF

Considered Cozumel's shallowest wall dive, this ½-mi reef at the end of Old San Francisco Beach is teeming with marine life. It is best dived between 35 and 50 ft.

SANTA ROSA WALL

A renowned spot for deep dives and drift dives, this wall—just north of Palancar—drops off abruptly at 50 ft to enormous coral overhangs and caves below. Sponges are especially populous here, as are angelfish, groupers, and eagle rays—along with a shark or two.

TORMENTOS REEF

Sea fans and other gorgonians and sponges live on this variegated reef, where the maximum depth reaches about 70 ft. One of the best locations for underwater photography, Tormentos hosts sea cucumbers, arrow crabs, green eels, groupers, and other marine life, which provide a terrifically colorful backdrop.

YUCAB REEF

About 400 ft long and 55 ft deep, this reef is less than 1½ km (1 mi) from shore, near Chankanaab. Coral, sponge, sea whips, and angelfish swim in these waters, where the currents can reach 2 or 3 knots.

Snorkeling

Snorkeling equipment is available at the Presidente Inter-Continental, La Ceiba, Chankanaab Bay, Playa San Francisco, and Club Cozumel Caribe hotels, and directly off the beach near the Fiesta Americana Cozumel Reef and Playa Corona for less than $10 a day.

Tour Operators

Snorkeling tours run from $25 to $50, depending on the length, and take in the shallow reefs off Palancar, Colombia, and Yucab. Contact **Apple Vacations** (⊠ Av. 11 and Av. 30, ☎ 987/24311 or 987/20725) for snorkeling, sunset cruises, or tours around the island, or **Caribe Tours** (⊠ Av. Rafael Melgar at Calle 5 S., ☎ FAX 987/23100 or 987/23154) for information and reservations. **Fiesta Cozumel** (⊠ Calle 11 Sur 598, between Avs. 25 and 30, ☎ 987/20725, FAX 987/21389) runs snorkeling tours from the 45-ft catamaran *El Zorro*. Rates begin at about $50 per day and include equipment, a guide, soft drinks and beer, and a box lunch. The *Zorro* and the 60-ft catamaran *Fury* are also used for sunset cruises; the cost is under $35 for unlimited domestic drinks and live entertainment. You can book either of these sunset cruises through Caribe Tours.

SHOPPING

As in other Mexican resort destinations, Cozumel's shops accept dollars as readily as pesos, and many goods are priced in dollars. You'll get a better price everywhere on Cozumel if you pay with cash or traveler's checks, although credit cards—MasterCard and Visa more often than American Express, Diners Club, or Discover—are widely accepted. If you use plastic, however, you may be asked to pay a surcharge. Authorities and experienced travelers alike warn against buying from street vendors, because the quality of their merchandise leaves much to be desired, although this may not be apparent until it's too late.

Cruise ships traditionally dock at Cozumel on Monday, but there is traffic here almost every weekday, and the shops are the most crowded 10–11 and 1–2. Traditionally, stores are open 9–1 and 5–9, but a number of them, especially those nearest the pier, tend to disregard siesta hours and even open on weekends, particularly during high season. Don't pay much attention to written or verbal offers of "20% discounts, today only" or "only for cruise-ship passengers," because they're nothing but bait to get you inside. Similarly, many of the larger stores advertise "duty-free" wares, but these are of greater interest to Mexicans from the mainland than to North Americans since the prices tend to be higher than retail prices in the United States.

A last word of caution: Cruise-ship activities directors tend to push the black coral "factories." These should be avoided, not only because they are usually overpriced but also because coral is an endangered species.

Department Stores

Relatively small and more like U.S. variety stores than department stores, the following nevertheless carry a relatively wide array of goods, from the useful to the frivolous. **Chachy Plaza** (⊠ Av. Benito Juárez 5, near church at the back of plaza, ☎ 987/20130) sells everything from liquor and perfume to snorkeling gear and snack food. **Duty Free Mexico** (⊠ Av. Rafael Melgar at Calle 3 Sur, ☎ 987/20796) emphasizes top-line fragrances. **Pama** (⊠ Av. Rafael Melgar Sur 9, ☎ 987/20090), near the pier, carries imported food, luggage, snorkeling gear, jewelry, and crystal. **Prococo** (⊠ Av. Rafael Melgar Norte 99, ☎ 987/21875 or 987/21964) offers a good selection of liquor, jewelry, and gift items.

Shopping Districts, Streets, and Malls

Cozumel has three main shopping areas: **downtown** along the waterfront, on Avenida Rafael Melgar, and on some of the side streets around the plaza (there are more than 150 shops in this area alone); at the **crafts market** (⊠ Calle 1 Sur, behind the plaza) in town, which sells a respectable assortment of Mexican wares; and at the cruise-ship **passenger terminal** south of town, near the Casa Del Mar, La Ceiba, and Sol Caribe hotels. There are also small clusters of shops at **Plaza del Sol** (on the east side of the main plaza), **Villa Mar** (on the north side of the main plaza), the **Plaza Confetti** (on the south side of the main plaza), and **Plaza Maya** (across from the Sol Caribe). As a general rule, the newer, trendier shops line the waterfront, while the area around Avenida 5a houses the better crafts shops. The **town market** (⊠ Calle Rosada Salas, between Avs. 20a and 25a) sells fresh produce and other essentials.

Specialty Stores

Clothing
Several trendy sportswear stores line Avenida Rafael Melgar (⊠ Between Calles 2 and 6). **Miro** (⊠ Av. Rafael Melgar, 1 block from town pier, ☎ 987/20260) has a wide variety of Mexican resort wear in the latest styles. **Explora** (⊠ Av. Rafael Melgar 49, ☎ 987/20316) offers a casual line of modish cotton sports clothing.

La Fiesta Cozumel (⊠ Av. Rafael Melgar Norte 164-B, ☎ 987/22032), a large store catering to the cruise ships, sells a variety of T-shirts as well as souvenirs.

Jewelry
Jewelry on Cozumel is pricey, but it tends to be of higher quality than the jewelry you'll find in many of the other Yucatán towns. **Casablanca** (⊠ Av. Rafael Melgar Norte 33, ☎ 987/21177) specializes in gold, silver, and gemstones, as well as expensive crafts. The elegant **Diamond Creations** (⊠ Av. Rafael Melgar Sur 131, ☎ 987/25330 or 800/322–6476, FAX 987/25334) lets you custom design a piece of jewelry from an extensive collection of loose diamonds—or emeralds, rubies, sapphires, or tanzanite. Customers can select a stone and pick out a mounting, and the store will have it set in an hour in a ring, earrings, necklace, or bracelet. Nothing but fine silver, gold, and coral jewelry—particularly silver bracelets and earrings—is sold at **Joyeria Palancar** (⊠ Av. Rafael Melgar Norte 15, ☎ 987/21468). Quality gemstones and striking designs are the strong point at **Rachat & Romero** (⊠ Av. Rafael Melgar 101, ☎ 987/20571). The toney **Van Cleef & Arpels** (⊠ Av. Rafael Melgar Norte 54, ☎ 987/21143) offers a superlative collection of high-end silver and gold jewelry.

Mexican Crafts
El Sombrero (⊠ Av. Rafael Melgar 29, ☎ 987/20374) stocks a fine selection of leather clothing and accessories.

Gordon Gilchrist (⊠ Studio I, Av. 25 Sur 981, at Calle 15 Sur, ☎ 987/22659), a local artist, displays—by appointment—limited editions of his black-and-white etchings of local Maya sites. He also sells handsome boxes of notepaper featuring these etchings.

Hammocks (⊠ Av. 5a Norte and Calle 4, no phone) are made by Manuel Azueta and sold from his front porch.

Los Cinco Soles (⊠ Av. Rafael Melgar Norte 27, ☎ 987/20132 or 987/22040) is your best bet for one-stop shopping. The nearly block-long store stocks an excellent variety of well-priced, well-displayed items, including blue-rim glassware, brass and tin animals from Jalisco, tablecloths and place mats, cotton gauze and embroidered clothing, onyx, T-shirts, papier-mâché fruit, reproduction Maya art, Mexican fashions, silver jewelry, soapstone earrings and beads, and other Mexican wares.

Na Balam (⊠ Av. 5a Norte 14, no phone) sells high-quality Maya reproductions, batik clothing, and jewelry.

Talavera (⊠ Av. 5a Sur 349, ☎ 987/20171) carries beautiful ceramics from all over Mexico—including tiles from the Yucatán—as well as masks from Guerrero, brightly painted wooden animals from Oaxaca, and carved chests from Guadalajara.

Unicornio (⊠ Av. 5a Sur 1, ☎ 987/20171) specializes in Mexican folk art, including ceramic notions and etched wooden trays, but you'll have to sift through a lot of souvenir junk to find the good quality items.

COZUMEL A TO Z

Arriving and Departing

By Cruise Ship
At least a dozen cruise lines call at Cozumel and/or Playa del Carmen, including, from Fort Lauderdale, **Chandris/Celebrity** (☎ 800/437–3111), **Cunard/Crown** (☎ 800/221–4770), and **Princess** (☎ 800/568–3262); from Miami, **Carnival** (☎ 800/327–9501), **Costa** (☎ 800/327–2537), **Dolphin/Majesty** (☎ 800/222–1003), **Norwegian** (☎ 800/327–7030), and **Royal Caribbean** (☎ 800/327–6700); from New Orleans, **Commodore** (☎ 800/327–5617); and from Tampa, **Holland America** (☎ 800/426–0327).

By Ferry
Passenger-only ferries depart from the dock at **Playa del Carmen** (no phone; ☞ Chapter 5) for the 40-minute trip to the main pier in Cozumel. They leave approximately every hour between 5:15 AM and 8:45 PM and cost about $5 one way, $7 round-trip. Return service to Playa operates roughly from 4 AM to 7:45 PM. Verify the regularly changing schedule. The car ferry from **Puerto Morelos** (☎ 987/21722), on the mainland to the north of Playa del Carmen, is not recommended unless you *must* bring your car. The three- to four-hour trip costs about $30, depending on the size of the car, or $4.50 per passenger. Again, schedules change frequently, so we advise you to call ahead. Tickets can be bought up to a day in advance.

By Hydrofoil
A water-jet catamaran and two large speed boats make the trip between Cozumel (downtown pier, at the zócalo) and Playa del Carmen. This service, operated by **Aviomar** (Av. 5a, between Calles 2 and 4, ☎ 987/20588 or 987/20477), costs the same as the ferry and takes almost as much time, but the vessel is considerably more comfortable and offers on-board videos and refreshments. The boats make at least 10 crossings a day, leaving Playa del Carmen approximately every one to two hours between 5:15 AM and 8:45 PM and returning from Cozumel between 4 AM and 8 PM. Tickets are sold at the piers in both ports one hour before departure; call to confirm the schedule as it tends to be erratic.

By Plane
The **Cozumel Airport** (☎ 987/20928) is 3 km (2 mi) north of town. **Continental** (☎ 987/20487) provides nonstop service from Houston. **Mexicana** (☎ 987/20157) flies nonstop from Miami and San Francisco; **Aerocaribe** (☎ 987/20503) and **Aerocozumel** (☎ 987/20928), both Mexicana subsidiaries, fly to Cancún and other destinations in Mexico, including Chichén Itzá, Chetumal, Mérida, and Playa del Carmen. The airport departure tax is $12.

BETWEEN THE AIRPORT AND HOTELS

Because of an agreement between the taxi drivers' and the bus drivers' unions, there is no taxi service from the airport; taxi service is available *to* the airport, however. Arriving passengers reach their hotels via the *colectivo,* a van with a maximum capacity of eight. Buy a ticket at the airport exit: the charge is $5 per passenger to the hotel zones, a little under $3 into town. If you want to get to your hotel without waiting for the van to fill and for other passengers to be dropped off, you can hire an *especial*—an individual van costing a little under $20 to the hotel zones, about $8 to the city. Taxis to the airport cost about $8 from the hotel zones and approximately $5 from downtown. Most car rental agencies (☞ Contacts and Resources, *below*) maintain offices in the terminal.

Getting Around

By Bicycle, Moped, and Motorcycle

Mopeds and motorcycles are very popular here, but also extremely dangerous because of heavy traffic, potholes, and hidden stop signs; accidents happen all too frequently. Mexican law now requires all passengers to wear helmets; it's a $25 fine if you don't. For mopeds, go to **Auto Rent** (⊠ Carretera Costera Sur, ☎ 987/20844, ext. 712), **Rentadora Caribe** (⊠ Calle Rosada Salas 3, ☎ 987/20955 or 987/20961), or **Rentadora Cozumel** (⊠ Calle Rosada Salas 3 B, ☎ 987/21503; Av. 10a Sur at Calle 1, ☎ 987/21120). Mopeds go for about $25 per day; insurance is included. Auto Rent and Rentadora Chac also rent bicycles for approximately $5–$8 per day.

By Bus

Because of a union agreement with taxi drivers, no public buses operate in the north and south hotel zones; local bus service runs mainly within the town of San Miguel, although there is a route from town to the airport. Service is irregular but inexpensive (under 20¢).

By Car

Open-air Jeeps and other rental cars, especially those with four-wheel drive, are a good way of getting down dirt roads leading to secluded beaches and small Maya ruins (although the rental insurance policy may not always cover these jaunts). The only gas station on Cozumel, at the corner of Avenida Juárez and Avenida 30a, is open daily 7 AM–midnight.

By Taxi

Taxi service is available 24 hours a day, with a 25% surcharge between midnight and 6 AM, at the main location (⊠ Calle 2 Norte, ☎ 987/20041 or 987/20236) or at the *malecón,* as the oceanside walkway is called, at the main pier in town. You can also hail taxis on the street, and there are taxis waiting at all the major hotels. Fixed rates of about $3 are charged to go between town and either hotel zone, about $8 from most hotels to the airport, and about $6–$12 from the northern hotels or town to Chankanaab park or San Francisco beach. However, cruiseship passengers taking taxis to or from the international terminal are often charged about twice as much as tourists staying on the island.

Contacts and Resources

Banks

Banks are open weekdays 9–1:30. Hours for foreign currency exchange vary; your best bet is between 10 AM and noon. Banks include **Banpaís** (⊠ Across from main pier, ☎ 987/21682); **Bancomer** (⊠ Av. 5a at the plaza, ☎ 987/20550); **Banco del Atlántico** (⊠ Av. Rafael Melgar 11, ☎ 987/20142); and **Banco Serfín** (⊠ Calle 1 Sur between Avs. 5a and 10a, ☎ 987/20930).

MONEY EXCHANGE

If you need to exchange money after banking hours, go to **Promotora Cambiaria del Centro** (⊠ Av. 5a Sur between Calle 1 Sur and A.R. Salas), which provides service Monday–Saturday 8 AM–9 PM.

Car Rentals

Following is a list of rental firms that handle two- and four-wheel-drive vehicles (all the major hotels have rental offices): **Budget** (⊠ Av. 5a at Calle 2 Norte, ☎ 987/20903; cruise-ship terminal, 987/21732; airport, 987/21742), **Hertz** (airport, ☎ 987/23888), **National Interrent** (⊠ Av. Juárez, Lote 10, near Calle 10, ☎ 987/23263 or 987/24101), and **Rentadora Aguilla** (⊠ Av. Rafael Melgar 685, ☎ 987/20729). Rental rates start at $50 a day.

Doctors and Dentists

The **Centro de Salud clinic** (⊠ Av. 20 at Calle 11, ☎ 987/20140) provides 24-hour emergency care, and the **Medical Specialties Center** (⊠ Av. 20 Norte 425, ☎ 987/21419 or 987/22919) offers 24-hour air ambulance service and a 24-hour pharmacy. Cozumel's newest medical treatment outlets are the **Cozumel Walk-In Clinic** (⊠ Calle 6 Norte and Av. 15, ☎ 987/24070) and **Cozumel Chiropractic** (⊠ Av. 5 Sur 24-A, between Calles 3 and 5, ☎ 987/25099); the latter offers bargain-priced therapeutic massage for overworked or injured muscles.

Emergencies

Police (⊠ Anexo del Palacio Municipal, ☎ 987/20092). **Red Cross** (⊠ Av. Rosada Salas at Av. 20a Sur, ☎ 987/21058). **Air Ambulance** (☎ 987/24070). **Recompression Chamber** (⊠ Calle 5 Sur 21-B, between Av. Rafael Melgar and Av. 5a Sur, ☎ 987/21430).

English-Language Bookstore

Publiciones Gracia (east side of the plaza, ☎ 987/20031) carries a limited selection of guidebooks and English-language publications and is open Monday–Saturday 8–2 and 4–10, and Sunday 9–1 and 5–10.

Guided Tours

See Travel Agencies and Tour Operators, *below,* for addresses and telephone numbers of the companies mentioned here.

AIR TOURS

A plane trip to **Chichén Itzá** (☞ Chapter 7) is offered by **Caribe Tours;** the price of $145 includes the flight, transfers to the ruins, buffet lunch, and a guide. The company also flies to the **Sian Ka'an Ecological Biosphere** (☞ Chapter 5); in addition to lunch, this $160 plane trip includes a boat ride through the biosphere's mangroves for a closer look at the flora and fauna of the region.

HORSEBACK TOURS

Rancho Buenavista (☎ 987/21537) runs four-hour guided horseback tours that visit three Maya ruins tucked away in Cozumel's tropical forest. The tour departs from Restaurant Acuario (⊠ Av. Rafael Melgar at Calle 11), weekdays at noon and Saturday at 11; the price ($60) includes transportation to the ranch and soft drinks or beer during the tour.

ORIENTATION

Tours of the island's sights, including San Gervasio ruins, El Cedral, Chankanaab Park, and the museum and Archaeological Park, cost about $35 and can be arranged through a travel agency such as **Fiesta Cozumel. Caribe Tours** sells a similar tour, focusing on the botanical gardens, archaeological replicas, and reef snorkeling at Chankanaab; the cost is about $40 and includes an open-bar lunch. Another option is to take a private taxi tour of the island; they range from $30 to $50 per day depending on which parts of the island you wish to visit.

SPECIALTY TOURS

Glass-bottom-boat trips are provided by **Turismo Aviomar** to people who don't want to get wet but do want to see the brilliant underwater life around the island. The air-conditioned semi-submarine *Mermaid* glides over a number of reefs that host a dazzling array of fish; the daily tour, which costs about $30, lasts 1 hour and 45 minutes and includes soft drinks. A similar trip aboard the *Nautilus IV* is available through **Fiesta Cozumel.**

Off-island tours to **Tulum and Xel-Há** (☞ Chapter 5), run by **Turismo Aviomar** and **Caribe Tours,** cost about $75 and include the 30-minute ferry trip to Playa del Carmen, the 45-minute bus ride to Tulum, 1½–2 hours at the ruins, entrance fees, guides, lunch, and a stop for snorkeling at Xel-Há lagoon.

Day trips to the eco-archaeological theme park of **Xcaret,** about halfway between Playa del Carmen and Tulum are offered by **Fiesta Cozumel.** The $50 price includes round-trip ferry to Playa del Carmen, entrance to the park, and a bilingual guide.

Late-Night Pharmacy
Farmacia Joaquín (✉ North side of the plaza, ☎ 987/22520) is open Monday–Saturday 8 AM–10 PM and Sunday 9–1 and 5–9.

Mail
The local **post office** (✉ Calle 7 Sur at Av. Rafael Melgar, ☎ 987/20106), six blocks south of the square, is open weekdays 8–8, Saturday 9–5, and Sunday 9–1. If you are an American Express cardholder, you can receive mail at **Fiesta Cozumel/American Express** (✉ Calle 11 Sur 598, between Avs. 25 and 30, ☎ 987/20925 weekdays 8–1 and 5–8, and Saturday 8–5.

Publications
At the tourist office and at most shops and hotels around town, you can pick up the *Blue Guide, Cozumel Today Guide, Vacation Guide to Cozumel,* and *Cozumel Island's Restaurant Guide.* These publications, all free, tend to be heavily advertiser-driven, but they are helpful all the same and contain good maps of the island and the downtown area.

Telephones
Long-distance calls can be placed from the well-signed **blue phones** around town. However, you'll save 10%–50% by making your calls at the **Calling Station** (✉ Av. Rafael Melgar 27 and Calle 3 Sur, ☎ FAX 987/21417). You can also exchange money and get one-day dry cleaning done at this handy outlet; it's open 8 AM–11 PM daily during high season (mid-December–April), Monday–Saturday 9 AM–10 PM and Sunday 9 AM–1 PM and 5 PM–10 PM the rest of the year.

Travel Agencies and Tour Operators
Apple Vacations (✉ 11 and Av. 30th 598, ☎ 987/24311 or 987/20725), **Caribe Tours** (✉ Av. Rafael Melgar at Calle 5 Sur, ☎ FAX 987/23100 or 987/23154), **Fiesta Cozumel Holidays/American Express** (in all major hotel lobbies; Calle 11 Sur 598, between Avs. 25 and 30, ☎ 987/20725), **Turismo Aviomar** (in several hotel lobbies, including El Presidente; Av. 5 Norte 8, between Calles 2 and 4, ☎ 987/20588).

Visitor Information
State tourism office (✉ Upstairs in the Plaza del Sol mall, at the east end of the main square, ☎ 987/20218), open weekdays 9–2:30. A good source of information on lodgings (and many other things) is the **Cozumel Island Hotel Association** (✉ Calle 2 Norte at 15a, ☎ 987/23132, FAX 987/22809), open weekdays 8–2 and 4–7. But *avoid* the "tourist information" booths on the main square: They're actually trying to sell time-share tours.

5 Mexico's Caribbean Coast

Although the eastern shore of the Yucatán from Cancún to Chetumal is no longer as pristine as it was in the past—what's been termed the Maya Coast is becoming more and more developed—it still offers plenty of secluded beach escapes. Take time to view the Maya ruins at Tulum, vestiges of an ancient civilization with a spectacular Caribbean backdrop. Visit the Sian Ka'an Biosphere Reserve to see the area's abundant wildlife, including crocodiles, jaguars, and wild boars, as well as more than 300 species of birds.

Updated by
Patricia Alisau

ABOVE ALL ELSE, BEACHES ARE WHAT DEFINE the eastern coast of the Yucatán peninsula. White, sandy strands with offshore coral reefs, bordered by tropical foliage and jungles filled with abundant wildlife, make the coastline of Quintana Roo a marvelous destination for lovers of the outdoors. The scrubby limestone terrain is mostly flat and dry, punctuated only by sinkholes, and the shores are broken by freshwater lagoons and cliffs.

The various destinations on the coast cater to different preferences. The once laid-back town of Playa del Carmen is now host to resorts as glitzy as those in Cancún and Cozumel, though still not quite as expensive, while the lazy fishing village of Puerto Morelos so far has been only slightly altered to accommodate foreign tourists. Rustic fishing and scuba diving lodges on the even more secluded Boca Paila and Xcalak peninsulas are gaining a well-deserved reputation for bone fishing and superb diving on virgin reefs. The beaches, from Punta Bete to Sian Ka'an, south of Tulum, are beloved of scuba divers, snorkelers, birders, and beachcombers, and offer accommodations to suit every budget, from campsites and bungalows to condos and luxury hotels. Ecotourism is on the rise, with special programs designed to involve visitors in preserving the threatened sea-turtle population.

Then there are the Maya ruins at Tulum, superbly situated on a bluff overlooking the Caribbean, and, a short distance inland, at Cobá, whose towering jungle-shrouded pyramids evoke its importance as a leading center of commerce in the Maya world. South of Tulum, smaller archaeological sites that were dominated by Kohunlich, the main Maya city in the southern part of the state, are being beautifully restored with new funding. At the Belizean border is Chetumal, a modern port and the capital of Quintana Roo; with its dilapidated clapboard houses and sultry sea air, it is more Central American than Mexican. The waters up and down the coast, abundant with shipwrecks and relics from the heyday of piracy, are dotted with mangrove swamps and minuscule islands where only the birds hold sway.

During your sojourn along the coast, you'll run into expats from around the world, running lodges and restaurants where you least expect to find them. Chat with them for a bit and they'll surely tell you how they succumbed to the spellbinding bewitchery of the Caribbean coast, unable to resist the urge to stay.

Pleasures and Pastimes

Beaches
The Caribbean coast beaches—most blessed with white sand and fringed by dense jungle foliage—are so various that they attract everyone from amateur archaeologists to professional divers and devoted sun worshipers.

Dining
Most of the restaurants along the Mexican Caribbean coast are simple beachside affairs with outdoor tables and *palapas* (thatched roofs). Little attention is paid to the niceties of decor you find in such resort destinations as Cancún, Cozumel, and even Isla Mujeres. In addition to their generally casual ambience, restaurants here offer bargains, especially when it comes to seafood, provided it is fresh and local, such as grouper, *mojarra,* snapper, dorado, and sea bass. Shrimp, lobster, oysters, and other shellfish are usually flown in frozen from the Gulf or Pacific coast, and often you can taste the difference. A number of

places that cater to the North American palate have sprung up where tourists congregate, especially in Playa del Carmen and Puerto Aventuras; their menus include such items as pizza and spaghetti. The few luxury hotels in the area have fancy restaurants offering Continental cuisine, elegant service, and, of course, high prices—almost as high as those in Cancún. Many of the restaurants have limited hours or close down in summer and during the hurricane season (September). Generally, all restaurants maintain a casual dress code and do not accept reservations.

CATEGORY	COST*
$$$$	over $20
$$$	$15–$20
$$	$8–$15
$	under $8

per person, excluding drinks and service

Diving and Snorkeling

Quintana Roo attracts scuba divers and snorkelers with its transparent turquoise and emerald waters strewn with rose, black, and red coral reefs and sunken pirate ships. Schools of black, gray, and gold angelfish, luminous green-and-purple parrot fish, earth-colored manta rays, and scores of other jewel-toned tropical species seem oblivious to the clicking underwater cameras. The visibility in these waters reaches 100 ft, so you can see the marine life and topography without even getting wet. There is particularly good diving in Akumal and Punta Bete. Those who want to get away from all distractions except fish head for Banco Chinchorro.

Fishing

Fishing ranks with diving and snorkeling as one of the most popular activities along the coast. For fly-fishing, boats can be rented from locals who run beachside stalls. Many local marinas run charters catering to those interested in Caribbean deep-sea fishing for such catches as marlin, bonito, and sailfish. Generally, larger hotels have dive shops on the premises. Serious anglers often book a week or more on the Boca Paila peninsula.

Lodging

Accommodations on the Caribbean coast run the gamut from campsites to simple palapas and bungalows to middle-range, strictly functional establishments to luxury hotels and condominiums. Many of these hotels include two or three meals in their prices. The fanciest accommodations are in Playa del Carmen, Akumal, and Puerto Aventuras, while the coastline (including the Tulum area) is sprinkled with small campgrounds and hotels on solitary beaches. Note that hotel rates drop as much as 25% in the low season (September to approximately mid-December). In the high season, it's virtually impossible to find hotels in the $ price range, especially in Playa del Carmen, unless you opt to camp out.

In Chetumal, the new Holiday Inn is striking; other than this one, probably you will not find much to impress you in the way of accommodations. Hotels tend to be old and lacking in character—or downright deteriorated. Accommodations reflect the town's origin as a pit stop for traders en route to or from Central America. Laguna de Bacalar is an alternative to Chetumal as your base for explorations in the area, although the accommodations are no better.

CATEGORY	COST*
$$$$	over $90
$$$	$60–$90
$$	$25–$60
$	under $25

All prices are for a standard double room in the high season (Dec.–Aug.) excluding service and the 12% tax.

Maya Ruins

Lovers of archaeology will not be disappointed here, as the magnificent remains of sacred cities attest to the power held by the coastal Maya in controlling trade routes along the Caribbean. Tulum, a walled city spread before the sea, Cobá, the largest inhabited city of the Maya peninsula, and the majestic stucco masks of Kohunlich are breathtaking. Mysterious temples with hidden chambers, stelae carved with god images, and the sounds of the jungles intermingle at these sites.

Nature-Watching

The wildlife on the Caribbean coast is unsurpassed in Mexico, except perhaps in Baja California. Along the more civilized stretches of road, wild pigs, turkeys, iguanas, lizards, and snakes appear in the clearings. Jaguars, monkeys, white-tail deer, armadillos, tapir, wild boars, peccaries, ocelots, raccoons, and badgers all inhabit the tropical jungle's most isolated retreats. Birders come to stare into the jungle and seaside marshes for glimpses of parrots, toucans, terns, herons, ibis, and hundreds of nesting pink flamingos. Onlookers are entertained by yellow, blue, and scarlet butterflies, singing cicadas and orioles, sparkling dragonflies, kitelike frigates, and night owls nesting in the trees.

The reefs, lagoons, cenotes (sinkholes), and caves along the Caribbean and down the Hondo river—which runs along the borders between Mexico, Belize, and Guatemala—are filled with alligators, giant turtles, sharks, barracuda, and manatees. During July and August sea turtles throng the beaches, laying thousands of eggs. Colorless crabs scuttle sideways toward the coconut groves, over pale white limestone and sand. Tiny mosquitoes and gnats, impervious to mild repellents, bore through the smallest rips in window screens, tents, and mosquito nets.

Exploring the Caribbean Coast

The coast is divided into two areas: Puerto Morelos to Tulum, which has the most sites and places to lodge; and Tulum to Chetumal, where civilization thins out quite a bit and you find the most alluringly beautiful but remote beaches, coves, inlets, lagoons, and tropical landscapes.

Numbers in the text correspond to numbers in the margin and on the Mexico's Caribbean Coast map.

Great Itineraries

Stays of three to five days will give you enough time to visit the Puerto Morelos to Tulum area, seven days can be spread out along the entire coast, and longer visits will allow you to visit every attraction and village mentioned in this chapter. Playa del Carmen is a good base from which to explore, as it is closest to the major ruins of Tulum and Cobá, and has the best bus, taxi, and rental car service outside of Cancún. Venturing south of Tulum on a seven-day or longer trek requires a car.

IF YOU HAVE 3 DAYS

Get a room in **Playa del Carmen** ③ and start out by visiting **Tulum** ⑭ to view the cliffside Castillo temple; afterward, climb down to the small beach alongside it for a dip in the ocean. On day two, head out to the cenote at **Xel-Há** ⑫, where you can snorkel, swim, or sunbathe. Follow this with a visit to the CEDAM museum at **Puerto Aventuras** ⑥, full of displays salvaged from old shipwrecks. Day three, head for **Akumal** ⑧ for a diving or deep-sea fishing excursion, snorkeling, or swimming; later in the day visit the tiny lagoons of **Xpuhá** ⑦ and **Yalkú** ⑨, which were around during the time of the Maya traders.

IF YOU HAVE 5 DAYS

Again basing yourself in Playa del Carmen, visit Tulum on the first day, and then spend day two touring **Xcaret** ④, an ecological theme park where you can swim with dolphins, snorkel in a cenote, and take in a Mexican rodeo show. On day three, start the morning at the archaeological ruins of **Cobá** ⑮ and spend the afternoon cooling off at **Xel-Há.** Day four, head for **Akumal** and its nearby lagoons. Day five, take a tour of the **Sian Ka'an Biosphere Reserve** ⑯.

IF YOU HAVE 7 DAYS

Follow the first five days of the above itinerary; on day six, drive to the enormous **Laguna de Bacalar** ㉑ to marvel at its transparent layers of turquoise, green, and blue waters (it should take about three hours if you drive straight through); visit the colonial San Felipe Fortress in the village of Bacalar and overnight in **Chetumal** ㉓. On day seven, in the early morning, visit the Museum of Maya Culture and then head for **Kohunlich** ㉔, which has huge stucco masks of its Maya rulers surrounded by jungle ruins. Make a small detour to **Dzibanché** ㉕ and then head back up the coast to Playa del Carmen, stopping at the **Cenote Azul** ㉒, the largest sinkhole in Mexico; at the town of **Felipe Carrillo Puerto** ⑱, where you can get a taste of present-day Maya culture; and finally at **Muyil** ⑰ with its pretty Maya temple.

When to Tour the Caribbean Coast

If driving your own vehicle, get an early start to travel to the various destinations before the tour buses arrive. This is true practically the whole year round, as nearby Cancún, which is responsible for most of the tours, is the most popular resort in the country. Reach your overnight destination before dark as the majority of the main coastal highway is only two lanes and is not lit at night—nor does it have road reflectors. A four-lane segment went into operation between Cancún and Playa del Carmen at the end of 1996.

THE CARIBBEAN COAST

Quintana Roo, Mexico's youngest state and the one that geographically enfolds the Caribbean coast, entered the modern era in the 1970s, when Mexican politicians decided to develop the area for tourism. (It did not become a state until 1974, the same year that the first two hotels popped up at Cancún.) From Cancún to Tulum, at most points the road is 1 or 2 km (½ to 1 mi) from the coast; thus there is little in sight but dense vegetation, assorted billboards, roadside artisans' markets, and signs marking the dirt-road entrances to the ruins, resorts, beaches, and campgrounds hidden off the road.

It won't stay that way for long. The Mexican government now allows development along the 130-km (81-mi) stretch of coastline known as the Cancún–Tulum Corridor; new hotel developments for the rest of the coastline south to Chetumal have also been announced. Each year more picture-coded international tourist signs crop up, pointing the way to more restaurants, gas stations, and hotels. Still, thanks to the federal government's foresight in setting aside a 22-mi strip of coastline and jungle called Sian Ka'an Biosphere Reserve, wildlife and travelers who seek the Yucatán of old still have somewhere to go.

Mexico's Caribbean Coast

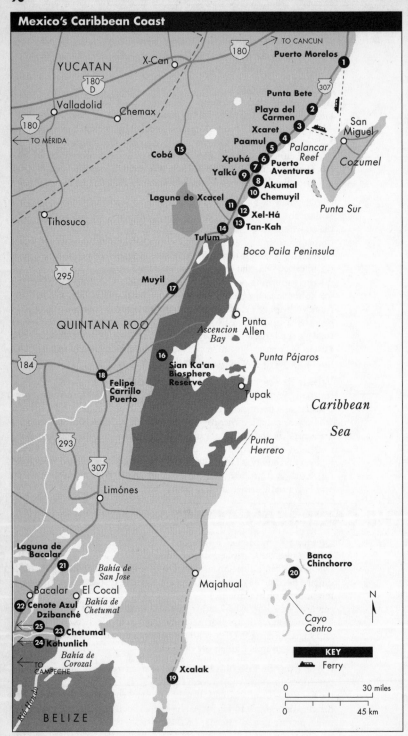

TO CANCUN

180

YUCATAN

X-Can

Puerto Morelos ①

307

Punta Bete

②

Playa del
Carmen

Xcaret ③

San
Miguel

180
D

Valladolid

Chemax

Paamul ④

⑤

Cozumel

180

TO MÉRIDA

Xpuhá

⑥ Puerto
Aventuras

Palancar
Reef

Cobá ⑮

Yalkú

⑦

⑨

⑧ Akumal

Punta Sur

Laguna de Xcacel

⑩ Chemuyil

Tihosuco

⑪

⑫ Xel-Há

⑬ Tan-Kah

Tulum

⑭

Boco Paila Peninsula

295

Muyil

⑰

QUINTANA ROO

Ascencion
Bay

Punta
Allen

184

⑯ Sian Ka'an
Biosphere
Reserve

Punta Pájaros

Felipe
⑱ Carrillo
Puerto

Tupak

Caribbean

Sea

293

Punta
Herrero

307

Limónes

Laguna de
Bacalar

⑳ Banco
Chinchorro

⑳

Bahía de
San Jose

Majahual

⑳

Bacalar

El Cocal

N

㉒ Cenote Azul
Dzibanché

Bahía de
Chetumal

Cayo
Centro

㉕

㉓ Chetumal

KEY

㉔ Kohunlich

Ferry

Bahía de
Corozal

TO
CAMPECHE

Xcalak

0   30 miles

⑲

0   45 km

BELIZE

The music, food, and cultural traditions of the Caribbean coast are Yucatecan. The northern portion has a decided Spanish influence. Cancún's transformation into a world-class resort has brought an international flair to the region; the Continental restaurants and glitzy shopping malls of the beach resort now flourish within 16 km (10 mi) of small Maya settlements. The coastline south of Tulum is more purely Maya: Seaside fishing collectives, jungles, and close-knit communities carry on ancient traditions. The far south, particularly Chetumal, is influenced by its status as a seaport and its proximity to Belize and Guatemala. The language spoken here is mainly Spanish and some Caribbean patois, and most visitors to the area are passing through to cross the border.

There isn't much in the way of nightlife on the coast unless you happen upon some entertainment in a luxury hotel bar. More and more restaurants in Playa del Carmen have live music at night on weekends, but there are no discos or nightclubs to speak of in the area. Xcaret offers a daily evening show chock full of folk dances and cultural lore on the Maya.

Nor are there many high-quality crafts available along the Caribbean coast, although the shopping situation has improved in Playa del Carmen, where more and more good folk-art shops are opening.

Our exploration of the Caribbean coast takes you from Puerto Morelos to Chetumal, with brief detours inland to the ruins of Cobá and Kohunlich. Route 307 parallels the entire coastline for the 382 km (233 mi) from Cancún to Chetumal. Although buses do traverse the region and are popular with backpackers, a rental car or four-wheel-drive vehicle allows you to explore more thoroughly and creatively.

Puerto Morelos

❶ *36 km (22 mi) south of Cancún.*

Many people know Puerto Morelos only as the small coastal town where they catch the car ferry to Cozumel. It has been left remarkably free of the large-scale development so common farther south, though each year more and more tourists stop here to take in its easygoing pace, cheap accommodations, and convenient seaside location near a superb offshore coral reef. For obvious reasons, this place is particularly attractive to divers, snorkelers, and anglers. The reef at Morelos is about 1,800 ft offshore. The caves of the sleeping sharks of documentary movie fame are also 8 km (5 mi) east of the town.

Morelos was once a point of departure for Maya women making pilgrimages by canoe to Cozumel, the sacred isle of the fertility goddess, Ixchel; today it is not very different from many small towns in the Spanish-speaking Caribbean. There is not much to it beyond a gas station, a central square, and auto repair shops. (However, the town square is much prettier now after having been remodeled at the beginning of 1997). If you wander down the dirt streets north and south of town, you will notice neighborhoods of new, Mediterranean-style houses and condos, home to part-time residents who enjoy the town's laid-back mode. Nature endowed Puerto Morelos with a fine deep-sea port (the principal port for the area until the road to Puerto Juárez was built), so today ferries and freight ships call regularly. Most of the action is centered on the long pier south of the square, where vehicles line up for hours waiting for the ferry to depart. Three lighthouses from different eras break up the long stretch of beach, and boats to take out to the surrounding reefs can be rented on the beach.

Dining and Lodging

$ ✕ **Los Pelicanos.** If you're looking for good fresh fish—fried, grilled, or steamed—stop by this thatch-roofed restaurant on the beach where you can spend hours feasting on the catch of the day and watching the boats go by. ⊠ *Oceanfront near main plaza,* ☎ *987/10014. MC, V.*

$$$$ ✕🖼 **Caribbean Reef Club at Villa Marina.** This rather functional-look-
★ ing white condo complex is one of the newest hideaways along the coast. The colonial-style suites have marble floors, air-conditioning, ceiling fans, blue-tile kitchenettes, floral pastel linens, and arched windows. Sliding glass doors lead to balconies outside, where you can slip in an afternoon nap on your own private hammock. The adjacent restau-rant is easily the most picturesque in town, with a balcony overlook-ing the sea, hand-painted tile tables, and candlelight at night. A Cuban chef prepares superb coconut shrimp, seafood gumbo, jerk chicken, and other Caribbean specialties. ⊠ *South of ferry dock,* ☎ *98/834999 in Cancún and* ☎ *987/10191 or 800/322–6286,* ⅢⅩ *987/10190. 21 suites. Restaurant, bar, pool, diving, snorkeling, fishing. MC, V.*

$ ✕🖼 **Posada Amor.** One of Puerto Morelos's first hotels, this family-run property near the pier has been operating for more than 15 years. The humble rooms in a two-story building behind the restaurant have screened windows with dark blue draperies (helpful for late sleepers) and cement slab beds. Only eight rooms offer private baths. The restau-rant, a neighborhood gathering spot, serves great home-style Mexican meals and has a full bar. ⊠ *Av. Xavier Rojo Góez (1st street on right as you enter town),* ☎ *987/10033,* ⅢⅩ *987/10178. Reservations, Box 806, Cancún, Quintana Roo 77580. 20 rooms. Restaurant. No credit cards.*

$$ 🖼 **Cabañas Playa Ojo de Agua.** This dive-oriented hotel is on a lovely beach just north of town. Most of the guest rooms have kitchenettes, ceiling fans, and views of the sea or the courtyard gardens. There is a freshwater pool on the premises, and 14 rooms were added in 1996. ⊠ *1 block north of town,* ☎ *987/10027. Reservations, Calle 12, No. 96, Mérida, Yucatán 97050,* ☎ *99/250292, 98/834999 in Cancún. 30 rooms. Pool, dive shop. No credit cards.*

$$ 🖼 **Los Arrecifes.** Located on an isolated (and sometimes windy) beach, Los Arrecifes is an older hotel that's been remodeled and redecorated. Its twelve one-bedroom apartments with kitchenettes, large living rooms, and balconies are in an ideal, private setting. Owner Vicki Sharp also has information on condo and house rentals in Puerto Morelos. ⊠ *8 blocks north of town on street closest to beach, no phone. Reser-vations, Box 986, Cancún, Quintana Roo 77500,* ☎ *98/834999 in Can-cún,* ☎ ⅢⅩ *987/101121. 12 apartments. Kitchenettes. No credit cards.*

Outdoor Activities and Sports

WATER SPORTS

Snorkeling gear, fishing tackle, and boats can be rented from the **Aqua Deportes** (no phone) dive shop on the town's main beach, by the plaza. The **Posada Amor** hotel can also fix you up with deep-sea fishing ex-cursions. The **Caribbean Reef Club** can arrange diving, fishing, snorkel-ing, or mountain biking.

Side Trips

Croco-Cun. The biologists running this crocodile farm and miniature zoo just north of Puerto Morelos have collected specimens of most of the animals and reptiles indigenous to the area, and offer immensely informative tours to visitors willing to spend an hour or two learning about the jungle's wildlife. Self-guided tours, a restaurant, and a gift shop are also available. ⊠ *Rte. 307, Km 30,* ☎ *98/841709.* 🎫 *$4.* ☺ *Tues.–Sun. 9–6.*

Dr. Alfredo Barrera Marín Botanical Garden. This 150-acre tropical forest a few miles south of Puerto Morelos off Highway 186 is the largest of its kind in Mexico. Named for a local botanist, the botanical garden is framed by mangroves on the east, facing the ocean, and harbors endangered species such as spider monkeys, toucans, and parrots. There's also a tree nursery, an orchid garden, a reproduction of a *chiclero* (gum collector), an authentic Maya house, and an archaeological site. ⊠ *Hwy. 186, sign at turnoff to garden, no phone.* 🎫 *$3.* ☺ *Daily 9–5.*

Punta Bete

❷ *22 km (16½ mi) south of Puerto Morelos.*

Punta Bete is a 6½-km (4-mi) white-sand beach between rocky lagoons. This point is the setting for several bungalow-style hotels that have almost become cult places for travelers who love being in or on the water. All the properties are set off from Route 307 at the end of a 2⅓-km (1½-mi) paved road; many of them are still recovering from the damage that Hurricane Roxanne caused in late 1995.

Lodging

$$$$ 🏨 **Posada del Capitán Lafitte.** Set on an invitingly long stretch of beach
★ just 10 km (6 mi) north of Playa del Carmen at Punta Bete, this lodging is known for its genuinely chummy, unpretentious atmosphere. It's no luxury resort, but a simple cluster of two-unit cabañas, each with its own private bath and ceiling fan;14 units have air-conditioning. A duplex at the south end of the property has four two-bedroom, two-bath units, ideal for families. Breakfast, dinner, tax, and tips are included in the room rate, so you rarely need to carry money. In the evening the European and American clientele congregate around a small but pretty pool bar decorated with red tiles and coral-pink stucco. Group activities include snorkeling trips, scuba certification and dives, horseback riding, fishing, and birding. All reservations must be prepaid. ⊠ *Dirt road (follow signs), about 3 km (2 mi) off Rte. 307, Km 62,* ☎ *987/ 30214,* ⅀ *987/4–5226. Reservations, Turquoise Reef Group, Box 2664, Evergreen, CO 80439,* ☎ *303/674–9615 or 800/538–6802,* ⅀ *303/674–8735. 47 rooms. Restaurant, bar, beach, pool, dive shop, airport shuttle, car rental. AE, MC, V.*

Outdoor Activites and Sports

WATER SPORTS

Posada del Capitán Lafitte (☎ 987/30214 or 800/538–6802), off Route 307 just north of Playa del Carmen, has an excellent, full-service dive shop called Buccaneer's Landing. Services include diving and snorkeling excursions and scuba resort courses.

Playa del Carmen

❸ *10 km (6 mi) south of Punta Bete and 68 km (41 mi) south of Cancún.*

Only a few decades ago, Playa del Carmen was a deserted beach where Indian families raised coconut palms to produce copra and the odd foreigner wandered in to get away from it all. There are still a few foreigners-gone-native around, but the town—now the fastest growing on the coast, with a population of over 30,000—has become the preferred destination of travelers who want easy access to gorgeous beaches and the archaeological sights of Yucatán. Its alabaster-white beach and small offshore reefs lend themselves to excellent swimming, snorkeling, and turtle-watching. Those traveling the coast by car can stock up on supplies here, while those taking the bus often use Playa as their base camp, since it's the easiest jumping off point for nearby sights. Prices, particularly at the hotels, have been increasing steadily; Playa is no longer a budget destination. But you still get more for your money here than in Cancún or Cozumel. Playa has 35 hotels now, or about 60 percent more than a few years ago.

The village of Playa del Carmen, which lies midway between Cancún and Tulum, has undergone not only a tourist boom but also a beautification effort that has greatly enhanced its natural charms. A new water and sewage system was completed in 1994, and many of the main streets in town have been paved. **Avenida 5,** the first street running parallel to the beach, has been closed to vehicular traffic from the plaza to Calle 8 and turned into a pedestrian walkway with quaint little cafés and lots of street art and entertainment. Driving to the beachfront hotels is difficult unless you know exactly where you're going, and parking has become a nightmare. Restaurants and shops—including **Rincón del Sol,** a colonial-style mall with a tree-filled courtyard and high-quality folk-art boutiques—are opening here as the area becomes established. Many new businesses are branches of Cancún establishments whose owners have taken up permanent residence in Playa or commute daily between the two resorts. **Avenida Juárez,** running from the highway to the beach, is the main commercial zone for the Cancún–Tulum corridor, with small food shops, hotels, pharmacies, auto-parts and hardware stores, and banks lining the curbs; the bus station is also here.

The busiest parts of Playa are down by the ferry pier, around the main plaza, and along the pedestrian walkway. Take a stroll north from the pier along the beach and you'll see the essence of the town: simple restaurants roofed with palm fronds, where people sit drinking beer for hours; a few campgrounds; and lots of hammocks. On the south side of the pier is the **Continental Plaza Playacar,** a first-class, lavish hotel that brought a sense of luxury and style to Playa del Carmen in 1991. Several more all-inclusive hotels, the **Diamond Resort** and the **Royal Maeva,** have opened in the immense Playacar complex; the development's 18-hole championship golf course opened in 1994.

If you walk away from the beach, you'll come upon the affluent section: several condominium projects and well-tended gardens and lawns can be seen from the street. From here, only the sandy streets, the small vestiges of Maya structures, and the stunning turquoise sea on the horizon suggest you're in the tropics. If you walk to the north end of town, you'll see new luxury hotels opening in another residential area, not quite as posh as Playacar but promising nevertheless. The streets at both ends of town peter out into the jungle. Playa has acquired the confident veneer of an up-and-coming beach destination, which can be attributed, in part, to the amiability of the locals (including the growing number of expatriates who manage many of the hotels and restaurants).

A series of cenotes, lies just off the highway between Playa del Carmen and Tulum. They sport such colorful names as **Car Wash, Dos Palamas, Dos Ojos** and **Cenote Azul.** Highway signs identify them so they can be easily visited.

Dining and Lodging

$$ ✕ **Da Gabi.** There are two Da Gabi restaurants on the planet—one in
★ Playa and the other in Boulder, Colorado—and both are successful. Locals flock here at night to dine under a romantic candle-lighted palapa on remarkable Italian cuisine. Enjoy the Maya chef's homemade fettuccine, spinach ravioli, angel hair pasta with fresh tomatoes, or oven-

baked pizza. You can't go wrong with the daily specials either—salmon antipasto or carpaccio with capers and Parmesan cheese slices, for example. Top your meal off with an espresso or cappuccino. Service is especially cordial here, and owner John Lackey is always around to keep things running smoothly. ☒ *Av. 1 and Calle 12, Da Gabi Hotel,* ☎ *987/30048. No credit cards. No lunch.*

$$ ✕ **La Parrilla.** The far end of the pedestrian walkway gained a social center when La Parrilla opened in 1994 at the Rincón del Sol plaza. A branch of an enduringly popular Cancún chain, the open-air restaurant sits a few feet above the street, and it's hard to resist stopping in for a beer, a platter of chicken fajitas, or lobster. This is one of the most animated places in town on weekends, with tables spilling out onto the street and a heavy noise level until the wee hours of the morning. ☒ *Av. 5 at Calle 8, no phone. MC, V.*

$$ ✕ **La Placita.** This attractive restaurant is about as authentic as they come in Playa. A narrow table-filled entranceway overlooking Avenida 5 opens up into a delightful patio in back where northern Mexican dishes such as *cabrito* (roasted kid), grilled fillets of meat and fish, and bone-marrow soup get top billing. Lobster, shrimp, squid, and U.S.-style rib eye and t-bone, which are in a display case out front, can also be ordered. Save room for desert and a flambéed *café* Maya made of Kahlua, *Xtabetum* (honey liqueur), and vanilla ice cream. The Mexican handicrafts—piñatas and colored-paper cutouts—used to decorate the place are so attractive that tourists often buy them right off the wall. And some people like the food so much that they ask to photograph the chef. There's live music nightly. ☒ *Av. 5 between Calles 4 and 6,* ☎ *987/31067. AE, MC, V.*

$$ ✕ **Limones.** A romantic little spot right off Avenida 5, this restaurant offers dining by candlelight, either alfresco in a courtyard or under the shelter of a palapa indoors. Wine bottles hanging from the ceiling and soft guitar music add to the amorous atmosphere. House favorites include copious entrées such as fettuccine, lasagna, and lemon-sautéed beef scaloppine. The daily dinner special is the best bargain in town. ☒ *Av. 5 at Calle 6, no phone. MC, V.*

$$ ✕ **Máscaras.** The wood-burning brick oven here produces exception-
★ ally good thin-crusted pizzas and breads; the homemade pastas are also excellent. Fresh-squeezed, sweetened lime juice, margaritas, wine, and beer help wash down the rich Italian fare. Be sure to try the smoked salmon pizza or calamari in garlic and oil or the four-cheese pizza—the most popular item on the menu. The wine cellar stocks good Italian reds. Masks from throughout the world cover the walls. Since it opened in 1983, Máscaras has been unfailingly popular with locals and the workers from the hotels, and is a central gathering spot with a view of the goings-on at the *zócalo* (main plaza). ☒ *Av. Juárez, across from plaza,* ☎ *987/30153. MC, V.*

$ ✕ **El Tacolote.** Opened in 1992, this fanciful, colorful open-air restaurant continues to expand, overtaking less popular eateries. Mariachis play on most evenings in front of the sidewalk tables, where diners feast on platters of grilled meats, fajitas, or tacos with all sorts of fillings. You can eat cheaply or splurge on a multi-course feast while watching the action on the plaza from an outdoor table. ☒ *Av. Juárez, across from plaza,* ☎ *987/30066. MC, V.*

$ ✕ **Sabor.** Owner Melinda Burns tried several locations for her café/bakery before she settled on the pedestrian-only stretch of Avenida 5, where patrons have a good view of local goings-on. Its home-made baked goods—chocolate cakes, brownies, and apple pies—have made this place famous. It's hard to find a seat at breakfast time, when locals and travelers drop by for granola, fruit salads, and whole-wheat muffins. Customers can be also be seen downing giant goblets of blended fruit drinks.

Stick with breakfast and snacks here, as the burgers, sandwiches, and other main dishes tend to be a bit dry. ⊠ *Av. 5 between Calles 3 and 4, no phone. No credit cards.*

$$$$ 🏨 **Continental Plaza Playacar.** Playa del Carmen became a first-class tourism destination when the Playacar hotel opened in October 1991. The centerpiece of an 880-acre master-planned resort, Playacar faces the sea on the south side of the ferry pier. A pastel, blush-colored palace, it possesses all the amenities of its competitors at the larger resort towns. The tropical-style rooms have ocean views and balconies or patios, marble baths, blonde-wood furnishings, satellite TV, and in-room safes. The beach is one of the nicest in Playa del Carmen, and far less crowded than those to the north. Mexican and international dishes are served at a restaurant in the main building and a palapa by the pool; the breakfast buffet is excellent. A full-scale scuba and water-sports facility offers diving, snorkeling, sailing, and waterskiing. Playacar's 18-hole championship golf course opened in 1994; ask about golf packages. ⊠ *Fraccionamiento Playacar, Playa del Carmen, Quintana Roo 77710,* 📞 *987/30100 or 800/882–6684. 188 rooms, 16 suites. 2 restaurants, bar, pool, 18-hole golf course, dive shop, shops, travel services, car rental. AE, MC, V.*

$$$$ 🏨 **Diamond Resort.** Opened in 1992 as part of the Playacar development, Diamond is an all-inclusive resort that sprawls down a sloping hill to the sea. The guest rooms are spread out in thatch-roofed villas along winding paths; the dining room, bar, lobby, and entertainment areas are housed in a gigantic multi-peaked palapa. Unlike many all-inclusive resorts, Diamond's design allows peace and privacy. One pool is used for games and activities, while another is reserved for quiet lounging. Guests get a bit rowdy at the karaoke bar and outdoor stage, but the noise does not reach the guest rooms. Electric carts are available for getting around the grounds. Buffet-style meals are plentiful and imaginatively prepared; there are also two à la carte restaurants. Playa del Carmen is a 20-minute walk or a $4 cab ride north. ⊠ *Playacar development,* 📞 *987/30039,* FAX *987/3–0346. Reservations, 901 Ponce de León Blvd., Suite 400, Coral Gables, FL 33134,* 📞 *800/858–2258,* FAX *305/444–4848. 296 rooms. 3 restaurants, bar, 2 pools, 4 tennis courts, dive shop, shops, children's program (ages 5–10), car rental. AE, MC, V.*

$$$$ 🏨 **Mayan Paradise.** The architecture of this new hotel at the north-
★ ern end of Playa is a successful updating of old Maya style; the rooms are set in two-story bungalows with thatched roofs, terraces, and dark hardwood siding, and they surround a pretty pool and jungle palms. Local hardwood from the sapodilla tree also lines the walls of the guest rooms, which have all the amenities of a luxury hotel at reasonable prices (low end of $$$$). Each has a small kitchenette, color satellite TV, two double beds, room safe, air-conditioning, and furnishings in rich fabrics; suites have whirlpool baths. The restaurant and bar are under a palapa and meals are served at a fixed time each day. Although not on the ocean, the hotel has its own private beach club and complimentary shuttle service for guests. ⊠ *Av. 10 between Calles 12 and Bis,* 📞 FAX *987/30933. 44 rooms and suites. Restuarant, bar, pool, travel services, free parking. MC, V.*

$$$$ 🏨 **Royal Maeva Playacar.** This all-inclusive Mexican club opened in 1996 in the Playacar development south of the ferry pier and already draws plenty of Italian and German vacationers. The complex looks like a small, salmon-colored Mexican village sprinkled liberally with red-tiled roofs and colonial arches. Several pools surround a thatched pavilion restaurant in the middle of the tropical garden, beyond which is a powder-sand beach that stretches several miles north to town. The friendly staff of guest-pleasers called "Amigoes" hail mainly from Eu-

In case you want to see the world.

At American Express, we're here to make your journey a smooth one. So we have over 1,700 travel service locations in over 120 countries ready to help. What else would you expect from the world's largest travel agency?

do more

Travel

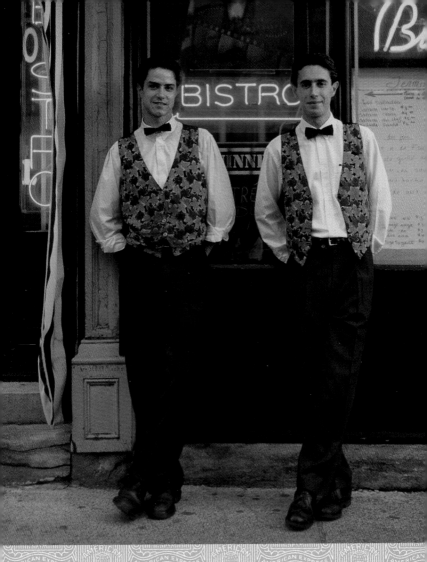

In case you want to be welcomed there.

We're here to see that you're always welcomed at establishments everywhere. That's why millions of people carry the American Express® Card – for peace of mind, confidence, and security, around the world or just around the corner.

do more®

Cards

And just in case.

We're here with American Express® Travelers Cheques and Cheques *for Two.*® They're the safest way to carry money on your vacation and the surest way to get a refund, practically anywhere, anytime.

Another way we help you...

do more

Travelers Cheques

rope and are fluent in several different languages. Maeva is adding free room service, in-room minibars, scuba diving, and snorkeling trips to compete with its all-inclusive neighbors down the beach. ⊠ *Playacar development,* ☎ *213/935–6089 or 800/466–2382,* FAX *213/935–6197. 300 rooms. 2 restaurants, 4 bars, 4 pools, 4 tennis courts, basketball, exercise room, volleyball, snorkeling, fishing, dance club, theater, children's program (ages 5-10), convention center, meeting rooms, travel services, car rental, free parking. AE, DC, MC, V.*

$$$$ 🏨 **Shangri-La Caribe.** Similar to Las Palapas (☞ *below*) next door, Shangri-La's attractive whitewashed bungalows, capped with palapa roofs, have hammocks out front and ceiling fans inside; the oceanfront cabañas also have sitting areas. Music blares from the tropical-style bar, where the French, German, and American clientele gather around the pool table. You can order American or Mexican food à la carte at the spacious restaurant. ⊠ *Dirt road off Rte. 307, midway between Punta Bete and Playa del Carmen. Reservations, Turquoise Reef Group, Box 2664, Evergreen, CO 80439,* ☎ *303/674–9615 or 800/538–6802,* FAX *303/674–8735. 70 bungalows. Restaurant, bar, coffee shop, pool, beach, dive shop, snorkeling, fishing, shops, car rental. AE, MC, V.*

$$$–$$$$ 🏨 **Baal Nah Kah.** This elegant three-story guest house opened in late
★ 1996. A real home-away-from-home, it offers guests the use of a big kitchen, game room, sitting/living room, and barbecue pit. Baal Nah Kah, which means "family house in a village" in Maya, is a block from the beach and has five bedrooms and one studio on various levels, affording complete privacy. Some rooms have spacious balconies with a panoramic view of the ocean; all come with tile baths, two fans or air-conditioning, double or king–size beds, and Mexican decor. A small café serving breakfast, snacks, and light meals is next door. ⊠ *Calle 12 between Av 5 and Av. 1,* ☎ *98730110,* FAX *987/30050. Reservations, Turquoise Reef Group, Box 2664, Evergreen, CO 80439,* ☎ *303/674– 9615 or 800/538–6802,* FAX *303/674–8735. 5 rooms, 1 apartment. No credit cards except with advance payment in U.S.*

$$$ 🏨 **Albatros Royale.** The nicest complex right on the beach, the Royale opened in 1991 but still looks brand new. Two-story palapa-covered buildings face each other along a pathway to the sand, resembling a small village. Sea breezes and ceiling fans cool the small rooms, simply decorated with white walls and tile floors; five have a view of the ocean. Guests can have included in the price of the room a breakfast buffet across the street at the sister **Pelicano Inn** hotel (☞ *below*). The Royale fills up quickly; advance reservations are advised. ⊠ *Calle 8 between beach and Av. 5,* ☎ *987/30001,* FAX *987/30002. Reservations, Turquoise Reef Group, Box 2664, Evergreen, CO 80439,* ☎ *303/674– 9615 or 800/538–6802,* FAX *303/674–8735. 31 rooms. Restaurant, in-room safes, dive shop, travel services. MC, V.*

$$$ 🏨 **El Tucan Condotel.** This lodging in the residential north end of
★ town looks like a very exclusive and expensive hotel but actually is the best deal for your money in Playa. Catering to lots of German tour groups, it is set around a huge jungle garden with a pool, even a cenote, and winding flagstone paths and offers the ultimate in tranquility well away from the noise of downtown Avenida 5; however, it's a mere 10-minute walk to get there. All rooms and apartments in the slate-colored buildings are fairly well separated from one another and have lots of attractive tile—burnished brown tile floors and hand-painted flower tile sinks in the bathrooms, for example. Each has a private terrace, overhead fan, and tiny kitchenette; groceries can be purchased at a small shopping center nearby. A Continental breakfast is included. ⊠ *Av. 5 between Calles 14 and 16, Quintana Roo 77710,* ☎ *987/30417,* FAX *987/30668. 32 rooms, 24 apartments. Restaurant, bar, grocery, pool. MC, V.*

$$$ 🏨 **Las Molcas.** This pretty hotel, which used to have a pet monkey as its mascot (now living in retirement in Cozumel), is in downtown Playa a half block from the ferry pier and one block south of the plaza. It has a colonial-style lobby and hallways with red tile floors. Pleasant air-conditioned rooms face the pool, the sea, or the street and have dark wood furniture, tile floors, and terraces; a new array of shops selling everything from gold jewelry to Cuban cigars lines the street outside. The hotel dining room—modern and unremarkable, with some outdoor tables overlooking the plaza—is a safe bet for standard international fare. ⊠ *Av. 5 at Calle 1, Box 79, Quintana Roo 77710,* ☎ *987/30070,* 🅵🅰🆇 *987/30138. 24 rooms. Restaurant, bar, pool, shops, travel services, car rental. AE, MC, V.*

$$$ 🏨 **Las Palapas.** German manager Gunter Spath has made Las Pala-
★   pas into an ideal get-away-from-it-all destination resort with his friendly personality and Teutonic attention to detail. Many guests stay for 10 days or more (a 3-night minimum stay is required). White cabañas are trimmed in blue, and duplexes have balconies or porches and hammocks. The thatch roofs and hexagonal shape of the buildings enhance the ocean breezes, making air-conditioning unnecessary. German tour groups keep the hotel's occupancy up to 80% year-round; make reservations early. Room rates include breakfast and dinner (the buffets can be elaborate, but we've had reports that the food was disappointing in low season). ⊠ *Rte. 307, Km 292, Box 116, Playa del Carmen, Quintana Roo 77710,* ☎ *987/3–0582, 800/433–0885,* 🅵🅰🆇 *987/3–0458. 55 cabanas. Restaurant, 2 bars, in-room safes, pool, beach. MC, V.*

$$$ 🏨 **Pelicano Inn.** Formerly Cabañas Albatros, this rather austere-looking hotel has been completely restructured into 1- to 3-story beach villas. It reopened in November 1995 and is the sister hotel to the Albatros Royale. The entrance is an odd tunnel painted with scenes from the deep. Six rooms face the ocean directly; the other 32 have peek-a-boo views of the sea. All are fairly spacious and offer ceiling fans, private bathrooms, and double beds. Breakfast is included in the price of the room. ⊠ *On beach at Calle 8,* ☎ *987/30001,* 🅵🅰🆇 *987/30002. Reservations, Turquoise Reef Group, Box 2664, Evergreen, CO 80439,* ☎ *303/674–9615 or 800/538–6802,* 🅵🅰🆇 *303/674–8735. 38 rooms. Restaurant. MC, V.*

$$ 🏨 **Alejari.** This two-story complex set amid lush gardens is one of the pleasantest accommodations on Playa's north beach. Some rooms have kitchenettes and fans or air-conditioning. Breakfast comes with the room. ⊠ *Calle 6N, no phone. Reservations, Box 166, Playa del Carmen, Quintana Roo 77710,* ☎ *987/30374,* 🅵🅰🆇 *987/30005. 29 rooms. Restaurant, kitchenettes. MC, V.*

$$ 🏨 **Delfín.** Though not on the beach, the Delfín is a good choice for its bright, airy rooms cooled by sea breezes and fans. The ones on the street side can be a bit noisy, as most restaurants along the pedestrian zone play blaring music until about 11 PM. Everything you need is within immediate walking distance, and the management is exceptionally helpful. ⊠ *Av. 5 at Calle 6, Playa del Carmen, Quintana Roo 77710,* ☎ 🅵🅰🆇 *987/30176. 14 rooms. MC, V (5% fee).*

$$ 🏨 **Maya-Bric.** Larger than most beachfront hotels in Playa, the Maya-Bric has a pretty landscaped courtyard and pool area, which affords a pleasant escape from the hot sandy beach; the staff, however, could benefit from charm school. The rooms have fans, and are comfortable and basic, with few frills. Try to avoid the rooms overlooking the parking lot as they get all the street noise at night. The gates are locked at night, making this one of the most private places around. The on-site dive shop runs snorkeling, diving, and sightseeing trips to the nearby reefs. ⊠ *5a Av. Norte between Calles 8 and 10, Playa del Carmen, Quintana Roo 77710,* ☎ 🅵🅰🆇 *987/30011. 29 rooms. Breakfast room, pool, dive shop. No credit cards.*

$ ☎ **Elefante.** Three blocks from the beach, this two-story, family-run hotel is well kept and the best deal around for price; the only sore spot is the unkempt field you pass on the way to the rooms. All the bare bones units overlook a small plant-filled walkway and have tile floors and bathrooms, two double beds, and fans; some have kitchenettes. There's a restaurant down the street. ⊠ *Av. 12 and Calle 10,* ☎ *987/91987. 38 rooms. No credit cards.*

Nightlife and the Arts

Campers from across the street and Playa residents head for the **Cafe Sofía** (⊠ Calle 2 between the beach and Av. 5, no phone) for U.S. video movies shown daily at 3, 5:30, and 8 in the evening. The movies are free with consumption of food; the menu has light fare such as tortas, sandwiches, hamburgers, soft drinks, and fruit juices, and the restaurant is open 24 hours.

Outdoor Activities and Sports

DIVING

Playa del Carmen's scuba scene has grown considerably in the past few years. Most shops offer similar services, but the quality of the equipment and dive instructors varies; those listed below are known to be reliable. The oldest shop in town, **Tank Ha** (⊠ Maya-Bric hotel, ☎ FAX 987/30011), with PADI-certified teachers, arranges diving and snorkeling trips to the reefs and caverns. **Wet Dreams** (⊠ Albatros Royale hotel, ☎ 987/30001) also has certified, bilingual instructors. Other shops are at the Shangri-La Caribe, Las Palapas, Cabañas Albatros, and Continental Plaza Playacar hotels.

GOLF

The **Casa Club de Golf** clubhouse (⊠ Continental Plaza Playacar Hotel, ☎ 987/30100) can arrange for golf.

MOUNTAIN BIKING

There are bike paths between Playa del Carmen and Xcaret. Contact the Casa Club de Golf clubhouse (☞ *above*) for bike rentals.

Shopping

Avenida 5 between Calles 4 and Calle 10 is definitely the best place to shop in Playa if not along the whole coast. Pretty shops and boutiques have sophisticated offerings from all of Mexico and hand-painted batiks from Indonesia. Even the ubiquitous T-shirts sold here have exotically creative designs. All shops close in the afternoon between 1 and 5 following a long-established tradition of the coast, and then stay open until 9 at night.

Xop (⊠ Rincón del Sol, Av. 5 at Calle 8, no phone) is one of the best places on the coast for handcrafted wooden masks and statues and incredibly carved amber pendants, along with earrings, necklaces, and bracelets set with silver and semi-precious stones. **El Vuelo de los Niños Pajaros** (⊠ Rincón del Sol, Av. 5 at Calle 8, ☎ 987/30445) has a great selection of regional music on CD and tape, along with handcrafted paper, cards, incense, and beaded baskets. **Museum Shop** (⊠ Av. 5 between Calles 4 and 6, ☎ 987/30446) has simple but elegantly crafted amber jewelry by a German designer who also keeps a shop in Chiapas near the mines that provide the raw material. **La Calaca** (⊠ Av. 5 between Calles 6 and 8 and Av. 5 and Calle 4, ☎ 987/30177 for both locations) probably has the biggest selection of playful wooden devils and angels in Playa.

Off Avenida 5, try **Gaitan** (⊠ West side of main plaza, no phone), a branch of a respected Mexico City leather shop that sells vests, boots, belts, purses, and wallets. **Promoshow** (⊠ Calle 6 between Av. 5 and

Av. 10, ☎ 987/31202) sells pre-Hispanic music instruments such as tambors, flutes, ocarinas, rain sticks, and a "tepozazki" made from an armadillo shell; it also stocks famous hand-made guitars from Paracho, Michoacan. **Artesanías Margarita** (⊠ Calle 2 and Av. 5 , no phone) has exquisite hand-painted sun hats and wind chimes designed by Luis de Ocampo. **El Dorado** (⊠ Calle 1 between Av. 5 and the ferry pier in the Las Molcas Hotel shopping arcade, no phone) has replicas of pre-Hispanic Inca and Maya jewelry fashioned in silver dipped in gold.

Xcaret

❹ *6 km (4 mi) south of Playa del Carmen and 72 km (50 mi) south of Cancún.*

A paved road leads to Xcaret, a sacred Maya city and port that has been developed into a 250-acre ecological theme park on a gorgeous stretch of coastline. Maya ruins are scattered over the lushly landscaped property, a vivid green oasis set against gray limestone and the turquoise sea.

One highlight of the park is the underground river ride, where visitors don life jackets (snorkels, masks, and fins come in handy as well) and float with the cool water's currents through a series of caves. At the educational Dolphinarium, visitors can attend a dolphin workshop ($20) and even swim with the dolphins ($60); only 36 people are allowed in the water with them each day, so arrive early to sign up for your slot. An artificially created beach, breakwater, and lagoons are perfect for snorkeling and swimming; instruction and water-sports equipment rentals are available. Xcaret also includes a botanical garden, a museum with reproductions of the Yucatán peninsula's main archaeological sites, a tropical aquarium, wild bird sanctuary, stables with riding demonstrations, a dive shop, and several restaurants. Its Butterfly Pavilion is the world's largest. Plan on spending the entire day. Transportation is available from Cancún and Playa del Carmen on colorfully decorated buses.

A new nighttime attraction is a sound-and-light show and walk through a candle-lighted Maya village, altar, and underground passageway. The evening winds up with a folkloric flourish, its highlight an exhibition by the famed Flying Indians of Papantla who swing by their feet from a tall pole in an ages-old mystical prayer to the gods of nature. The show is presented daily at 6 PM; tickets can be purchased in advance from travel agencies and major hotels at Playa del Carmen or Cancún. ☎ 98/830632 or 98/830765. ⊡ *Theme park Mon.–Sat. $30, including show; Sun. $25 (no show).* ⊗ *May–Oct., daily 8:30–5; Nov.–Apr., daily 8:30–8:30.*

Dining

$ ✕ **Restaurant Xcaret.** This small palapa restaurant, its walls lined with photos from diving expeditions, serves conch ceviche, lobster, poc chuc, and french fries at prices far lower than those inside the Xcaret theme park. ⊠ *Hwy. 307 at Xcaret turnoff, no phone. No credit cards.*

Paamul

❺ *10 km (6 mi) south of Xcaret.*

Beachcombers and snorkelers are fond of Paamul, a crescent-shaped lagoon with clear, placid waters sheltered by the coral reef at the lagoon's mouth. Shells, sand dollars, and even glass beads—some from the sunken pirate ship at Akumal—wash onto the sandy parts of the beach. Trailer camps, cabañas, and tent camps are scattered along the shore; a restaurant sells cold beer and fresh fish; and in the summer visitors may view one of Paamul's chief attractions: sea turtle hatchlings on the beach. You can also take the jungle path to the north, which leads to a lagoon four times the size of the first and even more private.

Lodging

$$ 🏨 **Cabañas Paamul.** If you're looking for seclusion and comfort, you'll be thrilled with this small hostelry on a perfect white sand beach. Seven bungalows painted white and peach face the sea. All have two double beds and ceiling fans, and hot-water showers. The hotel turns Mexican holidays into fiestas for the guests, and there are activities galore. A large palapa houses the restaurant, and there is a small market just off the main highway at the road to the hotel. The property includes 190 camping sites for motor homes and tents, and a full-service dive shop. ✉ *Hwy. 307, Km 85. Reservations, Box 83, Playa del Carmen, Quintana Roo 77710,* ☎ *99/259422,* 🖷 *987/256913. 7 rooms. Restaurant, dive shop. No credit cards.*

Puerto Aventuras

⑥ *12 km (7 mi) south of Paamul.*

Puerto Aventuras is a 900-acre self-contained resort, initiated by developers in 1988 by blasting through limestone to create a marina and channels. Ultimately, there are plans for a 250-slip marina, tennis club, beach club, 18-hole golf course, shopping mall, movie theater, and five deluxe hotels with a total of 2,000 rooms. At press time, facilities in operation included several restaurants and shops, nine holes of the golf course, an excellent dive shop, and a 95-slip marina. In addition, the **underwater archaeology museum** displays models of old ships as well as coins, canons, sewing needles, and nautical devices recovered from Mexican waters by CEDAM (Mexican Underwater Explorers Club) members; it's open daily 10–1 and 2–6. Also in operation are three hotels and several condo and time-share units, built in a combination of Mediterranean, Caribbean, and Mexican architectural styles and spread along the golf course and marina. Currently, the entire complex is losing money, and some of the services are not up to par.

Dining and Lodging

$$ ✗ **Carlos 'n Charlie's.** Having a branch of this popular restaurant chain in town is a sign of true resort status. Carlos Anderson's restaurants are known for being wacky, wild, and rowdy and for serving ample portions of well-prepared barbecued ribs and chicken, enchiladas, *carne asada,* and other Mexican dishes, and powerful tequila drinks. ✉ *Commercial center, no phone. MC, V.*

$$$$ 🏨 **Club de Playa.** This 30-room hotel underwent extensive renovations in 1995 and has become part of the Colony Resorts chain. The spacious rooms have stunning views of the Caribbean, and the swimming pool seems to flow right into the sea. Guests have use of a fitness room, and one of the coast's best dive shops is on the property. Guests can also enjoy the facilities (including nine holes of golf) and restaurants at the Club Oasis hotel on the other side of the marina. ✉ *On beach near marina,* ☎ 🖷 *987/35100 for reservations. 30 rooms. Restaurant, pool, exercise room, dive shop, dock. AE, MC, V.*

$$$$ 🏨 **Club Oasis Puerto Aventuras.** Opened in 1992 by the Spanish company that owns luxury hotels worldwide, this large hotel bustles with European tour groups on great package deals. The hotel is all-inclusive, with meals, domestic drinks, and most activities included in the rates. Some rooms have whirlpool baths on their balconies and kitchenettes with microwaves. A shuttle bus runs to the golf course, commercial center, and marina. ⊠ *On beach at north end of complex. Reservations, 3520 Piedmont Rd. NE, Suite 325, Atlanta, GA 30305,* ☏ *987/35050 or 800/446–2747,* ℻ *987/35051 or 404/240–4039. 275 rooms. 2 restaurants, 2 bars, deli, kitchenettes, 2 pools, dive shop, shops, car rental, travel services. AE, MC, V.*

$$$$ ☒ **Continental Plaza Puerto Aventuras.** Situated on the marina a short distance from the beach, the Continental Plaza has a variety of rooms, many with kitchenettes. Most guest quarters are decorated in soft shades of blue and peach and feature French doors opening onto balconies overlooking the pool. The hotel has a shuttle service to the beach; restaurants, shops, and water sports services are within walking distance. ⊠ *Marina, Puerto Aventuras, Quintana Roo 77710,* ☏ *987/35133 or 800/882–6684,* ℻ *987/35134. 56 rooms. Restaurant, bar, pool, bicycles, car rental. AE, MC, V.*

Outdoor Activities and Sports

DIVING

Mike Madden's CEDAM Dive Centers (⊠ Club de Playa Hotel, ☏ 987/35147 or 987/35129, ℻ 987/41339) is a full-service dive shop with certification courses; cave and cenote diving is a specialty.

Xpuhá

❼ *9 km (5½ mi) south of Puerto Aventuras.*

The little fishing village of Xpuhá, where residents weave hammocks and harvest coconuts, can be found along a narrow sandy road off Route 307. Some small, overgrown pre-Hispanic ruins in the area still bear traces of paint on the inside walls. A cluster of pastel-colored hotel buildings sit on the beach; inexpensive rooms are available on a first-come, first-served basis, although the smaller properties close for September and October. Hammocks are for sale along the main highway.

Akumal

❽ *37 km (22 mi) south of Playa del Carmen and 102 km (59 mi) south of Cancún.*

The name Akumal, meaning "Place of the Turtle," recalls ancient Maya times, when the beach was the nesting ground for thousands of turtles. The place first attracted international attention in 1926, when explorers discovered the *Mantanceros,* a Spanish galleon that sank in 1741. Three decades later, Akumal became headquarters for the Mexican Underwater Explorers Club (CEDAM) and a gathering spot for wealthy underwater adventurers who flew in on private planes and searched the waters for sunken treasures. Mexican diver/businessman Pablo Bush Romero, a lover of this pristine coast, was the founder of both CEDAM and of the first resort in the area, which predated the development of Cancún.

The long curved bay and beach are rarely empty now, especially at lunchtime, when tour buses stop here en route from Tulum. Even so it's far less crowded than Cancún. Those who stay here are seeking the comforts of an international resort without the high-rises; Europeans—who tend to gravitate toward Mexico's quieter side—are coming in ever greater numbers.

Akumal consists of three distinct areas. Half Moon Bay to the north is lined with private homes and condominiums and has some of the prettiest beaches and best snorkeling in the area. Akumal proper consists of a large resort and small Maya community with a market, grocery stores, laundry facilities, and pharmacy. There's also an ecology center next to the dive shop with a staff of ecologists. More condos and homes and an all-inclusive resort are at Akumal Aventuras to the south. People come to this part of Akumel to dive or simply to walk on the deliciously long beaches filled with shells, crabs, and migrant birds.

First and foremost, however, Akumal is famous for its diving. Area dive shops sponsor resort courses and certification courses, and luxury hotels and condominiums offer year-round packages comprising airfare, accommodations, and diving (hotel rooms are at a premium during the high season, December 15–April, and reservations should be made well in advance. Lower prices can be had during the medium season from May 1 to September 16 and low season from September 17 to December 14). The reef, which is about 425 ft offshore, shelters the bay and its exceptional coral formations and sunken galleon; the sandy bottom invites snorkelers to wade out at the rocky north end, where they can view the diverse underwater topography. Deep-sea fishing for giant marlin, bonito, and sailfish is also popular.

❾ Devoted snorkelers may want to walk to **Yalkú,** a practically unvisited lagoon just north of Akumal along an unmarked dirt road. Wending its way out to the sea, Yalkú hosts throngs of parrot fish in superbly clear water with visibility to 160 ft, but it has no facilities.

Dining and Lodging

$$ ✕ **La Lunita.** Locals and enterprising tourists congregate at the indoor and patio tables of this converted one-bedroom condo at Half Moon Bay for good conversation and innovative cuisine. Regulars swear by the fresh fish served with a lime and cilantro sauce or smothered in tomatoes and onions. The conversation typically includes everyone in the place, and you're sure to pick up a few tips on local events and secret beaches. You'll need a car, a cab, or strong legs to reach this place, but it's worth it. ✉ *Hacienda de la Tortuga; go through entranceway at Club Akumal Caribe, then turn left (north) at dirt road to Half Moon Bay,* ☎ *987/22421 for condo office. No credit cards.*

$$$$ ☷ **Club Oasis Akumal.** An all-inclusive luxury hotel managed by the Spanish hotel group Oasis, this sprawling property started as the private preserve of millionaire Pablo Bush Romero, a friend of Jacques Cousteau. Today the beach—protected by an offshore reef—and the pier are used as the starting point for canoeing, snorkeling, diving, fishing, and windsurfing jaunts. The U-shaped building, with nautical decor, has handsome mahogany furniture and sunken blue-tile showers between Moorish arches (no doors!). All rooms have balconies (you can choose a sea view or a garden view) and air-conditioning or ceiling fans (same price). The clientele consists primarily of Americans and Canadians on package deals, though non-group guests are also welcome. *Reservations, 3520 Piedmont Rd. NE, Suite 325, Atlanta, GA 30305,* ☎ *987/22828 or 800/446–2747,* ℻ *987/35051 or 404/240–5500. 120 rooms. Restaurant, 2 bars, 2 pools, tennis court, beach, dive shop, shops, recreation room, travel services, car rental. AE, MC, V.*

$$$$ ☷ **Hacienda de la Tortuga.** One of several condominium projects lining the shores of Half Moon Bay north of Akumal, this small complex on the beach has one- and two-bedroom units with tile kitchens and baths. Housekeeping service is part of the arrangement. The dive shops and restaurants at Club Akumal Caribe are within walking distance. ✉ *Dirt road about 10 min north of Club Akumal Caribe. Reservations,* ✉ *Box 18, Puerto Aventuras, Quintana Roo 77710,* ☎ *987/30858 or 800/521–2980,* ℻ *987/30989 or 810/683–5076. 9 condos. Restaurant, kitchenettes, pool. AE, MC, V.*

$$$$ ☒ **Villas de las Palmas.** Expatriate Americans Daniel Mincey and Karen Jenkins handle reservations and assist guests at several two-bedroom, two-bath condominiums along the beach just south of Club Oasis. The area is peaceful, and the units are a reasonably priced alternative for those wanting privacy, comfort, and the sense of being in a home away from home. *Reservations, ✉ Box 124, Playa del Carmen, Quintana Roo 77710, ☎ 987/41886, FAX 987/12092. 4 condo complexes. No credit cards.*

$$$ ☒ **Club Akumal Caribe & Villas Maya.** Accommodations at this resort, situated on the edge of a cove overlooking a small harbor, range from rustic but comfortable bungalows with red tile roofs and garden views (Villas Maya) to beachfront rooms in a modern three-story hotel building. All have air-conditioning, ceiling fans, and refrigerators. Also available are the more secluded one-, two-, and three-bedroom condominiums called the Villas Flamingo, on Half Moon Bay and 1 km (½ mi) from the beach. The bungalows and hotel rooms are cheerfully furnished in rattan and dark wood, with attractive tile floors; the high-domed, Mediterranean-style condominium units have kitchens and balconies or terraces overlooking the pool and beach. The property began as a few thatched cottages built for CEDAM, the Mexican divers' organization, and it still emphasizes diving. Two dive shops offer resort courses, PADI certification, and cenote or cave diving; snorkeling, windsurfing, kayaking, and deep-sea fishing are also available. The best of the three restaurants is **Lol Ha:** The grilled steak and seafood dinner entrées are bountiful. An optional meal plan includes breakfast and dinner. *✉ Hwy. 307, Km 104, ☎ 987/2–2532. Reservations, Akutrame, Box 13326, El Paso, TX 79913, ☎ 915/584–3552 or 800/351–1622, 800/343–1440 in Canada. 21 rooms, 40 bungalows, 4 villas, 5 condos. 3 restaurants, bar, grocery, ice cream parlor, pizzeria, snack bar, pool, beach, 2 dive shops, shops. AE, MC, V.*

Outdoor Activities and Sports

DIVING

Akumal Dive Center rents equipment, runs dive trips, and has certification programs. For dive packages, including accommodations, contact Akutrame Inc. (✉ Box 13326, El Paso, TX 79913, ☎ 915/584–3552 or 800/351–1622; in Canada, 800/343–1440). There is a **Mike Madden dive shop** at the Aventuras Akumal (☎ 987/22828).

Chemuyil

🔟 *7 km (4½ mi) south of Akumal.*

You can stop for lunch and a swim at the little cove at Chemuyil. The crescent-shaped beach, which has been declared an official sea turtle reserve, is popular with tour groups and campers who pitch their tents under the few remaining palms (most were destroyed by disease and have not been replaced). Fresh seafood is served here for lunch by a modest eatery on the beach.

Laguna de Xcacel

⓫ *7½ km (5 mi) south of Chemuyil.*

The Laguna de Xcacel perches on a sandy ridge overlooking yet another long white beach. A sunken ship sits offshore at the south end of the beach and farther into the surrounding jungle, there's a cenote for a cool dip. During the summer month, a sea-turtle protection program in force with beach patrols and turtle tagging. The calm waters of the beach provide excellent swimming, snorkeling, diving, and fishing; birders and beachcombers like to stroll in the early morning.

Camping is permitted, and there's a restaurant (closed Sunday) on the site. Tour buses full of cruise-ship passengers stop here for lunch, and the showers and dressing rooms get crowded at dusk.

Xel-Há

⑫ *2 km (about 1 mi) south of Laguna de Xcacel.*

Now managed by the same people that run Xcaret, Xel-Há (pronounced zhel-hah) is a natural aquarium cut out of the limestone shoreline. The national park consists of several interconnected lagoons where countless species of tropical fish breed; the rocky coastline curves into bays and coves in which enormous parrot fish cluster around an underwater Maya shrine. Several low wooden bridges over the lagoons have benches at regular points, so you can take in the sights at leisure. Though much of the fauna used to be threatened by suntan oil and garbage, 1995's hurricane Roxanne cleaned out the pollution, and wearing sun tan lotion is strictly forbidden, so now the waters are remarkably clear. Certain areas are off-limits to swimmers, but because the lagoons are quite large, in places you can swim fairly far out, or you can explore one of the underwater caves or the cenotes deep in the jungle. Lockers and dressing rooms are available, and you can buy snorkel gear (it is not available for rent) and underwater cameras (the $18 fee includes a roll of film).

The park holds other attractions as well. A shrine stands at the entrance, and there are other small Maya ruins throughout, including one named **Na Balaam** for a yellow jaguar painted on one of its walls. There is also a huge but overpriced souvenir shop, food stands, and a small museum housing artifacts from pre-Hispanic days. The enormous parking lot attests to the number of visitors who come here; you should plan to arrive in the early morning before all the tour-bus traffic hits. For a pleasant breakfast or lunch you may want to try one of the five restaurants, which all serve reasonably good ceviche, fresh fish, and drinks. ☎ 98/833280. ⌦ $10. ☺ *Daily 8–5.*

Tan-Kah

⑬ *9½ km (6 mi) south of Xel-Há.*

In the depths of the jungle stands a small grouping of pre-Hispanic structures that cover 10 square km (4 square mi) and once comprised a satellite city of Tulum. Tan-kah, as the place is known, has still not been fully explored, and while the buildings themselves may not warrant much attention, a curious bit of more recent history does. In the 1930s an airstrip was built here; Charles Lindbergh, who was making an aerial survey of the coast, was one of the first to land on it.

Tulum

⑭ *2 km (about 1 mi) south of Tan-kah, 130 km (80 mi) south of Cancún.*

One of the Caribbean coast's biggest attractions, Tulum is the Yucatán Peninsula's most visited Maya ruin, attracting more than 2 million people annually. It's the largest Maya city built on the coast, and the spectacle of those gray limestone temples against the blue-green Caribbean waters is nothing less than riveting. The modern name for the site, "Tulum" means "wall." The pre-Hispanic name was "Zama" from *zamul* (dawn), because the city faced the sunrise over the ocean.

Tulum entered a new phase in 1994 when an ecological park project was launched by private investors to save the site from further deterioration. The entrance and parking lot were moved away from the ruins.

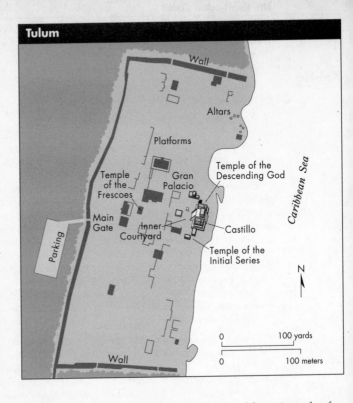

Tulum

In the past, tour buses and cars spewed noise and fumes just a few feet away from the crumbling temples. Now even the highway turnoff is new, and an enormous paved lot has separate designated areas for cars ($2 fee) and buses. Esthetically speaking, however, the new entrance is an eyesore. An enormous cement slab building is filled with burger joints and tacky shops selling the requisite overpriced T-shirts and junky souvenirs. An electric shuttle car costing $1 each way hustles visitors to the temples; otherwise it's a ½ km (¼ mi) hike. Clay reproductions of Maya gods, machine-produced serapes with pyramid designs, and wood carvings are laid out on the side of the road where the shuttle stops.

You can hire a guide to the ruins at the stand near the shuttle stop. Visitors are no longer allowed to climb or enter Tulum's most impressive buildings (only three, described below, really merit close inspection), so you can see the ruins in two hours. You may, however, wish to allow extra time for a swim or a stroll on the beach, where it's likely that the ancient Maya beached their canoes.

Tulum is the only Maya city known to have been inhabited when the conquistadors arrived. Juan de Grijalva and his men, who spotted it from their ships in 1518, were so intimidated by the enormity of its vivid 25-ft-high blue, white, and red walls that they were reluctant to land. What they had seen was four towns so close to one another that they appeared to be one continuous metropolis. The Postclassical (AD 900–1541) architecture at Tulum evinces strong influences of the Toltecs as a result of the encroaching empire of central Mexico. Although artistic refinements found elsewhere in the Maya world are missing here, the site is well preserved.

Tulum has long held special significance for the Maya. A key city in the League of Mayapán (AD 987–1194), it was never conquered by the Spaniards, although it was abandoned about 75 years after the Conquest. For 300 years thereafter, it symbolized the defiance of an otherwise subjugated people; it was one of the last outposts of the Maya during their insurrection against Mexican rule in the 1840s War of the Castes. Uprisings continued intermittently until 1935, when the Maya ceded Tulum to the government.

Tulum's fortifications attest to its military importance. It may once have been home to 2,000 people living in houses set on man-made platforms along the main artery. John L. Stephens, an American explorer, came upon Tulum in 1842, and his traveling companion, Frederick Catherwood, sketched its magnificence. Those sketches eventually illustrated a book by Stephens, which became the archaeological Bible of its time.

Visitors enter the archaeological site through a low limestone gateway in a crumbling wall. Even the Maya, who are typically short of stature, have to duck their heads. Apparently the design forced those who entered to bow in deference to the divinities within. Low-lying structures dot the site's 60-acre grassy field, wrapped on three sides by a 3,600-ft-long wall. Tulum's buildings seem unremarkable at first glance.

The first significant structure is the two-story **Temple of the Frescoes,** to the left of the entryway. The temple's vaulted roof and corbeled arch are examples of Classical Maya architecture. Faint traces of blue-green frescoes outlined in black on the inner and outer walls refer to ancient Maya beliefs (the clearest frescoes are hidden from sight now that visitors aren't allowed to walk into the temple). Reminiscent of the Mixtec style, the frescoes depict the three worlds of the Maya and their major deities, and are decorated with stellar and serpentine patterns, rosettes, and ears of maize and other offerings to the gods. One scene portrays the rain god seated on a four-legged animal—probably a reference to the Spaniards on their horses.

The largest and most famous building, the **Castillo** (castle), looms at the edge of a 40-ft limestone cliff just past the Temple of the Frescoes. Atop the castle, at the end of a broad stairway, sits a temple with stucco ornamentation on the outside and traces of fine frescoes inside the two chambers. (The stairway has been roped off, so it's no longer possible to walk through the top temple.) The front wall of the Castillo has faint carvings of the Descending God and columns depicting the plumed serpent god, Kukulcán, who was introduced to the Maya by the Toltecs. The regal structure overlooks the rest of Tulum and an expanse of dense jungle to the west; the blue Caribbean blocks access from the east. Footpaths are etched at the sides of the castillo wherever it's possible to catch a snapshot of the ruins against the sea. Researchers think the Castillo may have functioned as a watchtower to monitor enemy approaches by sea.

To the left of the Castillo is the **Temple of the Descending God**—so called for the carving of a winged god plummeting to earth over the doorway. The same deity is seen in stucco masks in the corners, and is thought either to be Ab Muzen Cab, the bee god, or to be associated with the planet Venus, guardian of the coast and of commerce.

The other buildings at the site typically have flat roofs resting on wood beams and columns. The architecture is considered commonplace, with few distinguishing features. Buildings were laid out along straight streets running the length of the site with a slight dip, or culvert, between two gentle slopes. The tiny cove to the left of the Castillo and Temple of the Descending God is a good spot for a cooling swim, but there are no changing rooms. A few small altars sit atop a hill at the north side of the cove and have a good view of the Castillo and the sea. ☎ *$5.50, free Sun. and holidays, parking $2, use of video camera $8.* ☉ *Daily 8–5.*

Tourist services are clustered at the old turnoff from Route 307 to the ruins, marked by restaurants and two hotels. The new road is a few yards farther south and is clearly marked with overhead signs. Still farther south is the turnoff for the Boca Paila Peninsula, the Sian Ka'an preserve, and several small waterfront hotels. The fourth turnoff you'll come to, about 4 km (2½ mi) south of the ruins, is for the present-day village of Tulum. The highway at the entrance to town has been widened to four lanes, and street lamps placed down the middle. As Tulum's importance as a commercial center increases, markets, auto-repair shops, and other businesses continue to spring up along the road. Growth has not been kind to the pueblo, however, and it has become rather unsightly and congested.

Dining and Lodging

$$ ✕ **Casa Cenote.** Don't miss this outstanding restaurant beside a large
★ cenote—this one's a mini-pool of fresh and salt water full of tropical fish. In fact, work up an appetite with a pre-meal swim in the cenote. With luck you may spot one of the three resident manatees, bashful critters who would prefer to be left in peace. Follow up with a spot of snorkeling in the sea, then rest in the shade under the restaurant's uniquely designed palapa roof—note the absence of center support. The restaurant's beef, chicken, and cheese are imported from the United States, and the burgers, chicken fajitas, and nachos are superb. On Sunday afternoon the expats living along the coast gather at Casa Cenote for a lavish barbecue featuring ribs, chicken, beef brisket, or lobster kebabs. The restaurant operates without electricity or a generator (perishables are packed in ice coolers) and closes at dark. ⊠ *Dirt road off Rte. 307, between Xel-Há and Tulum, no phone. Reservations not accepted. No credit cards.*

$$$ ✕🏨 **Cabañas Ana y José.** Several two-story buildings face the beach
★ at this small, well-loved hotel south of the ruins, owned by a Mexican couple who left the big city to build this retreat at the edge of the Sian Ka'an Biosphere Reserve. All rooms have fans, tile floors, hot-water showers, and hammock hooks; those on the second floor are cooler, thanks to the sea breezes. A new suite was added to this floor in 1995. The restaurant ($) is one of the best along this road, and management is more than helpful. Mountain bikes are available for rent, making it easy for those without cars to visit the ruins and secluded beaches in the area. The electricity goes on only five hours a day between 5 in the afternoon and 10 at night. ⊠ *Dirt road off Rte. 307 between ruins entrance and Tulum pueblo, 4 mi south of ruins, Box 15, Tulum, Quintana Roo 77780, ☎ 98/806022, FAX 98/806021. 16 rooms. Restaurant. No credit cards.*

$ ✕🏨 **Acuario.** This hotel and restaurant at the turnoff for the Tulum ruins has large, clean rooms with satellite TV, screen windows, ceiling fans, and hot water; the pool may be filled by the time you get here. The **Acuario** restaurant ($$) is well worth a visit because the owner takes pride in the preparation and quality of the food. Although the diner-like setting is unimpressive, Acuario offers a menu that includes above-average seafood, soup, tacos, nachos, guacamole, salads, and really good coconut ice cream. Buses to and from Playa del Carmen stop at Acuario's parking lot, and the management can arrange rental cars. ⊠ *Crucero de las Ruinas de Tulum, Hwy. 307, Km 127, Box 80, Tulum, Quintana Roo 77780, ☎ 98/844856. 27 rooms. Restaurant, bar, grocery, pool, shops. No credit cards.*

$ ▦ **Cabañas Tulum.** This property, idyllically situated in a coconut grove on a beach, is 7 km (4 mi) south of the Tulum ruins on the dirt road leading to Boca Paila. Eighteen palapa bungalows with private bathrooms (but without fans), and an indoor-outdoor restaurant, bar, and game room make a good package. ✉ *Box 10, Tulum, Quintana Roo 77780,* ☎ *98/258295. 18 cabanas. Restaurant, bar, recreation room. No credit cards.*

Shopping

The **Mercado de los Artesanías** at the Tulum ruins contains at least 50 stalls displaying woven rugs, clay reproductions of Maya gods, and a wide array of tacky souvenirs.

Cobá

⑮ *37 km (22½ mi) northwest of Tulum and 167 km (109 mi) southwest of Cancún.*

Beautiful but barely explored, Cobá was once one of the most important city-states in the entire Maya domain. It now stands in solitude; the spell this remoteness casts is intensified by the silence at the ruins, broken occasionally by the shriek of a spider monkey or the call of a bird. Processions of huge army ants cross the footpaths, and the sun penetrates the tall hardwood trees, ferns, and giant palms with fierce shafts of light. Cobá exudes the still, eerie ambience of a dead city.

The site is not inaccessible, however. Cobá is a 35-minute drive northwest of Tulum down a well-marked and well-paved road that leads straight through the jungle. Two tiny pueblos, **Macario Gómez** and **Balché,** with their clusters of thatch-roofed white huts, are the only signs of habitation en route. Both settlements have small markets. There is a tourist rest area en route to Cobá called **Lolche;** its entrance is marked by a parking lot and a tall wooden statue of a *campesino* (farmer) bearing a rifle. Inside, a large artisan's market is packed with pottery and hammocks. Check out the carved wooden jaguars, Cobá's signature souvenir. Cold drinks and snacks are sold at a small stand, and there are clean rest rooms. ☉ *Daily 6–6.*

Archaeologists estimate that some 6,500 structures are present in the Cobá area, but only 5% have been uncovered, and it will take decades before the work is completed. Discovered by Teobert Maler in 1891, Cobá was subsequently explored in 1926 by the Carnegie Institute but not excavated until 1972. At present there is no restoration work under way.

The city flourished from AD 400 to 1100, probably boasting a population of as many as 40,000 inhabitants. Situated on five lakes between coastal watchtowers and inland cities, its temple-pyramids towered over a vast jungle plain; one of them is 138 ft tall, the largest and highest in northern Yucatán. Cobá (meaning "ruffled waters") exercised economic control over the region through a network of at least 16 *sacbeob* (white stone roads), one of which, measuring 100 km (62 mi), is the longest in the Maya world. Cobá's massive, soaring structures and sheer size—the city once covered 210 square km (81 square mi)—made it a noteworthy sister nation to Tikal in northern Guatemala, to which it apparently had close cultural and commercial ties.

The main groupings are separated by several miles of intense tropical vegetation, so the only way to get a sense of the immensity of the city is to scale one of the pyramids. Maps and books about the ruins are sold at the makeshift restaurants and shops that line the parking lot. None of the maps are particularly accurate, and unmarked side trails lead temptingly into the jungle. Stay on the main, marked paths unless you have a guide; several men with guide licenses congregate by the entrance and offer their services. When you go, bring plenty of bug repellent, and, if you plan to spend some time here, bring a canteen of water (you can also buy sodas and snacks at the entrance).

The first major grouping, off a path to your right as you enter the ruins, is the **Cobá Group,** whose pyramids are built around a sunken patio. At the near end of the group, facing a large plaza, you'll see the 79-ft-high Iglesia (church), where some Indians still place offerings and light candles in hopes of improving their harvests. If you have strong legs and want a great view, scale this ruin—unless you want to save your energy for the far taller Nohoch Mul (☞ *below*).

Farther along the main path to your left is the **Chumuc Mul Group,** little of which has been excavated. The principal pyramid here is covered with the stucco remains of vibrantly painted motifs (*chumuc mul* means "stucco pyramid").

A kilometer (approximately ½ mile) past this site is the **Nohoch Mul (Large Hill) Group,** the highlight of which is the pyramid of the same name, the tallest at Cobá. The pyramid, which has 120 steps—equivalent to 12 stories—shares a plaza with Temple 10. The Descending God (also seen at Tulum) is depicted on a facade of the temple atop Nohoch Mul, from which the view is excellent; the temple seems to have been erected much later than the pyramid itself. It was from the base of this pyramid that the longest sacbe started; it extended all the way to Yaxuná, 20 km (12 mi) southwest of Chichén Itzá. Because of their great width (up to 33 ft), there is considerable speculation about the function of the sacbeob. The Maya had no beasts of burden; they carried all cargo on their own backs. Thus the roads may have been designed to allow people to walk abreast in processions, suggesting that they played a role in religion as well as in trade. The unrestored **Crossroad Pyramid** opposite Nohoch Mul was the meeting point for three sacbeob.

Beyond the Nohoch Mul Group is the **Castillo** (castle); its nine chambers are reached by a stairway. To the south are the remains of a ball court, including the stone ring through which the ball was hurled. From the main route follow the sign to **Las Pinturas Group,** named for the still discernible polychromatic friezes on the inner and outer walls of its large, patioed pyramid. An enormous stela here depicts a man standing with his feet on two prone captives. Take the minor path for a km (⅔ mi) to the **Macanxoc Group,** not far from the lake of the same name. The main pyramid at Macanxoc is accessible by a stairway. The portal of the temple at its summit is divided by a column; there are also a molded lintel and the remains of a stucco painting. Many of the stelae here are intricately carved with dates and other symbols of the history of Cobá.

Devotees of archaeology may wish to venture farther to the small **Kukulcán Group,** one of the larger satellites of Cobá, positioned just 5½ km (3½ mi) south of the Cobá group. Only five structures remain, and they are among the more puzzling ruins in the Maya world; their design and use have yet to be explained by archaeologists. The three-story temple is particularly intriguing because it is the only Maya structure in which the top story does not rest on filled-in lower stories.

Cobá can be comfortably visited in a half day, but if you want to spend the night, opt for the Villa Arqueológica Cobá (☞ Dining and Lodging, *below*), operated by Club Med and only a 10-minute walk from the site along the shores of Lake Cobá. Spending the night is highly advised—the nighttime jungle sounds will lull you to sleep, and you'll be able to visit the ruins in solitude when they open at 8 AM. Even on a day trip, consider taking time out for lunch and a swim at the Villa—an oasis of French civilization—after the intense heat and mosquito-ridden humidity of the ruins. Buses depart Cobá for Playa del Carmen and Valladolid twice daily. Check with your hotel and clerk at the ruins for times, which may not be exact. ☎ $6.50, free Sun. ☉ Daily 8–5.

Dining and Lodging

$$ ✕⊡ **Villa Arqueológica Cobá.** This Club Med property, a 10-minute
★ walk from the entrance to the Cobá ruins, overlooks one of the region's vast lakes, where turtles swim to the hotel's dock for a breakfast of bread and rolls. Tastefully done in white stucco and red paint, with bougainvillea hanging from the walls and museum-quality pieces throughout the property, the hotel has a clean, airy feel; corridors in the square, two-story building face a small pool and bar. The air-conditioned rooms are small but they feel cozy, not claustrophobic. A handsome library, housing books on the Maya and paperback novels, also contains a large VCR and a pool table. Dining choices near the isolated Cobá ruins are quite limited, so the restaurant here is an attractive option, though it should not be judged by the rather large, impersonal, and formal dining room. The food is very good (it's not included in the room rates as at most Club Med properties). For regional fare, try the grouper, ceviche, shrimp, *pollo píbil* (chicken baked in banana leaves), or enchiladas. On the more international side are pâtés, salad niçoise, marinated artichokes, and a superb chocolate mousse. *Reservations,* ☎ *800/258–2633,* ☎ 𝔽𝔸𝕏 *987/42087 in Cobá. 40 rooms. Restaurant, bar, pool, tennis court, shops. AE, MC, V.*

$ ✕⊡ **El Bocadito.** Though nowhere near as lavish as the Villa Arqueológica (☞ *above*), El Bocadito is a friendly, satisfactory budget alternative and only a five-minute walk from the ruins. The simple, tiled rooms fill up quickly—if you're thinking of spending the night, stop here before visiting the ruins. There is no hot water, and only fans to combat the heat, but the camaraderie of the clientele and staff make up for the discomforts. The restaurant is decent, clean, and popular with tour groups. ⊠ *On road to ruins, APDO 56, Valladolid, Yucatán 97780, no phone. 8 rooms. No credit cards.*

Sian Ka'an and the Boca Paila Peninsula

⓰ *15 km (9½ mi) south of Tulum to Punta Allen turnoff, located within Sian Ka'an; 137 km (84 mi) south of Cancún.*

Sian Ka'an, meaning "where the sky is born," was first settled by the Xiu tribe from Central America in the 5th century BC. In 1986 the Mexican Government established the 1.3-million-acre Sian Ka'an Biosphere Reserve as an internationally protected area; the next year, it was named a World Heritage Site by the United Nations Educational, Scientific, and Cultural Organization (UNESCO). In 1996 the reserve was extended by 200,000 acres.

The Man and the Biosphere program at UNESCO, of which this is part, was created to preserve biologically rich areas of the earth and promote the sustainable use of their natural resources. The reserves are particularly important in developing countries, where, for large segments of the population, encroaching on dwindling resources is the only way they know to survive. Maintaining and preserving the ecological diversity of these areas while educating the local people to do likewise is the challenge of the biosphere program.

Under the program, the land is divided for various purposes, including research, preservation, and economic activities in conjunction with conservation. Assisted by scientists, the local population makes a living through fishing, lobster harvests, and small farming and receives support from the low-impact tourism, biological research, and sustainable development programs.

The Sian Ka'an reserve constitutes 10% of the land in Quintana Roo and covers 100 km (62 mi) of coast. Freshwater and coastal lagoons, mangrove swamps, watery cays, savannahs, tropical forests, a barrier reef, hundreds of species of local and migratory birds, fish, other animals and plants, and fewer than 1,000 local residents—primarily Maya—share this area, one of the last undeveloped stretches of coastline in North America. Some of the approximately 27 sites of ruins scattered about are linked by a unique canal system—the only one of its kind in the Maya world in Mexico.

It's possible to see the reserve via guided tour: These can be arranged through the private, nonprofit **Amigos de Sian Ka'an** organization (⌧ Plaza América, Av. Cobá 5, Suites 48–50, Cancún, QR 77500, ☎ 98/849583, ⨎ℵ 98/873080). You'll get an excellent, informed tour; highlights include visiting a Maya temple and jumping off the boat into one of the channels to float downstream in the current.

The best way to explore on your own is to enter via the Punta Allen turnoff, south of Cancún on the coastal road; you'll be on a secluded 35-km (22-mi) coastal strip of land that is part of the reserve.

The narrow, rough dirt road down the peninsula is dotted with fishing lodges and deserted palapas and copra farms. It ends at **Punta Allen**, a fishing village whose main catch is spiny lobster, which was becoming scarce until ecologists taught the local fishing cooperative how to build and lay special traps to conserve the species. There are several small guest houses, but the road is filled with potholes; in the rainy season it may be completely impassable. Most fishing lodges along the way close for the rainy season in August and September, and accommodations are hard to come by. If you haven't booked ahead and want to explore, start out early in the morning so you can get back to civilization before dark.

Many species of the once-flourishing wildlife have fallen into the endangered category, but the waters here still teem with rooster fish, bonefish, mojarra, snapper, shad, permit, sea bass, and crocodiles. Fishing the flats for the wily bonefish and fly-fishing are especially popular, and the peninsula's few lodges run deep-sea fishing trips. Birders take launches out to **Cayo Culebra** (Rattlesnake Cay) or to **Isla de Pájaros** to view the pelicans, frigate birds, woodpeckers, sparrow hawks, and some of the 15 species of heron and egret. The beaches are wide and white, and although many of the palms have succumbed to the yellowing palm disease imported from Florida, the beautiful vegetation is growing back. Adventuresome travelers can explore some of the waterways' myriad caves or trek out to the tiny ruins of **Muyil** (☞ *below*).

Lodging

$$$$ 🏨 **Boca Paila Fishing Lodge.** This enclave of nine spacious cottages in the midst of the Sian Ka'an Biosphere Reserve offers clean, bright, and cheerful accommodations that include the basics: bed, dresser, and nightstand on tile floors. Catering principally to anglers, the lodge provides boats and guides for fly-fishing and bonefishing; guests can bring their own tackle or rent some at the lodge. Maya specialties, such as pollo píbil, are served at mealtime. (Meals are included in room rate.) A transfer service to and from the Cancún airport is available at an extra charge, or clients can rent a car in Cancún and drive to the lodge. A one week reservation with 50 % payment is required in the high season; bookings may be for less than a week during the low season. ⊠ *Boca Paila peninsula, no phone. Reservations, Frontiers, Box 959, Wexford, PA 15090, ☎ 412/935–1577 or 800/245–1950, ℻ 412/935–5388. 9 cottages. Restaurant, 2 bars. No credit cards.*

$$$$ ☒ **Caphé-Ha.** Built as a private home by an American architect, this
★ small guest house—between a lagoon and the ocean—is a perfect place to stay if you're interested in bonefishing or bird-watching. A two-bedroom house with kitchen, bath, and living room or a two-unit bungalow with shared bath are your choices; though neither has fans or electricity, all the windows have screens and catch the ocean breeze. A caretaker/chef from Mérida cooks meals that are served in the solar-powered community palapa; he will prepare vegetarian meals upon request. Fishing tackle and snorkeling gear are available from the property's small dock, but there's an extra charge for bonefishing. The room rates include breakfast and dinner; advance reservations must be accompanied by a 50% deposit, and a three-day or longer stay is required during high season. ⊠ *30 km (19 mi) south of Tulum, on road to Sian Ka'an, 5 km (3 mi) past bridge at Boca Paila and around next rocky point, ☎ 610/912–9392 for reservations. 1 villa, 1 bungalow. Dining room, fishing. No credit cards.*

$$$$ ☒ **Casa Blanca Lodge.** Punta Pájaros, to which this remote fishing re-
★ sort provides unique access, is reputed to be one of the best places in the world for light-tackle saltwater fishing. The American-managed, all-inclusive lodge—just 100 ft from the ocean—is set on a rocky outcrop covered with palm trees. Bonefish swarm in the mangrove swamps, flats, and shallow waters. The lodge's nine large, modern guest rooms, painted white with turquoise trim, and featuring slatted windows and tile and mahogany bathrooms, provide a pleasant tropical respite at dusk. An open-air thatched bar and a large living and dining area welcome anglers with drinks, fresh fish dishes, fruit, and vegetables at the start and end of the day. Rates are highest from March through June, lowest from January through March; the lodge is closed September through December, but will open during that time for groups of four or more. To get here, you must take a charter flight from Cancún to the Punta Pájaros airstrip, or rent a car in Cancún and drive to Punta Allen (three hours). From there, it's a one-hour boat trip across the bay. A one-week reservation and 50% prepayment are required during high season. *Reservations,* ⊠ *Frontiers, Box 959, Wexford, PA 15090, ☎ 412/935–1577 or 800/245–1950, ℻ 412/935–5388. 9 rooms. Restaurant, bar, fishing. No credit cards.*

Muyil

⑰ *43 km (27 mi) south of the marked Boca Paila turnoff on Route 307.*

The name of the archaeological site of Chunyaxché has been changed back into its ancient name of Muyil. Dating from the Late Preclassical era (300 BC–AD 200), it was connected by road to the sea and served as a port between Cobá and the Maya centers in Belize and Guatemala. A 15-ft-wide sacbe, built during the Late Postclassical period (AD 1250–1600), extended from the city to the mangrove swamp; today the remains of the sacbe get flooded during the rainy season. Structures were erected at 400-ft intervals along the white limestone road, almost all of them facing west. At the beginning of this century, the ancient stones were used to build a chicle (gum) plantation, which was managed by one of the leaders of the War of the Castes. Today, all that stands are the remains of the 56-ft **Castillo temple-pyramid**—one of the tallest on the Quintana Roo coast—at the center of a big patio.

From its summit you can see the Caribbean, 15 km (9 mi) in the distance. Muyil sits on the edge of a deep blue lagoon and is surrounded by a nearly impenetrable jungle inhabited by wildcats, white-tailed deer, wild boars, raccoons, badgers, pheasants, wild turkeys, ducks, herons, and parakeets. You can swim or fish in the lagoon. ☎ *$6.50, free Sun. and holidays.* ☉ *Daily 8–5.*

Felipe Carrillo Puerto

⑱   *24 km (15 mi) south of Muyil.*

The town of Felipe Carrillo Puerto is named for a local hero who preached rebellion. In 1920 Carrillo Puerto became governor of Yucatán and instituted a series of reforms to help the impoverished campesinos; these led to his assassination by the alleged henchman of the presidential candidate of an opposing party. Formerly known as Chan Santa Cruz, this town also played a central role in the 19th-century War of the Castes, during which it was not only a significant political and military center but also a religious capital. It was here that what became known as the Talking Cross first appeared, carved into a cedar tree near a cenote. The Indian priest Manuel Nahuat, translating from behind a curtain, interpreted the cross as a sign for the Indians to attack the *dzulob* (white Christians). Although Mexican soldiers cut down the tree and destroyed the cross, the Indians made other crosses from the trunk and placed them in neighboring villages, including Tulum. By 1904 half the local population had been annihilated in the war.

Today, the town exists primarily as the hub of three highways, and the only vestige of the momentous events of the last century is the small, uncompleted temple (on the edge of town in an inconspicuous, poorly marked park) begun by the Indians in the 1860s and now a monument to the War of the Castes. The church where the Talking Cross was originally housed also stands. Several humble hotels, some good restaurants, and a gas station may be incentives for stopping here on your southbound trek.

Dining and Lodging

$ ✕🏨 **El Faisán y El Venado.** Given the paucity of hotels in Felipe Carrillo Puerto, this one is your best bet. It's bare-bones, but you can choose between rooms with air-conditioning or with ceiling fans; they also come with color or black-and-white TVs and refrigerators. The pleasant restaurant does brisk business with locals at lunchtime because it is so centrally located. Yucatecan specialties such as poc chuc, *bistec a la yucateca* (Yucatecan-style steak), and pollo píbil are served in a simple but rustically decorated setting. ✉ *Av. Juárez 781, 77200,* ☏ *983/40702. 21 rooms. Restaurant. No credit cards.*

Xcalak

⑲   *69 km (43 mi) south of Felipe Carrillo Puerto (take Majahual exit south of Limones), then 56 km (35 mi) south of Majahual.*

Devoted divers who don't mind putting up with dirt, sand, and ruts to get to Xcalak, a fishing village near the tip of the Xcalak peninsula, which divides Chetumal Bay from the Caribbean Sea, will be aptly rewarded when they get there. The landscape is lush with mangrove swamps, tropical flowers, birds, and other wildlife. The Xcalak area offers some wonderfully deserted beaches, but the few small resorts ⑳ here cater mostly to divers who come to visit **Banco Chinchorro,** a 42-km (26-mi) coral atoll and national park some two hours by boat from

Xcalak. Strewn with shipwrecks, it's an undersea explorer's dream. Fishing is not permitted here.

Lodging

$$$$ ★ 🏨 **Costa de Cocos.** For the ultimate in privacy and gorgeous scenery, you can't beat the southern tip of the Xcalak peninsula, where divers and explorers congregate for trips to the famed Chinchorro Banks (weather permitting) and the nearby reefs. Costa de Cocos is one of the precious few resorts in this area and is easily the most hospitable and comfortable. Twelve cleverly crafted cabañas offer exquisite hand-crafted mahogany furnishings and an eclectic selection of paperbacks. The proprietors, Dave and Maria Randall, are immensely knowledgeable about the peninsula and the reef offshore. Small *pangas* (motor launches) transport divers to the nearby reefs, and day trips by boat to Belize can be arranged. The on-site dive shop has a compressor for air, and rents tanks, weights, and other equipment. There's an airstrip for those who want to arrive by small plane. It's best to make room reservations in advance; if you plan to drop by unannounced, be sure to start out for Xcalak early in the day so you can make it back to the main road before dark if the cabañas are full. ✉ *Xcalak Peninsula, 56 km (35 mi) south of Majahual, no phone. Reservations, Turquoise Reef Group, Box 2664, Evergreen, CO 80439, ☎ 303/674–9615 or 800/538–6802, FAX 303/674–8735. 12 cabanas. Restaurant, dive shop. No credit cards.*

Bacalar

112 km (69 mi) south of Felipe Carrillo Puerto, 320 km (200 mi) south of Cancún, and 40 km (26 mi) northwest of Chetumal.

㉑ The spectacularly vast **Laguna de Bacalar,** also known as the Lake of the Seven Colors, is the second-largest lake in Mexico (56 km, or 35 mi, long) and is frequented by scuba divers and other lovers of water sports. Seawater and fresh water mix in the lake, intensifying the aquamarine hues, and the water contrasts starkly with the dark jungle growth. If you drive along the lake's southern shores, you'll enter the affluent section of the town of Bacalar, with elegant turn-of-the-century waterfront homes. Also in the vicinity are a few hotels and campgrounds.

Founded in AD 435, **Bacalar** appears to be the oldest settlement in Quintana Roo. Of some historical interest is the **Fuerte de San Felipe,** a stone fort built by the Spaniards during the 18th century to ward off marauding pirates and Indians and later used by the Maya during the War of the Castes. The monolithic structure is right on the zócalo and overlooks the lake. Presently it houses government offices and a museum with exhibits on local history (ask for someone to bring a key if museum doors are locked). *No phone.* 💺 *Free.* ☉ *Daily 8–5.*

㉒ Just beyond Bacalar exists the largest sinkhole in Mexico, the **Cenote Azul,** 607 ft in diameter, with clear blue waters that afford unusual visibility even at 200 ft below the surface. Surrounded by lush vegetation and underwater caves, the cenote attracts divers who specialize in this somewhat tricky type of dive. There's a restaurant at the foot of the cenote where you can linger over fresh fish and a beer while gazing out over the deep, blue waters. Swimming can be done just beyond the restaurant from a rocky shore.

Lodging

$$$ 🏨 **Rancho Encantado.** On the shores of Laguna Bacalar, 30 minutes north of Chetumal, the Rancho comprises eight private *casitas* (cottages), each with its own patio and hammocks, kitchenette, sitting area, and bathroom. The casitas and public areas have hand-carved hard-

wood furnishings, woven Oaxacan rugs, and sculptures of Maya gods; lush green lawns border the water, where a gaggle of snow-white geese honk at passersby. Both breakfast and dinner are included in the room rate, and guests applaud the homemade breads and ice creams, curries, gumbo, lasagna, and other exotic fare (no red meat is served). You can swim and snorkel off the private dock leading into the lagoon. Adventure tours to the ruins in southern Yucatán, Campeche, and Belize are available through the U.S. office, and the ranch's staff are well informed on changes at the nearby archaeological sites. The ranch is also available for group retreats and meetings. When traveling by car on Route 307, watch for the road sign on your left. *Reservations,* ✉ *APDO 233, Chetumal, Quintana Roo 77000,* ☎ *983/80427. Reservations in U.S., Box 1644, Taos, NM 87571,* ☎ *800/748–1756,* 🅵🅰🆇 *505/751–0972. 8 units. Restaurant, bar, travel services. No credit cards.*

Chetumal

㉓ *58 km (36 mi) south of Bacalar and 382 km (240 mi) south of Cancún.*

Chetumal is the last town on Mexico's southern Caribbean shore. It was founded in 1898 as Payo Obispo in a concerted and only partially successful effort to gain control of the lucrative traffic in the region's precious hardwoods, arms, and ammunition, and also as a base of operations against the rebellious Indians. The city, which overlooks the Bay of Chetumal at the mouth of the Río Hondo, was devastated by a hurricane in 1955 and rebuilt as the capital of Quintana Roo and the state's major port. Though Chetumal remains the state capital to this day, it attracts few visitors other than those en route to Central America.

Overall, Chetumal feels more Central American than Mexican; this is not surprising, given its proximity to Belize. Run-down (but often charming) clapboard houses interspersed with low-lying ramshackle commercial establishments line the quiet streets. The mixed population includes many black Caribbeans, and the arts reflect this eclectic combination—the music includes reggae, salsa, and calypso (but little mariachi). The many Middle Eastern inhabitants have influenced the cuisine, which represents an exotic blend of Yucatecan, Mexican, and Lebanese. Although Chetumal's provisions are modest, the town has a pleasant, extended waterfront, since the city is surrounded by the Bay of Chetumal on three sides.

The town's most attractive thoroughfare, the wide **Boulevard Bahía**, runs along the water and is a popular gathering spot at night (though on the weekend Chetumal practically shuts down). The main plaza sits between the boulevard and Avenidas Alvaro Obregón and Héroes; unremarkable modern government buildings and patriotic statues and monuments to local heroes wall in the plaza on two sides. The water lapping at the dock creates a melancholy rhythm, but if you sit at one of the sidewalk cafés by the square, you will have an appealing view of the huge, placid bay.

Downtown Chetumal is getting spruced up to attract more tourists. It has been repainted and just opened its first five-star hotel, a Holiday Inn, as well as a tony new museum on the Maya. The **Museum of Maya Culture** is one of the best of its kind in the country. The first of eight salons in this interactive museum dwells on the art of war of the Maya, then leads into other sections devoted to the Maya view of life, death, and higher wisdom. A giant replica of the underworld is set in the depths of the museum; this is one of the most eerie and fascinating of all the lifelike displays. Vivid videos, stellae, multimedea displays, and models of major Maya cities guide the visitor through the early beginnings to the final demise of the civilization with the arrival of the Spanish conquistadors. ⊠ *Av. Héroes and Calle Mahatma Ghandi,* ☎ *983/26838.* 🖾 *$3.* ⊙ *Tues.–Thurs. 9–7, Fri. and Sat. 9–8, Sun. 9–2.*

The new attractions are aimed at boosting tourist dollars to replace the revenue Chetumal lost from losing its status as a duty-free port. Since Mexico joined GATT (General Agreement on Tariffs and Trade), all duty-free areas in the country have been eliminated. There is still shopping along Avenida Héroes, where most of the stores are, but the handicrafts tend to be a humdrum and uninteresting.

Laguna Milagrosa, a lovely lagoon with an island in the center and a shoreline graced by palms and bougainvillea, is 15 km (9 mi) west of Chetumal on the road to Bacalar. Restaurants and shops that rent out diving equipment are in the vicinity, too.

For many, Chetumal's major attractions are farther inland. The **Río Hondo** runs alongside the borders between Mexico and Belize and Guatemala; in its wildest parts, alligators roam the riverbeds and manatees breed.

Dining and Lodging

$$ ✕ **Casablanca.** This informal, air-conditioned restaurant is one of the favorite local hangouts. Overall, the food—mostly Mexican fare—is good, and the wine list is better. ⊠ *Av. Madero 293,* ☎ *983/23791. AE, MC, V.*

$$ ✕ **Emiliano's.** The seafood is excellent here, as evidenced by the packed house most days at lunchtime. Try the shrimp pâté (a smooth blend of cream cheese and grilled shrimp) and the huge chili relleno stuffed with seafood. For an all-out feast for two or more, go for the seafood platter. ⊠ *Av. San Salvador 557, at Calle 9,* ☎ *983/70267. MC, V.*

$$ ✕ **Mandinga.** One of the best places in town for the freshest seafood, Mandinga is best known for its octopus and conch seafood soup, a spicy blend of the daily catch. ⊠ *Av. Belice 214,* ☎ *983/24824. No credit cards.*

$$ ✕ **Sergio's.** This pizza parlor became so popular that the owners had to convert the small frame house into a bigger place while they added more dishes to the menu. Locals rave about the grilled steaks, barbecued chicken (made with Sergio's own sauce), and garlic shrimp, along with smoked oyster and seafood pizzas. ⊠ *Av. Alvaro Obregón 182, at Av. 5 de Mayo,* ☎ *983/22355. MC, V.*

$$$ 🏠 **Holiday Inn Chetumal Puerta Maya.** Chetumal's best hotel, this
★ started out as the Continental Caribe; a multi-million-dollar remodeling and U.S. franchise deal has added a glamorous sheen to its persona. The lobby is washed in cream-color marble and glass, and all public areas sparkle with a new identity. Rooms have new air-conditioning units, color satellite TV, minibars, and modern furnishings in somber grey and light brown. No-smoking rooms and rooms for people with mobility problems have been added, along with a gym and travel agency. A large swimming pool is on the lobby level. The hotel's restaurant, **La Cascada,** serves buffets as well as an international menu. The hotel has the largest banquet and conference facilities in town—it can accommodate 1,600 persons in the banquet room—and the staff is very courteous. ⊠ *Av. Héroes 171, 77000,* ☎ *983/21050 or 800/465–4329,* 🖾 *983/21676. 75 rooms, 10 suites. Restaurant, lobby lounge, pool, exercise room, meeting rooms, travel services, car rental. AE, MC, V.*

$$ 🖥 **Los Cocos.** Chetumal's second-best hotel lacks any semblance of glamour or glitz. But it does have comfortable rooms with powerful air-conditioning, in-room phones and TVs, and a pleasant garden area with a large swimming pool. However, some of the furnishings look slipshod, and dresser-drawer knobs are likely to come off at any moment. The waterfront is within easy walking distance, and the hotel's travel agency is a reliable source of information on the town. ⊠ *Av. Héroes 134, at Calle Chapultepec, 77000,* 🕾 *983/20544,* 𝔽𝔸𝕏 *983/20920. 80 rooms. Restaurant, bar, pool, shops, travel services. MC, V.*

With the exception of the Holiday Inn and Los Cocos, there are practically no acceptable hotels in town unless you want to put up with leaking air-conditioning units, missing toilet seats, and backed-up plumbing. For all this at budget prices, you can try the **Príncipe** (⊠ Av. Héroes 326, 77000, 🕾 983/24799, 𝔽𝔸𝕏 983/25191) which is between the bus station and downtown and is in the lower end of the $ price range.

Kohunlich

❷❹   *42 km (67 mi) west of Chetumal, on Route 186.*

Kohunlich is renowned for the giant stucco masks on its principal pyramid, the **Templo del Sol** (Temple of the Sun), for one of the oldest ball courts in Quintana Roo, and for the remains of a great hydraulic system at the **Plaza de las Estrellas** (Plaza of the Stars). The masks—about 6 ft tall—are set vertically into the wide staircases; first thought to be representations of the Maya sun god, they are most likely the faces of actual rulers of Kohunlich, according to new theories. Archaeologists say there are over 500 mounds on the site, most unexplored, and believe that Kohunlich was built and occupied during the Early and Late Classical periods, about AD 300–1200. Recent excavations have turned up 29 individual and multiple burial sites inside a building called **Templo de Los Viente-Siete Escalones** (Temple of the Twenty-Seven Steps). This site is usually deserted, and in the vicinity are scores of unexcavated mounds, stelae, and thriving flora and fauna. *No phone.* 🗺 *$3.* ☉ *Daily 8–5.*

Dzibanché

❷❺   *1 km (½ mi) east of turnoff for Kohunlich on Hwy. 186, follow road for Morocoy for 6 km (4 mi) north to site.*

Dzibanché and its sister city Kinichna (not open to the public yet) are considered to have been the most powerful alliance ruling southern Quintana Roo in the Classic period of the state. Opened to the public in 1996, Dzibanché has several plazas surrounded by temples, palaces and pyramids, all bearing the Peten style of architecture with crestcombs, and all open to the public. **Temple IV** has a large, impressive, carved lintel made from quebracho wood with eight glyphs dating to AD 618. *No phone.* 🗺 *$2.* ☉ *Daily 8–5.*

THE CARIBBEAN COAST A TO Z

Arriving and Departing

By Bus
CHETUMAL
The bus station (⊠ Av. Salvador Novo 179) in Chetumal is served by **ADO** (🕾 983/29877 or 983/71357), **Caribe Express** (🕾 983/20740), and other lines. Buses run regularly from Chetumal to Cancún, Villahermosa, Mexico City, Mérida, Campeche City, and Veracruz.

PLAYA DEL CARMEN

There is first-class and deluxe service on the **ADO** line (✉ Av. Juárez at Av. 5, ☎ 987/30109) between Playa del Carmen and Cancún, Valladolid, Chichén Itzá, Chetumal, Tulum, Xel-Há, Mexico City, and Mérida daily. **Autotransportes del Caribe** (✉ Av. Juárez, no phone) runs second-class buses to the above destinations, and deluxe express buses to Chetumal. **Autotransportes Oriente** (✉ Av. Juárez, no phone) has express service to Mérida eight times daily, and one bus daily to Cobá. **ATS**(✉ Av. Juárez at Av. 5, no phone) offers first–class service about every 20 minutes to Cancún.

By Ferry

Ferries and jet foils—which can be picked up at the dock—run between Playa del Carmen and Cozumel about every two hours (more frequently in the early morning and evening); trips on the old ferry take about 40 minutes, those on the two enclosed hydrofoils, 30 minutes. The fee varies depending on which boat you choose, but the one-way trip costs between $4 and $6.

By Plane

Almost everyone who arrives by air into this region flies into Cancún (☞ Chapter 2).

Getting Around

By Car

The entire coast, from Punta Sam near Cancún to the main border crossing to Belize at Chetumal, is traversable on Route 307. This straight road is entirely paved and has been widened into four lanes to Playa del Carmen; eventually, it will be widened as far south as Chetumal (but be careful—many motorists see the road's straightness as an opportunity to speed). Gas stations are becoming more prevalent, but it's still a good idea to fill the tank whenever you can; there are gas stations in Cancún, Puerto Juárez, Puerto Morelos, Playa del Carmen, Tulum, Felipe Carrillo Puerto, and Chetumal.

Good roads that run into Route 307 from the west are Route 180 (from Mérida and Valladolid), Route 295 (from Valladolid), Route 184 (from central Yucatán), and Route 186 (from Villahermosa and, via Route 261, from Mérida and Campeche). There is an entrance to the *autopista* toll highway between Cancún and Mérida off Hwy. 307 just south of Cancún. Approximate driving times are as follows: from Cancún to Felipe Carrillo Puerto, three hours; from Cancún to Mérida, 4½ hours (3½ hours on the new *autopista* toll road, $27); from Carrillo Puerto to Chetumal, 2 hours; from Carrillo Puerto to Mérida, about 4½ hours; from Chetumal to Campeche, 6½ hours. Be sure to stock up on groceries, pharmacy items, hardware, and auto parts in Puerto Morelos, Playa del Carmen, Felipe Carrillo Puerto, or Chetumal.

By Plane

In **Chetumal,** the airport is on the southwestern edge of town, along Avenida Alvaro Obregón where it turns into Route 186. **Bonanza** (☎ 983/28306) has daily flights from Chetumal to Cancún; **Aerocaribe** (☎ 983/26675) has flights to Cancún four times a week.

The airstrip in **Playa del Carmen** is near the Continental Plaza Hotel, and there is occasional shuttle service to Cozumel. A small airline called **Aero Saab** (Playa del Carmen airstrip, ☎ 987/30501) offers daily scheduled air tours to Tulum, Uxmal, and Chichén Itzá if enough passengers turn up to fill the four- and five-seat Cessnas. The company also offers charter flights to Cozumel, Mérida, Belize, and Guatemala.

By Taxi

Taxis can be hired in Cancún to go as far as Playa del Carmen, Tulum, or Akumal, but the price is steep unless you have many passengers. Fares run about $55 or more to Playa alone; between Playa and Tulum or Akumal, expect to pay at least $25. It's much cheaper from Playa to Cancún, with taxi fare running about $30; negotiate before you hop into the cab. There's a taxi stand at the entrance to Akumal.

Contacts and Resources

Banks

CHETUMAL

Banco del Atlántico (⊠ Av. Héroes 37, ☎ 983/22776 or 983/20631) and **Bancomer** (⊠ Av. Alvaro Obregón 222 at Av. Juárez, ☎ 983/25300 or 983/25318) provide banking services, including foreign currency exchange.

PLAYA DEL CARMEN

Banco del Atlántico (⊠ Av. 10a and Av. Juárez, no phone) cashes traveler's checks weekdays 10–noon; a new **Bancomer** (⊠ Av. Juaréz and Calle 25) does the same. Both banks have ATM machines that accept some U.S.bank cards.

Car Rental

In **Playa del Carmen,** car rental agencies are beginning to appear around the ferry pier and Avenida Juárez. Rental agencies include **Budget** (⊠ Hotel Continental Plaza Playacar); **Hertz** (⊠ Escape Travel, ☎ 987/31080 and 987/30558; ⊠ Hotel Continental Plaza Playacar, ☎ 987/30566, ☎ 987/30033); and **National** (⊠ Hotel Molcas, ☎ 987/ 30360). If you want air-conditioning, reserve your car in advance.

Hertz also has offices in Puerto Adventuras (☎ 987/35050) and Akumal (☎ 987/59000).

Emergencies

CHETUMAL

Police (⊠ Av. Insurgentes and Av. Belice, ☎ 983/21500). **Red Cross** (⊠ Av. Efraín Aguilar at Av. Madero, ☎ 983/20571).

PLAYA DEL CARMEN

Police (⊠ Av. Juárez, between Avs. 15a and 20a, next to post office, ☎ 987/30021). **Red Cross** (⊠ Av. Héroes de Chapultapec at Independencia, ☎ 987/30045).

English-Language Bookstores

In **Playa del Carmen,** the newsstand at the Rincón del Sol Plaza (⊠ Av. 5 at Calle 8, no phone) has an excellent selection of English-language books and periodicals; used books are sold at a discount. **Duty Free** (⊠ main plaza, no phone) has English–language periodicals. The **gift shop** at the Playacar hotel (☎ 987/21583) has a modest selection of magazines and paperbacks. However, expect to pay double what you pay in the United States.

Guided Tours

Although some guided tours are available in this area, the roads are quite good for the most part, so renting a car is an efficient and enjoyable alternative: Most of the sights you'll see along this stretch are natural, and you can hire a guide at the ruins sites.

ECOTOURISM

Naviera Asterix (☎ 98/864847 and 99/864270 in Cancún) offers guided yacht tours to Contoy Island. **Ecolomex Tours** (☎ 98/843805 and 98/871776 in Cancún) does off-the-beaten-path trips to little–known areas along the coast. **Ava Tours** (☎ 98/848676 and 98/848696 in Cancún) specializes in aerial tours of the coast. All will pick up at hotels along the coast from Puerto Morelos to Playa del Carmen.

MAYA RUINS

Mayaland Gray Line Tours (✉ Hotel America, Av. Tulum at Calle Brisa, ☎ 98/872450 or 800/235–4079, FAX 98/872438 in Cancún or Las Molcas Hotel, Calle 1 Sur between Av. 5 and the ferry pier, ☎ 987/31106 or 800/235–4079 in Playa del Carmen), one of the Yucatán's leading tour companies, is now running tours to Chichén Itzá from hotels around Punta Bete, Playa del Carmen, and Akumal. Tours include pickup at your hotel, transportation on a deluxe bus, lunch at the Mayaland hotel, and use of the hotel's facilities (including swimming pool), and free beer, wine, and soft drinks on the ride home.

The first-class hotels in Playa del Carmen and Puerto Aventuras can arrange **day tours** to Tulum, Chichén Itzá, and Cobá.

In Chetumal, try **Viajes Calderitas** (✉ Los Cocos Hotel, Av. Héroes 138, ☎ 983/22540, FAX 983/22006) or **Turistica Maya de Quintana Roo** (✉ Holiday Inn Chetumal Puerta Maya, ☎ 983/20555 or 983/22058, FAX 983/29711) for tours to Kohunlich, Dzibanché, the Laguna de Bacalar and Fort of San Felipe, and Belize.

In Playa del Carmen, **Aero Fenico** Airlines (☎ 987/ 30636) has day and half-day tours to Uxmal, Chichén Itzá and Tikal in Guatemala; tour guide and lunch are included.

Mail
The post office in **Chetumal** (✉ Plutarco Elias Calles, ☎ 983/22578) is open Monday–Saturday 8–1 and 3–6. In **Playa del Carmen** (✉ Av. Juárez, next to police station, no phone), it's open weekdays 9–1 and 3–6, Saturday 9–1.

Medical Clinics
Chetumal: Hospital General (✉ Avenida Andres Quintana Roo, ☎ 983/21932). **Playa del Carmen: Centro de Salud** (✉ Avenida Juárez at Avenida 15a, ☎ 987/21230, ext. 147) or **Dr. Victor Macias**, a bilingual physician (✉ Av. 35 between Calles 21 and 4, ☎ 987/987/30493).

Pharmacies
Chetumal: Farmacia Social Mechaca (✉ Av. Independencia 134C, ☎ 983/20044). **Playa del Carmen:** There's a pharmacy at the **Plaza Marina** shopping mall and several on **Av. 5 between Calles 4 and 8.**

Telephones
Electricity and telephones are still the exception rather than the rule in this region, although most hotels have radio or cellular phone communication with the outside world.

In **Chetumal,** the government-run telephone office, TELMEX, is at Avenida Juárez and Lázaro Cárdenas. For long-distance and international calls, you might also try the booths on Avenida Héroes: One is on the corner of Ignacio Zaragoza and the other is just opposite Avenida Efraín Aguilar, next to the tourist information booth.

In 1992, after many years of having only one phone line, **Playa del Carmen** finally received telephone service. Hotels, restaurants, and shops were still adding extra lines for phones and fax machines at press time; numbers are included here where available. There are Ladatel long-distance phone booths in front of the post office on Avenida Juárez and at the corner of Avenida Juárez and Avenida 5.

Travel Agencies

There are more major travel agencies and tour operators up and down the coast than before, and first-class hotels in Playa del Carmen, Puerto Aventuras, and Akumal usually have their own in-house travel services.

CHETUMAL

Viajes Calderitas (⊠ Los Cocos Hotel, Av. Héroes 138, ☎ 983/22540, FAX 983/22006) or **Turistica Maya de Quintana Roo** (⊠ Holiday Inn Chetumal Puerta Maya, ☎ 983/20555 or 983/22058, FAX 983/29711).

PLAYA DEL CARMEN

Mayaland Gray Line Tours (⊠ Las Molcas Hotel, Calle 1 Sur between Av. 5 and the ferry pier, ☎ 987/31106); **Escape Travel** (⊠ Av. 5 between Calle 6 and 8, ☎ 987/31080 or 987/30558); and **Amazing Tours** (⊠ Av. 5 and Calle Juaréz, ☎ 987/30925).

Visitor Information

CHETUMAL

Both the **tourist office** (⊠ Palacio del Gobierno, 2nd floor, ☎ 983/20266, FAX 983/20855) and **tourist information booth** (⊠ Avenida Héroes, opposite Avenida Efraín Aguilar, ☎ 983/23663) are open weekdays 9–2:30 and 4–7.

PLAYA DEL CARMEN

The **tourist information booth** (⊠ Av. 5, 1 block from beach, no phone) has sporadic hours. The **Playa del Carmen Hotel Association** (☎ 987/30646) has a new information service at Avenue 30 and Calle 6 Sur, open weekdays 9–1 and 3:30–5:30 and Saturday 9–2. In the United States, call 800/467–5292.

6 Campeche

Ruins of the fortifications built to fend off the pirates who ravaged Yucatán's gulf coast make the walled city of Campeche well worth exploring. Among the remnants of Maya settlements that dot the rest of this little-explored state, Edzná is the best known and most interesting.

Updated by
Patricia Alisau

CAMPECHE, THE LEAST-VISITED PART of the Yucatán, is not for everybody, but the adventuresome visitor will discover both charm and mystery here. Three-hundred-year-old cannons point across the Gulf of Mexico from fortress battlements, recalling pirate days and lending an air of romance to the walled capital city of Campeche. Beyond the city, ancient pyramids and ornate temple facades from the area's Maya past lie hidden deep in tropical forests.

Most of the State of Campeche is flat—never higher than 1,000 ft above sea level—but more than 60% of its territory is covered by jungle, where precious mahogany and cedar abound. The Gulf Stream keeps temperatures at about 26°C (78°F) year-round; the humid, tropical climate is eased by evening breezes. Campeche's economy is based on agriculture, fishing, logging, salt, tourism, and—since the 1970s—hydrocarbons, of which it is the largest producer in Mexico. But most of the oil industry is concentrated at the southern end of the state, near Ciudad del Carmen.

Campeche City's location on the gulf has played a pivotal role in its history. Ah-Kin-Pech (Maya for "Lord of the Serpent Tick")—from which the Spanish name of Campeche is derived—was the capital of an Indian chieftainship long before the Spaniards arrived in 1517. Earlier explorers had visited the area, but it was not until 1540 that the conquerors—led by Francisco de Montejo and, later, his son—established a real foothold at Campeche (originally called San Lazaro), using it as a base for their conquest of the peninsula.

Because Campeche City was the only port and shipyard on the gulf, the Spanish ships, with their rich cargoes of plunder from the Maya, Aztec, and other indigenous civilizations, dropped anchor here en route from Veracruz to Cuba, New Orleans, and Spain. News of this wealth spread, and soon the shores were overrun with pirates. From the mid-1500s to the early 1700s, such notorious corsairs as Diego the Mulatto, Lorenzillo, Peg Leg, Henry Morgan, and Barbillas swooped down repeatedly from their base on Tris—or Isla de Términos, as Isla del Carmen was then known—pillaging and burning the city and massacring its people.

Finally, after appealing for years to the Spanish crown, the citizens of Campeche received funds that enabled them to build a protective wall (with four gates and eight bastions). For some time thereafter, the city thrived on its exports, especially *palo de tinte*—a dyewood used by the nascent European textile industry—but also hardwoods, chicle, salt, and henequen. However, when the port of Sisal on the northern Yucatán coast opened in 1811, Campeche's monopoly of the gulf traffic ended, and its economy fell into decline.

The shape of modern-day Campeche is still defined by history. Remnants of the wall and other military structures divide it into two main districts, intramural (the old city) and extramural (the new). Because the city was long preoccupied with defense, colonial architecture is less developed here than elsewhere in Mexico. Churches are more somber; streets (a few still paved with flagstones) are narrow because of the confines of the walls; houses are more practical than aesthetic in their design. Although the face of the city has altered over the centuries, as landfill was added and walls and bastions demolished to make room for expansion, it still retains an aura of antiquity.

The state as a whole has a population of only about 635,000, most of it scattered through villages and small towns. Maya traditions still reign in the countryside, which is dotted with windmills and fields of tobacco, sugarcane, rice, indigo, maize, and cocoa. Wildlife flourishes here, too: Jaguars (though diminished in number), tapir, and armadillos roam free, while the sea provides fishing boats with butterfly shrimp, barracuda, swordfish, and other catch.

Thousands of Guatemalan refugees who fled to Campeche were settled into four camps, one of which was involved in excavating the Maya archaeological site of Edzná. Since the Guatemalan government granted an armistice to the refugees in 1993, many of them have returned home. Recently, however, settlements of Chol Maya homesteaders relocated from Chiapas after the Zapatista uprising have appeared on the edge of southern Campeche's Calakmul Biosphere Reserve.

Pleasures and Pastimes

Architecture
Nowhere in the Yucatán does Spanish colonial history feel more immediate than in the city of Campeche. Not only does the architecture of the Old City remain unchanged since the 17th century, for the most part it has not even been painted. The present-day population is predominantly Maya, a race of people with considerable experience at living among the ruins of past glories. Heritage blends easily with pragmatism here. You are likely to come across colonial mansions being used as auto body shops and karate studios. Yet the constant proximity of architecture from an earlier era makes this charmingly decrepit city more evocative in its own way than many self-consciously preserved historic districts around the world.

Dining
There is nothing fancy about Campeche's restaurants, but the regional cuisine is renowned throughout Mexico—particularly the fish and shellfish stews, shrimp cocktails, squid and octopus, crabs' legs, *panuchos* (tortillas stuffed with beans and topped with meat or fish), and other Yucatecan specialties. Other unusual seafood delicacies include the famous Champotón baby shrimp from the coastal town of Champotón, which are a highly rated delicacy in other parts of the world; red snapper wrapped in banana leaves; baby shark, cooked, shredded, and served over tortillas and tomato sauce (called *pan de cazon*); *moro* crab, hard to find because it's a hot export item; and crayfish claws. *Botanas,* or canapés, include cooked eggs with pumpkin seed and tomato sauce, fruit conserves in syrup with chili, ceviche (raw marinated fish), and *chicharrón* (fried pork rind). The addition of cumin, marjoram, bay leaf, cayenne pepper, and allspice imparts an exotic flavor to entrées. Fruits are served fresh, added to breads, made into liqueurs, or marinated in rum or vinegar. Look for mango, papaya, *zapote* (sapodilla), mamey, guanabana, tamarind, watermelon, jicama, melon, pineapple, and coconut, to name only a few. Because regional produce is plentiful, most restaurants—including all those listed below—fall into the $ to $$ price categories. Casual dress—though not always shorts—is fine in restaurants throughout Campeche, and reservations are not required.

CATEGORY	COST*
$$	$8–$15
$	under $8

per person, excluding drinks and service

Ecotourism

Southern Campeche contains one of the last vestiges of primeval rain forest in Mexico, now legally protected under UNESCO's Man and the Biosphere program as the Calakmul Biosphere Reserve. It adjoins the much larger Maya Biosphere Reserve across the Guatemalan border, as well as a smaller reserve in Belize. The deep forest in the heart of the reserve is almost impossible to reach, but the outskirts offer plenty of opportunity to see a wide range of orchids and jungle wildlife including spider monkeys, peccaries, boa constrictors, and hundreds of species of birds. Ecotourism in the area is still in its infancy, but there's likely to be rapid growth in environmentally aware tourism in southern Campeche over the next few years.

Lodging

Most of Campeche City's hotels are old (and several are in disrepair), reflecting the city's lackadaisical attitude toward tourism. Hotels tend to be either luxury accommodations along the waterfront, with air-conditioning, restaurants, and other standard amenities, or basic downtown accommodations offering only ceiling fans and a no-credit-card policy. Those in the latter category tend to be either seedy and undesirable or oddly charming, with some architectural and regional detail unique to each.

CATEGORY	COST*
$$$	over $90
$$	$40–$90
$	under $40

*All prices are for a standard double room, excluding service and the 15% tax.

Ruins

A thousand years ago, as today, the Maya people were a diverse race. In Campeche, archaeology buffs will find several styles of ruins that are completely different from any in the states of Yucatán or Quintana Roo. The Chenes style, found in central and southern Campeche, features facades in the shape of giant masks of jaguars, birds, and other creatures, often called "monster mouth" temples. Secret passageways let priests emerge suddenly from the jaws of the beast. The Río Bec style, found in the southern rain forest, has temples with facades built in the shape of double pyramids with as many as 12 levels. An architectural trick called false perspective makes them appear far larger and more imposing than they actually are. Visiting most Campeche ruins is much easier now than a few years ago as, with a few exceptions, they are reachable via good paved roads. A few do require driving hundreds of highway miles to the most remote part of the Yucatán Peninsula—not for the faint-hearted, but ideal for adventurous souls.

Exploring Campeche

Campeche City, the most accessible place in the state, makes a good hub for exploring other areas, many of which lack restaurants and lodging. For purposes of exploration, the sights in the state of Campeche are arranged in three distinct regions: the northern interior along Routes 261 and 180, containing the ruins of Edzná and other ancient cities as well as many modern Maya villages that can be visited easily en route between Campeche City and Mérida or Uxmal; the southern coast along Route 180—the only part of the Campeche coastline that is accessible by road—with several small beach resorts and fishing villages that are all but eclipsed by oil industry development; and the southern interior along Route 186, a remote rain forest area with numerous large Maya ruins that have started to get more visitors after opening to the public a few years ago. Route 186 also runs through to the coast of Quintana Roo, linking the ruins of southern Campeche with the ancient Maya cities of southern Quintana Roo, which are definitely worth visiting. These ruins are under extensive research through a 1995 government grant. Previous to this, visitors to the Yucatán Peninsula rarely reached these areas because of their remoteness.

Numbers in the text correspond to numbers in the margin and on the State of Campeche and Campeche City maps.

Great Itineraries

Our Campeche itinerary highlights attractions in Campeche City, then takes you into the countryside. While it may sound dauntingly ambitious to accomplish the city tour in one day, many of the sights described here can be seen in just a few minutes. The more leisurely visitor may wish to schedule two days. Traveling throughout the State of Campeche could take from two to five days, depending on how much time you devote to some of the towns that are farther off the beaten path.

IF YOU HAVE 1 DAY

The city of Campeche is easy to explore in a day, as almost all sights of interest to visitors are located within the compact historical district. Start out at the **Baluarte San Carlos** ⑪ at the southern edge of the **Ciudad Viejo** for an overview of the history of the port. Then head north into the heart of the old city center and take in its time-worn bastions, museums, and colonial buildings, ending up at the pretty **Parque Principal** ② for a stop at the **catedral** ③. Take a break for lunch at the Miramar restaurant. After lunch, browse in the **Mercado Municipal** ⑮, then (around 4, after the siesta when everything including taxi service comes to a halt) hop in a cab for a late afternoon visit to the **Fuerte de San Miguel** ⑰ and its new Museum of Maya Culture. Come evening, join the locals in a breezy walk along the **malecón** ⑭.

IF YOU HAVE 3 DAYS

After spending the first day in Campeche City, head inland the next morning to visit **Edzná** ㉔, a magnificently restored ceremonial center an hour's drive from the city. Return to your Campeche City hotel—accommodations are crude or nonexistent in the area—and set out the next day to the **Hopelchén** ㉕ region, beyond Edzná, where you can explore the little-known Maya temples at **Hochob** ㉗ and **Dzibilnocac** ㉘, as well as **Bolonchén de Rejón** ㉖, one of the large cave systems on the peninsula. From Hopelchén, it is as easy to continue north toward Uxmal and Mérida (☞ Chapter 7) as it is to return to Campeche City.

IF YOU HAVE 7 DAYS

In addition to the capital and the northern region, you'll have time to explore the southern part of the state. Follow the coast highway and plan to spend the night on **Isla del Carmen** ㉜, hardly a great beach resort but far more pleasant than the only real alternative—the grimy truck stop town of Escárcega. As you head east across the base of the Yucatán Peninsula toward Chetumal, you will find a number of impressive Maya sites. To appreciate the natural beauty of the rain forest and the myriad ruins, plan to spend at least two or three days at the one small ecotourism resort in the area. **Becán** ㉝, **Chicanná** ㉞, and **Xpujil** ㉟ are just off the highway and can all be explored in a single full day. Local guides can take you to more remote sights such as **Hormiguero** ㊱ and **Río Bec** ㊲ on day trips, or on more ambitious journeys to sites such as **Calakmul** ㊳ and **El Tigre** ㊴, deep in the forests of the Calakmul Biosphere Reserve. From the Xpujil area, it is easier to continue to the Caribbean coast than it is to return to Campeche City, unless you're in a four-wheel-drive vehicle.

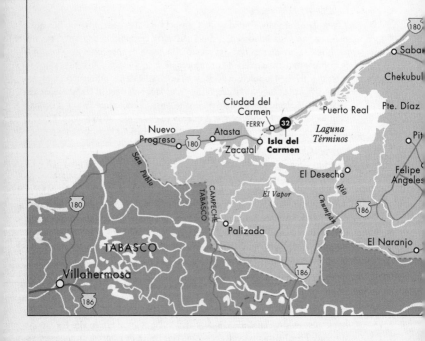

0   40 miles

0   60 km

Golfo
de
México

180

Saba

Chekubul

Ciudad del Carmen

Puerto Real   Pte. Díaz

FERRY   32   *Laguna Términos*

Nuevo Progreso   180   Atasta

Zacatal   **Isla del Carmen**

Pit

San Pablo

El Desecho

Felipe Angeles

CAMPECHE TABASCO

El Vapor

Río Chumpán

186

180

Palizada

El Naranjo

TABASCO

186

Villahermosa

186

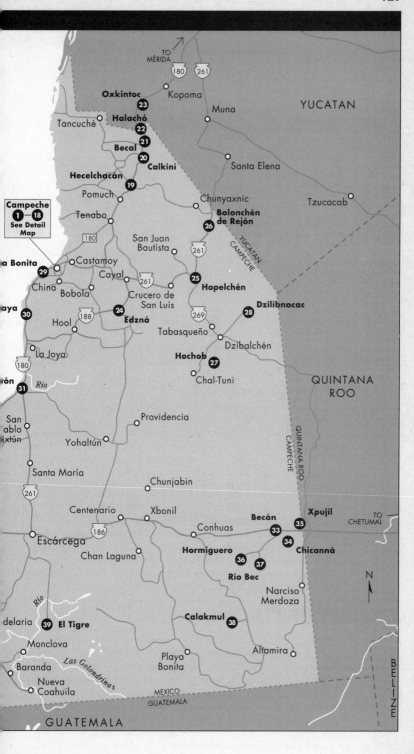

TO MÉRIDA

180 261

Oxkintoc ◯ Kopoma

23

YUCATAN

◯ Muna

Tancuché

Halachó

22

Becal

21

20 **Calkiní**

◯ Santa Elena

Hecelchacán

19

Pomuch

◯ Chunyaxnic

Tenabo

Bolonchén de Rejón

26

◯ Tzucacab

Campeche
1 — **18**
See Detail
Map

180

San Juan Bautista

YUCATAN
CAMPECHE

261

a Bonita

29

Castamoy

China

Cayal

261

25

Hopelchén

Bobola

Crucero de San Luis

24

188

Edzná

Hool

269

28 **Dzilibnocac**

aya

30

La Joya

Tabasqueño

Dzibalchén

180

Río

Hochob

27

vón

31

Chal-Tuni

QUINTANA ROO

San ablo ixtún

◯ Providencia

Yohaltún

QUINTANA ROO
CAMPECHE

Santa María

261

◯ Chunjabin

Centenario

Xbonil

Becán

Xpujil

TO CHETUMAL

186

Conhuas

33

35

Escárcega

Hormiguero

34 **Chicanná**

Chan Laguna

36

37

Río Bec

Narciso Merdoza

Río

Calakmul

38

delaria

39 **El Tigre**

Altamira

Monclova

Las Golondrinas

Baranda

Playa Bonita

Nueva Coahuila

MEXICO
GUATEMALA

N

B E L I Z E

GUATEMALA

Baluarte de la
Soledad, **1**

Baluarte San
Carlos, **11**

Baluarte
Santiago, **5**

Calle 59, **6**

Catedral, **3**

Congreso del
Estado, **12**

Ex-Templo de
San José, **9**

Fuerte de San
Miguel, **17**

Fuerte San
José, **18**

Iglesia de San
Francisco, **16**

Iglesia de San
Francisquito, **7**

Iglesia de San
Román, **10**

Malecón, **14**

Mansión
Carvajal, **4**

Mercado
Municipal, **15**

Palacio del
Gobierno, **13**

Parque
Principal, **2**

Puerta de
Tierra, **8**

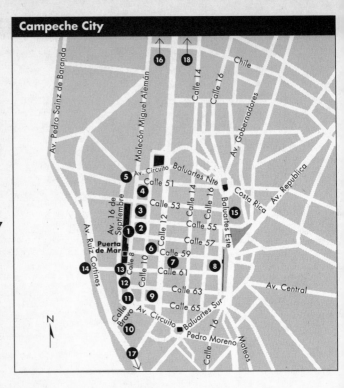

Campeche City

When to Tour Campeche

Both the capital and outlying villages of Campeche state, with their predominantly Maya population, celebrate the Day of the Dead (November 1 and 2) with special fervor because it corresponds to a similar observance in ancient Maya tradition. Colorfully embroidered regional dress, street celebrations, special meals, and altars of offerings to deceased loved ones are typical.

November also marks the end of the rainy season (the strongest rains fall July to September), when the risk of hurricanes is over and the rain forests of the interior are at their most luxuriant. Any time from November through March is good for traveling, though as everywhere in Mexico, the Christmas and Holy Week holidays mean extremely crowded hotels and public transportation. The rainy season often renders unpaved side roads impassable in central and southern Campeche unless you're in a four-wheel drive vehicle.

CAMPECHE CITY

The city of Campeche has a time-weathered and lovely feel to it: No self-conscious, ultramodern tourist glitz here, just a friendly city by the sea (population 270,000), proud of its heritage and welcoming all to share in it. That good-humored, open-minded attitude is enshrined in the Spanish adjective *campechano*, meaning hearty and jovial. The city gets only about 20,000 tourists a year, its strongest attraction being its sense of history. You can easily imagine pirates attacking the formidable stone walls that surround the downtown, and several Maya ruins and undisturbed Maya towns are within easy driving distance. The city's coastline is cluttered with commercial fishing operations, and there are a few popular public beaches. It is possible to see much of Campeche City in a day or two, but you will probably want to stay longer to absorb the traditional lifestyle, whiling away the hours at a café near the plaza.

Because it has been walled (though not successfully fortified) since 1686, most of the historic downtown is neatly contained in an area measuring just five blocks by nine blocks. Today, for the most part, streets running north–south are even-numbered, and those running east–west are odd-numbered. The city is easily navigable (on foot, at least); the historical monuments and evocative name plaques above street numbers serve as handy guideposts. The old city looks fresh and pretty with newly painted and remodeled buildings and new signs guiding tourists to attractions along the streets. Lacking the large-scale tourism that has sustained Cancún and Mérida, Campeche was hit harder than any other part of the Yucatán by Mexico's 1995 recession but is showing definite signs of recovery.

On various corners in the old city, or Viejo Campeche, stand seven *baluartes* (bastions) in various stages of disrepair or reconstruction. These were once connected by a 3-km (2-mi) wall in a hexagonal fortification that was built to safeguard the city against the pirates who kept ransacking it. Only short stretches of the wall exist, and two stone archways—one facing the sea, the other the land—are all that remain of the four gates that provided the only means of access to Campeche. Although these walls helped protect the residents, it was not until 1771, when Fuerte San Miguel was built on a hilltop on the outskirts of town, that pirates finally ceased their attacks for good.

Campeche was one of few walled cities in North or Central America and was built along the traditional lines of defensive Spanish settlements, such as Santo Domingo in the Dominican Republic, Cartagena in Colombia, and Portobelo in Panama. The walls also served as a class demarcation. Within them lived the ruling elite. Outside were the barrios of the Indians who aided the conquistadors, and whose descendants continued to serve the upper class. The mulattoes brought as slaves from Cuba also lived outside.

A Good Walk

The Ciudad Viejo, the old city center, is the best place to start a walking tour, beginning with the **Baluarte de la Soledad** ① and its fascinating Maya stelae museum. From the nearby **Parque Principal** ②, the city's central plaza, a short stroll will show you some of the Yucatán Peninsula's most stately Spanish Colonial architecture, including the **catedral** ③ and the **Mansión Carvajal** ④, as well as the remaining sections of the **baluartes** ⑤ ⑪, fortress walls built to protect the city. Walk up **Calle 59** ⑥ past the **Iglesia de San Francisquito** ⑦ to the **Puerta de Tierra** ⑧, then follow the walls around the south side of the historic district to search out some more masterpieces of colonial religious architecture—the **Ex-Templo de San José** ⑨ and the **Iglesia de San Román** ⑩—juxtaposed against the strange modernistic designs of the **Congreso del Estado** ⑫ and the **Palacio del Gobierno** ⑬. End your tour with a stroll along the **Malecón** ⑭.

Sights to See

① **Baluarte de la Soledad.** On the south side of Parque Principal, this old bastion houses the **Museo de los Estela Dr. Roman Pina Chan** in a separate section. The largest of the bastions, this one has comparatively complete parapets and embrasures that offer a sweeping view of the cathedral, the municipal buildings, and the Gulf of Mexico. Artifacts housed inside and around the outside of the museum—named for a renowned archaeologist from the State of Campeche—include 20 beautiful and well-proportioned Maya stelae and other pieces from various periods, such as a sculpture of a man wearing an owl mask, columns from Edzná and Jaina, a perfectly sculpted pumpkin, and a phallus. This museum is a real find and not to be missed. ⊠ *Calles 8 and 57, no phone.* 🖾 *50¢.* ☉ *Tues.–Sat. 8–8, Sun. 8–1.*

⓫ **Baluarte San Carlos.** This bastion, where Avenida 16 de Septiembre curves around and becomes Circuito Baluartes, houses the **Sala de las Fortificaciones** (Chamber of the Fortifications), containing scale models of the original defense system, and the **Museo Graficode la Ciudad,** or City Museum, with photographs of the city as it developed. Don't miss the dungeon inside the bastion, where captured pirates were jailed.

❺ **Baluarte Santiago.** The last of the bastions to be built (1704) has been transformed into a botanical garden. A film explaining the garden's 250 plant species is shown throughout the day (when the projector is working). The original bastion was demolished at the turn of the century, but it was rebuilt in the 1950s. Architecturally this fort looks much the same as the others in Campeche: a stone fortress with thick walls, watchtowers, and gunnery slits. ⊠ *Calles 8 and 49,* ☏ *981/66829.* 🖾 *Free.* ☉ *Tues.–Sat. 9–1 and 4:30–8, Sun. 9–1.*

❻ **Calle 59.** On this city street, between Calles 8 and 18, once stood some of Campeche's finest homes, many of them two stories high, with the ground floors serving as warehouses and the upper floors as residences. Geometric motifs decorate the cornices, and the windows are gaily adorned with iron latticework. The richest inhabitants built as close to the sea as possible, in case escape became necessary. (Legend has it that beneath the city a network of tunnels crisscrossed, linking the eight bastions and providing temporary refuge from the pirates. Although the tunnel network has never been found, rumors still persist that it once existed.) These days, behind the genteel lace curtains of some of the homes, you can glimpse equally genteel scénes of Campeche life, with faded lithographs on the dun-colored walls and plenty of antique furniture and clutter.

❸ **Catedral.** An exception to the generally somber architecture rule of colonial Campeche is the cathedral, which took two centuries (from 1650 to 1850) to build and incorporates Neoclassical and Renaissance elements. The present cathedral occupies the site of Montejo's original church, which was built in 1540 on what is now Calle 55, between Calles 8 and 10. The simple exterior lines terminate in two bulbous towers rising to each side of the gracefully curved stone entrances, the fluted pilasters echoing those on the towers. Sculptures of saints set in niches recall the French Gothic cathedrals. The interior is no less impressive, with a single limestone nave, supported by Doric capitals and Corinthian columns, arching toward the huge octagonal dome above a black-and-white marble floor. The pièce de résistance, however, is the magnificent Holy Sepulchre, carved from ebony.

⓬ **Congreso del Estado.** A modernistic building resembling a flying saucer, the State Congress building is where government activities take place.

❾ **Ex-Templo de San José**. It occupies the full city block between Calles 10 and 12 and Calles 63 and 65. The Jesuits built this fine Baroque church in 1756, and today its facade stands as an exception to the rather plodding architectural style of most of the city's churches. Its immense portal is completely covered with blue Talavera tiles and crowned by seven narrow, stone finials that resemble the roof combs on many Maya temples. (The roof combs, in turn, are reminiscent of the combs Spanish women used to wear in their elaborate hairdos.) The convent-school next door is now used for cultural events and art exhibitions.

Campeche's first lighthouse, built in 1864, sits atop a brick pillar next to the church. ۞ *Tues.–Fri. 9–2 and 5–10.*

⑰ Fuerte de San Miguel. A well-marked scenic drive turns off Avenida Ruíz Cortines near the south end of the city and winds its way to a hilltop, where the fort commands one of the grandest views in the Yucatán, overlooking the city and the Gulf of Mexico. Built in 1771, the fort was positioned to bombard enemy ships with cannonballs before they could get close enough to attack Campeche; as soon as it was completed, pirates stopped attacking the city without a fight. Its impressive cannons were fired only once, in 1842, when General Santa Anna used Fuerte San Miguel to put down a revolt by Yucatecan separatists seeking independence from Mexico. More recently, the hilltop location has made the fort's parking lot a nighttime hangout for amorous local teenagers. Besides a great view and imposing architecture, the fort now houses the **Museo Cultura Maya,** for which you should allow at least two hours. Dedicated solely to the Campeche Maya and with explanations in English, the archaeological collection should not be missed. Six exquisite jade funeral masks found at various tombs at Calakmul comprise the most striking exhibit. Other Calakmul discoveries include urns decorated with cleverly worked king-buzzard, tapir, monkey, turtle, and other animal figures. Yet other museum pieces include a sizeable collection of the small, well-proportioned human funerary figures from the island of Jaina and stucco masks from the Río Bec ruins. A gift shop sells some reproductions of museum pieces. ⊠ *South of downtown on Av. Resurgimiento s/n, no phone.* 🎟 *50¢.* ۞ *Tues.–Sun. 8–8.* ۞ *Tues.–Sat. 8–8, Sun. 8–1.*

⑱ Fuerte San Jose. This lofty fortress at the opposite end of town from the Fuerte San Miguel is now home to a new museum—the **Museo de Armas y Barcos,** which is half of the exhibit that used to be in the Museo Regional. The display focuses on the 18th-century military weapons of seige and defense in the many wars fought against the pirates. Scale ships-in-a-bottle, manuscripts, and religious art can also be seen. The view is terrific from the top of the ramparts, which were used for spotting the ships of the invaders. ⊠ *Av. Francisco Morazon s/n, north of town, no phone.* 🎟 *50¢,* ۞ *Tues.–Sun. 8–8.*

⑯ Iglesia de San Francisco. Away from the city center, in a residential neighborhood, stands the beautifully restored church, the oldest one in Campeche. It marks the spot where, some say, the first Mass on the North American continent was said in 1517 (the same claim has been made for Veracruz and Cozumel). One of Cortés's grandsons was baptized here, and the baptismal font still stands. ⊠ *Avs. Gustavo Díaz Ordaz and Francisco I. Madero.*

❼ Iglesia de San Francisquito. Just east of Calle 12, this tiny, architecturally exquisite church does justice to historic Calle 59's old-fashioned beauty.

⑩ Iglesia de San Román. This church sits just outside the intramural boundary in the barrio of the same name at Calle 10 and Calle Bravo. San Román, with a bulbous bell tower typical of other Yucatán churches, was built to house the *naboríos* (Indians brought by the Spaniards to aid in the Conquest and later used as household servants); the barrio, like other neighborhoods, grew up around the church. Though it was built earlier in the 16th century, the church became central to the lives of the Indians only when an ebony image of Christ, the "Black Christ," was brought in about 1565. The Indians had been skeptical about the Christian saints, but this Christ figure came to be associated with miracles. The legend goes that a ship that refused to carry the tradesman and his precious statue was wrecked, while the ship that did take him on board reached Campeche in record time. To this day, the Feast of San Román—when the icon is carried through the streets as part of a colorful and somber procession—is the biggest such celebration in Campeche. People still come to see the black wood Christ mounted on a silver filigree cross. There's a Saturday mass at 7:30 PM and Sunday masses at 10 AM and 7:30 PM.

⑭ Malecón. This is Campeche's waterfront boulevard along Avenida Ruíz Cortines. The broad sidewalk runs the length of the waterfront, from the Ramada Inn south to the outskirts of town, and is popular with joggers and strollers enjoying the cool sea breezes and view at sunset. On weekend nights, the malecón turns into an extended college mixer, with hundreds of university students hanging out around their cars, which line the boulevard from end to end.

❹ Mansión Carvajal. Built in the early 20th century by one of the wealthiest plantation owners in Yucatán, the eclectic mansion did time as the Hotel Señorial before arriving at its present role as an office for the Family Institute run by the state governor's wife and her staff. Take a stroll: The black-and-white tile floor, Art Nouveau staircase with Carrara marble steps and iron balustrade, and blue-and-white Moorish arcades speak volubly of the city's heyday, when Campeche was the peninsula's only port. ⊠ *Calle 10 s/n, between Calles 53 and 55, no phone.* ☎ *Free.* ☉ *Mon.–Sat. 8–2:30 and 5–8:30.*

⑮ Mercado Municipal. To take in the heart of a true Mexican inner city, stroll through the market where locals congregate en masse to shop for seafood, produce, and housewares. Beside the market is a small bridge aptly named **Dog Bridge**—four bright yellow plaster dogs guard the area. The market is open daily from dawn to dusk. Try to arrive early, before it gets uncomfortably crowded.

⑬ Palacio del Gobierno. One block inland from the malecón, on Avenida 16 de Septiembre, the Congreso del Estado shares a broad plaza with this much taller building, dubbed *El Tocadiscos* ("The Jukebox") by locals because of its outlandish facade. The eccentric architecture of these two state capital buildings stands in odd contrast to the graceful colonial skyline of the adjacent Ciudad Viejo historic district.

❷ Parque Principal or Plaza de la Independencia. This is the centerpiece of the old city, the southern side of which—Calle 57—is lined with several agreeable cafés and hotels; the park is the focal point for the town's activities. Concerts are held on Sunday evenings, when it seems all the city's residents come out for a stroll. ⊠ *Bounded by Calles 10, 8, and 55.*

❽ Puerta de Tierra. This is where old Campeche ends—the only one of the four city gates that still stands with its basic structure intact; the walls, arches, and gates were refurbished in 1987. This stone arch intercepts a long stretch of the partially crenelated wall, 26 ft high and 10 ft thick, that once encircled the city; looking through it, you can just barely see across town to its counterpart, the **Puerta de Mar,** through which all seafarers were forced to pass. Because the latter stands alone, without any wall to shore it up, it looks like the Arc de Triomphe. The wall that is standing today around the Puerta de Tierra was built in 1957 to replace the one demolished in 1893. ⊠ *Calles 18 and 59.* ☎ *Light and sound show $2.* ☉ *Show weekdays at 8:30.*

Dining and Lodging

$$ ✕ **La Pigua.** A favorite with local professionals lingering over long
★ lunches, La Pigua is perhaps the best seafood restaurant in town, with
the most pleasant ambience. The long, glass-walled dining room is sur-
rounded by trees and plants. A truly ambitious lunch would start with
a seafood cocktail or plate of cold crab claws, followed by *pescado rel-
leno*, a fish fillet stuffed with finely diced shellfish, and then local peaches
drenched in sweet liqueurs. ⊠ *Av. Miguel Alemán 197-A,* ☎ *981/13365.
MC, V. No dinner.*

$ ✕ **La Perla.** Right down the street from the Instituto Campecheño uni-
versity, this is a popular student hangout. Fresh *licuados* (fruit drinks),
soups, salads, and sandwiches are priced for student budgets. ⊠ *Calle
10, No. 345,* ☎ *981/64092. No credit cards.*

$ ✕ **Marganzo.** This rustically furnished restaurant, conveniently situated
★ a half block south of the plaza, is a popular tourist spot—which is not
to its detriment. It's impeccably clean, with a colorful decor, and the
seafood dishes served at lunch and dinner are characteristic of the cui-
sine for which this region is known. You can't go wrong with such spe-
cials as *pan de casón* (tortillas with shredded baby shark). Waitresses
dressed in colonial Mexican–style skirts and embroidered blouses keep
in step with Marganzo's regional theme. ⊠ *Calle 8, No. 267,* ☎ *981/
13898. AE, MC, V.*

$ ✕ **Miramar.** This restaurant across from Hotel Castelmar attracts lo-
cals and foreign visitors with its fabulous *huevos motuleños* (fried
eggs smothered in refried beans and garnished with peas, chopped ham,
shredded cheese, and tomato sauce), red snapper, shellfish, soups, and
meat dishes. The heavy wooden tables and chairs and the paintings of
coats-of-arms give Miramar a colonial feel. ⊠ *Calle 8, No. 293A,* ☎
981/62883. MC, V.

$$–$$$ 🏨 **Ramada Inn.** The luxurious Ramada has undergone major reno-
★ vations: In 1994, 30 rooms and new kitchen facilities were added, and
improvements were made to the swimming pool and grounds. Fairly
large rooms, with all the necessary amenities, are decorated in shades
of blue and have rattan furnishings; balconies overlook the pool or the
bay. The lobby restaurant, **El Poquito,** is extremely popular with lo-
cals at breakfast and at night before the disco Atlantis opens. ⊠ *Av.
Ruíz Cortines 51, on waterfront,* ☎ *981/62233 or 800/228–9898,* FAX
*981/11618. 149 rooms. Restaurant, coffee shop, pool, exercise room,
shops, dance club, travel services. AE, MC, V.*

$ 🏨 **Alhambra.** A great choice away from the bustle of the city, the Al-
hambra is a modern hotel facing the waterfront near the university. A
wide-screen TV plays softly in the lobby; TVs in the rooms get U.S.
stations, sometimes including CNN. Rooms are carpeted and clean,
with king- and double-size beds. ⊠ *Av. Resurgimiento 85, between Avs.
Universidad and Augusto Melgar,* ☎ *981/66822,* FAX *981/66132. 98
rooms. Restaurant, bar, pool, tennis court. MC, V.*

$ 🏨 **Baluartes.** This big, square hotel is in the middle of a much-needed
refurbishing. Most rooms have been redecorated in cool blue tones and
have had their worn carpeting replaced with new terra-cotta tile and
new bathroom plumbing; air-conditioning has been installed in the ma-
jority of them. All have double-size beds, in-room phones, and TVs
that receive one U.S. network. The renovation has not reached the com-
mon areas, though. The hallways are on the dismal side, the creaking
elevators are amazingly slow, and the restaurant smells of cigarettes.
Still, there is a half-way decent sandwich shop, and the location is ideal.
Sandwiched between the waterfront malecón and the Puerto del Mar
gateway to the old city, Baluartes is within easy walking distance of

everything in the historic district. ✉ *Av. Ruíz Cortines 61,* ☎ *981/63911,* FAX *981/65765. 102 rooms. Restaurant, bar, coffee shop, pool, travel services, free parking. MC, V.*

$ ★ 🏨 **Colonial.** This building—the former home of a high-ranking army lieutenant—dates back to 1850 but was made over as a hotel in the 1940s, when its wonderful tiles were added. There's a plaque outside the front door identifying it as an important historical monument of the town. All rooms are delightfully different in structure, as befits a colonial mansion, but they are also pastel-colored and spacious with ceiling fans or air-conditioning, cool cotton bedding, good mattresses, tile bathrooms, window screens, and phones. In addition, Rooms 16, 18, 28, and 27 have lots of windows with ambient light and wonderful views of the cathedral and city at night. The well-kept public areas include two foliated patios, a small sun roof, and a sitting room on the second floor for reading. Guests breakfast at a small eatery down the street. ✉ *Calle 14, No. 122, between Calles 55 and 57,* ☎ *981/62222 or 981/62630. 30 rooms. No credit cards.*

$ 🏨 **Debliz.** Those traveling by car may wish to stay outside town at this modern hotel in a residential area north of the city. The four-story, elevator-equipped property, renovated in 1994, is refreshingly decorated with cream-color walls, beige carpets, dark wood furnishings, and paintings of flowers. Room amenities include color TV, reading lamps, and double beds. The bar and garden are popular gathering places for hotel guests. The Debliz can seem deserted and lonely—until the tour buses that frequent the place pull into the parking lot. ✉ *Av. Las Palmas 55, off Av. Pedro Sainz de Baranda, near baseball stadium,* ☎ *981/52222,* FAX *981/52277. 120 rooms. Restaurant, bar, coffee shop, pool, free parking. AE, MC, V.*

$ 🏨 **Del Paseo.** Located in the quiet San Román neighborhood, a block from the ocean, this new hotel is cheerful and well-lit. Rooms, painted in a soft rose with tasteful rattan furniture, have balconies, cable TV, and air-conditioning. A glass-roofed atrium next to the lobby is lovely, with its globe lamps, park benches, and many plants. ✉ *Calle 8, No. 215,* ☎ *981/10084 or 981/10100,* FAX *981/10097. 40 rooms. Restaurant, bar, shops. MC, V.*

$ 🏨 **El Regis.** This new seven-room hotel a mere two blocks from the plaza has to be the best bargain in town with prices at the low end of the $ category. Opened in March 1996, the Regis is a lovely old two-story colonial home with a humongous wooden entrance door, wrought-iron staircase, high ceilings, balconies, and an airy inner atrium. All rooms are spic-and-span with new black-and-white tile floors, two double beds with floral-print bedspreads, a cupboard closet, shower in the bathroom and cream-color walls. Four rooms come with air-conditioning and a TV with Spanish channels. The rest have overhead fans. The front doors close at 11 at night but there's a night watchman who opens up for guests who come in later. There's a coffee shop a half-block away. ✉ *Calle 12, No. 148, between Calles 55 and 57,* ☎ *981/53175. 7 rooms. No credit cards.*

$ 🏨 **Lopez.** Cheerful pink, yellow, and white walls and an open, airy ambience make this little two-story hotel a pleasant place to stay. Standard rooms include colonial-style desks and armoires, luggage stands, and easy chairs. Although the restaurant serves basic Continental fare, it's a convenient enough stop for breakfast, lunch, or dinner. ✉ *Calle 12, No. 189, between Calles 61 and 63,* ☎ *981/63344,* FAX *981/62488. 39 rooms. Restaurant. No credit cards.*

Nightlife and the Arts

Discos

If you're in the mood to dance, try Campeche's two discos, **Atlantis** (⌧ Ramada Inn, ☎ 981/62233), the only chic club in town, where politicians go to party, or the more student-oriented **El Dragon** (⌧ Sajuge complex, on Av. Resurgimiento, ½ block from the Alhambra Hotel, ☎ 981/11810 or 981/64289). Both places are open Thursday through Saturday nights only.

Movies

Campeche has five movie theaters. Two of the most conveniently located are **Cine Estelar** (⌧ Av. Miguel Alemán and Calle 49-B) and **Cine Alhambra** (⌧ At the shopping center at the Hotel Alhambra, Av. Resurgimiento 85). Both show films made in the United States, with Spanish subtitles, and are only open on weekend nights.

Outdoor Sports and Activities

Hunting, fishing, and birding are popular throughout the State of Campeche. Contact Don Jose Sansores at his office in the Hotel Castelmar (⌧ Calle 61, No. 2, ☎ 981/62356, ℻ 981/10624). Doves, ducks, and ocellated turkey are hunted October through the end of January; brocket deer and peccary in March and April. Sansores also can arrange sports-fishing excursions for snook and tarpon through his Campeche office or his Snook Inn hotel in Champotón (☎ 982/80018, ℻ 981/10624), an area with good fishing. Licenses and gun permits are required for big game—and arrangements for bringing any firearm and ammunition into Mexico are daunting—so make your inquiries well in advance.

Shopping

Because Campeche is a seaport, folk art here varies somewhat from the rest of Yucatán's handicrafts. Black coral and mother-of-pearl jewelry, sea shells, and ships-in-a-bottle are everywhere. You can also find basketry, leather goods, embroidered cloth, and clay trinkets. With a few exceptions, listed below, most of the shops sell cheap-looking trinkets.

Local Crafts

For handicrafts, try the brand-new **Casa de Artesanía** (⌧ Calle 55, No. 25, no phone), located in a lovely old mansion and operated by the government-run Family Institute; here's where you'll find well-made embroidered dresses and blouses, regional dress for men and women, hammocks, jipijapa (Panama) hats, lawn chairs, jewlery, baskets, leather goods, stucco reproductions of Maya motifs, and much more. **Veleros** (formerly called Aresanía Boutique, ⌧ Ah-Kin-Pech shopping center, ☎ 981/12446) is owned by craftsman David Pérez. It stocks his miniature ships, lots of black and red coral jewelry, sea shells, furniture with nautical motifs, and, new to the market, jewelry fashioned from sanded and polished bull's horns. The horn looks a lot like tortoise shell (which it is no longer legal to import to the United States) in thickness and color; although it's not as beautiful, it's a good, legal substitute. Pérez's first shop, Artesanía Típica Naval (⌧ Calle 8, No. 259, ☎ 981/65708), is still thriving, but it's much smaller and more cramped than the new store. Neither shop accepts credit cards.

Shopping Districts and Malls

Campeche City has two large, modern shopping malls: the **Plaza Comercial Ah-Kin-Pech** (⌧ Between Calles 51 and 49), on the stretch of the waterfront boulevard known as Avenida Pedro Sáinz de Baranda, and **Plaza del Mar,** across the parking lot from Ah-Kin-Pech on Avenida

Ruíz Cortines. Between them, they house a supermarket, a pastry shop, a beauty salon, a travel agency, a sporting-goods store, and clothing shops. Visit the **municipal market** (⊠ Circuito Baluartes at Calle 53), at the eastern end of the city, for crafts and food.

ALONG ROUTE 180 TOWARD MÉRIDA

The so-called short route to or from Mérida takes you past several villages and minor archaeological sites. After Halochób, the rest of the way to Mérida consists of relatively monotonous terrain, with the occasional clusters of white, thatched-roof huts, speed bumps, windmills, and spearlike henequen plants.

Hecelchacán

⑲ *75 km (56 mi) north of Campeche, along Route 180 toward Mérida.*

Although the pretty 15th-century town of Hecelchacán boasts a lovely church and former convent, it is known primarily for the **Museo Arqueológico del Camino Real.** This museum holds an impressive collection of clay figurines from the island of Jaina (a giant cemetery for the Maya) and stelae from the Puuc region. Don't make a special trip just to tour the museum, since the hours are erratic; it's often closed when it should be open. But if you're en route to Mérida and are an archaeology buff, it's worth the short detour off the highway to check out. Jaina itself is still off limits to walk-in visitors but can be visited with prior written permission from the National Institute of Anthropology and History in Campeche; the tourist office can help with the request. Even then, it can only be visited on guided boat. ⊠ *Rte. 180 to Hecelchacán, no phone.* 🎫 *Free.* ⊙ *Daily 8–4.*

Calkiní

⑳ *24 km (15 mi) north of Hecelchacán.*

Inside the fortress–convent built in Calkiní by the Franciscans between 1548 and 1776 is an exquisite cedar altarpiece on which the four Evangelists have been carved, and the columns and cornices adorning the convent have been painted in rich gold, red, and black. The portal is Plateresque (a 16th-century Spanish style whose elaborate ornaments suggest silver plate), while the rest of the structure is Baroque. Interestingly enough, Calkiní dates back much earlier, to the Maya Ah-Canul dynasty. According to a local codex, the Ah-Canul chieftainship was founded here in 1443 beneath a ceiba, a tree sacred to the Maya and frequently mentioned in their legends. The Ah-Canul was the most important dynasty at the time of the Conquest; the fighters rebelling against Montejo were put down in Mérida, dealing a great blow to the Maya spirit.

Becal

㉑ *10 km (6 mi) north of Calkiní.*

The small town of Becal is noted for the famous jipijapa (Panama-style) hats made here by local Indians. The Indians weave reeds of the guano palm in caves beneath their houses, because the humidity there keeps the reeds flexible. First produced in the 19th century by the García family, the hats have become a village tradition. Who can resist photographing the statue of three giant hats in the center of the town plaza? For a tour of a family hat workshop, just wander into any of the hat establishments on the town's main street and ask; the merchants will be more than happy to take you to their caves.

Halachó

㉒ *6 km (4 mi) north of Becal.*

Just across the Yucatán state line from Becal, in Halachó, townspeople weave motifs from central Mexico into their baskets. The centerpiece of this dusty little Maya town is a magnificent white 18th-century mission church dedicated to Santiago Matamoros, the patron saint of the Spanish conquistadors. Thousands of pilgrims come to Halachó each year to pay homage to the equestrian statue of the saint, located up a flight of stairs behind the altar.

Oxkintoc

㉓ *14 km (9 mi) north of Halachó.*

The archaeological site of Oxkintoc, which is actually in the state of Yucatan, is 2 km (1 mi) off the main highway near the present-day village of Maxcanú and contains the ruins of an important Maya capital that dominated the region from about AD 300 to 1100. Little was known about Oxkintoc until excavations began there in 1991. Structures that have been excavated so far include two tall pyramids, a palace with stone statues of several ancient rulers, and a temple that serves as the entrance to a mysterious subterranean labyrinth. ⊠ *Off Rte. 184, 1½ km (1 mi) west of Rte. 180, no phone.* 🕿 *$2, free Sun.* ☉ *Daily 8–5.*

ALONG ROUTE 261 TOWARD MÉRIDA

This is by far the longer—and more interesting—way to reach the Yucatán capital. The highway takes you through green hills covered by low scrub with occasional stands of tall, dark forest. In the valleys, cornfields and citrus orchards surround the occasional thatched-roof hut.

Edzná

㉔ *55 km (34 mi) southeast of Campeche City.*

The Maya ruin of Edzná deserves more fame than it has. Archaeologists consider it one of the peninsula's most important ruins because of the crucial transitional role it played among several architectural styles. Its obscurity can be attributed to two factors: Excavation began here relatively recently (in 1943), and restoration work is going ahead now. A new tourist facility with a cafeteria, rest rooms, and bookshop went up in 1996 here as well as at the rest of Campeche's major ruin sites.

Edzná, occupied from 300 BC to AD 900, was discovered in 1927. The 6-square-km (2-square-mi) expanse of savanna, broken up only by the occasional tall tree, is situated in a broad valley prone to flooding and flanked by low hills. Surrounding the site are vast networks of irrigation canals, the remnants of a highly sophisticated hydraulic system that channeled rainwater and water from the Champotón River into human-made *chultunes,* or wells.

Commanding center stage in the **Gran Acrópolis**, or Great Acropolis complex, is the **Pirámide de los Cinco Pisos** (Five-Story Pyramid), which rises 102 ft. The man-made platform consists of five levels, each narrower than the one below it, terminating in a tiny temple crowned by a roof comb. Hieroglyphs carved into the vertical face of the 15 steps between each level describe astronomy and history, while the numerous stelae depict the opulent attire and adornment of the ruling class—quetzal feathers, jade pectorals, and skirts of jaguar skin. Over the course of several hundred years, Edzná grew from a humble agricultural settlement into a major politico-religious center.

A Campeche archaeologist discovered recently that the temple was so constructed that, during certain dates of the year, the setting sun would illuminate the mask of the sun god, Itzamná, located inside one of the pyramid's rooms. This happens annually on May 1, 2, and 3—the beginning of the planting season for the ancient Maya, when they invoked the god to bring rain. It also occurs on August 7, 8, and 9, when the harvest was brought in and the Maya thanked the god for his help. Today, a local anthropologist, Elvira del Carmen Tello, stages an ancient Maya production at Edzná each May to commemorate the phenomenon. Check with the tourist office or travel desk at the Ramada Inn in Campeche City for more information.

Carved into **Building 414** of the Great Acropolis are some grotesque masks of the sun god with huge and sinister protruding eye sockets, the effect of which is enhanced by the oversized incisors or tongues extending from the upper lips. Local lore holds that Edzná, which means the House of the Gestures, or Grimaces, may have been named for these images.

A variety of architectural styles have been discerned at this site. The Petén style of northern Guatemala and Chiapas is reflected in the use of acropoli as bases for pyramids; of low-lying structures that contrast handsomely with soaring temples; and of corbeled arch roofs, richly ornamented stucco facades, and roof combs. The Río Bec style, which dominated much of Campeche, can be seen in the slender columns and exuberant stone mosaics. The multistory edifices, arched passageways, stone causeways, and hieroglyph-adorned stairways represent both the Chenes and Puuc styles.

If you're not driving, consider taking one of the inexpensive day trips offered by most travel agencies in Campeche; this is far easier than trying to get to Edzná by bus. If you do go by bus, be forewarned that you must walk about 1 km (½ mi) from the main road to the ruins. Check and double check with the driver about return buses—they are few and far between, and many tourists have been stranded until the next day. ⊠ *Rte. 261 east from Campeche City for 44 km (27 mi) to Cayal, then Rte. 188 southeast for 18 km (11 mi).* ⊠ *$2.* ⊙ *Daily 8–5.*

Hopelchén

㉕ *41 km (25 mi) north of the Edzná turnoff on Route 261.*

Hopelchén—the name means Place of the Five Wells—is a traditional Maya town noted for the lovely Franciscan church built in honor of St. Francis of Padua in 1667. Corn, beans, tobacco, fruit, and henequen are cultivated in this rich agricultural center.

Bolonchén de Rejón

㉖ *34 km (21 mi) north of Hopelchén.*

Just short of the state line between Campeche and Yucatán and a few miles before Bolonchén de Rejón is the Grutas de Xtacumbilxunán caverns ("hidden women" in Maya), where legend says a Maya girl never came back after going into the caverns for water. In ancient times, cenotes (sinkholes) deep in the extensive cave system provided an emergency water source during droughts. Only a few chambers are open to the public because the rock surfaces are dangerously slippery. Visitors can admire the delicate limestone formations in the upper part of the cave on an easy, two-hour guided tour booked through a travel agency in the city of Campeche; there are no guides at the site. ⊠ *$2.* ⊙ *Daily 8–5.*

Hochob

㉗ *41 km (25 mi) south of Hopelchén.*

The small Maya ruin of Hochob is an excellent example of the Chenes architectural style, which flowered in the classical period from about AD 200 to 900. Found throughout central and southern Campeche, Chenes-style temples are easily recognized by their elaborate stucco facades forming giant masks of jaguars, birds, or other creatures, with doorways representing the beasts' open jaws. Since work began at Hochob in the early 1980s, eight temples and palaces have been excavated at the site, including two that have been restored to their original grandeur. ⊠ *South of Hopelchén on Dzibalchén–Chenko road, no phone.* ✆ *Free.* ⊘ *Daily 8–5.*

Dzibilnocac

㉘ *25 km (16 mi) east of Hochob.*

The rarely visited archaeological site of Dzibilnocac, reached by a good but unpaved road, was a fair-size ceremonial center between AD 250 and 900. Although at least seven temple pyramids have been located here, the only one that has been excavated is the **Palacio Principal,** an unusual rounded pyramid resembling a smaller version of the one at Uxmal and combining elements of the Puuc and Chenes architectural styles. ⊠ *East of Hochob on Iturbide road, no phone.* ✆ *Free.* ⊘ *Daily 8–5.*

ROUTE 180 TO VILLAHERMOSA

Heading south from Campeche, Route 180 hugs the coast, offering a wonderful view of the Gulf of Mexico. The deep green sea is so shallow that the continental shelf is almost visible at low tide, and because waves and currents are rare, the gulf resembles a lake more than the vast body of water that it is.

Playa Bonita

㉙ *13 km (8 mi) south of Campeche City.*

The first beach south of Campeche City, Playa Bonita can be reached by public buses from the market (⊠ Circuito Baluartes, between Calles 53 and 55); the buses depart daily (6 AM–11 PM). The beach has lockers, changing rooms, showers, and a snack bar, but is crowded on weekends and badly littered at all times. A few beaches are private property where trespassing is not allowed. This is the case with Playa San Lorenzo, which is about 5 km (3 mi) south of Playa Bonita. You are allowed to walk the 3-km (2-mi) trail between the two beaches, however.

Seybaplaya

㉚ *20 km (12 mi) south of Playa Bonita.*

Wooden motor launches fill the beach at the traditional fishing port of Seybaplaya; its palm-lined setting is probably the prettiest seascape on the Campeche coast. A couple of miles beyond lies **Payucán,** a beach with fine white sand and moderate waves. It has a campsite and a snack bar that only opens during holiday periods like Holy Week, Christmas Week, and July and August; otherwise, there are no facilities. There's a new paved road from Seyaplaya to Payucán.

Champotón

③ *35 km (22 mi) south of Seybaplaya.*

The highway curves through a hilly region before reaching Champotón's immensely satisfying vista of open seas. Champotón is a charming little town with a bridge, palapas right on the water, and plenty of swimmers and launches in sight. The Spaniards dubbed the outlying bay the *Bahía de la Mala Pelea,* or Bay of the Evil Battle, because it was here that the troops of the Spanish conqueror and explorer Hernández de Córdoba were trounced for the first time in Mexico in 1517 by belligerent Indians armed with arrows, slingshots, and darts.

The 17th-century Church of **Nuestra Señora de las Mercedes** and the ruins of the **Fuerte de San Luis** still stand in Champotón. This area, ideal for fishing and hunting, teems with shad and bass as well as deer, wild boar, doves, and quail, and is sustained by an economy based largely on chicle, water coconut, sugarcane, bananas, avocados, corn, and beans. The famous Champotón baby shrimp are harvested here. You may be lucky enough to spot the "green ray" of light making up the sunset.

Isla del Carmen

③ *115 km (71 mi) south of Champotón.*

It was on this barrier island protecting the lagoon from the gulf that the pirates who raided Campeche hid from 1663 until their expulsion in 1717. The island has served as a depot for everything from dyewoods and textiles to hardwoods, chicle, shrimp, and (for the last 20 years) oil. Its major development is at **Ciudad del Carmen,** on the eastern end, now connected by two bridges to the mainland; the second, inaugurated in November 1994, eliminates an hour's detour around the lagoon when driving north.

There is a surprising variety of things to do on Isla del Carmen, which has several fine white-sand beaches with palm groves and shallow waters, excellent fishing (sailfish, swordfish, shrimp, oyster, and conch), water sports, restaurants, hotels, and even some nightlife. Catamarans regularly ply the inner canals; **dolphins** can be spotted at Zacatal, a hotel on the lagoon side of the island; a Moorish 18th-century pavilion marks the center of **Zaragoza Park;** and the **Museum of Anthropology and History** (⊠ Av. Gobernadores 289, no phone) displays pre-Hispanic and pirate artifacts. Archaeological sites on the island include **Xicalango,** where Cortés's mistress, Malinche, eventually lived, and **Itzankanac,** where the last Aztec emperor, Cuauhtémoc, supposedly met his demise (although other sources place Itzankanac on the mainland). The tourist office can arrange for a guide to take visitors through the **Laguna de Terminos,** past mangroves and an estuary; there's a stop to see how oysters grow and a short visit to a crocodile farm to get a look at its most famous couple, "Sasha" and "Conan," who measure 9 ft each. The best beaches for swimming are **El Playon** and **Playa Benjamin.**

Dining and Lodging

$$ ✕ **Piamonte.** An exception to the rule that says hotel restaurants are bound to be inferior, the dining room at the Eurohotel serves some of Ciudad del Carmen's finest fare, featuring Italian pastas as well as seafood. Grilled, cooked, and oven-broiled lobster and shrimp from the nearby gulf get top billing with local oil entrepreneurs who frequently book business lunches. Soft music plays in the evening. ⊠ *Calle 22, No. 208,* ☎ *938/23044. AE, MC, V.*

$ ✕ **La Flama.** In addition to fresh fish and seafood dishes, this casual restaurant serves barbecued chicken and beef ribs and brochettes. The house special is fish fillet filled with seafood. La Flama is open every night until 2 AM. ⊠ *Calle 35, No. 39,* ☎ *938/27152. AE, MC, V.*

$$$ ⊞ **Eurohotel.** Geared to the Mexican business traveler, this contemporary, upscale hotel is close to the center of town and offers secretarial services and meeting rooms. It also affords lots of after-work relaxation options, including a disco, bar, and pool. Standard modern guest rooms are air-conditioned, with cable TV and phones. ⊠ *Calle 22, No. 208, 1 block from Terminos lagoon,* ☎ *938/23044 or 938/23078,* ℻ *938/23021. 92 rooms and suites with bath. Restaurant, coffee shop. AE, DC, MC, V.*

$ ⊞ **Hotel Zacarias.** This bare-bones downtown hotel has its priorities down: None of the rooms have phones, half of them have air-conditioning, and all have cable TV. Most of the older accommodations offer only sofa beds, but there are 18 rooms in a new wing with standard-size beds. ⊠ *Calle 24, No. 58, on Plaza Principal,* ☎ *938/23506. 58 rooms. Restaurant. No credit cards.*

ALONG ROUTE 186 TOWARD CHETUMAL

Campeche's archaeological sites, particularly those near the Quintana Roo border, are attracting more attention from scientists and travelers alike. The vestiges of at least 10 little-known Maya cities lie hidden off Route 186 between Francisco Escárcega and Chetumal. Becán and the neighboring sites of Chicanná and Xpujil are just off Highway 186 near the Quintana Roo border, and you can now take a paved road all the way to Calakmul near the Guatemala border south of Xpujil, but the others are more difficult to reach; a four-wheel-drive vehicle—and much enthusiasm—are required. All three sites are easily viewed in a day if you're en route between Escárcega and Chetumal. The ruins at Hormiguero and Río Bec are reached by expeditions of several hours along four-wheel-drive-only roads on the edge of the Calakmul Biosphere Reserve. Both sites are best visited on guided Land Rover tours. A half-day Hormiguero trip or an all-day Río Bec expedition can be arranged a day in advance at either the small, nameless cabaña lodge at Xpujil or the Ramada Ecovillage (☞ *below*). For now, this secluded but accessible area is perfect for those who want to get a sense of the ruins as they appear in the wild. This area is gradually being developed for visitors, with attempts made to minimize the impact of tourism on the surrounding areas.

Becán

③ *293 km (182 mi) southeast of Campeche, 132 km (82 mi) west of Chetumal.*

Becán, which means "path of the serpent" in Maya, may have served as a religious and ceremonial center as early as 150 AD, based on the period in which its defensive moat was constructed. Most of Becán's temples date from 600 to 900 AD. The site has some of Campeche's largest Maya buildings, connected by underground passages and secret rooms. A deep moat ½ km long (1 mi long) surrounds the ruins, which have been extensively restored. A visitor center with snack bar and rest rooms has opened at this pristine site. ⊡ *$2.* ⊙ *Daily 8–5.*

Chicanná

③④ *3 km (2 mi) east of Becán.*

A small city of the same era as Becán, Chicanná (Maya for "house of the serpent's mouth") dates from the Late-Classical period. The main temple at this intimate site has lovely sculpted reliefs and faces with long twisted noses caressing its facade. Masks most likely representing an earth monster are on the facades of several temples. The Chenes-style main temple is virtually identical to the one at Hochob, far to the north. A small snack shop with rest rooms has been added. ⌨ *$2.* ☉ *Daily 8–5.*

Xpujil

③⑤ *7 km (4 mi) east of Chicanná.*

Xpujil (or "cat's tail") comprises three large towers in one structure overlooking the jungle, along with several other building groups that have not yet been excavated. The site, which can be clearly seen from the highway, blends architectural elements of both the Chenes architectural style, characterized by elaborate facades with "monster mouth" doorways, and the Río Bec style, with facades decorated with massive false pyramids. A visitor center with a snack bar and restrooms is now in operation. ⌨ *$2.* ☉ *Daily 8–5.*

Lodging

$$ 🏨 **Ramada Ecovillage Resort.** Until recently, the complete absence of overnight accommodations and the distance from major towns made visiting the Maya ruins in southern Campeche very difficult. The opening of this jungle lodge in early 1995 has changed that. The lodge's rooms, in two-story stucco duplexes with thatched roofs, are secluded in a rain forest. Each of the large units has a separate bedroom with one king-size or two double beds, overhead fan, plus one or two hammocks on a porch or balcony. Lush gardens surround the outdoor swimming pool. Solar energy powers the hot water, there's an artificial lagoon for water storage and an organic waste-treatment plant. There are no phones or TVs at the lodge, though public long-distance phones and fax service are available at the small village of Xpujil. ⌨ *Off Rte. 186 at Zona Arqueológico Xpujil, 3 km (2 mi) north of village of Xpujil,* ☎ *981/62233 or 800/228–9898,* ℻ *981/11618. Restaurant, bar, pool. AE, MC, V.*

Hormiguero

③⑥ *19 km (12 mi) southeast of Xpujil.*

Hormiguero (Spanish for "anthill," referring to the looters' tunnels that honeycombed the ruins when archaeologists discovered them) has five temples, two of which have been excavated to reveal ornate facades. During the rainy season, the unpaved road from Xpujil is impassable. ⌨ *Free.*

Río Bec

③⑦ *15 km (10 mi) south of Xpujil, same distance from Hormiguero.*

The sprawling Río Bec archaeological zone covers nearly 78 square km (30 square mi) along the banks of the river of the same name. The zone includes five major ceremonial centers and 15 smaller temple groups, but although archaeologists have done extensive surveys of the area, little clearing or excavation has been done. The only structure that has been completely excavated and restored, known as **Río**

Bec B, is a 55-ft-tall temple. Similar in design to the temples found at Becán, Xpujil, and other sites in the area, it typifies the so-called Río Bec architectural style, with two false-pyramid towers flanking the front entrance. Ancient builders created miniaturized, impossibly steep stairways and used an optical illusion known as forced perspective to give the towers the appearance of huge pyramids towering hundreds of feet. Experts now believe the center of the Río Bec culture was actually Calakmul (☞ *below*), about 95 km (60 mi) to the southeast, but the architectural style was given this name before Calakmul was discovered. ✉ *Free.*

Seeing all the main ceremonial centers at Río Bec requires about eight hours of hiking through difficult rain forest terrain; an all-day trip that includes Río Bec B and its unexcavated look-alike, Río Bec N, involves only a few miles of relatively easy hiking. Guide services, essential for this trip, can be arranged (do this at least a day in advance) at the Ramada Ecovillage (☞ *above*); the nameless little restaurant and cabin compound at Xpujil; or Rancho Encantado at Bacalar, Quintana Roo (☞ Chapter 5).

Calakmul

③⑧ *70 km (43 mi) southwest of Xpujil.*

Remote Calakmul (Twin Towers) is in the isolated region near the Guatemala border. The area surrounding the ancient Maya city has been declared a biosphere reserve; boasting 1.8 million acres, it is the second largest reserve of its kind on the continent (☞ Sian Ka'an *in* Chapter 5). Flora and fauna, including several different species of wildcats (jaguar, puma, ocelot) and 120 varieties of orchids, proliferate here. Although structures will be excavated, the dense jungle surrounding them will be left in its natural state. Extensive information on the site's ecosystem is presented in tours conducted by local guides. You have a better chance of getting an English-speaking guide if you hire one through a travel agency in Campeche City.

Archaeologists and anthropologists estimate that the region may once have been inhabited by more than 50,000 Maya, and have thus far uncovered more than 6,000 structures, including what may be the largest Maya building on the peninsula; more than 100 stelae have also been found. Twin pyramids or temples facing each other across a plaza, similar to those found at Tikal, Guatemala, have been discovered here. However, the sites' bulky Río Bec architectural style is not as graceful or aesthetically appealing as that at Tikal. Perhaps the most monumental discovery so far is a 1,000-year-old mummy, found in 1994 locked away in a royal tomb. It's the first known example of this type of burial in the Maya world to date, and the remains are under study at the government's anthropology institute in Mexico City. At present, special permission is needed from the Instituto Nacional de Antropología e História in the city of Campeche for entry into Calakmul; the tourist office in Campeche can help with the permit, but it generally takes a couple of weeks to obtain. The entrance road to the site has been paved, and a standard module with snack bar, rest rooms, and bookshop was opened in the beginning of 1997. It's best to take a tour offered by the Ramada Ecovillage (☞ Xpujil, *above*) or to book one through a travel agency in the city of Campeche.

Calakmul was a formidable military power in its time. It's estimated to have been first settled around 1500 BC. Experts say it was probably the capital city of the mighty Serpent Head dynasty; the glyph with this symbol has been found on stelae in other parts of the ancient Maya empire, suggesting that Calakmul dominated a large number of vassal city-states. It reached the pinnacle of its power in the late Classic period when it held sway over Palenque in Chiapas and superpower Tikal in Guatemala. Stelae under study also indicate that the new heads of vassal states were obligated to journey to Calakmul to be formally consecrated in their new duties by the leader of the Serpent Head lineage. Epigraphers also have discovered inscriptions relating the defeat of Calakmul's most famous ruler, Jaguar Paw, at the hands of arch rival Tikal in 695 AD. The city-state went into decline after this.

All visitors entering Calakmul must register at the entrance gate. From there, vehicles drive about 10 minutes along a newly paved road to the parking area. Then it's a good 20-minute hike to the first building. The site is shrouded in thick rain forest, but paths with signposts lead to various temples. Only about a half-dozen structures can be visited, including Temples I and II–twin pyramids separated by an immense plaza. Temple II, the tallest so far at 175 ft, has to be climbed via a ragged rock incline as the steps have not been restored yet. It's worth it though, because the view from the top of the surrounding canopy of rain forest is spectacular; you can see into Guatemala 35 km (22 mi) away. The facade and steps of slightly smaller Temple I have been restored, so it's easier to climb. A pair of royal tombs has been extracted from here, one of a female regent. There's a stela at the base of the pyramid overlooking the plaza. Parts of temples are scattered around one of the rain forest paths, probably the work of grave robbers who got away with the choice pieces. It's hard to thwart these criminals since to do so would require a large corps of guards at the site, and there is no budget available for hiring them. This site is also perfect for birdwatchers. ⊠ *97 km (51 mi) east of Escárega to turnoff at Cohuas, then 65 km (40 mi) south to Calakmul.* 🖾 *$2.50.* ⊙ *Daily 8–5.*

El Tigre

③⑨ *30 km (19 mi) from Escárcega.*

El Tigre is difficult to reach and barely explored. The ruins may have been the site of postclassical Itzankanac, capital of the province of Acalán, where Spanish conquistador Cortés supposedly hanged Cuauhtémoc, the last Aztec emperor. El Tigre comprises a 656-ft-long ceremonial plaza and dozens of mounds in the jungle near Lake Salsipuedes and Vieja Lagoon in the Candelaria River basin. Hire a *cayuca* (dugout canoe) from one of the locals to take you from Candelaria across the river to the site. A four-wheel-drive vehicle is best for traversing the 30½ km (19 mi) of dirt road to the river from Francisco Escárcega. 🖾 *Fee at all sites when someone is there to collect it.*

CAMPECHE A TO Z

Arriving and Departing

By Bus

ADO (⊠ Av. Gobernadores 289 at Calle 45, along Rte. 261 to Mérida, ☎ 981/62802), a first-class line, runs buses to Campeche City from Coatzacoalcos, Ciudad del Carmen, and Mérida every half hour, and from Mexico City, Puebla, Tampico, Veracruz, and Villahermosa regularly, but less frequently. The deluxe **Expreso del Caribe** (☎ 981/13973) travels between Campeche, Mérida, Villahermosa, and Cancún. Buses depart from the Plaza Ah-Kim-Pech on Avenida Pedro Sainz de Baranda 120. There is less desirable second-class service on **Autobuses del Sur** (☎ 981/63445) from Chetumal, Ciudad del Carmen, Escárcega,

Mérida, Palenque, Tuxtla Gutiérrez, Villahermosa, and intermediate points throughout the Yucatán Peninsula.

By Car

Campeche can be reached from Mérida in about 1½ hours along the 160-km (99-mi) *via corta* (short way, Route 180). The alternative route, the 250-km (155-mi) *via larga* (long way, Route 261), takes at least three hours but crosses the major Maya ruins of Uxmal, Kabah, and Sayil. From Chetumal, take Route 186 west to Francisco Escárcega, where you pick up Route 261 north; the drive takes about seven hours. Villahermosa is about six hours away if you drive inland via the town of Francisco Escárcega, but longer if you hug the gulf and cross the bridge at Ciudad del Carmen.

By Plane

Aeromexico (☎ 981/65678) has one flight daily from Mexico City to Campeche City.

Getting Around

By Bus

The municipal bus system covers all of Campeche City, but you can easily visit the major sights on foot. Public buses run along Avenida Ruíz Cortines and cost under $1.

By Taxi

Taxis can be hailed on the street in Campeche City, or—more reliably—commissioned from the main taxi stand (⊠ Calle 8, between Calles 55 and 53, ☎ 981/62366 or 981/65230) or at stands by the bus stations and market. Because of the scarcity of taxis, it's quite common to share them with other people headed in the same direction as you. Don't be surprised to see one already occupied slow down to where you are standing if the cab driver thinks he can pick up another fare.

Contacts and Resources

Banks

Campeche City banks are open weekdays 9–1 Those where you can exchange money include **Banamex** (⊠ Calle 53, No. 15, at Calle 10, ☎ 981/65251) and **Bancomer** (⊠ Av. 16 de Septiembre, No. 120, ☎ 981/66622).

Car Rental

There is a **Hertz** representative at the Torres de Crital building in Campeche City (⊠ Av. Ruíz Cortines 112, ☎ 981/12106) and the airport (☎ 981/68848).

Emergencies

Throughout the state, call 06 locally in case of emergency.

Campeche City: Police (⊠ Av. Resurgimiento s/n, ½ block from Hotel Alhambra, ☎ 981/62329); **Red Cross** (⊠ Av. Resurgimiento s/n, ☎ 981/52411).

Guided Tours

Trolley tours of the city leave from the Plaza Principal daily at 9:30, 6, and 8. They last 1½ hours, have a bilingual guide, and cost $6.

Emerald Planet (⊠ 4076 Crystal Court, Boulder, CO 80304, ☎ 303/541–9688, FAX 303/449–7805) and **Siteseer Journeys** (⊠ 27210 SW 166 Ave., Homestead, FL 33031, ☎ 800/615–4035, FAX 305/242–9009) arrange tours to the **Calakmul Reserve** to see the conservation projects such as beekeeping and organic gardening. The projects' sponsor, **Pronatura** (⊠ Calle 1-D 254-A, Campestra, ☎ FAX 99/443390 and

99/443580) leads overnight trips to Calakmul with advance reservations and an obligatory donation to their conservation fund.

Mail

The **post office** (⊠ Av. 16 de Septiembre, between Calles 53 and 55, ☎ 981/62134) in Campeche City is open weekdays 9–6, Saturday 9–1.

Medical Clinics

In Campeche City, **Hospital General** (⊠ Av. Central at Circuito Baluartes, ☎ 981/60920 or 981/64233) and **Social Security Clinic** (⊠ Av. Lopez Mateos s/n, ☎ 981/65202) are both open 24 hours for emergencies.

Pharmacies

In Campeche City, **Clínica Campeche** (⊠ Av. Central 65, near the Social Security Clinic, ☎ 981/65612) is open 24 hours. The **Farmacia Alhambra** in the Hotel Alhambra (⊠ Av. Resurgimiento 85, between Av. Universidad and Av. Augusto Melgar, ☎ 981/11246), open 7 AM–11 PM, will deliver to guests of other hotels.

Telephones

There are several public booths for making long-distance calls in Campeche City: In addition to the ones at Avenida Gobernadores s/n (8 AM–10 PM) and at the corner of Calle 12 at Calle 59 (9 AM–10 PM), there are phones at the post office and all international courier service offices.

Travel Agencies and Tour Operators

Campeche City: **American Express/VIPs** (⊠ Prolongación Calle 59, Edificio Belmar, Depto. 5, ☎ 981/11010 or 981/11000, FAX 981/68333); **Destinos Maya** (⊠ Av. Miguel Aleman 162, Locale 106, ☎ 981/13726 or 713/440–0291 or 713/440–0253 in the U.S., FAX 981/10934); **Viajes Campeche** (⊠ Calle 10, No. 339, ☎ 981/65233, FAX 981/62844).

Visitor Information

The **tourist office** has moved to a new location (⊠ Av. Ruiz Cortines s/n, across the street from the Palacio de Gobierno, ☎ 981/65593 or 981/66829); it's open daily 9–3 and 5–8. There's an information booth at the Baluarte de Santiago at the Botanical Gardens.

Ciudad del Carmen: The **tourist office** (⊠ Palacio Municipal on the main plaza, ☎ 938/20311 or 938/21137) is open weekdays 9–3 and 6–9.

7 Mérida and the State of Yucatán

Long a favorite of archaeologists, the state of Yucatán contains the two most spectacular Maya ruins, Chichén Itzá and Uxmal. Travelers are also coming to recognize the charms of Mérida, with its excellent restaurants and markets and its unique mix of Spanish, Maya, and French architectural styles.

VISITORS WHO VENTURE away from the Caribbean coast soon find themselves in a strange land of women in white, oval thatched-roof huts, iguanas

Updated by
Patricia Alisau

and stray pigs, and stately old mission churches. Mysterious "lost cities" lie hidden in the forests. Small fishing villages dot beaches that are oblivious to the tourist industry. In the midst of this exotic landscape stands the graceful old city of Mérida, for centuries the main stronghold of Spanish colonialism in the land of the Maya.

There is a marvelous eccentricity about Mérida. Fully urban, with maddeningly slow-moving traffic, it has a self-sufficient, self-contented air that would suggest a small town more than a state capital of some 600,000 inhabitants (locals say there are about 1 million). Gaily pretentious turn-of-the-century buildings have an Iberian-Moorish flair for the ornate, but most of the architecture is low-lying, and although the city sprawls, it is not imposing. Grandiose colonial facades adorned with iron grillwork, carved wooden doors, and archways conceal marble tiles and lush gardens; horse-drawn carriages hark back to the city's heyday as the wealthiest capital in Mexico.

Mérida is a city of subtle contrasts, from its opulent yet faded facades to its residents, very European yet very Maya. The Indian presence is unmistakable: People are short and dark-skinned, with sculpted bones and almond eyes; women pad about in *huipiles* (hand-embroidered, sacklike white dresses), and craftsmen and vendors from the outlying villages come to town in their huaraches. So many centuries after the conquest, Yucatán remains one of the last great strongholds of Mexico's indigenous population. To this day, in fact, many Maya do not even speak Spanish, primarily because of the peninsula's geographic and, hence, cultural isolation from the rest of the country. Additionally, the Maya—long portrayed as docile and peace-loving—for centuries provided the Spaniards and the mainland Mexicans with one of their greatest challenges. Yucatán tried to secede from the rest of Mexico in the 1840s and, as late as the 1920s and 1930s, rebellious pockets of Maya communities held out against the outsiders, or *dzulobs*. Yucatecos speak of themselves as *peninsulares* first, Mexicans second.

The Maya civilization—one of the great ancient cultures—had been around since before 1500 BC, but it was in a state of decline when the conquistadors arrived in AD 1527, burning defiant warriors at the stake, severing limbs, and drowning and hanging women. Huge agricultural estates brought riches to the Spaniards, and Mérida soon became a strategic administrative and military foothold, the gateway to Cuba and to Spain. Francisco de Montejo's conquest of Yucatán took three gruesome wars, a total of 24 years. "Nowhere in all America was resistance to Spanish conquest more obstinate or more nearly successful," wrote the historian Henry Parkes. By the 18th century, huge maize and cattle plantations flourished throughout the peninsula, and the wealthy *hacendados* (plantation owners), left largely to their own devices by the viceroys in faraway Mexico City, accumulated fortunes under a semifeudal system. As the economic base shifted to the export of dyewood, henequen, and chicle, the social structure—based on Indian peonage—barely changed.

Insurrection came during the War of the Castes in the mid-1800s, when the enslaved indigenous people rose up with religious fervor and massacred thousands of whites. The United States, Cuba, and Mexico City finally came to the aid of the ruling elite, and between 1846 and 1850 the Indian population of Yucatán was effectively halved. Those

Maya who did not escape into the remote jungles of Quintana Roo or get sold into slavery in Cuba found themselves worse off than before under the dictatorship of Porfirio Díaz, who brought Yaqui prisoners from Northern Mexico to the peninsula as forced labor under the rapacious grip of the hacendados. Díaz's legacy is still evident in the pretentious French-style mansions that stretch along Mérida's Paseo de Montejo.

Yucatán was then and still is a largely agricultural state, although oil, tourism, and the *maquiladora* (assembly plants, usually foreign-owned) now play more prominent roles in the economy. Some 93 offshore oil-drilling platforms dot the continental shelf surrounding the peninsula, and soon there will be as many as 50 factories. The capital accounts for about half the state's population, but the other half lives in villages, maintaining conservative traditions and lifestyles. The state exports honey, textiles, henequen, orange-juice concentrate, fresh fish, hammocks, and wood products.

Physically, too, Yucatán differs from the rest of the country. Its geography and wildlife have more in common with Florida and Cuba—with which it was probably once connected—than with the central Mexican plateau and mountains. A mostly flat limestone slab possessing almost no bodies of water, it is rife with underground cenotes (sinkholes), caves with stalactites, small hills, and intense jungle. Wild ginger and spider lilies grow in profusion, and vast flamingo colonies nest at swampy estuaries on the northern and western coasts, where undeveloped sandy beaches extend for 370 km (230 mi). Deer, turkeys, boars, ocelots, tapirs, and armadillos flourish in this semitropical climate (the average temperature is 82°F, or 28°C).

But it is, of course, the celebrated Maya ruins, Chichén Itzá and Uxmal especially, that bring most tourists to Mérida. Indeed, the Puuc hills south of Mérida have more archaeological sites per square mile than any other place in the hemisphere. The roads in this region rank among the best in the country, and local travel agencies are adept at running tours.

Pleasures and Pastimes

Beaches

Although Yucatán's beach resorts are no match for those of Cancún and the Caribbean coast, the north coast of the peninsula has long stretches of wide, soft white-sand beaches shared by sunbathers and fishermen. Progreso, where Mérida residents go to beat the heat, is unpretentious and affordable, and on summer weekends it can be as lively as anyplace on the Mexican Caribbean. Empty beaches stretch for about 64 km (40 mi) to the east, punctuated by half-abandoned fishing villages that never really recovered from Hurricane Hugo in 1988. Other popular beach destinations are Celestún and Sisal.

Bird-Watching

More than 300 bird species are abundant in the Yucatán, both along the coast and inland. The most extraordinary are flamingos, which can be seen in the natural parks at Celestún and Río Lagartos at any time of year. The largest flocks of both flamingos and birding enthusiasts can be found during the spring months, when thousands of the birds— 90 percent of the entire flamingo population of the Western Hemisphere—come to Río Lagartos to nest.

Dining

Dining out is a pleasure in Mérida. The city's 50-odd restaurants offer a superb variety of cuisine—primarily Yucatecan, of course, but also

Lebanese, Italian, French, Chinese, and Mexican—at very reasonable prices. Generally, reservations are advised for those places marked $$$, but only during the high season. Casual but neat dress is acceptable at all Mérida restaurants.

Beach towns north of Mérida like Progreso, Yucaltepen, Sisal, Telchac Puerto, and Río Lagartos and Celestún to the west offer the most mouth-watering seafood around, always fresh-caught the same day. A real gourmet dish is the blue crab at Celustún. However, you can't go wrong in any of these restaurants, whether they be thatched-roof affairs along the beach or in-town eateries.

Beware the restaurants in Pisté, the village nearest to Chichén Itzá; they're overpriced, and the food is only fair. It's better to try one of the *palapa* (pre-Hispanic thatched roof) cafés along the main road or the small markets and produce stands, which can provide the makings for a modest picnic.

The restaurants near the ruins in Uxmal are nothing to write home about either. The exception is Los Almendros, in Ticul, which is well worth the 15-minute drive.

All restaurants are open for breakfast, lunch, and dinner unless otherwise noted. People who like eating with the locals might stop in at one of the many *loncherías* (diners) in the small towns and downtown districts of cities for *panuchos* (cooked tortillas stuffed with beans and topped with shredded meat or fish), *empanadas* (meat-filled turnovers), tacos, or *salbutes* (fried tortillas smothered with diced turkey, pickled onion, and sliced avocado). However, take care with the *habanero* chilies. This native species will have smoke coming out of your ears if not used in moderation.

CATEGORY	COST*
$$$$	over $20
$$$	$15–$20
$$	$8–$15
$	under $8

per person, excluding drinks and service

Fishing

Those interested in sportfishing for such catch as grouper, red snapper, and sea bass, among others, will be sated in **Yucalpetén,** west of Progreso. **Río Lagartos** also offers good fishing in its murky waters. In the Parque Natural del Flamenco Mexicano in **Celestún,** you have your choice of river or gulf fishing.

Lodging

Outside of Mérida you'll find that accommodations fit the low-key, simple pace of the region. Internationally affiliated properties are the exception rather than the rule; instead, charmingly idiosyncratic old mansions or former haciendas like the Hacienda Katanchel, recently restored and opened as a hotel (☞ Dining and Lodging *in* Mérida, *below*) offer visitors a base from which to explore the countryside. However, the new all-inclusive Mayan Beach Resort in Telchac Puerto, which is patterned after a Club Med, has diversified the hotel offerings.

Mérida's 60-odd hotels offer a refreshingly broad range, from the chain hotels at the top end and the classic, older hotels housed in colonial or turn-of-the-century mansions suffused with genteel charm, to fleabags adequate only for the budget traveler unconcerned with creature comforts. As in the rest of Mexico, the facade rarely reveals the character of the hotel behind it, so check out the interior before turning away.

Location is very important in your choice of hotels: If you plan to spend most of your time enjoying Mérida, stay in the vicinity of the main square or along Calle 60. If you're a light sleeper, however, choose a hotel away from the plaza and parks or one that has double-pane windows to cut out traffic noise; you're better off staying in one of the places along or near Paseo de Montejo, about a 30-minute stroll from the *zócalo* (main square). If being assured of hot water is a major concern, test the faucets before renting a room. In general, the public spaces in Mérida's hotels are prettier than the sleeping rooms. All hotels have air-conditioning unless otherwise noted. More budget hotels are installing air-conditioning in at least a few rooms nowadays to keep up with the competition.

Properties in Mérida have a Yucatán 97000 mailing address.

CATEGORY	COST*
$$$$	over $90
$$$	$60–$90
$$	$25–$60
$	under $25

All prices are for a standard double room, excluding service and the 15% tax.

Ruins

Ancient Maya ruins from the Classic Period, about AD 250 to AD 900, are Yucatán's greatest claim to fame. The Maya-Toltec city of Chichén Itzá, midway between Cancún and Mérida, was the first Yucatán ruin to be excavated and extensively restored for public viewing in the late 1930s. Its main pyramid has become one of the most familiar images of Mexico. Uxmal, south of Mérida, is at least equally spectacular. Public interest in these ruins has inspired a boom in ruins restoration since the early 1980s. The archaeological sites along the Puuc Route south of Uxmal, though not large, are among the most beautiful in Mexico, and recently discovered sites such as Oxkintok invite adventuresome travelers to explore where few visitors have set foot in recent centuries.

NOTE: New discoveries about the Mayas, one of the most mysterious cultures of Mesoamerica, are constantly coming to light through the diligent work of many archaeological investigators. The Mexican government has earmarked several million dollars for research since 1992, and it is paying off. So keep in mind that many dates of major events reported in the Exploring sections, *below,* are only good estimates unless precise dates have been found in Maya writings. Unfortunately, with the near total destruction of the Maya codices (or books) by a fanatic bishop in the 16th century, many of these historical records have been lost.

Maya temples are not the only ruins that tug at the imagination in Yucatán. Grandiose Spanish colonial mission churches, built—often on the same site—with stones scavenged from ancient pyramids, dominate Maya villages throughout the state. The opulence of a more recent era can be seen at haciendas where wealthy plantation owners grew *henequen,* a fiber used to make rope. Some plantations still operate on a small scale today, but most of the lavish mansion houses either have become museums or have been allowed to crumble.

Shopping

Yucatecan artisans produce some of the finest crafts in Mexico. For the most part, Mérida is the best place in Yucatán to buy local handicrafts at reasonable prices. The main products include *hamacas* (hammocks), *guayaberas* (loose dress shirts for men), *huaraches* (woven leather sandals), *huipiles* (hand-embroidered dresses), baskets, *jipis* (Panama hats made from guano palm) that can be rolled up in your suitcase, leather goods, gold and silver filigree jewelry, masks, painted gourds, vanilla, and piñatas. A word about hammocks, one of the most popular craft items sold here: They are available in cotton, nylon, and silk as well as in the very rough and scratchy henequen fiber. Silk, which is very expensive, is unquestionably the best choice but is hard to find. Double-threaded hammocks are sturdier and stretch less than single-threaded ones, a difference that can be identified by studying the loop handles. Hammocks come in different sizes: *sencillo,* for one person; *doble,* very comfortable for one but crowded for two; *matrimonial,* which will decently accommodate two; and *familiares* or *matrimoniales especiales,* which can theoretically sleep an entire family. Unless you're an expert, avoid the hammocks sold by street vendors and head for one of the specialty shops in Mérida.

Exploring the State of Yucatán

Mérida is the hub of Yucatán and the best base for exploring the rest of the state. From there, highways radiate in every direction. To the east, along Route 180 to Cancún, are the famous Chichén Itzá ruins and the low-key colonial city of Valladolid. Heading south on Route 261, you come to Uxmal and the Puuc Route, a series of the most beautiful ruins in Yucatán. If you follow Route 261 north, it will take you to the seaport and beach resort of Progreso. To the west, separate secondary highways go to Celestún and Sisal, two fishing villages with white-sand beaches on the edge of the Parque Natural Celestún wildlife preserve.

Numbers in the text correspond to numbers in the margin and on the State of Yucatán and Mérida maps.

Great Itineraries

IF YOU HAVE 3 DAYS

Spend two days in Mérida, savoring the city's unique character as you make your way among the historic churches and mansions and enjoy the parks and restaurants. You can easily devote a full day to exploring the **zócalo** ① and its surrounding colonial bank, religious, and government buildings. Proceed up Calle 60 to **Parque Hidalgo** ⑨, the neighboring **Museo de la Ciudad** ⑧ and **Iglesia de Jesús** ⑩, finally working your way back past the zócalo to the **Mercado de Artesanías "García Rejón"** ⑥ and the nearby **Mercado Municipal** ⑦, where it's easy to get pleasantly lost for hours. In the evening, you're likely to find a theater or dance performance at the **Teatro Peón Contreras** ⑪, the atrium of the **Universidad Autonoma de Yucatán** ⑫, or (on Thursday) **Parque de Santa Lucía** ⑬ or (on Sunday) the main square. Take a second, more leisurely day to visit the Museum of Anthropology and History in the **Palacio Cantón** ⑮ and perhaps the **Museo de Artes Populares** ⑯ or the El Centenario Zoo. On the third day, drive or take a tour to one of Yucatán's most famous Maya ruins—either **Chichén Itzá** ⑲ or **Uxmal** ㉓. Each is within about two hours of Mérida, making for an ideal day trip.

IF YOU HAVE 7 DAYS

First explore the sights of Mérida, and then take two separate overnight excursions from the city. Spend the night at one of the archaeological hotels near **Uxmal** ㉓, and the next day explore the Ruta Puuc, the series of lost cities south of Uxmal that includes **Kabah** ㉔, **Sayil** ㉕, and **Labná** ㉖, as well as the fascinating **Loltún Caves** ㉗, returning to Mérida through **Ticul** ㉘. On the second excursion, to **Chichén Itzá** ⑲, allow as much as a full day en route to explore some of the present-day Maya villages along the way, especially **Izamal** ⑱. After visiting Chichén Itzá, you may wish to beat the afternoon heat by exploring the **Cave**

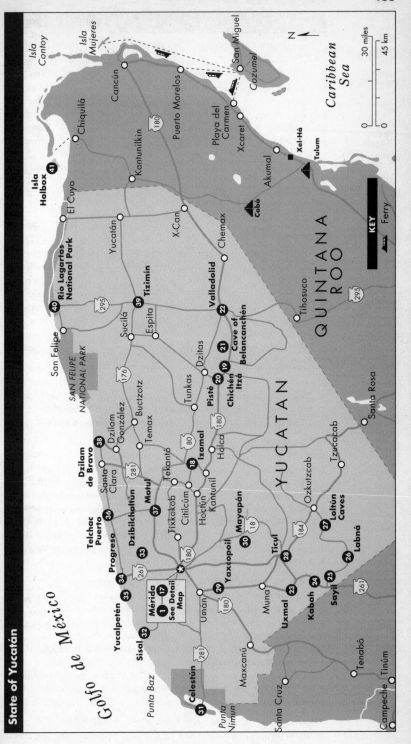

State of Yucatán

Casa de Montejo, **2**

Catedral, **5**

Ermita de Santa Isabel, **17**

Iglesia de Jesús, **10**

Mercado de Artesanías "Garcia Rejón," **6**

Mercado Municipal, **7**

Museo de Artes Populares, **16**

Museo de la Ciudad, **8**

Palacio Cantón, **15**

Palacio del Gobierno, **4**

Palacio Municipal, **3**

Parque de Santa Lucía, **13**

Parque Hidalgo, **9**

Paseo de Montejo, **14**

Teatro Peón Contreras, **11**

Universidad Autonoma de Yucatán, **12**

Zócalo, **1**

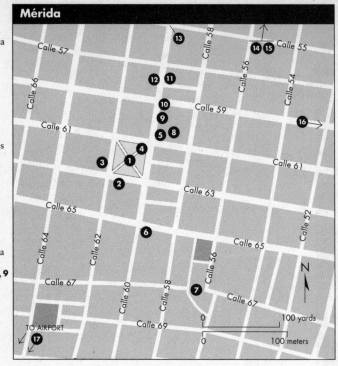

Mérida

of **Balancanchén** ㉑ or swimming in one of the cool subterranean cenotes nearby; you might also head north from **Valladolid** ㉒ to see the flamingo nesting grounds at **Río Lagartos National Park** ㊵.

IF YOU HAVE 10 DAYS

In addition to visiting the sights noted above, you may also want to add one or more beach days into your itinerary. An obvious choice is nearby **Progreso** ㉞, with a stop en route from Mérida to see the ruins of **Dzibilchaltún** ㉝, and perhaps side trips to explore smaller, more traditional North Coast beach towns such as **Yucalpetén** ㉟, **Telchac Puerto** ㊱, and **Dzilam de Bravo** ㊳. If you prefer a secluded fishing village, try either **Celestún** ㉛ or **Sisal** ㉜. Guided boat trips are available from both villages into Parque Natural del Flamenco Mexicano, a tropical wetlands teeming with birds and sea life.

When to Tour Mérida and the Yucatán

Sundays are special in Yucatán. Mérida blocks off traffic in the downtown area as what seems to be the entire population of the city mingles in the zócalo and other parks and plazas for entertainment, food, and celebration of life. Sidewalk cafés along this route are perfect vantage points from which to watch the passing parade of people as well as the folk dancers and singers. Sunday is also the day when admission to archaeological sites is free, an important consideration if you plan to explore the Puuc Route, where you can visit six Maya sites, each of which charges a separate admission on other days of the week.

Thousands of visitors ranging from international sightseers to Maya shamans swarm to Chichén Itzá for the vernal equinox (the first day of spring) to witness the optical illusion that makes a representation of the plumed serpent god Kukulcán appear to descend the stairway of the main pyramid. The phenomenon also occurs on the first day of fall, but the rainy weather typical at that time of year tends to discourage visitors.

High season generally corresponds to high season in the rest of Mexico: the Christmas period, Easter week, and the months of July and August. Rainfall is heaviest between June and October, bringing with it an uncomfortable humidity. The best months for visiting are the coolest: November–April.

MÉRIDA

Travelers to Mérida are a loyal bunch, content to return again and again to favorite restaurants, neighborhoods, and museums. The city's traffic and noise are frustrating, particularly after a peaceful stay on the coast or at one of the archaeological sites, but its merits far outweigh its flaws. Mérida is the cultural and intellectual center of the peninsula, with museums, schools, and attractions that greatly enhance the traveler's insights into the history and character of Yucatán. Consider making it one of the first stops in your travels, and make sure your visit includes a Sunday, when traffic is light and the city seems to revert to a more gracious era.

Most streets in Mérida are numbered, not named, and most run one way. North-south streets have even numbers, which ascend from east to west; east-west streets have odd numbers, which ascend from north to south. Street addresses are confusing because they don't progress in even increments by blocks; for example, the 600s may occupy two or even 10 blocks. A particular location is therefore usually identified by indicating the street number and the nearest cross street, as in "Calle 64 at Calle 61" (the "at" may appear as "x") or "Calle 64 between 61 and 63."

Zócalo and Surroundings

The zócalo is the oldest part of town and has now been officially dubbed the Centro Historico (Historic Center) by city officials. The city is restoring all colonial buildings in the area to their original splendor, and it's not uncommon to see work proceeding on facades in several streets at once.

A Good Walk

Start at the **zócalo** ①; the **Casa de Montejo** ② is on the south side, the **Palacio Municipal** ③ on the west side, the **Palacio del Gobierno** ④ on the northeast corner, and the **catedral** ⑤ catercorner to the Governor's Palace. Step out on Calle 61 from the cathedral and walk east to the **Museo de la Ciudad** ⑧; then double back west on Calle 61 and walk a half block north on Calle 60 to the **Parque Hidalgo** ⑨ and the **Iglesia de Jesús** ⑩ in the same block. Continue north along Calle 60 for one short block to the **Teatro Peón Contreras** ⑪, which lies on the right side of the street; the **Universidad Autonoma de Yucatán** ⑫ is directly across the street on the left side of Calle 60. A block farther north on the left side of Calle 60 is the **Parque de Santa Lucía** ⑬. From the park, walk due north three blocks and turn right on Calle 47 for two blocks to **Paseo de Montejo** ⑭. Once on this street, continue north for two blocks to the **Palacio Cantón** ⑮. From here, you can either hire a *calesa* (horse-drawn carriage) or cab parked outside the museum to take you back past the zócalo to the **Mercado de Artesanías "García Rejón"** ⑥ and the **Mercado Municipal** ⑦, or walk if you are up to it.

Sights to See

❷ **Casa de Montejo.** This stately palace sits on the south side of the plaza, on Calle 63. Montejo—father and son—conquered the peninsula and founded Mérida in 1542; they built their "casa" 10 years later. The property remained with the family until the late 1970s, when it was restored by banker Agustín Legorreta and converted into a bank. Built in the French style during Mérida's heyday as the world's henequen capital, it now represents the city's finest—and oldest—example of colonial Plateresque architecture, which typically features elaborate ornamentation. It also incorporates a great deal of *porfiriato,* architectural details characteristic of the reign of dictator Porfirio Díaz that mimicked 19th-century French style in such traits as mansard roofs, gilded mirrors, and the use of marble. A bas-relief on the doorway—which is all that remains of the original house—depicts Francisco de Montejo the younger, his wife and daughter, and Spanish soldiers standing on the heads of the vanquished Maya. Even if you have no banking to do, step into the building weekdays between 9 and 5 to glimpse the lushly foliated inner patio, which resembles a small jungle.

❺ Catedral. Begun in 1561, this is the oldest cathedral on the North American mainland. It took several hundred Maya laborers, working with stones from the pyramids of the ravaged Maya city, 36 years to complete it. Designed in the somber Renaissance style by an architect who had worked on the Escorial in Madrid, its facade is stark and unadorned, with gunnery slits instead of windows, and faintly Moorish spires. Inside, the black **Cristo de las Ampollas** (Christ of the Blisters), now occupying a side altar to the left of the main one, is a replica of the original, which was destroyed during the Revolution (this was also when most of the gold that typically burnished Mexican cathedrals was carried off). According to one of many legends, the Christ figure was carved from a tree that had burned all night yet appeared the next morning unscathed. A later fire left the statue covered with the blisters for which it is named. For those who are fond of near-superlatives, the crucifix above the main altar is reputedly the second largest in the world.

☾ El Centenario Zoological Park. Mérida's great children's attraction, this is a large, somewhat tacky amusement complex consisting of playgrounds; rides (including ponies and a small train); a roller skating rink; snack bars; and cages with more than 300 marvelous native monkeys, birds, reptiles, and other animals. There are also picnic areas, pleasant wooded paths, and a small lake where you can rent rowboats. Come on Sunday if you enjoy the spectacle of people enjoying themselves. The French Renaissance–style arch (1921) commemorates the 100th anniversary of Mexican independence. ⊠ *Av. Itzaes between Calles 59 and 65, entrances on Calles 59 and 65.* ☜ *Free.* ☾ *Daily 9–6.*

⓱ Ermita de Santa Isabel. At the far south of the city stands the hermitage (circa 1748), part of a Jesuit monastery also known as the Hermitage of the Good Trip, which was restored in 1966. A resting place in colonial days for travelers heading to Campeche, and the most peaceful place in the city, the restored chapel is an enchanting spot to visit at sunset (when it is open) and perhaps a good destination for a ride in a calesa. Next door there's a huge garden with a waterfall and footpaths bordered with bricks and colored stones. ⊠ *Calles 66 and 77.* ☜ *Free.* ☾ *The church hours are irregular. The garden is almost always open during the day.*

⓾ Iglesia de Jesús. Facing Parque Hidalgo on the north side is one of Mérida's oldest buildings and the first Jesuit church in the Yucatan. The church was built in 1618 of limestone from a Maya temple that had previously stood on the site, and faint outlines of ancient carvings are still visible on the stonework of the west wall. Although it is a favorite place for society weddings because of its antiquity, the church's interior is not very ornate. The former convent rooms in the rear of the building now host a pair of small art museums—the **Juan Gamboa Guzmán Painting Museum** and the adjoining **Gottdiener Mu-**

seum. You might pass on the former, which contains oil paintings of past governors and other public figures but rarely identifies them. The latter, on the other hand, displays striking bronze sculptures of the Yucatán's indigenous people by its most celebrated 20th-century sculptor, Enrique Gottdiener. The museums' hours are sporadic, and they often do not keep to their published schedule. ⊠ *Calle 59 between Calles 60 and 58, no phone.* ▧ *Free.* ☉ *Tues.–Sun. 8–8.*

❻ Mercado de Artesanías "García Rejón." Shops, somewhat sterile in appearance, selling dry goods, straw hats, and hammocks occupy both sides of Calle 65. Here you'll find local handicrafts and souvenirs. ⊠ *Calles 60 and 65.*

❼ Mercado Municipal. On Calle 65, between Calles 56 and 58, stand two picturesque 19th-century edifices housing the main post office and telegraph buildings. Behind them sprawls the pungent, labyrinthine Mercado Municipal, a place filled with local color, where almost every patch of ground is occupied by Indian women selling chilies, herbs, and fruit. On the second floor of the main building is the **Bazar de Artesanías Municipales,** the principal handicrafts market, where you can buy jewelry (gold or gold-dipped filigree earrings), pottery, embroidered clothes, hammocks, and straw bags.

❶❻ Museo de Artes Populares. Those who love Mexican crafts may want to trek several blocks east of the main square to this museum. Housed in a fine old mansion, the museum has a ground floor devoted to Yucatecan arts and crafts, displaying weaving, straw baskets, filigree jewelry, carved wood, beautifully carved conch shells, exhibits on huipil manufacture, and the like. The second floor focuses on the popular arts of the rest of Mexico. ⊠ *Calles 59 and 52, no phone.* ▧ *Free.* ☉ *Tues.–Sat. 8–8.*

❽ Museo de la Ciudad. History lovers should stop in at the small but informative museum. Once a hospital chapel for the only convent in the entire bishopric, it now houses prints, drawings, photographs, and other displays that recount the history of Mérida. ⊠ *Calles 61 and 58, no phone.* ▧ *Free.* ☉ *Tues.–Sun. 8–8.*

❶❺ Palacio Cantón. The most compelling of the mansions on Paseo de Montejo, the pale peach palacio presently houses the **Museum of Anthropology and History.** Its grandiose airs seem more characteristic of a mausoleum than a home, but in fact it was built for a general between 1909 and 1911 and was designed by Enrique Deserti, who also did the blueprints for the Teatro Peón Contreras. Marble shows up everywhere, as do Doric and Ionic columns and other Italianate Beaux Arts flourishes. From 1948 to 1960 the mansion served as the residence of the state governor; in 1977 it became a museum dedicated to the culture and history of the Maya; although it's not as impressive as its counterparts in other Mexican cities, it can serve as an introduction to ancient Maya culture before you visit nearby Maya sites. Exhibits explain the Maya practice of dental mutilation and incrustation. A case of "sick bones" shows how the Maya suffered from osteoarthritis, nutritional maladies, and congenital syphilis. The museum also houses conch shells, stones, and quetzal feathers that were used as money. There's also a bookstore. ⊠ *Calle 43 and Paseo de Montejo,* ☎ *99/230557.* ▧ *$2.* ☉ *Tues.–Sat. 9–6, Sun. 9–2; bookstore weekdays 9–3.*

❹ Palacio del Gobierno (State House). Occupying the northeast corner of the main square is this structure, built in 1885 on the site of the Casa Real (Royal House). The upper floor of the State House contains Fernando Castro Pacheco's murals of the history of Yucatán, painted in 1978. On the main balcony stands a reproduction of the **Bell of Do-**

lores **Hidalgo,** where Mexican independence was rung out on September 16, 1810. Every year on that date, the state governor tolls the bell to commemorate the great occasion. ⊠ *Calle 61 between Calles 60 and 62.* 🎫 *Free.* ☯ *Daily 8 AM–9 PM.*

❸ Palacio Municipal (City Hall). The west side of the main square is occupied by the this 17th-century building (⊠ Calle 62 between Calles 61 and 63), which is painted yellow and trimmed with white arcades, balustrades, and the national coat of arms. Originally erected on the ruins of the last surviving Maya structure, it was rebuilt in 1735 and then completely reconstructed along colonial lines in 1928. It remains the headquarters of the local government.

❸ Parque de Santa Lucía. The rather plain park at Calle 60 and Calle 55 draws crowds to its Thursday-night serenades, performed by local musicians and folk dancers. The small church opposite the park dates from 1575 and was built as a place of worship for the African and Caribbean slaves who lived here; the churchyard functioned as the cemetery until 1821.

❾ Parque Hidalgo. Only half a block north of the main plaza is the small, cozy park, officially known as Cepeda Peraza. Renovated mansions-turned-hotels and sidewalk cafés stand at two corners of the park, which comes alive at night with marimba bands and street vendors.

❶❹ Paseo de Montejo. North of downtown, the 10-block-long street known by this name exemplifies the Parisian airs the city took on in the late 19th century, when wealthy plantation owners were building opulent, impressive mansions. The broad boulevard, lined with tamarinds and laurels, is sometimes wistfully referred to as Mérida's Champs-Elysées. Inside the mansions, the owners typically displayed imported Carrara marble and antiques, opting for the decorative and social standards of New Orleans, Cuba, and Paris over styles that were popular in Mexico City. (At the time there was more traffic by sea via the Gulf of Mexico and the Caribbean than there was overland across the lawless interior.) Although the once-stunning mansions fell into disrepair a few years ago, they are being restored to stateliness by a city-wide beautification program. This part of town is also where the posh new hotels are opening.

❶❶ Teatro Peón Contreras. This Italianate theater was designed in 1908 along the lines of the grand European turn-of-the-century theaters and opera houses. In the early 1980s the marble staircase and the dome with frescoes were restored to their past glory. Today, in addition to performing arts, the theater also houses temporary art exhibits and the main **Centro de Información Turística** (☎ 99/249122), which is to the right of the lobby. The information center distributes maps and can provide details about local attractions. A café serving cappuccino and other coffees, plus light snacks and some meals, spills out to a patio from inside the theater to the right of the information center.

❶❷ Universidad Autonoma de Yucatán. The arabesque university plays a major role in the city's cultural and intellectual life. The folkloric ballet performs on the patio of the main building. A Jesuit college built in 1618 previously occupied the site; the present building, dating from 1711, features Moorish-style crownlike upper reaches and uncloistered archways.

❶ Zócalo (main square). The Meridanos also traditionally call it the Plaza Principal and Plaza de la Independencia, and it's a good spot from which to begin any tour of the city. Ancient, geometrically pruned laurel trees and *confidenciales* (S-shaped benches designed for tête-à-têtes) invite

Pick up the phone.

Pick up the miles.

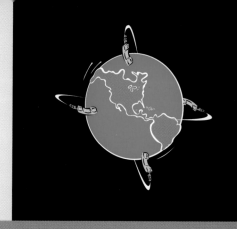

MCI Calling Card

415 555 1234 2244
J.D. SMITH

WorldPhone

Use your MCI Card® to make an international call from virtually anywhere in the world and earn frequent flyer miles on one of seven major airlines.

Enroll in an MCI Airline Partner Program today. In the U.S., call **1-800-FLY-FREE**. Overseas, call MCI collect at **1-916-567-5151**.

1. To use your MCI Card, just dial the WorldPhone access number of the country you're calling from.
   (For a complete listing of codes, visit www.mci.com.)
2. Dial or give the operator your MCI Card number.
3. Dial or give the number you're calling.

# American Samoa	633-2MCI (633-2624)
# Antigua	#2
(Available from public card phones only)	
# Argentina (CC)	0800-5-1002
# Aruba ÷	800-888-8
# Bahamas	1-800-888-8000
# Barbados	1-800-888-8000
# Belize	557 from hotels
	815 from pay phones
# Bermuda ÷	1-800-888-8000
# Bolivia ♦	0-800-2222
# Brazil (CC)	000-8012
# British Virgin Islands ÷	1-800-888-8000
# Cayman Islands	1-800-888-8000
# Chile (CC)	
To call using CTC ■	800-207-300
To call using ENTEL ■	800-360-180
# Colombia (CC) ♦	980-16-0001
Columbia IIIC Access in Spanish	980-16-1000
# Costa Rica ♦	0800-012-2222
# Dominica	1-800-888-8000
# Dominican Republic (CC) ÷	1-800-888-8000
Dominican Republic IIIC Access in Spanish	1121
# Ecuador (CC) ÷	999-170
El Salvador ♦	800-1767
# Grenada ÷	1-800-888-8000
Guatemala (CC) ♦	9999-189

# Guyana	177
# Haiti (CC) ÷	193
Haiti IIIC Access in French/Creole	190
Honduras ÷	122
# Jamaica ÷	1-800-888-8000
(From Special Hotels only)	873
# Mexico	
Avantel (CC)	91-800-021-8000
Telmex ▲	95-800-674-7000
Mexico IIIC Access	91-800-021-1000
# Netherlands Antilles (CC) ÷	001-800-888-8000
Nicaragua (CC)	166
(Outside of Managua, dial 02 first)	
Nicaragua IIIC Access in Spanish	★2 from any public payphone
# Panama	108
Military Bases	2810-108
# Paraguay ÷	008-112-800
# Peru	0-800-500-10
# Puerto Rico (CC)	1-800-888-8000
# St. Lucia ÷	1-800-888-8000
# Trinidad & Tobago ÷	1-800-888-8000
# Turks & Caicos ÷	1-800-888-8000
# Uruguay	000-412
# U.S. Virgin Islands (CC)	1-800-888-8000
# Venezuela (CC) ÷ ♦	800-1114-0

Is this a great time, or what? :-)

MCI

Urban planning.

CITYPACKS

The ultimate guide to the city—a complete pocket guide plus a full-size color map.

www.fodors.com

lingering. The plaza was laid out in 1542 on the ruins of T'hó, the Maya city demolished to make way for Mérida, and is still the focal point around which the most important public buildings cluster. The plaza is bordered to the east and west by Calles 60 and 62, and to the north and south by Calles 61 and 63.

Dining and Lodging

$$ ✕ **Alameda.** Middle Eastern and vegetarian specialties share the menu with standard Yucatecan fare at this side-street café, where businessmen linger over grilled beef shish kebab, pita bread, and breakfast coffee. The street action is visible from tables at the front; those in the back patio are quieter. Everything is served without side dishes—if you want beans or potatoes with your eggs you must ask for them. Meat-free dishes include tabbouleh and spinach and cauliflower casseroles. Only open until 6:30 PM. ⊠ *Calle 58, No. 474, across from Posada Toledo,* ☎ *99/283635. No credit cards.*

$$ ✕ **Alberto's Continental Patio.** You can probably find this restaurant
★ praised in just about every guidebook, and it merits the kudos: The setting is romantic and the food is excellent. The building, which dates from about 1727, is adorned with such fine details as mosaic floors from Cuba. Two beautiful dining rooms are tastefully decorated with dark wood trim, copper utensils, stone sculpture, and candles in glass lanterns on the tables. An inner patio surrounded by rubber trees is ideal for starlit dining. Most of the guests are tourists, but that need not detract from the surroundings or the food. If you order Lebanese food, your plate will be heaped with servings of shish kebab, fried kibi, cabbage rolls, hummus, eggplant, and tabbouleh, accompanied by pita bread, almond pie, and Turkish coffee. Black bean soup, enchiladas, fried bananas, and caramel custard make up the Mexican dinner; there are also a Yucatecan dinner, an Italian dinner, and à la carte appetizers and entrées. ⊠ *Calle 64, No. 482, at Calle 57,* ☎ *99/285367. AE, MC, V.*

$$ ✕ **Amaro.** Formerly called Ananda Maya Ginza and strictly vegetarian, Amaro has expanded its menu to include poultry and red meats. Still, the menu is heavy on health drinks, made mostly with local vegetables, fruit, and herbs. Regular coffee and Yucatecan beers are also served, and the salads are made with fresh local veggies washed with purified water. Recommended dishes include eggplant curry and soup made with *chaya,* a local vegetable that looks like spinach. The terrace of this old historic home provides a quiet dining atmosphere beneath a big tree. ⊠ *Calle 59, No. 507, between Calles 60 and 62,* ☎ *99/282451. No credit cards. Closed Sun.*

$$ ✕ **La Bella Epoca.** For a truly special dinner, nothing matches the ele-
★ gance and style of the second-story dining room, the former ballroom of an old mansion that has been restored well beyond its original grandeur. Crystal chandeliers sparkle over tiny balcony tables overlooking Parque Hidalgo. An ambitious menu includes French, Mexican, Middle Eastern, Yucatecan, vegetarian, and unusual Maya dishes—try the *sikil-pak,* a dip with ground pumpkin seeds, charcoal-broiled tomatoes, and onions; or the succulent *pollo píbil* (chicken baked in banana leaves). Arrive for dinner before 8 PM to claim one of the small balcony tables overlooking the street. The restaurant has taken over the building's ground floor, which is outfitted more casually with plain wooden tables and chairs but which has the same fine menu and windows overlooking the street. ⊠ *Hotel del Parque, Calle 60 between Calles 57 and 59,* ☎ *99/281928. AE, MC, V.*

$$ ✕ **La Casona.** This pretty mansion-turned-restaurant near Parque Santa Ana has an inner patio, arcade, and swirling ceiling fans; a new bar features live romantic music nightly. The accent is Yucatecan, with *poc chuc* (slices of pork marinated in sour orange juice and spices), pollo píbil, and *huachinango* (sea bass baked in banana leaves) among the recommended dishes. Some Italian offerings include homemade pasta—ravioli, manicotti, and linguine. Vegetables or pasta accompany most orders. ⊠ *Calle 60, No. 434, between Calles 47 and 49,* ☎ *99/ 239996. AE, MC, V.*

$$ ✕ Los Almendros. A Mérida classic, this restaurant—a spinoff from an original location in the Maya village of Ticul—takes credit for the invention of poc chuc. The food tends to be on the greasy side, and some international travelers may feel that local spices such as achiote overwhelm the main ingredients. Nonetheless, the restaurant provides a good introduction to the variety of Yucatecan cuisine, including *conchinita píbil* (pork baked in banana leaves), panuchos, pork sausage, *papadzules* (corn tortillas with pumpkin-seed sauce), and *pollo ticuleño* (boneless, breaded chicken in tomato sauce filled with fried beans, peas, red peppers, ham, and cheese). All dishes are described in English with pictures on the paper menus. Sangria—with or without alcohol— washes it all down. The two dining rooms have both ceiling fans and air-conditioning. ⊠ *Calle 50-A, No. 493, between Calles 57 and 59,* ☎ *99/238135 or 99/285459. AE, DC, MC, V.*

$$ ✕ Pancho's. The waiters in this steak and seafood restaurant—Mérida's version of the Carlos 'n' Charlie's chain—dress in what looks like Hollywood's idea of "Bandito" costumes. The bar, with its fancy drinks, attracts the international singles set; dancing is possible some nights on the outdoor patio. People go here more for the atmosphere than the food, which is standard Mexican fare. ⊠ *Calle 59, No. 509, between Calles 60 and 62,* ☎ *99/230942. AE, MC, V. No lunch.*

$$ ✕ Pórtico del Peregrino. A red tile floor, iron grillwork, and lots of plants
★   set the tone in both the indoor and outdoor patio sections of this Colonial-style restaurant with only 12 tables. The menu features lime soup, baked eggplant with chicken, shrimp, chicken pibil, shish kebab, mole enchiladas, seafood stew, chicken liver brochettes, and spaghetti. For dessert, try the coconut ice cream with Kahlúa. ⊠ *Calle 57, No. 501, between Calles 60 and 62,* ☎ *99/286163. MC, V.*

$ ✕ Bar La Ruina. Perfect for a quick pick-me-up, this spotlessly clean watering hole behind the new ADO bus terminal has an old-fashioned cantina atmosphere. Free hot and cold *botanas,* or snacks, are served nonstop from 11 AM opening to 7 PM closing with beer or mixed drinks. In keeping with Mexican tradition, only men are allowed in the front bar; women and families are ushered to the back rooms. ⊠ *Calles 69 and 72, no phone. No credit cards.*

$ ✕ Cafetería Pop. Across the street from the university and a favorite
★   with the student crowd, this place with wood tables always seems to be crowded. The busiest time is 8 AM–noon, but for late risers the breakfast menu can be ordered à la carte all day, and the noteworthy coffee is freshly brewed round the clock. In addition, sandwiches, hamburgers, spaghetti, chicken, fish, beef, and tacos are available. Beer, sangria, and wine are served only with food orders. ⊠ *Calle 57, No. 501, between Calles 60 and 62,* ☎ *99/286163. MC, V.*

$ ✕ Express. Young and middle-aged Méridano men in guayaberas have made this their "in" place and spend hours in this plain café-style restaurant that reeks of Madrid café ambience (and of cigar smoke as well). That ambience is reinforced by the paintings of old Spain and old Mérida, the ceiling fans, and the old-fashioned globe lights. On the menu are broiled garlic chicken, sandwiches, shrimp, and red snapper. Its name notwithstanding, service at this restaurant can be slow; Express is a place for lingering. ⊠ *Calle 60, No. 502, at Calle 59,* ☎ *99/281691. No credit cards.*

$ ✕ **Nicte-Ha.** Metal chairs and tables with plastic tablecloths sit under an arcade right on the main square, making this modest eatery a fine place for people-watching. A good selection of Yucatecan fare—soups, *huevos motuleños* (eggs with peas and ham), poc chuc, seafood, *antojitos* (appetizers), and a combination platter—is offered at budget prices. Afterward, stop in at the *sorbetería* next door for a sherbet. ⊠ *Calle 61, No. 500, at Calle 60,* ☎ *99/230784. No credit cards.*

$ ✕ **Pizza Bella.** In the same arcade in the main square as Nicte-Ha (☞ *above*), this restaurant serves Mexican and American breakfasts, espresso, and cappuccino as well as pizza. Checkered tablecloths atop wooden tables and an eclectic collection of wall decorations (from maps to beer advertisements) add atmosphere to this otherwise standard pizza joint. ⊠ *Calle 61, No. 500, Depto. E-2,* ☎ *99/236401. No credit cards.*

$ ✕ **Santa Lucía.** Locals crowd this small five-table dining room, a few
★ steps below the sidewalk, at lunch time, when the bountiful *comida corrida* is served. The bargain three-course lunch usually includes such Yucatecan specialties as *sopa de lima* (lime soup) and pollo pibil. Before you order, browse through the book of guests' comments to get tips on favorite meals—the pepper steak constantly wins rave reviews. Soft tropical music plays in the background, and the service is friendly and efficient. There's a live band Thursday through Sunday nights. ⊠ *Calle 60, No. 481, next to Parque de Santa Lucía,* ☎ *99/285957. MC, V.*

$$$$ ✕🏨 **Hacienda Katanchel.** Katanchel is a rambling 17th-century henequen
★ hacienda on 220 acres that has been lovingly restored to its former splendor by Anibal Gonzalez and his wife Monica Hernandez. At the same time, the couple is replanting the property with endangered Maya plants, trees, and medicinal herbs and restoring a small ruin they found on the estate. The guest rooms are set in small pavilions built along a garden walkway; the floors are made of local hardwoods, the roofs of red Marseilles tile, and there are overhead fans, hammocks, and double beds that look like pieces of modern sculpture. The bathrooms stock the hacienda's own homemade soaps and talc. The rest of the hotel, likewise, is turned out in an eclectic but elegant manner. The chef, a devotee of French cooking master Paul Boucuse, prepares contemporary Mexican cuisine such as vol-au-vent puff pastry stuffed with *huitlacoche* (mushrooms that grow on ripe corn) and tarragon sauce or cold avocado cream soup with prawns and goat cheese; for dessert, there's *cajeta* (caramel candy) mousse with toasted almonds. ⊠ *25 km (15 mi) east of Mérida on Hwy. 180 toward Izamal,* ☎ *99/200997, 800/223–6510 in the U.S.,* 🕾 *99/200995. 34 rooms. Restaurant, bar, pool, mineral baths, airport shuttle. AE, MC, V.*

$$$$ 🏨 **Fiesta Americana Mérida.** Opened in early 1995 across the street
★ from the Hyatt Regency, this is the town's newest posh hotel, catering to business travelers, groups, and conventions, but also attracting the locals who come to see and be seen. Its lovely pink facade mirrors the architecture of Paseo de Montejo mansions on an epic scale. The echoes of classic grandeur carry into the spacious upperlobby with its massive columns and gleaming marble and brass work and its 300-ft-high glass-roof atrium. Rich floral prints, dark wood furnishings, and slightly larger-than-life proportions maintain the theme of bygone elegance in the guest rooms, but the units are carpeted and have all the modern conveniences, including modems. They all offer L-shaped conversation areas, separate dressing rooms, and remote-control TVs concealed in armoires. ⊠ *Paseo de Montejo and Av. Colón,* ☎ *99/202194 or 800/343–7821,* 🕾 *99/202198. 350 rooms and suites. Restaurant, bar, health club, shops, business services, meeting rooms, travel services. AE, DC, MC, V.*

$$$$ ⊡ **Hyatt Regency Mérida.** The north end of Paseo de Montejo is the new hotel district; the 17-story Hyatt was the first to open in 1994, bringing a new level of service to Mérida. Guests staying on one of the two Regency Club floors receive complimentary Continental breakfast, beverages, and snacks, as well as concierge service. The rooms are regally decorated with russet-hued bed quilts and rugs set off by modern blond-wood furniture and cream-colored walls. Satellite TV, direct-dial long-distance phone service and minibars have been artfully integrated into each unit; club floor rooms also contain personal safes. Amenities not commonly found in Mérida include 24-hour room service and a state-of-the-art business center, plus the city's only tapas bar. Each evening guests head to the piano bar in the marble lobby for live entertainment, or to the **La Peregrina** restaurant on Tuesday night, when an upbeat Yucatecan folk dance troupe is featured along with a buffet. One of the country's most exclusive silver shops, **Tane,** is also on the premises. ⊠ *Calle 60, No. 344, at Av. Colón,* ☎ *99/420202 or 800/228–9000,* FAX *99/257002. 299 rooms and suites. 2 restaurants, 2 bars, pool, exercise room, tennis, shops, travel services, car rental. AE, DC, MC, V.*

$$$ ⊡ **Casa del Balam.** This very pleasant hotel on well-heeled Calle 60
★ was built more than 60 years ago as the home of the Barbachano family, pioneers of Yucatán tourism. Today the hotel—owned and managed by Carmen Barbachano—has a lovely courtyard ornamented with a fountain, arcades, ironwork, and a black-and-white tile floor. Rocking chairs in the hallways impart a colonial feeling, as do the mahogany trimmings and cedar doorways. The rooms are capacious and well maintained, with painted sinks, wrought-iron accessories, and minibars. The suites are especially agreeable, with large bathrooms, tiny balconies, arched doorways, and mahogany bureaus. All rooms now have hair dryers and have recently been soundproofed with double-pane windows. Cocktails and light meals are served in the lobby courtyard. ⊠ *Calle 60, No. 488, Box 988,* ☎ *99/248844, 99/242150, or 800/223–4084,* FAX *99/245011. 54 rooms. Restaurant, 2 bars, minibars, pool, shops, travel services, car rental. AE, MC, V.*

$$$ ⊡ **Holiday Inn.** The beautifully remodeled and redecorated hotel, which opened 16 years ago, is a half-block from Paseo de Montejo, near the swanky Hyatt and Fiesta Americana. Not only is it located on a choice piece of real estate, it has reasonable room rates for this part of town. The lodge has a decidedly Mexican flavor; the staff—from bellboys to waiters—exhibit good old fashioned Mexican warmth and courtesy. There's a nightly Fiesta Mexicana in the patio. This is probably the most light-filled hotel in Mérida, with floor-to-ceiling windows throughout the lobby area. Rooms and suites face an open Mexican-style courtyard; units have mini bars, marble bathrooms, and color TVs with U.S. channels. There's a new business center and meetings wing. ⊠ *Av. Colon and Calle 60, No. 468, 97127,* ☎ *99/ 256877 or 800/465–4329,* FAX *99/257755. 214 rooms. 2 restaurants, bar, shops, business services, meeting rooms, travel services, car rental. AE, DC, MC, V.*

$$ ⊡ **Caribe.** An old Mérida standard, the Caribe is done in typical colonial style, including tile floors, dark wood furniture, and a large inner courtyard with arcades. It is on Parque Hidalgo, but most of its rooms (38 of them with air-conditioning) overlook the inner courtyard and restaurant, as do the open balconies, which are lined with comfortable chairs. The rooftop sundeck and swimming pool have a great view of the plaza and downtown. The hotel's outdoor café, **El Meson,** is one of the better restaurants in Parque Hidalgo. ⊠ *Calle 60, No. 500,* ☎ *99/249022 or 800/826–6842,* FAX *99/248733. 56 rooms. Restaurant, outdoor café, pool, travel services, free parking. AE, DC, MC, V.*

$$ 🏨 **Casa Mexilio.** Two partners—one Mexican, one American—have brought the best of their respective architectural and decorating traditions to bear on this choice bed-and-breakfast with eight guest rooms. From the dark entrance you approach a tiny pool adjacent to a charming kitchen. At the top of the narrow stairs is a sundeck laden with cacti; one entire wall of the house is covered with vines. Middle Eastern wall hangings, French tapestries, colorful tile floors, black pottery, tile sinks, rustic furniture, and white walls make up the eclectic decor, which reaches its pinnacle in an immensely cozy sitting room on the second floor. Casa Mexilio lacks the amenities of the larger hotels (only three rooms have air-conditioning), but if you enjoy a casual ambience and the feeling of staying in a private home, you'll be happy here. Short tours to Celestún and historic convents and monasteries are offered. This place fills up fast; reservations as well as a minimum three nights' stay are required Christmas week, the month of February, and Easter week. Room rates include breakfast. ⊠ *Calle 68, No. 495, between Calles 59 and 57,* ☎ *303/674–9615 or 800/538–6802 for reservations,* ☎ FAX *99/282505,* FAX *303/674–8735. 8 rooms. Pool. AE, MC, V accepted only with prior payment in the U.S.*

$$ 🏨 **Gran Hotel.** Cozily situated on Parque Hidalgo, this legendary 1901 ★ hotel is the oldest in the city, and it still lives up to its name. The three-story neoclassical building exudes charm; its centerpiece is an Art Nouveau courtyard complete with wrought-iron bannister, variegated tile floors, Greek columns, and myriad potted plants. High ceilings in rooms drenched in cedar antique furniture provide a sense of spaciousness. Thirteen units have balconies—request one of these if you don't mind noise from the park; most of the others have no windows at all, and 24 have air-conditioning. The rooms on the second floor in the back are the quietest. Porfirio Díaz and Fidel Castro stayed in sumptuous Room 17, and Room 13 has an enormous sitting room. The hotel's **Patio Español** serves good sopa de lima plus paella on Sunday. ⊠ *Calle 60, No. 496,* ☎ *99/236963 or 99/247632,* FAX *99/247622. 31 rooms. Restaurant. MC, V.*

$$ 🏨 **Hotel El Conquistador.** Located on the Paseo de Montejo, the El Conquistador is within easy walking distance of the Fiesta Americana and the Hyatt and caters to German tour groups. Don't expect the top-notch amenities of those hotels—beds and pillows in the contemporary-style rooms are lumpy, and the electrical outlets are iffy. Still, views of the city from the rooftop solarium and pool area are superlative, the dining room is renowned for its daily breakfast buffet, the staff is helpful, and the prices are somewhat lower than those at the area's other hotels. ⊠ *Paseo de Montejo, No. 458,* ☎ *99/262155 or 99/269199,* FAX *99/268829. 161 rooms. Restaurant, coffee shop, 2 bars, pool, shops, travel services, free parking. MC, V.*

$$ 🏨 **María del Carmen.** This modern Best Western hotel caters to business travelers, bus groups, and those traveling by car who desire secured parking. The plaza, market, and other major sights are within easy walking distance. The modern remodeled rooms are decorated with ornate Oriental-style lamps and lacquered furniture. ⊠ *Calle 63, No. 550, between Calles 68 and 70,* ☎ *99/239133 or 800/528–1234,* FAX *99/239290. 89 rooms. Restaurant, bar, pool, travel services. AE, MC, V.*

$$ 🏨 **Mérida Misión Park Inn Plaza.** Part of the city's landscape for decades (in its earlier incarnation it was the Hotel Mérida), the Misión has two major assets: an excellent location in the heart of downtown and a genuine colonial ambience, with chandeliers, wood beams, archways, patios, and fountains in public areas, along with a pool and a bar with romantic music nightly. Rooms in the modern 11-story annex don't have as much character, but the ones on the upper floors offer good city views. Forty–five units in the old colonial section are set around a pretty courtyard, which gives them much more appeal. In addition, all rooms in the hotel were remodeled in 1996. ⊠ *Calle 60, No. 491,* ☎ *99/237665 or 800/221–6509,* ℻ *99/239500. 145 rooms. Restaurant, bar, snack bar, pool, shop, meeting rooms, travel services, car rental, free parking. AE, DC, MC, V.*

$$ 🏨 **Residencial.** Location is the major draw at this bright pink hotel, opened in 1991. It sits on Calle 59, the main entrance to town, and has a gated parking lot. The decor's French Colonial theme is most evident in the small dining room with its silken drapes, linen cloths, and high-backed chairs. Rooms have powerful showers, comfortable beds, and mirrored doors on the spacious closets. While the recently remodeled bar and small swimming pool in the central courtyard are pleasant for encountering fellow guests, they are far from private.Not all rooms have air-conditioning. ⊠ *Calle 59, No. 589, at Calle 76,* ☎ *99/243899 or 99/243099,* ℻ *99/240266. 66 rooms. Restaurant, bar, pool, free parking. AE, MC, V.*

$ 🏨 **Casa Bowen.** A great find if you want to be near the bus station and market, Casa Bowen is a converted home with a simple addition. All accommodations have fans, private baths, and good screens; air-conditioning has been added to a few rooms. Eight of the units are small apartments with refrigerators. There are plenty of sitting areas in the courtyard and lobby, and there's a pay phone in the lobby. ⊠ *Calle 66, No. 521-B,* ☎ *99/286809. 25 rooms. No credit cards.*

$ 🏨 **Dolores Alba.** A comfortable, friendly standby at the low end of the moderate range, the Dolores Alba is owned by the Sanchez family, who live on the premises and who also own the budget hotel Janiero in Mérida and the Dolores Alba at Chichén Itzá (☞ *below*). The basic rooms, some with air-conditioning, frame a courtyard where guests' cars can be parked. A full breakfast ($3.50) is served in the dining room; guests can keep cold drinks in the lobby refrigerator. ⊠ *Calle 63, No. 464, between Calles 52 and 54,* ☎ *99/285650,* ℻ *99/283163. 40 rooms. Breakfast room, pool. No credit cards.*

$ 🏨 **Hotel Mucuy.** Mérida's budget hotels have become affordable again because of favorable foreign exchange rates, but the Mucuy still remains one of the best bargains around. The delightful owners make you feel like part of the family and are eager to share information about the city, as well as some good tips on inexpensive tours to the ruins. The rooms, which are always immaculate, have overhead fans and good screens on the windows; they face a tranquil, flower-filled garden perfect for reading or sunning. There's a book exchange and communal refrigerator in the lobby, and the owners live at the front of the hotel. ⊠ *Calle 57, No. 481, between Calles 56 and 58,* ☎ *99/285193,* ℻ *99/237801. 22 rooms. No credit cards.*

$ 🏨 **Posada Toledo.** This inn occupies a beautiful old colonial house with high ceilings, floors of exquisite Moorish patterned tile, and old-fashioned carved furniture that evoke its former elegance. The dining room, where breakfast is served, is particularly fine, with stained-glass door frames. Antiques clutter the halls, along with warm, faded portraits of 19th-century family life, so that one feels more like a personal guest of the establishment than another nameless hotel client. However, guest room quality varies much more than the rates do, so be sure to inspect your room before checking in. If you're traveling with a few people, consider No. 5, an elegant two-room suite that was originally the mansion's master bedroom. The posada's popularity is becoming a drawback; as in many hotels in converted mansions, noise reverberates through the halls. If you're a light sleeper, ask for a room away from the courtyard. You have a choice of a ceiling fan or air-conditioning. ⊠ *Calle 58, No. 487, at Calle 57,* ☎ *99/231690. 23 rooms. Breakfast room. MC, V.*

$ ▣ **Trinidad Galería.** Eccentricity holds sway at this impossibly origi-
nal, slightly ramshackle little hotel, nearly unidentifiable unless you are
looking for it. In its previous lives it has been a hacienda, an auto rental
shop, and a furniture store, but in the late 1980s owner Manolo Rivero
made it into a hotel, or more precisely, "a post-contemporary museum
hotel." An adjacent art gallery has four yearly expositions of new, young
talent to which all hotel guests receive formal invitations. The large,
chaotic lobby is filled with modern art such as oil paintings of some
distinction, plants, a fountain, and yellow wicker furniture. Making
your way through the maze that is the rest of the hotel, you'll encounter
painted wooden angels, curved columns, and even a green satin shoe
mounted on a pedestal. The rooms are small and equally odd; they have
neither phones nor TVs, and only eight offer air-conditioning. (Rivero
has a second 17-room hotel, the Trinidad, a block away; guests have
access to the Trinidad Galería's swimming pool). ⊠ *Calles 60 and 61,*
☎ *99/232463,* ℻ *99/242319. 34 rooms. Pool. MC, V.*

Nightlife and the Arts

Mérida enjoys an unusually active and diverse cultural life, including
free government-sponsored music and dance performances nightly,
plus sidewalk art shows in four local parks. For information on these
and other performances, consult the tourist office, the local newspapers, or the billboards and posters at the **Teatro Peón Contreras** (⊠ Calle
60 at Calle 57) or **Café Pop** (⊠ Calle 57 between Calles 60 and 62).

Dancing

If you want pop music mixed with salsa, try **Saudaje** (⊠ Prolongación
Montejo, No. 477, ☎ 99/264330 or 99/292310). A number of restau-
rants feature live music and dancing, including **El Tucho** (⊠ Calle 60,
No. 482, between Calles 55 and 57, ☎ 99/242323), **Xtabay** (⊠ Above
El Tucho, ☎ 99/280961), and **Pancho's** (⊠ Calle 59 between Calles
60 and 62, ☎ 99/230942).

Film

Downtown movie theaters include **Cine Fantasio** (⊠ Calle 59 at Calle
60) and **Cine Rex** (⊠ Calle 57, No. 553); sometimes English films with
Spanish subtitles are shown.

Folkloric Shows

The **Hyatt Regency Hotel** (⊠ Calle 60, No. 344, at Av. Colon, ☎ 99/
420202) stages folkloric dances Tuesday nights beginning at 8 at the
La Peregrina restaurant along with a buffet dinner. Among a variety
of performances presented at the **Teatro Peón Contreras** is "The Roots
of Today's Yucatán," a combination of music, dance, and theater presented by the Folkloric Ballet of the University of Yucatán on Tuesday
at 9 PM. Another theater that regularly hosts cultural events is the **Teatro
Daniel Ayala** (⊠ Calle 60 between Calles 59 and 61).

Outdoor Activities and Sports

Baseball

Baseball is played with enthusiasm from February or March through
July at the stadium in the **Kukulcán Sports Center** (⊠ Calle 14, No.
17, ☎ 99/240306), next to the Carta Clara brewery. Tickets can also
be purchased through the local Lion's Club (☎ 99/253809 or
99/253409).

Bullfights

Bullfights are most often held from November through January, or during other holiday periods at the **bullring** (⊠ Paseo de la Reforma near
Avenida Colón, ☎ 99/257996). Contact the travel desk at your hotel

or one of the tourist information centers; prices range from $6 to $9 for seats in the sun and from $10 to $15 for seats in the shade.

Golf

There is an 18-hole championship golf course (and restaurant, bar, and clubhouse) at **Club de Golf de Yucatán** (⊠ Carr. Mérida-Progreso, Km. 14.5, ☎ 99/220053 or 220071), 16 km (10 mi) north of Mérida on the road to Progreso.

Tennis

The **Holiday Inn** (⊠ Av. Colón, No. 498, at Calle 60, ☎ 99/256877) and the **Hyatt Regency** (⊠ Calle 60 344 at Av. Colon, ☎ 99/420202) have tennis courts, as do the **Club Campestre de Mérida** (⊠ Calle 30, No. 500, ☎ 99/443494), the **Centro Deportivo Bancario** (⊠ Carr. a Motul s/n, Frac. del Arco, ☎ 99/430382 or 99/430550), and the **Deportivo Libanés Mexicano** (⊠ Calle 1-G, No. 101, ☎ 99/442940 or 99/442942).

Shopping

Malls

Mérida now has several shopping malls; the largest is **Gran Plaza** with about 90 shops. It's just outside of town, on the highway to Progreso (called Carretera a Progreso beyond the Mérida city limits).

Markets

On the second floor of the **Mercado Municipal** (⊠ Between Calles 65 and 56 and Calles 54 and 59) you'll find crafts, food, flowers, and live birds, among other items. Note: Men and boys often approach tourists by this market, offering to provide a guided tour or introduction to a shopkeeper with the "best" of whatever you're looking for. These unofficial guides will expect a tip from you (and will receive a commission from the seller if you buy anything), and won't necessarily guide you to the best deals. You're better off visiting some specialty stores first to learn about the quality and types of hammocks, hats, and other crafts; then, you'll have an idea of what you're buying—and what it's worth—if you want to bargain in the market.

If you're interested solely in handicrafts, visit the **Bazar García Rejón** (⊠ Corner of Calles 65 and 62), which has neat rows of indoor stalls with leather items, palm hats, and handmade guitars, among other things. On Sunday in Mérida, you will find an array of wares. Starting at 9, the **Handicraft Bazaar** (⊠ In front of the Municipal Palace across from the main square) is filled with huipiles, hats, and costume jewelry. Also starting at 9, the **Popular Art Bazaar** (⊠ Parque Santa Lucía, corner of Calles 60 and 55), a very small flea market, offers paintings, engravings, and woodcuts by local artists.

Specialty Stores

CLOTHING

Tastefully designed batik dresses and pillow covers with Maya motifs, along with a nice selection of white *manta* (Mexican cotton) clothing and silver jewelry, can be found at **El Paso** (⊠ Calle 60, No. 501, corner of Calle 61, ☎ 99/285452). You might not wear a guayabera to a business meeting as some men in Mexico do, but the shirts are cool, comfortable, and attractive; for a good selection, try **Camisería Canul** (⊠ Calle 62, No. 484, between Calles 57 and 59, ☎ 99/230158). Pick up a jipi at the well-known **El Becalenö** (⊠ Calle 65, No. 483, between Calles 56A and 58, ☎ 99/850581), where the famous hats are made at Becal, Campeche, by the González family. For stunningly beautiful embroidered dresses inspired by the old-fashioned Yucatecan dresses of the haciendas, visit **Georgia Charukas** (⊠ Fiesta Americana Hotel,

Paseo de Montejo and Av. Colon, ☎ 99/257671); the U.S. designer has become an icon of high fashion in Mérida over the last 25 years.

CRAFTS

The best place for hammocks is **Hamacas El Aguacate** (✉ Calle 58, No. 604, at Calle 73, ☎ 99/286429), a family-run establishment selling a wide variety of sizes and designs. **Tejidos Y Cordeles Nacionales** (✉ Calle 56, No. 516-B, ☎ 99/285561) is another good hammock emporium.

Casa de Artesanías (✉ Calle 63, No. 503, between Calles 64 and 66, ☎ 99/235392) purveys folk art from throughout Mexico, such as hand-painted, wooden mythical animals from Oaxaca; handmade beeswax candles and leather bags from Mérida; and hand-embroidered vests, shawls, blouses, and place mats from Chiapas. The streets north of the main square, especially **Calle 60,** are lined with crafts and jewelry stores.

GALLERIES

The **Teatro Daniel Ayala** (✉ Calle 60, between Calles 59 and 61, ☎ 99/214391) showcases contemporary paintings and photography. **Galería Manolo Rivero** (✉ Hotel Galería Trinidad, Calle 60 at Calle 61, ☎ 99/232463) displays paintings and sculptures by young, new wave contemporary artists from all over the world.

JEWELRY

La Perla Maya (✉ Calle 60, No. 485–487, between Calles 50 and 61, ☎ 99/285886) is one of the few jewelry shops selling difficult-to-find old-fashioned Yucatecan filigree earrings and bracelets—in silver dipped in gold. The store also stocks lots of quality silver jewelry in modern designs. **Tane** at the Hyatt Regency Hotel (✉ Calle 60, No. 344, at Av. Colon, ☎ 99/420202) is an outlet for exquisite (and expensive) silver earrings, necklaces, and bracelets, some using ancient Maya designs.

TO CHICHÉN ITZÁ AND VALLADOLID

Although it's possible to reach Chichén Itzá (120 km, or 75 mi, east of Mérida) along the shorter Route 180, it's far more scenic to follow Route 80 until it ends at Tekantó, then head south to Citilcúm, east to Dzitas, and south again to Pisté. These roads have no signs, but are the only paved roads going in these directions. Among the several villages you'll see along Route 80 is Tixkokob, a Maya community famous for its hammock weavers.

Izamal

 68 km (42 mi) southeast of Mérida.

One of the best examples of a Spanish Colonial town in the Yucatán, Izamal is nicknamed Ciudad Amarillo (Yellow City) because its buildings are painted earth-tone yellow. In the center of town stands the enormous 16th-century **Monastery of St. Anthony de Padua,** perched on—and built from—the remains of a pyramid devoted to Itamná, god of the heavens, day and night. The monastery's church, which was visited by Pope John Paul II in 1993, boasts a gigantic atrium (supposedly second only to that of the Vatican in size), newly discovered frescoes of saints, and rows of 75 yellow arches. The Virgin of the Immaculate Conception to whom the church is dedicated is the patron saint of the Yucatán; miracles are ascribed to her, and a yearly pilgrimage takes place in her honor. Horse-drawn carriages surround the town's large **main square,** which fronts the cathedral; there are far worse ways to spend an afternoon than to trot around this pleasant town and then lounge in the square enjoying the local action. **Kinich**

Kakmó, a pyramid that's all that remains of a royal Maya city that flourished here hundreds of years ago, is located a few blocks from the monastery; it's currently being excavated, but it's worth walking over for a look. If you're traveling here via Route 80 from Mérida, cut south at Tekantó and east again at Citilcúm (the road has no number, and there are few signs).

Chichén Itzá

🔟 *116 km (72 mi) southeast of Mérida.*

Probably the best-known Maya ruin, Chichén Itzá was the most important city in Yucatán from the 10th to the 12th century. Its architectural mélange encapsulates pre-Hispanic Mexican history, showing foreign domination and the intermingling of cultures. Chichén was altered by each successive wave of inhabitants, and archaeologists are able to date the arrival of new inhabitants by the changes in the architecture; however, they have yet to explain the long gaps of time when the buildings seem to have been uninhabited. The site is believed to have been first settled in AD 432, abandoned for an unknown period of time, then rediscovered in 964 by the Maya-speaking Itzás, believed to have come from the Petén rain forest around Tikal, in what is now northern Guatemala; *Chichén Itzá* means "the mouth of the well of the Itzás." The Itzás also abandoned the site, and later in the 10th century it was rediscovered by the central-Mexican Toltecs, who ruled the local Maya population for more than 200 years but abandoned the site forever in 1224. Francisco de Montejo established a short-lived colony here in the course of his conquest of Yucatán in the mid-1500s. At the turn of this century, U.S. Consul General Edward Thompson purchased Chichén Itzá and carried out some of the earliest excavations at the site, basing himself at a hacienda on the grounds (now the Hacienda Chichén) and carting most of the treasure away to the Peabody Museum at Harvard University.

The majesty and enormity of this site are unforgettable. It incarnates much of the fascinating and bloody history of the Maya, from the steep temple stairways down which sacrificial victims may have been hurled, to the relentlessly ornate beauty of the smaller structures. Its audacity and vitality are almost palpable. Chichén Itzá encompasses approximately 6 square km (2 square mi), though only 20 to 30 buildings of the several hundred at the site have been fully explored. These buildings include the largest ball court in Mesoamerica; a sacrificial well once filled with precious offerings (it was dredged by Mexican diver Pablo Bush Romero, and many of its treasures are now at Harvard); and a round building—one of the only ones in the Maya lands—that was possibly the most elegant and sophisticated of the Maya observatories. Other features of the site include stone sculptures of the feathered serpent god, reclining *chac mools,* steam baths for ritual purification, ruined murals, astronomical symbols, and broad *sacbeob,* (literally "white roads" used for ceremonial purposes and as trade arteries) leading to other ancient centers.

Chichén Itzá is divided into two parts, called Old and New, although architectural motifs from the classical period are found in both sections. A more convenient distinction is topographical, since there are two major complexes of buildings separated by a dirt path. The martial, imperial architecture of the Toltecs and the more cerebral architectural genius and astronomical expertise of the Maya are married in the 98-ft-tall pyramid called **El Castillo** (the castle), which dominates the site and rises above all the other buildings.

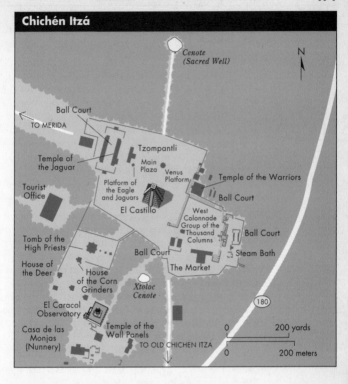

Chichén Itzá

Cenote (Sacred Well)

N

Ball Court

TO MERIDA

Tzompantli

Temple of the Jaguar

Main Plaza

Venus Platform

Temple of the Warriors

Tourist Office

Platform of the Eagle and Jaguars

Ball Court

El Castillo

West Colonnade Group of the Thousand Columns

Ball Court

Tomb of the High Priests

Ball Court

Steam Bath

House of the Deer

The Market

House of the Corn Grinders

Xtoloc Cenote

180

El Caracol Observatory

Casa de las Monjas (Nunnery)

Temple of the Wall Panels

TO OLD CHICHEN ITZA

0   200 yards

0   200 meters

Atop the castle is a temple dedicated to Kukulcán (the Maya name for Quetzalcóatl), the legendary priest-king from Tula in the Valley of Mexico who was incarnated by the plumed serpent. According to ancient lore, Quetzalcóatl went into exile, disappearing to the east, but promising to return one day. The Spaniards—whom the Aztecs (who adopted the cult of Quetzalcóatl after the Toltecs) mistook for gods—transformed that prophecy into a nightmarish reality. Four stairways, each facing a different cardinal point, provided access to the temple; two are used today. Those who fear heights can hold on to a rusty chain running down the center. Each access way consists of 91 very steep and narrow steps, which, when one adds the temple platform itself, makes a total of 365 (one for each day of the Mayas' extraordinarily accurate solar calendar). Fifty-two panels on the sides stand for the years of a sacred cycle, while the 18 terraces symbolize the months of the year. An open-jawed plumed serpent rests on the balustrade of each stairway, and serpents reappear at the top of the temple as sculptured columns.

At the spring and fall equinoxes (March 21 and September 21), the afternoon light and shadow strike one of these balustrades in such a way as to form a shadow representation of Kukulcán undulating out of his temple and down the pyramid to bless the fertile earth. The sound-and-light show in the evening was completely revamped in 1993, with a new computerized light system that highlights the architectural details in the Castillo and other buildings with a clarity the eye doesn't see in daylight. An entirely new sound system enables visitors to understand the formerly incomprehensible accompanying narration, drawn from the works of Bishop Landa and from the few surviving Maya texts, including the Books of Chilam Balam and Popul Vuh. Landa initially burned all the Maya manuscripts he collected but later, overcome with remorse and admiration for the Maya, wrote their history. Tens of thousands of people travel to Chichén Itzá for the equinoxes, particularly in the spring when there is little likelihood of rain. Hotel reservations for the event should be made well in advance; a year ahead is not unreasonable.

In 1937, archaeologists discovered a more ancient temple inside the Castillo. A humid, slippery stairway leads upward to an altar that once held two statues: a chac mool and a bejeweled red tiger. The tiger, which had jade encrusted discs embedded into its body and a turquoise disc laid on top of it, probably as an offering, is now housed in the Anthropology Museum in Mexico City. The inner temple is open to the public for only a few hours in the morning and again in the afternoon. Claustrophobes should think twice before entering: The stairs are narrow, dark, and winding, and there is often a line of tourists going both ways, making the trip somewhat frightening.

The temple rests on a massive trapezoidal square, on the west side of which is Chichén Itzá's largest **ball court,** one of seven on the site. Its two parallel walls are each 272 ft long, with two stone rings on each side, and 99 ft apart. The game played here was something like soccer (no hands were used), but it had a strictly religious significance. Bas-relief carvings at the court depict a player being decapitated, the blood spurting from his severed neck fertilizing the earth. Acoustics are so good that someone standing at one end of the court can hear the whispers of another person clearly at the other end. Sadly, the western wall of the court has been blackened by acid rain blown eastward from the oil fields on the Gulf of Mexico.

Between the ball court and El Castillo stands a **Tzompantli,** or stone platform, carved with rows of human skulls. In ancient times it was actually covered with stakes on which the heads of enemies were impaled. This motif was otherwise unknown in the Maya region, though a similar platform was found at the Templo Mayor or religious center of Tenochtitlán, the Aztec capital (modern-day Mexico City). The influence of the Toltecs, who preceded the Aztecs in the Valley of Mexico, is once again apparent.

The predilection for sacrifice was once believed to have come from the Toltecs, but recent research verifies that the pre-Toltec Maya had already been indulging in their own forms of the ritual. Legend has it that the **Sacred Well,** a cenote (sinkhole) 65 yards in diameter that sits ½ mi north of El Castillo at the end of a 900-ft-long *sacbe* ("white road" in Maya) was used for human sacrifices; another cenote at the site supplied drinking water. Skeletons of about 50 people were found in the first well. The sacrificial victims, many of them children of both sexes, were drugged before being dropped into the well. It is said that, if any of the victims survived, they were fished up out of the well in the hopes that they would recount the psychic visions they had experienced. (Hunac Ceel, the notorious ruler of Mayapán in the 1250s, hurled himself into its depths to prove his divine ascendancy, and survived.) Many archaeologists now believe that the sacrifices were carried out by local chiefs hundreds of years after Chichén Itzá was abandoned. Thousands of artifacts made of gold, jade, and other precious materials, most of them not of local provenance, have been recovered from the brackish depths of the cenote. Long on display at Harvard's Peabody Museum, many of the finds have now been returned to the Mexican government. Trees and shrubs have washed into the well over the centuries, and their remains have prevented divers from getting to the bottom; because the cenote is fed by a network of underground rivers, it cannot be drained. More treasure undoubtedly remains. The well's excavation launched the field of underwater archaeology, later honed by Jacques Cousteau.

Returning to the causeway, you will see on your left the **Group of the Thousand Columns** with the famous **Temple of the Warriors,** a masterful example of the Toltec influence at Chichén Itzá. This temple so resembles Pyramid B at Tula—the Toltecs' homeland, north of Mexico City—that scholars believe the architectural plans must have been carried 1,280 km (800 mi) overland or have come by sea (legend has it that Kukulcán arrived by the boat). Indeed, they can cite no other case in the pre-Columbian world of identical temples built by two such distant tribes. Masonry walls carved with feathered serpents and frescoes of eagles and jaguars consuming human hearts are among the unmistakably Toltec details. Using columns and wood beams instead of the Maya arches and walls to divide space enabled the Toltec-Maya architects to expand the interior and exterior spaces dramatically. Murals of everyday village life and scenes of war can be viewed here, and an artistic representation of the defeat of the Maya can be found on the interior murals of the adjacent **Temple of the Jaguar.**

To get to the less visited cluster of structures at "New" Chichén Itzá—often confused with "Old" Chichén Itzá (☞ *above*)—take the main road south from the Temple of the Jaguar past El Castillo and turn right onto a small path opposite the ball court on your left. Archaeologists are currently working in this area, restoring several buildings including the **Tomb of the High Priest,** where several tombs with skeletons and jade offerings were found. As work continues, certain ruins will be roped off and closed to tourists.

The most impressive structure within this area is the astronomical observatory called **El Caracol.** The name, meaning "snail," refers to the spiral staircase at the building's core. Built in several stages, El Caracol is one of the few round buildings constructed by the Maya. Although definitely used for observing the heavens (judging by the tiny windows oriented toward the four cardinal points, and the alignment with the planet Venus), it also served a religious function, since the Toltec cult of Kukulcán (Quetzalcóatl), the god of wind, often involved circular temples.

After leaving El Caracol, continue south several hundred yards to the beautiful **Casa de las Monjas** (Nunnery) and its annex, which have long panels carved with flowers and animals, latticework, hieroglyph-covered lintels, and Chaac masks (as does the nunnery at Uxmal). It was the Spaniards who gave the structure this sobriquet; no one knows how the Maya used it.

At "Old" Chichén Itzá, south of the remains of Thompson's hacienda, "pure Maya" style—a combination of Puuc and Chenes styles, with playful latticework, Chaac masks, and gargoyle-like serpents on the cornices—dominates. (This style also crops up at Uxmal, Kabah, Labná, and Sayil, among other sites.) Highlights include the **Date Group** (so named because of the complete series of hieroglyphic date inscriptions), the **House of the Phalli,** and the **Temple of the Three Lintels.** Maya guides will lead you down the path by an old narrow-gauge railroad track to even more ruins, barely unearthed, if you ask. A fairly good restaurant and great ice-cream stand are in the entrance building, and there are refreshment stands by the cenote and on the pathway near El Caracol. ⌸ *Site and museum $4, free Sun. and holidays; sound-and-light show $1 in Spanish, $5 in English; parking $1; use of video camera $8. ☉ Daily 8–5; sound-and-light show (Spanish) at 7, English at 9.*

Lodging

$$$ 🏨 **Mayaland.** The hotel closest to the ruins, this charming 1920s lodg-
★   ing belongs to the Barbachano family, whose name is practically synonymous with tourism in Yucatán. In addition to a main hotel building,

there are a wing and several bungalows set in a large garden on the 100-acre site. Colonial-style rooms in the main building have decorative tiles, ceiling fans, air-conditioning, and television. Eighteen bungalows were added in 1996; thirteen of them have television and air-conditioning. Tour buses fill the road in front of the hotel, so choose a room at the back. Light meals served poolside and at tables overlooking the garden are a far better choice than the fixed-price meals served in the dining room. ⊠ *Carretera Mérida–Cancún, Km 120,* ☎ *985/10129. Reservations, Mayaland Tours, Av. Colón 502, Mérida,* ☎ *99/236851 or 800/235–4079,* 𝖥𝖠𝖷 *99/642335. 83 rooms. Restaurant, bar, pool. AE, DC, MC, V.*

$$ 🏨 **Hacienda Chichén.** A converted 17th-century hacienda, this hotel
★ once served as the home of U.S. Consul General Edward S. Thompson; later it was the headquarters for the Carnegie expedition to Chichén Itzá. The rustic cottages have been modernized, and all rooms, which are simply furnished in colonial Yucatecan style, have private bathrooms and verandas. Rooms are air-conditioned but have no phones or TVs; there's a color satellite TV in the lobby area. Four rooms were added in 1997. An enormous old pool sits in the midst of the landscaped gardens. Fairly good meals are served on the patio overlooking the grounds, and there's an air-conditioned restaurant; stick with the Yucatecan specialties. ⊠ *Km 120 Carretera Mérida–Puerto Juarez, Yucatán 97000,* ☎ *985/10045, 99/248844, 99/242150, or 800/223–4084,* 𝖥𝖠𝖷 *99/245011. 18 rooms. Restaurant, bar, pool, free parking. No credit cards.*

Pisté

⑳   *About 1 km (⅗ mi) west of Chichén Itzá on Route 180.*

The town of Pisté serves mainly as a base camp for travelers to Chichén Itzá. Hotels, campgrounds, restaurants, and handicrafts shops tend to be cheaper here than south of the ruins. At the west end of town are a Pemex station and a bank. On the outskirts of Pisté, a short walk from the ruins, **Pueblo Maya,** a pseudo Maya village, provides a shopping and dining center for tour groups. The restaurant serves a bountiful buffet at lunch ($10).

Lodging

$$ 🏨 **Pirámide Inn Resort.** The rooms in this American-owned two-story motel in Pisté are being completely refurbished; ask for one that is finished. All have air-conditioning. The garden contains a small Maya pyramid, a swimming pool, and a tennis court, and the restaurant is one of the best in Pisté. The RV park has been closed. ⊠ *Km 117 Carretera Mérida–Puerto Juarez. Reservations, Box 433, Mérida,* ☎ *985/10115. 44 rooms. Restaurant, pool, tennis court, travel services. MC, V.*

$ 🏨 **Dolores Alba.** The best low-budget choice near the ruins is this family-run hotel, a long-time favorite in the country south of Pisté. The rooms are simple, clean, and comfortable; some have air-conditioning. Hammocks hang by the small pool, and breakfast and dinner are served family-style in the main building. Free transportation to the ruins is provided. ⊠ *Carretera Pisté-Cancún, 1½ mi south of Chichén Itzá. Reservations, Calle 63, No. 464, Mérida,* ☎ *99/285650,* 𝖥𝖠𝖷 *99/283163. 28 rooms. Dining room, pool. MC, V.*

Cave of Balancanchén

㉑   *4½ km (3 mi) northeast of Chichén Itzá.*

The Cave of Balancanchén, a shrine whose Maya name translates as "hidden throne," remained virtually undisturbed from the time of the

Conquest until its discovery in 1959. Inside is a large collection of artifacts—mostly vases, jars, and incense burners once filled with offerings. You'll walk past tiers of stalactites and stalagmites forming the image of sacred ceiba trees until you come to an underground lake. The lake is filled with blindfish (small fish with functionless eyes), and an altar to the rain god rises above it. In order to explore the shrine you must take one of the guided tours, which depart almost hourly, but it's necessary to be in fairly good shape, because some crawling is required; claustrophobes should skip it, and those who go should wear comfortable shoes. Also offered at the site is a sound-and-light show that fancifully recounts Maya history. You can catch a bus or taxi to the caves from Chichén Itzá. ✆ *Caves (including tour) $7, free Sun.; show $3.* ☉ *Daily 9–5; English tour at 11, 1 and 3, Spanish at 9 and noon, French at 10.*

Valladolid

② *44½ km (23 mi) east of Chichén Itzá.*

The second-largest city in the State of Yucatán, Valladolid is a picturesque, pleasant provincial town (population 70,000). It's enjoying growing popularity among travelers en route to or from Chichén Itzá or Río Lagartos who are harried by more touristy places. Montejo founded Valladolid in 1543 on the site of the Maya town of Sisal. The city suffered during the Caste War, when virtually the entire Spanish population was killed by the rebellious Maya, and again during the Mexican Revolution.

Today, however, placidity reigns in this agricultural market town. The center is mostly colonial, although it has many 19th-century structures. The main sights are the colonial churches, principally the large **cathedral** on the central square and the 16th-century **San Bernardino Church and Convent** three blocks southwest. Both were pillaged during the Caste War. A briny, muddy cenote in the center of town draws only the most resolute swimmers; instead, visit the adjacent **ethnographic museum.** Outside town, you can swim in **Cenote Dzitnup**, located in a cave lit by a small natural skylight ($4).

Valladolid is renowned for its cuisine, particularly its sausages; try one of the restaurants within a block of the square. You can find good buys on sandals, baskets, and the local liqueur, Xtabentún, flavored with honey and anise.

Lodging

$$ 🏨 **El Mesón del Marqués.** This building, on the north side of the main square, is a well-preserved, very old hacienda built around a lovely courtyard. Rooms in the modern addition at the back of the hotel have air-conditioning and are attractively furnished with rustic and colonial touches; rooms in the older section have ceiling fans. Unusually large bathrooms boast bathtubs—a rarity in Mexican hotels. ⊠ *Plaza Principal, Calle 39, No. 203, 97780,* ☎ *985/62073,* 🖷 *985/62280. 26 rooms, 12 suites. Restaurant, bar, pool, shops. MC, V.*

$ 🏨 **María del Luz.** Another choice by the main plaza, this hotel is built around a small swimming pool and courtyard. The rooms have been renovated with new floors, fresh paint, and tiled bathrooms; air-conditioning and color televisions (local channels only) are being added. The street-side restaurant is attractively furnished with high-backed rattan chairs and linen cloths; Mexican dishes are predictable and inexpensive. ⊠ *Plaza Principal, Calle 2, No. 195, 97780,* ☎ *985/ 62071. 33 rooms. Restaurant, bar, pool. No credit cards.*

TO UXMAL AND THE PUUC ROUTE

As soon as they pass through the large Maya town of Uman on Mérida's southern outskirts, travelers find themselves in one of the least populated areas of the Yucatán. From the highest point on the peninsula, the 500-ft crest between the present village of Muna and the ruins of ancient Uxmal, an unbroken expanse of forest reaches all the way to the southern horizon. The highway to Uxmal and Kabah is a fairly traffic-free route through uncultivated woodlands, punctuated here and there by oval thatched-roof huts and roadside stands where women sell hand-embroidered white cotton dresses.

The forest seems to become more dense beyond Uxmal, which was in ancient times the largest and most important city of the Puuc region. Raised and cobbled ceremonial roads connected it to a number of smaller ceremonial centers that, despite their apparent subservience to the Lords of Uxmal, boasted lofty pyramids and ornate palaces of their own. Several of these satellite sites, including Kabah, Sayil, and Labná, are open to the public along a side road known as the "Ruta Puuc," which winds eastward and eventually joins busy Route 184, a major highway linking Mérida with Felipe Carrillo Puerto, Quintana Roo, on the Caribbean coast, and serving the largest concentration of present-day Maya agricultural towns on the peninsula. From the east end of the Ruta Puuc near Loltún Caves, it takes motorists less than an hour to either retrace their route back to Uxmal or return to Mérida on Route 184.

Uxmal

㉓ *78 km (48 mi) south of Mérida on Route 261.*

If Chichén Itzá is the most impressive Maya ruin in Yucatán, Uxmal is arguably the most beautiful. Where the former has a Toltec grandeur, the latter seems more understated and elegant—pure Maya. The architecture reflects the late classical renaissance of the 7th-9th centuries and is contemporary with that of Palenque and Tikal, among other great Maya metropolises of the southern highlands. Although the name translates as "thrice built" (referring to the three levels of the Pyramid of the Magician, in which older temples were buried), the site was actually rebuilt, abandoned, and reoccupied in several stages, for reasons still unknown. Toltec (Itzá) invaders briefly occupied Uxmal in the 10th century; the site reemerged as a Maya ceremonial center in the postclassical era and was deserted for the last time some 90 years before the Conquest. When John Lloyd Stephens came upon Uxmal in 1840, it was owned by a descendant of the same Montejo family that had conquered Yucatán three centuries earlier.

The site is considered the finest and largest example of Puuc architecture, which embraces such details as ornate stone mosaics and friezes on the upper walls, intricate cornices with curled noses, rows of columns, and soaring vaulted arches. Lines are clean and uncluttered, with the horizontal—especially the parallelogram—preferred to the vertical. Many of the flat, low, elongated buildings were built on artificial platforms and laid out in quadrangles. The cult of the rain god, Chaac, who is depicted here with a long curled nose and whose image appears throughout Yucatán, became obsessive in this parched region. But the area lacks cenotes; though the Maya dug cisterns, called *chultunes*, for collecting rainwater, drought may be the reason that Uxmal was so often occupied and then abandoned. Some phallic figures—very common in Maya art because of the importance of fertility —are found here.

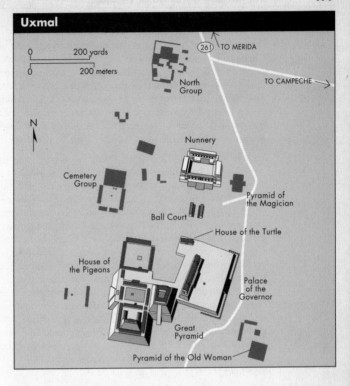

Uxmal

0   200 yards
0   200 meters

N

North
Group

261 TO MERIDA

TO CAMPECHE

Nunnery

Cemetery
Group

Pyramid of
the Magician

Ball Court

House of the Turtle

House of
the Pigeons

Palace
of the
Governor

Great
Pyramid

Pyramid of the Old Woman

While most of Uxmal remains unrestored, three buildings in particular merit attention. The most prominent, the **Pyramid of the Magician,** is, at 125 ft high, the tallest structure at the site. Unlike most Maya pyramids, which are stepped and angular, it has a strangely elliptical design. Built five times, each time over the previous structure, the pyramid has a stairway on its western side that leads through a giant mask of Chaac with its mouth wide open to two temples at the summit. The mask motif is repeated on one side of the stairs. You get a magnificent panoramic view of Uxmal and the hills by climbing up to the top. According to legend, the pyramid derived its name from a dwarf magician who built it overnight; it is especially lovely at night, when its pale beige slope glows in the moonlight.

West of the pyramid lies the **Nunnery,** or Quadrangle of the Nuns, considered by some to be the architectural jewel of Uxmal. Its name implies that early archaeologists may have surmised it had been a residence of the Maya priesthood, but no one knows for sure what role it played. You may enter the four buildings; each comprises a series of low, gracefully repetitive chambers that look onto a central patio. The building on the southern side is broken by a tall corbeled arch that is formed by placing ceiling stones increasingly close to and on top of one another until they meet at a central supporting capstone. Elaborate decoration—in the form of stone latticework, masks, geometric patterns reminiscent of ancient Greek ornamentation, representations of the classic Maya thatched hut (*na*), coiling snakes, and some phallic figures—blankets the upper facades, in contrast with the smooth, sheer blocks that face the lower walls. The mosaics that thrust into the upper facade are huge, sometimes surpassing several feet in size.

Continue walking south; you'll pass the ball court before reaching the **Palace of the Governor,** which archaeologist Victor von Hagen considered the most magnificent building ever erected in the Americas. Interestingly, the palace faces east while the rest of Uxmal faces west. Archaeologists believe this is because the palace was used to sight the planet Venus. Covering five acres and rising over an immense acropolis, the palace lies at the heart of what must have been Uxmal's administrative center. Its 320-ft length is divided by three corbeled arches, which create narrow passageways or sanctuaries. Decorating the facade are intricate friezes (along the uppermost section), geometrically patterned carvings overlaid with plumed serpents, stylized Chaac masks, and human faces. These mosaics required more than 20,000 individually cut stones.

First excavated in 1929 by the Danish explorer Franz Blom, the site served in 1841 as home to John Lloyd Stephens, who wrote of it: "The whole wears an air of architectural symmetry and grandeur. If it stood at this day on its grand artificial terrace in Hyde Park or the Garden of the Tuileries, it would form a new order . . . not unworthy to sit side by side with the remains of Egyptian, Grecian, and Roman art." Today a sound-and-light show recounts Maya legends, including the kidnapping of an Uxmal princess by a king of Chichén Itzá, and focuses on the people's dependence on rain—thus the cult of Chaac. The artificial colored light brings out details of carvings and mosaics that are easy to miss when the sun is shining—for example, the stone replicas of nas, which bear a remarkable resemblance to contemporary huts, on one facade of the nunnery. The show is performed nightly in English and is one of the better such productions. ✉ *Site and museum $4, free Sun. and holidays; sound-and-light show in Spanish $1.50, in English $5; parking $1; use of video camera $8.* ⊙ *Daily 8–5; sound-and-light show (Spanish) at 7, English at 9.*

Dining and Lodging

$$ ✕ **Nicte-Ha.** This café beside the Hacienda Uxmal hotel is the least expensive dining option by the ruins, serving pizzas, sandwiches, and Mexican snacks. Diners are welcome to use the swimming pool by the restaurant. Stop by after your morning tour, have lunch and a swim, and return to the ruins in late afternoon when the groups are gone and the sun is less intense. ✉ *Hacienda Uxmal, Hwy. 261,* ☎ FAX *9099/494754. MC, V.*

$ ✕ **Las Palapas.** A great alternative to the hotel dining rooms at Uxmal, this family-run restaurant specializes in delicious Yucatecan dishes served with homemade tortillas. When tour groups request it in advance, the owners prepare a traditional feast, roasting the chicken or pork pibil-style in a pit in the ground. If you see a tour bus in the parking lot, stop in—you may chance upon a memorable fiesta. ✉ *Hwy. 261, 5 km (3 mi) north of ruins, no phone. No credit cards.*

$$$ 🏨 **Hacienda Uxmal.** The oldest hotel at the Maya site, built in 1955 and still owned and operated by the Barbachano family, this pleasant colonial-style building has lovely floor tiles, ceramics, and iron grillwork. The rooms—all with ceiling fans and air-conditioning—are tiled and decorated with worn but comfortable furniture. Inside the large courtyard are a garden and pool. Across the road and about 100 yards south you'll find the ruins. Ask about packages that include free or low-cost car rentals for the nights you spend at Uxmal and at the Mayaland hotel in Chichén Itzá. ✉ *Within walking distance of ruins,* ☎ FAX *9099/494754. Reservations, Mayaland Tours, Av. Colón 502, Mérida,* ☎ *99/462331 or 800/235–4079,* FAX *99/462335. 80 rooms. Restaurant, bar, pool, shops. AE, DC, MC, V.*

$$ 🏨 **Villa Arqueológica Uxmal.** The hotel closest to the ruins is this two-story Club Med property built around a large Mediterranean-style pool. The functional rooms have cozy niches for the beds, tiled bathrooms, and powerful air conditioners. Maya women in traditional dress serve well-prepared French cuisine in the restaurant, and large cages around the hotel contain tropical birds and monkeys. For a fee, day-trippers can use the pool, then dine in the restaurant. ⊠ *Km 76 Carrerera Uxmal, Yucatán 97000, within walking distance of ruins,* ☎ *99/247053, 800/258–2633 for reservations in the U.S. 44 rooms. Restaurant, bar, pool, tennis court, shops. AE, MC, V.*

Kabah

㉔ *23 km (14 mi) south of Uxmal on Route 261.*

Kabah is the largest restoration project currently under way in the Yucatán; a ceremonial center of soft, almost Grecian beauty, it was once linked to Uxmal by a sacbe, at the end of which looms a great independent arch across the highway from the main ruins. The 151-ft-long **Palace of the Masks** (also known as **Codz-Poop** or "coiled mat") is so called because of its 250 Chaac masks, most without curled noses. ▨ *$1.25, free Sun.* ☉ *Daily 8–5.*

Sayil

㉕ *5 km (3 mi) south of Kabah on Route 261.*

Sayil, or "home of ants," is the oldest site of the Puuc group, renowned primarily for its majestic three-story **palace** with 70 rooms. The structure recalls Palenque in its use of multiple planes, its columned porticoes and sober cornices, and in the play of its long, graceful horizontal masses. ▨ *$1.25, free Sun. and holidays.* ☉ *Daily 8–5.*

Labná

㉖ *9 km (6 mi) south of Sayil on Route 31 East.*

The striking, monumental structure at Labná, called *La Puerta* or "The Gateway," is a fanciful corbeled arch rising high into a near peak with elaborate latticework and a small chamber on each side of it. One of the true curiosities of Maya civilization is that the Maya never discovered the true, or curved, arch. ▨ *$1.25, free Sun.* ☉ *Daily 8–5.*

Loltún Caves

㉗ *18 km (11 mi) northeast of Labná.*

The Loltún Caves is the largest known cave system in the Yucatán. This series of caverns contains wall paintings and stone artifacts from Maya and pre-Maya times (around 2500 BC), as well as stalactites and stalagmites. ▨ *$3, free Sun.* ☉ *Tues.–Sun. 9–4, tour at 9:30, 11, 12:30, 2, and 3.*

Ticul

㉘ *27 km (16½ mi) northwest of the Loltún Caves, 28 km (17 mi) east of Uxmal.*

Most of the pottery you'll see around the Yucatán is produced in Ticul, where huipiles and shoes are also made. Many descendants of the Xiu dynasty, which ruled Uxmal before the Conquest, still live here. One of the larger towns in Yucatán, Ticul has a handsome 17th-century church.

Dining

$$ ✕ **Los Almendros.** If you're traveling along the Puuc route, it's a good
★ idea to save your appetite for this place, considered by many the best

regional restaurant in the Yucatán. It offers fresher and tastier foods than do the other members of the Los Almendros chain. Although the interior is simple and clean, with whitewashed walls, the scenery behind the restaurant gives you a real taste of Yucatán: It's not unusual to see old Maya women in their huipiles and baseball hats patting corn tortillas by hand. The poc chuc and cochinita pibil are good choices, and the prices are the same as in the other branches. This is one place, however, where you can expect to wait in line for a table, especially during high season. ⊠ *Calle 23, No. 196,* ☎ *99/20021. MC, V.*

Yaxcopoil

㉙ *62 km (38 mi) north of Uxmal.*

Yaxcopoil, a restored 17th-century hacienda, offers a nice change of pace from the ruins. The building, with its distinctive Moorish double arch out front, has been used as a film set and is the best-known henequen plantation in the region. Visit the museum inside, which displays archaeological pieces and machinery used in the processing of henequen. ⊠ *Km 33, Rte. 261.* 🎟 *$2.* ☉ *Mon.–Sat. 8–sunset, Sun. 9–1.*

Mayapán

㉚ *49 km (30 mi) east of Ticul.*

Those who are really enamored of Yucatán and the ancient Maya can detour at Ticul on Route 18 to the ruined city of Mayapán, the last of the great city-states on the peninsula. There have been few excavations here, however, so archaeological evidence of past glory is limited to a few fallen statues of Kukulcán, and today the site is mainly of historical interest. ⊠ *Before Telchaquillo, Mayapán is off road to left; follow signs.* 🎟 *$1.25, free Sun.* ☉ *Daily 8–5.*

PROGRESO AND THE NORTH COAST

Three separate routes lead from the Mérida area to towns along the north coast. Less traveled roads dead-end at the forgotten former seaport of Sisal and the laid-back fishing village of Celestún, gateway to a flamingo reserve, while the busiest route leads due north to the modern shipping port and local beach playground of Progreso. All three towns have wide, white shadeless beaches that are crowded with bathers from Mérida on weekends, during Holy Week, and in the summer, but nearly vacant on winter weekdays.

The terrain in this part of the peninsula is absolutely flat. Tall trees are scarce, because the region was almost entirely cleared for sugar cane in the early 19th century and again for henequen in the early 20th century. Today local Maya people still tend some of the old fields of henequen, a spike-leaf agave plant, even though there is little profit to be made from the rope fiber it produces. Other former plantation fields have run wild, overgrown with scrub and marked only by the low, white stone walls erected to mark their boundaries. Bird life is abundant in the area, and butterflies swarm in profusion throughout the dry season.

Celestún

㉛ *90 km (56 mi) southwest of Mérida.*

The fishing town of Celestún sits at the end of a spit of land separating the Celestún estuary from the gulf on the western side of Yucatán. It is the only point of entry to the **Parque Natural del Flamenco Mex-**

icano, a 147,500-acre wildlife reserve with extensive mangrove forests and salt flats and one of the largest colonies of flamingos in North America. From June through March clouds of pink wings soar over the pale blue backdrop of the estuary, up to 18,000 at a time; it's also the fourth largest wintering ground for ducks of the gulf coast region, with over 200 other species of birds and a large sea turtle population. Conservation programs sponsored by the United States and Mexico not only protect the birds and turtles but other species like the blue crab and endangered crocodiles. Rocks, islets, and white-sand beaches enhance the park's lovely setting. There is good fishing in both the river and the gulf, and you can see deer and armadillo roaming the surrounding land. Bring your bathing suit if you want to enjoy a swim in one of the cenotes. Most Mérida travel agencies offer boat tours of the *ría* (estuary) in the early morning or late afternoon.

Popular with Mexican vacationers, the park's sandy beach is pleasant during the day but tends to get windy in the afternoon, with choppy water and blowing sand. To see the birds, hire a fishing boat at the dock outside town.

Sisal

③ *79 km (49 mi) northwest of Mérida.*

Sisal gave its name to the henequen that was shipped from this port in great quantity during the mid-19th century. With the rise of Progreso, Sisal dwindled into little more than a fisherman's wharf. However, it is beginning to take on importance again because of a large, exclusive residential development being built here by the same people who created the Continental Plaza Playacar (☞ Chapter 5). Sisal livens up in July and August when Méridanos come to swim and dine. Attractions include a **colonial customs house** and the private 1906 **lighthouse. Madagascar Reef,** one of three offshore reefs, offers excellent diving.

Lodging

$ 🏨 **Hotel Felicidades.** A few minutes' walk up the beach east of the pier, this somewhat dingy hotel caters to tourists during the vacation months and can be fun when a crowd arrives. ⊠ *Av. 6, No. 104, no phone. 10 rooms. No credit cards.*

Dzibilchaltún

③ *14 km (9 mi) north of Mérida.*

Dzibilchaltún ("the place where there is writing on flat stones") is one of the largest archaeological sites in the north Maya area, occupying more than 65 square km (25 square mi) of land cluttered with thousands of mounds, low platforms, piles of rubble, plazas, and stelae. It is also the longest-occupied city of this area, established around 375 BC in the pre-classical era and only abandoned when the conquistadors arrived.

For now, Dzibilchaltún's significance lies in the stucco sculpture and ceramics, from all periods of Maya civilization, that have been unearthed here. The **Temple of the Seven Dolls** (circa AD 500) is the only structure excavated on the site to date. Low and trapezoidal, the temple exemplifies the late pre-classical style, which predates such Puuc sites as Uxmal. The remains of stucco masks adorn each side, and there are vestiges of sculptures of coiled serpents representing Kukulcán. During the spring and fall equinoxes, sunbeams fall at the exact center of two windows opposite each other inside one of the temple rooms, an example of the highly precise mathematical calculations for which the

Mayas were known. The stone cube atop the temple and the open chapel built by the Spaniards for the Indians are additional points of interest. Twelve sacbeob lead to various groups of structures. Bones and ceremonial objects unearthed by divers from the National Geographic Society suggest that the **Xlacah cenote** was used for ceremonial offerings; these days, it's ideal for taking a dip if you're walking around the ruins in the heat.

An excellent museum called **Pueblo Maya** opened in December 1994 at the entrance to the site; it's part of a national program dedicated to establishing museums devoted—and accessible—to the country's native peoples. It's fronted by a garden featuring a number of the artifacts found on the site; in the back, two thatched roof huts (*nas*) let you see how the Maya live today. The museum's collection (marked in English as well as Spanish) includes figurines, bones, jewelry, and potsherds found in the cenote as well as the seven crude dolls that gave the temple its name; it also traces the area's Hispanic history and highlights contemporary crafts from the region. ✉ *$3, free Sun. and holidays.* ☉ *Daily 8–8.*

Progreso

㉝ *16 km (10 mi) north of Dzibilchaltún, 30 km (19 mi) north of Mérida.*

Progreso, the waterfront town closest to Mérida, is not particularly historical; it's also noisy with traffic and not at all picturesque. On weekdays during most of the year the town is deserted, but when school is out (Easter week, July, and August) and on summer weekends it becomes a popular vacation destination for families from Mérida. Progreso has fine sand and shallow waters that extend quite far out, making for nice walks, although its beaches are inferior to those of Quintana Roo. Because it is so close to Mérida and because its interest is limited, there is really no reason to spend the night here, but a couple of attractions in the small town may interest you.

The approach requires crossing some foul-smelling swamps, and these remind you of Progreso's main raison d'être: It has been the chief port of entry for the peninsula since its founding in 1872, when the shallow port at Sisal, to the southwest, proved inadequate for handling the large ships that were carrying henequen cargo. In 1989 the 2-km-long (1-mi-long) pier was extended 7 km (4 mi) out to sea to accommodate the hoped-for cruise-ship business and to siphon some of the lucrative tourist trade from Cozumel, but at the moment it looks as though all the millions invested have produced a white elephant because most cruise ships require deeper waters.

Progreso's attractions include its **malecón** (waterfront walkway), Calle 19, which is lined with seafood restaurants. Fishermen sell their catch on the beach east of the city between 7 and 8 AM. Some 120 km (75 mi) offshore are the **Alacranes Reef,** where divers can explore sunken ships, and **Pérez Island,** which supports a sizable population of sea turtles and seabirds.

Dining and Lodging

$$ ✕ **Capitán Marisco.** This large and pretty restaurant-bar on the malecón sports a nautical motif, with a ship's rudder in the center of the main dining room and a fountain adorned with seashells. The house specialty is *filete a la hoja de plátano* (fish fillet—usually grouper, sea bass, or pompano—cooked in banana leaves), but the entire menu is dependable. For a superb view of the sea, visit the outdoor terrace on the second floor. ✉ *Malecón on Calle 19, between Calles 60 and 66,* ☎ *993/50639. MC, V.*

$$ ✕ **Soberanis.** This branch of a respected Mexican chain of seafood houses is a dependable choice for fish dishes and traditional Mexican meals. ⊠ *Calle 30, No. 138, between Calles 27 and 29,* ☎ *993/50582. AE, MC, V.*

$$ 🏨 **Sian Ka'an.** These thatched-roof, two-story villas, right on the beach in Chelem (just west of Yucalpetén and near Progreso), all come with kitchenettes, ceiling fans, and terraces that overlook the water. Decorated in rustic Mexican-Mediterranean style, the suites have hand-woven bedspreads, *equipales* (leather chairs from Jalisco), and blown glassware. Prices include breakfast. Ask about discounts, which can be significant in the off-season. ⊠ *Calle 17, s/n, Progreso, 97320,* ☎ *993/54017. 7 suites. Restaurant, pool, beach. No credit cards.*

$ 🏨 **Progreso.** This clean, modest-but-tasteful three-star hotel in the heart of Progreso opened in 1990. The rooms, some with balconies, are furnished in pine, with arched window frames and tiled baths; they have either air conditioners or ceiling fans. ⊠ *Calles 29 and 28, 97320,* ☎ *993/50039,* 🗋 *993/52019. 9 rooms. Restaurant. MC, V.*

Yucalpetén

㉟ *3 km (2 mi) west of Progreso.*

If you approach Yucalpetén, which lies at the end of a narrow, marshy promontory, from the west, you'll pass a number of dead palm trees that were obliterated by the yellowing palm disease that has swept the peninsula in recent years. The harbor here dates only from 1968, when it was built to provide shelter for small fishing boats during the hurricane season. Little goes on here other than some activity at the yacht marina, where sportfishing for such catch as grouper, red snapper, dogfish, sea bass, and pompano is popular. Just beyond Yucalpetén, the even tinier village of **Chelem** has a few beachfront bungalow hotels.

Dining and Lodging
Take advantage of one of the several seafood restaurants on the beach strip. Rooms are available at **Hotel Gutiérrez** (⊠ Calle 12, No. 22, ☎ 99/280419) and **Hotel María del Carmen** (⊠ Calle 12, parallel to beach; look for sign for RESTAURANT VISTA DEL MAR, no phone).

Telchac Puerto

㊱ *43 km (27 mi) east of Progreso.*

This poverty-stricken little fishing village is worth visiting for its proximity to **Laguna Rosada**, where the flamingos come to nest, and it also has lovely, empty beaches. A new luxury hotel has brought some measure of prosperity back to the area.

More and more foreigners are getting wind of the inexpensive rental homes in the nearby fishing village of **Chicxulub Puerto**, with its inviting beach and low winter rates. Chicxulub has also gotten press among scientists who theorize that debris raised by an asteroid that landed here some 65 million years ago may have caused the extinction of the dinosaurs.

Dining and Lodging
$$$$ ✕🏨 **Mayan Beach Resort.** This Mexican version of a Club Med, run by Club Maeva, which also has hotels in Huatulco and Manzanillo, is smack on the beach and draws lots of Canadian travelers with its nonstop activities and all the food and drink you can consume included in the price of a room. Its friendly staffers, called "Amigos," take charge of water sports, classes, beach games, and the nightly musical revues.

Rooms are airy and have modern furniture and air-conditioning. The club also runs land excursions and provides airport transfer to and from Mérida. ⊠ *Telchac Puerto, domicilio conocido, Estado,* ☎ *99/249555 in Mérida, 800/466–2382 in the U.S.,* FAX *99/249477 in Mérida. 163 rooms. Restaurant, coffee shop, bar, pool, shops, dance club, travel services, car rental. AE, DC, MC, V.*

Motul

❸❼ *32 km (20 mi) south of Telchac Puerto, 51 km (32 mi) northeast of Mérida.*

Motul is the birthplace of the assassinated Socialist governor of Yucatán, Felipe Carrillo Puerto, who is also known for his romance with U.S. journalist Alma Reed in the 1930s. His former house is now a museum containing displays on his life and times. ⊙ *Daily 8–noon and 4–6.* 🖾 *Free.*

Dzilam de Bravo

❸❽ *40 km (25 mi) east of Telchac Puerto, 113 km (70 mi) northeast of Mérida.*

The pirate Jean Laffite supposedly lies buried just outside the village of Dzilam de Bravo; at least there's a grave so marked, and two locals claim to be his descendants. Stop here for a swim in the gentle waters.

Tizimín

❸❾ *108 km (67 mi) southeast of Dzilam de Bravo.*

Tizimín, renowned as the seat of an indigenous messianic movement during the 1840s Caste War, is situated at the junction of highways 176 and 295. The town boasts a 17th-century church dedicated to the Three Wise Men, who are honored here during a festival that is held December 15–January 15.

Río Lagartos National Park

❹⓿ *52 km (32 mi) north of Tizimín.*

If you're a flamingo fan (flamingo season runs from June through March), don't miss Río Lagartos National Park. Actually encompassing a long estuary, not a river, the park was developed with ecotourism in mind, though the alligators for which it and the village were named have long since been hunted into extinction. In addition to flamingos, birders can spot egrets, herons, ibis, cormorants, pelicans, and even peregrine falcons flying over these murky waters; fishing is good, too, and hawksbill and green turtles lay their eggs on the beach at night. Hotel Nefertiti, one of five hotels in town, offers boat tours, or you can hire a boat from the docks near the hotel.

Isla Holbox

❹❶ *141 km (87 mi) northeast of Valladolid.*

The tiny Isla Holbox (25 km, or 16 mi, long) sits at the eastern end of the Río Lagartos estuary and just across the Quintana Roo state line. A fishing fan's heaven because of the pompano, bass, barracuda, and shark thronging its waters, the island also pleases seekers of tranquillity who don't mind rudimentary accommodations (rooms and hammocks for rent) and simple palapa restaurants. Seabirds fill the air, the long sandy beach is strewn with seashells, and the swimming is good on the gulf side. To get here from Río Lagartos, take Route 176 to Kantunilkin, then head north on the unnumbered road for 44 km (27 mi) to Chiquilá. Continue by ferry to the island; schedules vary, but there are two crossings (time: one hour) a day.

MÉRIDA AND THE STATE OF YUCATÁN A TO Z

Arriving and Departing

By Bus

The **main bus station** (⊠ Calle 69, No. 544, between Calles 68 and 70, ☎ 99/247868) in Mérida offers frequent first- and second-class service to Akumal, Cancún, Chichén Itzá, Playa del Carmen, Puerto Morelos, Tulum, Uxmal, Valladolid, and Xel-Há. The new (opened 1994) **ADO bus terminal,** nearby at Calle 70, between Calles 69 and 71, can also be reached by phone (☎ 99/247868). Several lines, such as Expreso del Oriente (☎ 99/232287) and Super Expreso (☎ 99/248391) now offer deluxe service with air-conditioning, refreshments, and movies shown en route. **Autotransportes del Sureste** (☎ 99/281595) has the best coverage for out-of-the-way destinations, with daily service to the Guatemalan border, Palenque, and San Cristóbal de las Casas, and four buses daily to Uxmal. As its name suggests, the **Progreso bus station** (⊠ Calle 62, No. 557, between Calles 65 and 67, ☎ 99/281344) has departures for Progreso. Buses for Dzibilchaltún leave regularly from the San Juan Plaza. A new bus service called Nuevos Horizontes with deluxe service to Cancún, Campeche City, Tuxtla Gutierréz, Villahermosa, and Palenque leaves conveniently from the Fiesta Americana Hotel (Calle 56A and Av. Colon, local no. 56, ☎ 99/200100), where you can also buy your ticket. The Viajes Carmen travel agency (☎ 99/200126) in the lobby of the same hotel will sell you ADO bus tickets but departure is from the downtown bus terminal.

By Car

Route 180, the main road along the gulf coast from the Texas border to Cancún, runs into Mérida. Mexico City lies 1,550 km (960 mi) to the west; Cancún, 320 km (200 mi) due east.

The *autopista,* a four-lane toll highway between Cancún and Mérida, was completed in 1993. Beginning at the town of Kantuníl, 65 km (40 mi) southeast of Mérida, it runs somewhat parallel to Route 180 and cuts driving time between Cancún and Mérida—formerly around 4½ hours—by about one hour. Access to the toll highway is off Highway 180, about 24 km (15 mi) east of Mérida at Kantuníl. The highway has clearly marked exits for Valladolid and Pisté (Chichén Itzá), as well as rest stops and gas stations. At press time, tolls between Mérida and Cancún totaled about $16. From Campeche, it takes a little more than two hours to reach Mérida via Route 180, which is the fastest route. Another option is the three-hour drive along Route 261 from Campeche, which passes the ruins of Uxmal and other ancient Maya sites as well as present-day Maya villages. From Chetumal, the most direct way— it takes approximately nine hours—is Route 307 to Felipe Carrillo Puerto, then Route 184 to Muna, continuing north on Route 261. These paved highways are in good shape.

By Plane

The Mérida airport is 7 km (4 mi) west of the city's central square, about a 20-minute ride. The following airlines serve Mérida: **Aeromexico** (☎ 99/279000) flies direct from Miami with a stop (but no plane change) in Cancún; **Mexicana** (☎ 99/286790 and 99/281817) has a connecting flight from Newark via Cancún, and a number of connecting flights from the United States via Mexico City; **Aerocaribe** (☎ 99/286786 and 99/286790), a subsidiary of Mexicana, has flights from Cancún, Chetumal, Cozumel, Oaxaca, Tuxtla Gutiérrez, and Villahermosa; **Aviateca** (☎ 99/258062 and 99/258059), a Guatemalan carrier, flies from Houston and Guatemala City; and **Taesa** (☎ 99/202077) flies from Mexico City.

BETWEEN THE AIRPORT AND CITY CENTER

A private taxi costs about $7; there is only collective service for groups (usually a Volkswagen minibus), about $3. For both, pay the taxi-ticket vendor at the airport, not the driver. The inexpensive but irregular No. 79 bus goes from the airport to downtown. If you're driving into town, take the airport exit road, make a right at the four-lane Avenida Itzaes (the continuation of Route 180), and follow it to the one-way Calle 59, just past El Centenario Zoo. Turn right on Calle 59 and go straight until you reach Calle 62, where you again turn right, and drive a block to the main square. (Parking is difficult here.)

Getting Around

By Bus

Mérida's municipal buses run daily from 5 AM to midnight, but service is somewhat confusing until you master the system. In the downtown area, buses go east on Calle 59 and west on Calle 61, north on Calle 60 and south on Calle 62. You can catch a bus heading north to Progreso on Calle 56. Unfortunately, there is no bus service from the hotels around the plaza to the long-distance bus station.

By Car

Driving in Mérida can be frustrating because of the one-way streets (many of which end up being one-lane because of the parked cars) and because traffic is dense. But having your own wheels is the best way to take excursions from the city. Prices are sometimes lower if you arrange your rental in advance through one of the large international companies.

By Carriage

Horse-drawn calesas can be hailed along Calle 60. A ride to the Paseo de Montejo and back will cost about $7 to $9, and you can bargain.

By Taxi

Taxis don't cruise the streets for passengers; instead, they are available at 13 taxi stands around the city, or from the main taxi office (☎ 99/285324) or in front of the Hyatt Regency/Holiday Inn and Fiesta Americana hotels, which are strung out on the same block. Individual cabs cost $3 minimum.

Contacts and Resources

Banks

Most banks throughout Mérida are open weekdays 9–1:30. **Banamex** has its main offices, open weekdays and Saturday 9–5, in the handsome Casa de Montejo, on the south side of the main square, with a branch at the airport and the Fiesta Americana Hotel. The downtown and Fiesta Americana Banamex now have automatic teller machines that can be accessed with Cirrus, MasterCard, and Visa bank cards. Several other banks can be found on Calle 65 between Calles 62 and 60 and on Paseo Montejo.

MONEY EXCHANGE

There are several exchange houses, including **Del Sureste** (⊠ Calle 56 at Calle 57), open weekdays 9–5 and Saturday 9–1; **Centro Cambri-**

ano Canto (⊠ Headquarters at Paseo de Montejo at corner of Av. Perez Ponce; downtown branch at Calle 61 at Calle 52), both open weekdays 9–1 and 4–7; **Casa de Cambio del Pasaje Pichetti** (⊠ On the main square), open weekdays 9–5 and Saturday 9–1; and two on the ground level of the Fiesta Americana Hotel (Calle 56A and Av. Colon), open weekdays 9–5. By all means avoid the exchange house operated by GBM Atlantico in the same building complex as Centro *Cambiario* Canto as it's under investigation for possible fraudulent practices.

Car Rentals

There are almost 20 car-rental agencies in town, including **Budget** (⊠ Hyatt Regency, Calle 60, No. 344, at Av. Colon, ☎ 99/421226; the Holiday Inn next to the Hyatt, ☎ 99/255453, and airport, ☎ 99/461380); **Dollar** (⊠ Hotel Mérida Misión, ☎ 99/286759; airport, ☎ 99/461323), **National** (⊠ Fiesta Americana, ☎ 99/421111, ext. 6737; airport, ☎ 99/461791); and **Thrifty** (⊠ Calle 60 between Calle 51 and 49, ☎ 99/232440; airport, ☎ 99/462515.

Consulates

United States (⊠ Paseo de Montejo 453, ☎ 99/255011, 99/258677, or 99/255409). **United Kingdom** (⊠ Calle 58, No. 450, at Calle 53, ☎ 99/286152).

Emergencies

In Mérida: **Police** (☎ 99/252555); **Red Cross** (Calle 68, No. 583, at Calle 65, ☎ 99/249813); **Fire** (☎ 99/249242); **general emergency** (☎ 06).

Hospital O'Horan (⊠ Av. Internacional and Av. Itzaes, ☎ 99/244111, 99/242911, or 99/244800).

English-Language Bookstores

Librería Dante has several branches around Mérida (⊠ Calle 59 at Calle 68; Parque Hidalgo; in Teatro Peón Contreras, at corner of Calles 60 and 57; and on main square, next to Pizza Bella), all of which carry a small selection of English-language books and a Mexico City daily newspaper. For newspapers and magazines from Mexico City and the United States, visit **Rockerias** (⊠ Calle 58, No. 516, between Calles 61 and 63) and the newsstand under the portals in Plaza Pichetti on the main square.

Guided Tours

There are more than 50 tour operators in Mérida, and they generally offer the same destinations. What differs is how you go—in a private car, a van, or a bus—and whether the vehicle is air-conditioned. A two- to three-hour city tour, including museums, parks, public buildings, and monuments, will cost between $7 and $20. Or you can pick up an open-air sightseeing bus at Parque de Santa Lucía for $5; departures are Monday–Saturday at 10, 1, 4, and 7 and Sunday at 12:30 and 5. A day trip to Chichén Itzá, with guide, entrance fee, and lunch, runs approximately $40. For about the same price you can see the ruins of Uxmal and Kabah in the Puuc region, and for a few more dollars you can add on the neighboring sites of Sayil, Labná, and the Loltún Caves. Afternoon departures to Uxmal allow you to take in the sound-and-light show at the ruins and return by 11 PM, for $40–$50 (including dinner). There is also the option of a tour of Chichén Itzá followed by a drop-off in Cancún for about $50. Most tour operators take credit cards.

SPECIAL-INTEREST TOURS

Several of the tour operators in Mérida run overnight excursions to archaeological sites farther afield, notably Cobá, Tulum, Edzná, and Palenque. Tours of the Ruta Maya including sites in Mexico, Guatemala, and Belize are offered by **VN Travel** (⊠ Calle 58, No. 488, ☎ 99/239061 or 99/245996) and **Mayaland Tours** (⊠ Holiday Inn, Av. Colón, No. 502, ☎ 99/236851 or 800/235–4079, ℻ 99/462335), which also offers self-guided tours with economical rental car rates. **Ecoturismo Yucatán** (⊠ Calle 3, No. 235, at Col. Pensiones, ☎ 99/252187, ℻ 99/259047) specializes in nature tours, including bird-watching, natural history, anthropology, and the Mundo Maya. Owners Roberta and Alfonso Escobedo are especially adept at organizing group and individual trips to out-of-the-way archaeological sites and natural parks in Yucatán, Campeche, Chiapas, Tabasco, Belize, and Guatemala.

Emerald Planet (⊠ 4076 Crystal Court, Boulder, CO 80304, ☎ 303/541–9688, ℻ 303/449–7805) and **Siteseer Journeys** (⊠ 27210 S.W. 166 Ave., Homestead, FL 33031, ☎ 800/615–4035, ℻ 305/242–9009) offer bird-watching tours and other trips into wildlife reserves in the state of Yucatan. Part of the profits go towards funding Pronatura projects. With two weeks' advance notice **Pronatura** (⊠ Calle 1-D, No. 254-A, Campestra, ☎ ℻ 99/443390 and 99/443580) will arrange guided one- or two-day trips to Celustun or Rió Lagartos accompanied by a bilingual biologist; a donation is expected in addition to the fee.

Mail

In addition to the **main post office** (⊠ Calle 65 at Calle 56, ☎ 99/285404), there are branches at the airport (☎ 99/211556) and at the main bus station (⊠ Calle 69 between Calles 68 and 70, no phone), all open weekdays 8–5, Saturday 8–2.

Spanish-Language School

Intensive Spanish classes for foreigners are available in Mérida through the **Centro de Idiomas** (⊠ Calle 14, No. 106, at Calle 25, Col. Mexico 97128, Mérida, Yuc., Mexico, ☎ 99/230954 or 99/261156) and the **Academia de Cultura e Idiomas de Mérida** (⊠ Apdo. Postal 78-4, 97100 Mérida, Yuc., Mexico, ☎ ℻ 99/443148). Classes last a minimum of two weeks; advanced classes in special areas of study are available. Students stay with local families or in hotels.

Telephones

Local phone numbers are gradually changing throughout Mérida, causing much confusion. If you need information, talk with the operator or your hotel staff. There are several long-distance **Ladatel phone booths** around town: at the airport, at all bus stations, at Avenida Reforma and Avenida Colón, Calle 57 at Calle 64, Calle 59 at Calle 62, and Calle 60 between Calles 55 and 53. Both local and international direct calls can be made at some of these public phones, which accept new peso coins. Some phones accept Ladatel cards, electronic phone cards that can be purchased at some hotels and at the newsstands by the main square on Calle 61.

Travel Agencies and Tour Operators

Mérida's local agencies and operators include **American Express** (⊠ Calle 56-A, No. 494, ☎ 99/284222, ℻ 99/284373), **Buvisa** (⊠ Paseo de Montejo, No. 475, ☎ 99/277933, ℻ 99/277414), **Ceiba Tours** (⊠ Calle 60, No. 495, ☎ 99/244477 or 99/244499, ℻ 99/244588), **Holiday Inn** (⊠ Av. Colón, No. 502, ☎ 99/244477), **Intermar Caribe** (⊠ Prolongación Paseo de Montejo 74, at Calle 30, ☎ 99/445249 or 99/445222, ℻ 99/445259), **Mayaland Tours** (⊠ Av. Colón, No. 502, ☎ 99/462331 or 800/235–4079, ℻ 99/462335; Casa del Balam hotel, Calle 60, No. 488, ☎ 99/244919), **Turismo Aviomar** (⊠ Calle 58A, 500-C, ☎ 99/200444 or 99/200443, ℻ 99/246887), **Viajes Novedosos** (⊠ Calle 58, No. 488, ☎ 99/245996, ℻ 99/239061), and **Yucatán Trails** (⊠ Calle 62, No. 482, ☎ 99/241928 or 99/282582, ℻ 99/244919 or 99/285913).

24-Hour Pharmacies

Farmacia Yza Aviación (⊠ Calle 71 at Av. Aviación, ☎ 99/238116), **Farmacia Yza Tanlum** (⊠ Glorieta Tanlum, ☎ 99/251646), and **Farmacia Canto** (⊠ Calle 60, No. 514, at Calle 63, ☎ 99/248265).

Visitor Information

MÉRIDA

Tourist Information Center (⊠ Teatro Peón Contreras, Calle 59 between Calles 62 and 64, ☎ 99/249290), open daily 8–8. **Information kiosks:** At the airport (☎ 99/246764), open daily 8–8; and at Calle 59 and 62 (no phone), open weekdays 8–8 and weekends 9–7.

PROGRESO

Tourist office (⊠ Calle 30, No. 176, at Calle 37, ☎ 993/50104), open Monday–Saturday 9–3 and 6–9.

8 Portraits of the Yucatán Peninsula

*Chronology of the Maya
and History of Yucatán*

The Three Faces of the Yucatán

CHRONOLOGY OF THE MAYA AND HISTORY OF YUCATÁN

11,000 BC Hunters and gatherers settle in Yucatán.

Preclassic Period: 2000 BC–AD 200

2,000 BC Maya ancestors in Guatemala begin to cultivate corn and build permanent dwellings.

1500–900 BC The powerful and sophisticated Olmec civilization develops along the Gulf of Mexico in the present-day states of Veracruz and Tabasco.

Primitive farming communities develop in Yucatán.

900–300 BC Olmec iconography and social institutions strongly influence the Maya populations in neighboring areas. The Maya adopt the Olmecs' concepts of tribal confederacies and small kingships as they move across the lowlands.

600 BC Edzná is settled. It will be inhabited for nearly 900 years before the construction of the large temples and palaces found there today.

400 BC–AD 100 Dzibilchaltún develops as an important center in Komchen, an ancient state north of present-day Mérida. Becán, in southern Campeche, is also settled.

300 BC–AD 200 New architectural elements, including the corbeled arch and roof comb, develop in neighboring Guatemala and gradually spread into the Yucatán.

300 BC–AD 900 Edzná becomes a city; increasingly large temple-pyramids are built.

AD 200 A small temple is built on Isla Cancún.

Classic Period: 200–900

The calendar and the written word are among the achievements that mark the beginning of the classic period. The architectural highlight of the period is large, stepped pyramids with frontal stairways topped by limestone and masonry temples, arranged around plazas and decorated with stelae (stone monuments), bas-reliefs, and frescoes. Each Maya city is painted a single bright color, often red or yellow.

200–600 Economy and trade flourish. Maya culture achieves new levels of scientific sophistication and some groups become warlike.

250-300 A defensive fortification ditch and earthworks are built at Becán.

300 The first structures are built at San Gervasio on Cozumel.

300–600 Kohunlich rises to dominate the forests of southern Quintana Roo.

400–1100 Cobá grows to be the largest city in the eastern Yucatán.

432 The first settlement is established at Chichén Itzá.

6th Century Influenced by the Toltec civilization of Teotihuacán in Central Mexico, larger and more elaborate palaces, temples, ball courts, roads, and fortifications are built in southern Maya cities, including Becán, Xpujil, and Chicanná in Campeche.

600–900 Northern Yucatán ceremonial centers become increasingly important as centers farther south reach and pass developmental climax; the influence of Teotihuacán wanes. Three new Maya architectural styles develop: Puuc (exemplified by Chichén Itzá and

Edzná is the dominant style; Chenes (in northern Campeche, between the Puuc hills and the Río Bec area) is characterized by ornamental facades with serpent masks; and Río Bec (at Río Bec and Becán) features small palaces with high towers exuberantly decorated with serpent masks.

850–950 The largest pyramids and palaces of Uxmal are built. By 975, however, Uxmal and most other Puuc sites are abandoned.

Postclassic Period: 900–1541

900–1050 The great classic Maya centers of Guatemala, Honduras, and southern Yucatán are abandoned. The reason for their fall remains one of archaeology's greatest mysteries.

circa 920 The Itzá, a Maya tribe from the Petén rain forest in Guatemala, establish themselves at Champotón and then at Chichén Itzá.

987 According to legend, Toltecs leave their capital at Tula in central Mexico under the leadership of an exiled priest-king believed to be an incarnation of Quetzalcóatl, the "feathered serpent" god. The Yucatec Maya recognize him as the incarnation of their snake god, Kukulcán, and he becomes the ruler of Chichén Itzá. The Toltecs will rule Chichén Itzá for two centuries, until 1185.

987–1007 The Xiu, a Maya clan from the southwest, settle near ruins of Uxmal.

1224 An Itzá dynasty known as Cocomes emerges as a dominant group in northern Yucatán, building their capital at Mayapán.

1224–44 The Cocomes force the Toltec rulers out of Chichén Itzá, but the Itzá Maya soon return to the abandoned city as squatters.

1263–1440 Mayapán, under the rule of Cocomes aided by Canul mercenaries from Tabasco, becomes the most powerful city-state in Yucatán. The league of Mayapán—including the key cities of Uxmal, Chichén Itzá, and Mayapán—is formed in northern Yucatán. Peace reigns for almost two centuries. To guarantee the peace, the rulers of Mayapán hold members of other Maya royal families as lifelong hostages.

1441 Maya cities under Xiu rulers sack Mayapán, ending centralized rule of the peninsula. Yucatán henceforth is governed as 18 petty provinces, with constant internecine strife. The Itzá return to Lake Petén Itzá in Guatemala and establish their capital at Tayasal (modern-day Flores), one of the last un-Christianized Maya capitals, which will not be conquered by the Spanish until 1692.

15th Century The last ceremonial center on Cancún island is abandoned. Other Maya communities are developing along the Caribbean coast.

1502 A Maya canoe is spotted during Columbus's fourth voyage.

1511 Spanish sailors Jerónimo de Aguilar and Gonzalo Guerrero are shipwrecked off Yucatán's Caribbean coast and taken to a Maya village on Cozumel.

1517 Fernández de Córdoba discovers Isla Mujeres.

Trying to sail around Yucatán, which he believes to be an island, Córdoba lands at Campeche, marking first Spanish landfall on the mainland. He is defeated by the Maya at Champotón.

1518 Juan de Grijalva sights the island of Cozumel but does not land there.

1519 Hernán Cortés lands at Cozumel, where he rescues Aguilar. Guerrero chooses to remain on the island with his Maya family.

1527, Unsuccessful Spanish attempts to conquer Yucatán.
1531, 1541

1540 Francisco de Montejo founds Campeche, the first Spanish settlement in Yucatán.

Colonial Period: 1541–1821

1542 Maya chieftains surrender to Montejo at T'ho; 500,000 Indians are killed during the conquest of Yucatán. Indians are forced into labor under the *encomienda* system, by which conquistadors are charged with their subjugation and Christianization. The Franciscans contribute to this process.

Mérida is founded on the ruins of T'ho.

1543 Valladolid is founded on the ruins of Zací.

1546 A Maya group attacks Mérida, resulting in a five-month-long rebellion.

1562 Bishop Diego de Landa burns Maya codices at Maní.

1600 Cozumel is abandoned after smallpox decimates population.

1686 Campeche's city walls are built for defense against pirates.

1700 182,500 Indians account for 98% of Yucatán's population.

1736 Indian population of Yucatán declines to 127,000.

1761 The Cocom uprising near Sotuta leads to death of 600 Maya.

1771 The Fuerte (fort) de San Miguel is completed on a hill above Campeche, ending the pirates' reign of terror.

1810 Port of Sisal opens, ending Campeche's ancient monopoly on peninsular trade and its economic prosperity.

Postcolonial/Modern Period: 1821–Present

1821 Mexico wins independence from Spain by diplomatic means. Various juntas vie for control of the new nation, resulting in frequent military coups.

1823 Yucatán becomes a Mexican state encompassing the entire peninsula.

1839–42 American explorer John Lloyd Stephens visits Yucatán's Maya ruins and describes them in two best-selling books.

1840–42 Yucatecan separatists revolt in an attempt to secede from Mexico. The Mexican government quells the rebellion, reduces the state of Yucatán to one-third its previous size, creates the federal territories of Quintana Roo and Campeche, and recruits Maya soldiers into a militia to prevent further disturbance.

1846 Following years of oppression, violent clashes between Maya militiamen and residents of Valladolid launch the War of the Castes. The entire non-Indian population of Valladolid is massacred.

circa 1848 Twenty refugee families from the Caste War settle in Cozumel, which has been almost uninhabited for centuries. By 1890, Cozumel's population numbers 500.

1850 Following the end of the Mexican War with the United States in 1849, the Mexican army moves into the Yucatán to end the Indian uprising. The Maya flee into the unexplored forests of Quintana Roo. Military attacks, disease, and starvation reduce the Maya population of the Yucatán Peninsula to less than 10,000.

1863 Campeche achieves statehood.

1872 The city of Progreso is founded.

1880–1914 Yucatán's monopoly on henequen, enhanced by plantation owner's exploitation of Maya peasants, leads to its Golden Age as one of the wealthiest states in Mexico. Prosperity will last until the beginning of World War II.

Waves of Middle Eastern immigrants arrive in Yucatán and become successful in commerce, restaurants, cattle ranching, and tourism.

Payo Obispo (present-day Chetumal) is founded on the site of a long-abandoned Spanish Colonial outpost.

1901 The Caste War virtually ends with the defeat of the Chan Santa Cruz Maya in Quintana Roo.

U.S. Consul Edward Thompson buys Chichén Itzá for $500 and spends the next three years dredging the Sacred Cenote for artifacts.

1902 Mexican President Porfirio Díaz asserts federal jurisdiction over the Territory of Quintana Roo to isolate rebellious pockets of Indians and increase his hold on regional resources.

1915–24 Felipe Carrillo Puerto, Socialist governor of Yucatán, institutes major reforms in land distribution, labor, women's rights, and education during Mexican Revolution.

1923–48 A Carnegie Institute team led by archaeologist Sylvanus Moreley restores the ruins of Chichén Itzá.

1934–40 President Lázaro Cárdenas implements significant agrarian reforms in Yucatán.

1935 Chan Santa Cruz rebels in Quintana Roo relinquish Tulum and sign a peace treaty.

1940–70 With collapse of the world henequen markets, Yucatán gradually becomes one of the poorest states in Mexico.

1968 Cancún is selected by FONATUR as the site of Mexico's largest tourist resort.

1974 Quintana Roo achieves statehood. The first resort hotels at Cancún open for business.

1988 Hurricane Gilbert shuts down Cancún hotels and devastates the north coast of the Yucatán. The reconstruction is immediate. Within three years, the number of hotels on Isla Cancún triples.

1993 Quintana Roo's newly elected environmentalist governor, Mario Villanueva, toughens ecological protection in the state and orders a moratorium on new hotel construction on Cancún Island.

1994 Mexico joins the United States and Canada in NAFTA (North American Free Trade Association), which will phase out tariffs over a 15-year period.

Popular PRI presidential candidate Luis Donaldo Colosio assassinated while campaigning in Tijuana. Ernesto Zedillo, generally thought to be more of a technocrat and "old boy"-style PRI politician, replaces him and wins the election.

Zedillo, blaming the economic policies of his predecessor, devalues the peso in December.

1995   Recession sets in as a result of the peso devaluation. The former administration is rocked by scandals surrounding the assassinations of Colosio and another high-ranking government official; ex-President Carlos Salinas de Gortari moves to the United States.

1996   Mexico's economy, bolstered by a $28 billion bailout led by the United States, turns around, but the recovery is fragile. The opposition National Action Party (PAN), which is committed to conservative economic policies, gains strength. New details emerge of scandals within the former administration.

1997   Mexico's top antidrug official is arrested on bribery charges. The U.S. nonetheless recertifies Mexico as a partner in the war on drugs. Party elections are scheduled for midyear.

THE THREE FACES OF THE YUCATÁN

AS ANCIENT and mysterious as a stone idol, as stately as a cathedral, as sleek and modern as a sailboard slicing across a brilliant blue-green sea, the Yucatán Peninsula is a land with a complicated soul.

Vestiges of ancient Maya wisdom show in the eyes of country people carrying loads of wood along the roadside. A timeless innocence glows in the faces of children playing soccer amid the ruins of thousand-year-old ball courts and plunging merrily into cenotes, virtually bottomless water holes believed by their ancestors to possess mystical powers.

The ghost of Don Quixote dances in the faces of the men who drive *calesas,* old-fashioned horse-drawn carriages, along the traffic-choked Spanish Colonial streets of Mérida in competition with modern taxi cabs. The spirit of the conquistadors lives on in the cold, proud gaze of the bullfighters who keep Mexico's earlier tradition of blood ritual alive throughout the peninsula—even in that most modern of Yucatecan cities, Cancún.

The eyes of the people speaking English, French, Italian, German, Swedish, and a babel of other languages up and down the seemingly endless beaches of Isla Cancún hide behind dark glasses—bloodshot, most likely, from a pre-dawn airline flight or a late-night tour of the local discos. International visitors are equal partners in the unique multicultural mix of the Yucatán Peninsula today: From Cancún on the east coast to Celestún on the gulf coast, tourism is by far the region's largest industry.

The palm-lined beaches, warm turquoise waters, and dazzling coral reefs along the Corridor Turistico, the stretch of Caribbean coastline from Cancún south, offer sufficient reason for millions of vacationers to come to the Yucatán each year—North Americans and Europeans to escape the winter cold, Mexicans to find respite from the summer heat. But beyond the realm of tourist resorts lies a land with a cultural heritage rich and mysterious enough to fascinate casual sightseers and veteran adventurers alike.

Perhaps no civilization known to have inhabited Earth is more enigmatic and fascinating than that of the Maya.

We know that their accomplishments during the Classic Period (AD 250–900) were profound. Besides the monumental architecture and artwork we can see today at Classic Period sites, the Maya developed astronomy so advanced that some of their calculations did not become known to modern scientists until the 1930s. Their hieroglyphs were the only true written language used in the Western Hemisphere before Columbus. Their calendar, an ingenious refinement of the earlier Olmec calendar used by many ancient Mexican cultures, was more sophisticated than calendars used in Europe at the time. Their mathematics made use of the digit "zero," a concept unknown to European mathematicians in those days. And the Maya were probably the first people to discover the secret of cultivating corn. By freeing them from the need to wander in an endless, nomadic search for food, corn may have enabled the Maya to develop their sophisticated arts and sciences.

But who were these people? The early Mormon Church held that the Maya were the lost tribes of Israel. Some 19th-century scholars believed that their origins might lie in Egypt, Cambodia, or even the lost continent of Atlantis. In the 20th century, there are those who theorize that the Maya were influenced by mystical prophecies or by "gods" from outer space.

Most modern archaeologists now agree that the Maya were a purely American Indian race who inhabited the Yucatán Peninsula from about 2000 BC and were the ancestors of the native people who live in the Yucatán today. Maya people also lived in the adjoining areas of present-day Belize, Guatemala, Honduras, El Salvador and the Mexican state of Chiapas.

Still, the more that has been learned about the ancient Maya, the less certain experts have grown about the exact nature of their society. Were the Maya peace-loving or warlike? Were their rulers priests and artists or barbarian warlords? Did they sacrifice human beings to the gods, or was this solely a practice of Toltec invaders? Was it civil war, disease, famine, political collapse, environmental disaster, or urban decay that brought the Classic Maya civilization to an end? Archaeologists may argue endlessly about such matters, but nobody knows for sure. So much the better for today's visitors to the Yucatán: Touching the stones of lost cities with your own hands and letting ancient forest temples tug at your imagination, you can come up with your own answers.

Follow the highway for 87 miles south of Cancún, and you will find yourself among the ruins of Tulum, an ideal introduction to the world of the ancient Maya. Here a temple known as El Castillo ("The Castle") stands silent watch atop jagged charcoal-gray cliffs at the highest point on the coast of the Yucatán Peninsula. The youngest restored archaeological zone in the Yucatán—its main temples were built 300 years after the fall of the Classic Maya empire—Tulum was the center of a seagoing culture that traded up and down the coast in long canoes nearly 800 years ago. At midday, fleets of tour buses from Cancún parade into the parking lot and camera-clicking multitudes seize the place like an invading army. Yet, even at the most crowded times, a profound sense of strangeness wraps Tulum.

CONSIDER, THEN, that the art and architecture of Tulum are pale imitations of the grandeur that can still be seen at the ruins of older, much larger Maya cities throughout the Yucatán Peninsula. Tulum tantalizes the traveler with just enough hints of ancient glory to make the idea of a trip to other Maya sites such as Cobá, Chichén Itzá, and Uxmal irresistible.

Less than an hour from Tulum, on a side road where few tour buses venture, Cobá could not be more different from its neighbor. As Tulum is a young site, Cobá is a very old one, perhaps one of the first Maya capitals on the Yucatán Peninsula. As Tulum's temples are small, graceless, and slightly crooked, Coba's are some of the tallest in the Yucatán. And as Tulum is compact enough to visit on a half-day excursion from Cancún, Cobá's ruins stand at the shoreline of several lakes and require miles of hiking along jungle trails.

If you have time to visit only one Maya ruin during a brief trip to the Yucatán, choose Chichén Itzá, the most magnificently restored of all ancient ruins on the peninsula, ranking alongside Egypt's Valley of the Kings and the temples of ancient Greece as one of the foremost wonders of the archaeological world. The enormous scale and intricate detail of the site, with its Roman-looking columns, its murals recording rituals of human sacrifice, and its giant, dragonlike stone heads carved in the style of the Toltecs who occupied this part of the peninsula in the late part of the Classic Maya era, is awe-inspiring.

If Tulum and Cobá are studies in contrast, so too are Chichén Itzá and Uxmal, which lies south of Mérida. Although the largest structures at both sites were built around the same time, Uxmal's architecture is purely Maya, free from any hint of the Toltec influences that characterize Chichén Itzá. Instead of Chichén's plumed serpent sculptures, sacrificial altars, and carvings of warrior heroes, Uxmal is ornamented with complex geometric designs and small, symbolic sculptures of turtles, parrots, rattlesnakes, and human faces peering from the jaws of beasts. There are few hieroglyphs or other physical clues to the history of Uxmal, making it a great place to let your imagination roam.

One of the few things archaeologists know for sure about Uxmal is that it was the center of a state known as the Puuc (Maya for "Hills"). Wide, limestone-paved ancient roadways, or *sacbeob,* connected Uxmal with smaller communities throughout the hill country. Several of the most impressive, including Kabah, Sayil, and Labná, lie within a few minutes' drive from Uxmal along winding roads that were paved in the late 1970s to make the ruins accessible for visitors. Ongoing restoration has transformed Kabah from rubble to majesty and keeps on revealing new temples down winding forest footpaths. Sayil and Labná, just a few miles apart, have been cleared but not extensively restored. Two of the most lavish palaces in the ancient Maya Yucatán have been excavated there.

Fascinating as it is, ancient civilization in the Yucatán is only one aspect of the region's complex historical and cultural tapestry. Whatever miracles or visions may have given rise to the high Maya civilization, whatever catastrophe may have brought about its decline and fall, cannot have been any more dramatic than the events that have swept the region since it became a Spanish colony nearly five centuries ago. Travelers in the Yucatán are never far from reminders of the Spanish Colonial era. Besides the more than 70 old Franciscan mission churches still in use in towns and villages throughout the region, the abandoned mansion houses of overgrown plantations are a familiar sight along Yucatán highways and back roads. In Mérida, as well as in the smaller cities of Valladolid and Campeche, most downtown buildings date back to colonial times.

IT BEGAN QUIETLY in 1511, when two shipwrecked Spanish sailors, Jerónimo de Aguilar and Gonzalo Guerrero, were washed up half-drowned on a beach near Tulum. The first Europeans ever to set foot on the American mainland, they were promptly captured by seagoing Maya traders who brought them to the island of Cozumel, which became their home for eight years. In 1519, Hernán Cortés stopped on Cozumel in the early days of the expedition that would end with the conquest of Mexico. Aguilar was rescued, but Guerrero chose to stay with his Maya wife and family. Aguilar became a military advisor to Spanish army expeditions in the Yucatán, while Guerrero counseled the Maya chiefs on how to resist the Spanish invaders.

Guerrero's advice must have been effective, because it took 21 years for conquistador Francisco de Montejo to establish the first permanent Spanish outpost in the Yucatán. This early settlement became Campeche, now the capital city of the state of the same name. Mérida, capital of the entire peninsula in colonial times and of the state of Yucatán today, was founded two years later, in 1542, and Chetumal, capital of Quintana Roo, in 1544. Montejo's mansion still stands in downtown Mérida, across the *zócalo* from the cathedral and the government palace.

The Spanish conquest seemed to spell the end of the ancient Maya heritage. Franciscan missionaries, under the direction of notorious inquisition leader Bishop Diego de Landa, destroyed dozens of Maya temples and used the stones to build the imposing mission churches that still tower over many Maya villages today, including the great cathedral at Izamal, on the route between Mérida and Chichén Itzá and still one of the Yucatán's most impressive sights. Landa also burned the sacred books used by the native priests; only four of these Maya books are known to have been saved from the flames. At the same time, smallpox and other epidemics wiped out half the Indian population of the peninsula and drove the survivors to regroup in new communities under church guidance. The ways of the ancient Maya were forgotten—or so the conquerors believed.

For a time, the greatest problem facing the people of the Yucatán was piracy. As on the other side of the Atlantic, the British Navy fought the Spanish Armada for the right to colonize North America; England commissioned "privateers"—free-lance fighting ships—to rob Spanish gold shipments and loot Spanish seaport towns from Florida to Colombia. As lawlessness increased on the Caribbean sea route known as the Spanish Main, Dutch and French mercenaries as well as renegade Spaniards joined in the plunder.

The Yucatán became both a perfect hideout and an easy target. Campeche, the Yucatán's largest port city in Colonial times, was sacked by pirates repeatedly despite the construction of the massive stone walls that still surround the old city center today.

It was only after 1771, when two impregnable fortresses were built on the hills overlooking the city and the harbor, that pirates quit looting and burning Campeche. At the same time, the uninhabited north and east coasts provided safe havens for other infamous pirates including Jean Laffite, whose grave is in the small Yucatán fishing village of Dzilam de Bravo, and Edward "Blackbeard" Teach, who is credited with founding the isolated community of Punta Allen in what is now Quintana Roo's Sian Ka'an Biosphere Reserve.

Although they never intermarried as Indians and soldiers did in other parts of Mexico, for nearly three centuries the Spanish and Maya people of the Yucatán co-existed in peace—the Spanish as sugar cane plantation owners, the Maya as sharecroppers or church servants. But in 1821, following Mexico's declaration of independence from Spain, the new government banished the clergy, ending church protection of the Indians. Soon many Maya people found themselves brutalized as slaves. The anger that began to seethe would soon erupt in events so devastating that they would leave the Spanish Colonial culture of the Yucatán in ruins alongside the debris of the ancient Maya civilization.

After a failed 1840 attempt by civic leaders in the Yucatán to secede from Mexico and form an alliance with the breakaway republic of Texas, the Mexican government segmented the peninsula into thirds, with boundaries so straight that the three states—Yucatán on the north, Campeche on the west, and Quintana Roo on the east—look like a sliced pie. The government also established a militia of Maya army recruits in order to keep the region under federal control.

THE PLAN BACKFIRED when, in 1847, Maya soldiers turned their guns against their oppressors in history's bloodiest Indian war. The Maya people killed the entire Spanish-speaking population of the city of Valladolid, and every plantation owner in the Yucatán either fled or died. As the last remaining Spanish residents of the peninsula huddled within the besieged walls of Mérida, with the Maya insurgents poised to annihilate them, a strange thing happened: Maya astronomers announced that the time for planting had arrived. The rebel Maya army suddenly abandoned the siege of Mérida and went home to plant corn.

The conflict that became known as the War of the Castes—a reference to the complicated Spanish Colonial caste system, at this point reduced simply to Spanish versus Indian—dragged on for more than 50 years, until 1901. Except for Mexican army patrols, few Spanish-speaking people ever ventured far from the protection of the capital cities. The army systematically killed the Maya wherever they were found. By the end of the century, not only had the Spanish-speaking population of the Yucatán been reduced to half of what it had been in colonial times, but the Maya people had been almost wiped out; authorities believed that there were fewer than 300 living Maya left in the Yucatán.

But they were wrong. As many as 10,000 Indians had taken refuge deep in the forests of Quintana Roo, where, unknown to the Spanish, they had built a capital city called Chan Santa Cruz and returned to ancient Maya religious practices in newly built temples. The war ended with the Spanish capture of Chan Santa Cruz, which became the town of Felipe Carrillo Puerto. The memory of the War of the Castes lives on in rural areas of the Yucatán today in an undercurrent of distrust between the Maya and the Mexicans.

Outsiders' fascination with the Yucatán began in 1841 with the publication of *Incidents of Travel in Central America, Chiapas and Yucatán* by American explorer John Lloyd Stephens, the first popular account in English describing Maya ruins. The book and its sequel, *Incidents of Travel in Yucatán,* published two years later, ranked among the top best-sellers of their day. They would have sparked a wave of tourism in the mid-19th century had the War of the Castes not put the Yucatán off limits to gringos for the next half-century.

Popular interest in the Yucatán was revived in 1901, when the U.S. Consul to Mérida, Edward Thompson, bought the ranch where the overgrown ruins of Chichén Itzá lay and proceeded to dredge the Sacred Cenote on his property. His discoveries—not only of huge quantities of Maya artifacts, but also of enough human skeletons to give rise to romantic legends about sacrificial virgins—were taken to Harvard University with so much fanfare that Maya artifacts came into high demand on the international art market. As the War of the Castes drew to an end, hordes of archaeologists and treasure-hunters descended upon the Yucatán.

At the same time as the Maya civilization was being rediscovered, Mexican plantation owners were riding a wave of prosperity based on henequen, a plant fiber native to northern Yucatán used to make rope. Demand for rope boomed during World War I, which led to the financing of the construction of factories to strip the plants into fiber and railroad spurs to ship it to the seaport of Sisal. In a region whose economy had been destroyed by a protracted war, henequen built the elegant mansions along Mérida's Paseo de Montejo and created jobs for thousands of Maya.

But as synthetic rope materials were developed during World War II, the market for henequen collapsed, plunging landowners into bankruptcy. Plantations were abandoned and native laborers were without work. Famine swept the Yucatán, which once again became the poorest region of Mexico.

The region's terrible poverty was one reason the government decided to locate its most ambitious tourism project on the coast of the Yucatán. The ruins of Chichén Itzá and Uxmal, as well as the picturesque fishing villages, sparkling beaches, and lovely coral reefs of Cozumel and Isla Mujeres, had been attracting small numbers of adventurous travelers for decades. In 1968, FONART, the Mexican federal agency in charge of promoting resorts, ran a computer analysis and concluded that the most promising site in Mexico for development was an uninhabited barrier island the Maya people called *Can-Cun* (meaning "Bowl of Snakes").

THE ISLAND LIES ON the Caribbean, exactly the kind of turquoise, transparent, bathwater-warm sea people daydream about. And it has a unique beach. Scientists have found that its white sand contains snowflake-shaped fossils of extinct microorganisms from Jurassic times, giving it a luxuriant, almost fluffy feel. Not far offshore, coral reefs at Punta Nizuc and Punta Cancún are havens for myriad colorful fish. On the side of Isla Cancún that faces the mainland lies a wild coastline where water flows from hidden freshwater springs to form a labyrinth of channels among the mangroves. Snowy egrets and great blue herons stand statuelike or glide overhead on silent wings.

FONART presented their plan for a megaresort to more than 80 international luxury hotel corporations based in Mexico, the United States, Great Britain, Germany, and Japan: Mexico would build a huge international airport in the jungle and pave the highway all the way to Cancún, and the hotel chains would take care of the rest. Workers hacked away with machetes at the bushes to clear the way for new construction.

The plan worked brilliantly. With the opening of the first hotels in 1974, the Yucatán Peninsula was transformed from the poorest region of Mexico to the wealthiest. Since then, Cancún has taken its place among the world's leading beach resort areas, in recent years drawing more international visitors than all other destinations in Mexico combined.

Tourism has overflowed Cancún's Zona Hotelería (Hotel Zone). It fills the narrow cobblestone streets of Isla Mujeres with daily groups of sightseers. It has poured down the Caribbean coast along the segment of Highway 307 that slices straight through the jungle, flanking beaches and rocky points at a discreet distance, for 87 miles south of Cancún. It has spurred large-scale resort development on the island of Cozumel and along once-remote expanses of sand that have been transformed into sprawling hotel and recreation complexes at Playacar, Akumal, and Puerto Aventuras; this stretch of highway is now officially called the Corridor Turistico.

Yet this is no tropical paradise lost. Large-scale resort development is confined to a few, small glitzy pockets along the Corridor Turistico where the government has provided electricity, water, and other services. Far more of the coastline remains isolated and undeveloped. At plenty of remote, picture-perfect beaches along this route, the only accommodations are thatched-roof Maya-style huts with few modern conveniences. Other great beaches in the area are so little known that if you go there, yours may be the only footprints in the sand.

Visitors whose idea of the perfect vacation includes shopping for local crafts and folk art may wish to venture beyond the tourist zone. In the interior, from Chichén Itzá's souvenir stalls to the big public market in downtown Mérida, the Yucatán is a wonderland of traditional handicrafts, including beautifully embroidered dresses, hammocks, guayabera shirts, Panama hats, and carved wood replicas of ancient Maya sculptures. Such items are rare and overpriced in Cancún and the Corridor Turistico, a government designated free-trade zone where French perfumes, Italian designer fashions, Cuban cigars, and other international imports dominate the stores. Here the local art form is the T-shirt, available in dozens of colors and literally thousands of designs celebrating beaches, tequila, the sea . . .

But not snakes. The tourist office assures us that the snakes that gave Cancún its name have all moved to the southern part of the state. The reptiles most often encountered on Isla Cancún these days are little lizard-like beasts called geckos, which bring good luck according to local belief. They also attract mosquitos and eat them—which may help explain why they are unofficial local mascots. Searching for that final reminder of your Yucatán vacation? Nothing says Cancún like a gecko T-shirt.

— Richard Harris

SPANISH VOCABULARY

Note: *Mexican Spanish differs from Castilian Spanish.*

English	Spanish	Pronunciation

Basics

English	Spanish	Pronunciation
Yes/no	Sí/no	see/no
Please	Por favor	pore fah-**vore**
May I?	¿Me permite?	may pair-**mee**-tay
Thank you (very much)	(Muchas) gracias	(moo-chas) grah-see-as
You're welcome	De nada	day **nah**-dah
Excuse me	Con permiso	con pair-**mee**-so
Pardon me/ what did you say	¿Como?/Mánde?	**coh**-mo/**mahn**-dey
Could you tell me?	¿Podría decirme?	po-**dree**-ah deh-**seer**-meh
I'm sorry	Lo siento	lo see-**en**-toe
Good morning!	¡Buenos días!	**bway**-nohs **dee**-ahs
Good afternoon!	¡Buenas tardes!	**bway**-nahs **tar**-dess
Good evening!	¡Buenas noches!	**bway**-nahs **no**-chess
Goodbye!	¡Adiós!/ ¡Hasta luego!	ah-dee-**ohss**/ **ah**-stah-**lwe**-go
Mr./Mrs.	Señor/Señora	sen-**yor**/sen-**yore**-ah
Miss	Señorita	sen-yo-**ree**-tah
Pleased to meet you	Mucho gusto	**moo**-cho **goose**-to
How are you?	¿Cómo está usted?	**ko**-mo es-**tah** oo-sted
Very well, thank you	Muy bien, gracias	**moo**-ee bee-**en**, **grah**-see-as
And you?	¿Y usted?	ee oos-**ted**
Hello (on the telephone)	Bueno	**bwen**-oh

Numbers

1	un, uno	oon, **oo**-no
2	dos	dos
3	tres	trace
4	cuatro	**kwah**-tro
5	cinco	**sink**-oh
6	seis	sace
7	siete	see-**et**-ey
8	ocho	**o**-cho
9	nueve	new-**ev**-ay
10	diez	dee-**es**
11	once	**own**-sey
12	doce	**doe**-sey
13	trece	**tray**-sey
14	catorce	kah-**tor**-sey
15	quince	**keen**-sey

16	dieciséis	dee-es-ee-**sace**
17	diecisiete	dee-**es**-ee-see-**et**-ay
18	dieciocho	dee-**es**-ee-**o**-cho
19	diecinueve	dee-**es**-ee-new-**ev**-ay
20	veinte	**vain**-tay
21	veinte y uno/ veintiuno	**vain**-te-oo-no
30	treinta	**train**-tah
32	treinta y dos	train-tay-**dose**
40	cuarenta	kwah-**ren**-tah
43	cuarenta y tres	kwah-**ren**-tay-**trace**
50	cincuenta	seen-**kwen**-tah
54	cincuenta y cuatro	seen-**kwen**-tay **kwah**-tro
60	sesenta	sess-**en**-tah
65	sesenta y cinco	sess-**en**-tay **seen**-ko
70	setenta	set-**en**-tah
76	setenta y seis	set-**en**-tay **sace**
80	ochenta	oh-**chen**-tah
87	ochenta y siete	oh-**chen**-tay see-**yet**-ay
90	noventa	no-**ven**-tah
98	noventa y ocho	no-**ven**-tah **o**-cho
100	cien	see-**en**
101	ciento uno	see-en-toe **oo**-no
200	doscientos	doe-see-**en**-tohss
500	quinientos	keen-**yen**-tohss
700	setecientos	set-eh-see-**en**-tohss
900	novecientos	no-veh-see-**en**-tohss
1,000	mil	meel
2,000	dos mil	dose meel
1,000,000	un millón	oon meel-**yohn**

Colors

black	negro	**neh**-grow
blue	azul	ah-**sool**
brown	café	kah-**feh**
green	verde	**vair**-day
pink	rosa	**ro**-sah
purple	morado	mo-**rah**-doe
orange	naranja	na-**rahn**-hah
red	rojo	**roe**-hoe
white	blanco	**blahn**-koh
yellow	amarillo	ah-mah-**ree**-yoh

Days of the Week

Sunday	domingo	doe-**meen**-goh
Monday	lunes	**loo**-ness
Tuesday	martes	**mahr**-tess
Wednesday	miércoles	me-**air**-koh-less
Thursday	jueves	who-**ev**-ess
Friday	viernes	vee-**air**-ness
Saturday	sábado	**sah**-bah-doe

Months

January	enero	eh-**neh**-ro
February	febrero	feh-**brair**-oh
March	marzo	**mahr**-so
April	abril	ah-**breel**
May	mayo	**my**-oh
June	junio	**hoo**-nee-oh
July	julio	**who**-lee-yoh
August	agosto	ah-**ghost**-toe
September	septiembre	sep-tee-**em**-breh
October	octubre	oak-**too**-breh
November	noviembre	no-vee-**em**-breh
December	diciembre	dee-see-**em**-breh

Useful Phrases

Do you speak English?	¿Habla usted inglés?	**ah**-blah oos-**ted** in-**glehs**
I don't speak Spanish	No hablo español	no **ah**-blow es-pahn-**yol**
I don't understand (you)	No entiendo	no en-tee-**en**-doe
I understand (you)	Entiendo	en-tee-**en**-doe
I don't know	No sé	no **say**
I am American/ British	Soy americano(a)/ inglés(a)	soy ah-meh-ree-**kah**-no(ah)/in-**glace**(ah)
What's your name?	¿Cómo se llama usted?	**koh**-mo say **yah**-mah oos-**ted**
My name is . . .	Me llamo . . .	may **yah**-moh
What time is it?	¿Qué hora es?	keh **o**-rah es
It is one, two, three . . . o'clock	Es la una; son las dos, tres	es la **oo**-nah/sone lahs dose, trace
Yes, please/	Sí, por favor/	**see** pore fah-**vor**/
No, thank you	No, gracias	no **grah**-see-us
How?	¿Cómo?	**koh**-mo
When?	¿Cuándo?	**kwahn**-doe
This/Next week	Esta semana/ la semana que entra	**es**-tah seh-**mah**-nah/ lah say-**mah**-nah keh **en**-trah
This/Next month	Este mes/ el próximo mes	**es**-tay mehs/ el **proke**-see-mo mehs
This/Next year	Este año/ el año que viene	**es**-tay **ahn**-yo/el **ahn**-yo keh vee-**yen**-ay
Yesterday/today/ tomorrow	Ayer/hoy/mañana	ah-**yair**/oy/mahn-**yah**-nah
This morning/ afternoon	Esta mañana/ tarde	**es**-tah mahn-**yah**-nah/**tar**-day
Tonight	Esta noche	**es**-tah **no**-cheh
What?	¿Qué?	keh
What is it?	¿Qué es esto?	keh es **es**-toe
Why?	¿Por qué?	pore **keh**

Who?	¿Quién?	kee-**yen**
Where is . . . ?	¿Dónde está . . . ?	**dohn**-day es-**tah**
the train station?	la estación del tren?	la es-tah-see-**on** del **train**
the subway station?	la estación del Metro?	la es-ta-see-**on** del **meh**-tro
the bus stop?	la parada del autobús?	la pah-**rah**-dah del oh-toe-**boos**
the post office?	la oficina de correos?	la oh-fee-**see**-nah day koh-**reh**-os
the bank?	el banco?	el **bahn**-koh
the . . . hotel?	el hotel . . . ?	el oh-**tel**
the store?	la tienda . . . ?	la tee-**en**-dah
the cashier?	la caja?	la **kah**-hah
the . . . museum?	el museo . . . ?	el moo-**seh**-oh
the hospital?	el hospital?	el ohss-pea-**tal**
the elevator?	el ascensor?	el ah-**sen**-sore
the bathroom?	el baño?	el **bahn**-yoh
Here/there	Aquí/allá	ah-**key**/ah-**yah**
Open/closed	Abierto/cerrado	ah-be-**er**-toe/ ser-**ah**-doe
Left/right	Izquierda/derecha	iss-key-**er**-dah/ dare-**eh**-chah
Straight ahead	Derecho	der-**eh**-choh
Is it near/far?	¿Está cerca/lejos?	es-**tah** sair-kah/ **leh**-hoss
I'd like . . .	Quisiera . . .	kee-see-**air**-ah
a room	un cuarto/ una habitación	oon **kwahr**-toe/**oo**-nah ah-bee-tah-see-**on**
the key	la llave	lah **yah**-vay
a newspaper	un periódico	oon pear-ee-**oh**-dee-koh
a stamp	un timbre de correo	oon **team**-bray day koh-**reh**-oh
I'd like to buy . . .	Quisiera comprar . . .	kee-see-**air**-ah kohm-**prahr**
cigarettes	cigarrillo	ce-gar-**reel**-oh
matches	cerillos	ser-**ee**-ohs
a dictionary	un diccionario	oon deek-see-oh-**nah**-ree-oh
soap	jabón	hah-**bone**
a map	un mapa	oon **mah**-pah
a magazine	una revista	**oon**-ah reh-**veess**-tah
paper	papel	pah-**pel**
envelopes	sobres	**so**-brace
a postcard	una tarjeta postal	**oon**-ah tar-**het**-ah post-**ahl**
How much is it?	¿Cuánto cuesta?	**kwahn**-toe **kwes**-tah
It's expensive/cheap	Está caro/barato	es-**tah** kah-roh/ bah-**rah**-toe

A little/a lot	Un poquito/ mucho . . .	oon poh-**kee**-toe/ **moo**-choh
More/less	Más/menos	mahss/**men**-ohss
Enough/too much/ too little	Suficiente/de masiado/muy poco	soo-fee-see-**en**-tay/ day-mah-see-**ah**-doe/ **moo**-ee **poh**-koh
Telephone	Teléfono	tel-**ef**-oh-no
Telegram	Telegrama	teh-leh-**grah**-mah
I am ill/sick	Estoy enfermo(a)	es-**toy** en-**fair**-moh(ah)
Please call a doctor	Por favor llame un médico	pore fa-**vor ya**-may oon **med**-ee-koh
Help!	¡Auxilio! ¡Ayuda!	owk-**see**-lee-oh/ ah-**yoo**-dah
Fire!	¡Encendio!	en-**sen**-dee-oo
Caution!/Look out!	¡Cuidado!	kwee-**dah**-doh

On the Road

Highway	Carretera	car-ray-**ter**-ah
Causeway, paved highway	Calzada	cal-**za**-dah
Route	Ruta	**roo**-tah
Road	Camino	cah-**mee**-no
Street	Calle	**cah**-yeh
Avenue	Avenida	ah-ven-**ee**-dah
Broad, tree-lined boulevard	Paseo	pah-**seh**-oh
Waterfront promenade	Malecón	mal-lay-**cone**
Wharf	Embarcadero	em-bar-cah-**day**-ro

In Town

Church	Templo/Iglesia	**tem**-plo/e-**gles**-se-ah
Cathedral	Catedral	cah-tay-**dral**
Neighborhood	Barrio	**bar**-re-o
Foreign exchange shop	Casa de Cambio	**cas**-sah day **cam**-be-o
City Hall	Ayuntamiento	ah-yoon-tah-mee- **en**-toe
Main square	Zócalo	**zo**-cal-o
Traffic circle	Glorieta	glor-e-**ay**-tah
Market	Mercado (Spanish)/ Tianguis (Indian)	mer-**cah**-doe/ tee-**an**-geese
Inn	Posada	pos-**sah**-dah
Group taxi	Colectivo	co-lec-**tee**-vo
Group taxi along fixed route	Pesero	pi-**seh**-ro

Items of Clothing

Embroidered white smock	Huipil	whee-**peel**
Pleated man's shirt worn outside the pants	Guayabera	gwah-ya-**beh**-ra
Leather sandals	Huarache	wah-**ra**-chays
Shawl	Rebozo	ray-**bozh**-o
Pancho or blanket	Serape	seh-**ra**-peh

Dining Out

A bottle of . . .	Una botella de . . .	**oo**-nah bo-**tay**-yah deh
A cup of . . .	Una taza de . . .	**oo**-nah **tah**-sah deh
A glass of . . .	Un vaso de . . .	oon **vah**-so deh
Ashtray	Un cenicero	oon sen-ee-**seh**-roh
Bill/check	La cuenta	lah **kwen**-tah
Bread	El pan	el pahn
Breakfast	El desayuno	el day-sigh-**oon**-oh
Butter	La mantequilla	lah mahn-tay-**key**-yah
Cheers!	¡Salud!	sah-**lood**
Cocktail	Un aperitivo	oon ah-pair-ee-**tee**-voh
Dinner	La cena	lah **seh**-nah
Dish	Un plato	oon **plah**-toe
Dish of the day	El platillo de hoy	el plah-**tee**-yo day oy
Enjoy!	¡Buen provecho!	bwen pro-**veh**-cho
Fixed-price menu	La comida corrida	lah koh-**me**-dah co-**ree**-dah
Fork	El tenedor	el ten-eh-**door**
Is the tip included?	¿Está incluida la propina?	es-**tah** in-clue-**ee**-dah lah pro-**pea**-nah
Knife	El cuchillo	el koo-**chee**-yo
Lunch	La comida	lah koh-**me**-dah
Menu	La carta	lah **cart**-ah
Napkin	La servilleta	lah sair-vee-**yet**-uh
Pepper	La pimienta	lah pea-me-**en**-tah
Please give me . . .	Por favor déme	pore fah-**vor** **day**-may
Salt	La sal	lah sahl
Spoon	Una cuchara	oo-nah koo-**chah**-rah
Sugar	El azúcar	el ah-**sue**-car
Waiter!/Waitress!	¡Por favor Señor/ Señorita!	pore fah-**vor** sen-**yor**/ sen-yor-**ee**-tah

INDEX

✕ = restaurant, ▣ = hotel

A

Accessibility, *xvii*
Acuario ✕▣, 108
Air tours. ☞ Plane tours
Air travel. ☞ Plane travel
Akumal, 102–104
Alacranes Reef, 182
Alameda ✕, 161
Albatros Royale ▣, 97
Alberto's Continental Patio ✕, 161
Alejari ▣, 98
Alhambra ▣, 136
Amaro ✕, 161
Antillano ▣, 30
Apartments, *xxiv*
Aquatic Procession (festival), 10
Archaeological sights, 5–6. ☞ Maya sites and artifacts
Archaeological tours, *xxx*
Architectural heritage, 125
Arrecife ✕, 66
Art galleries and museums
Cancún, 36
Mérida, 158–159, 169
the Arts
Campeche, 137
Cancún, 31
Caribbean coast, 99
Cozumel, 74
Isla Mujeres, 51
Mérida, 167
ATMs (automated teller machines), *xxv*
Augustus Caesar ✕, 21

B

Baal Nah Kah ▣, 97
Bacalar, *115–116*
Bahía ▣, 73
Baluarte de la Soledad, *131–132*
Baluartes ▣, *135–136*
Baluarte San Carlos, 132
Baluarte Santiago, 132
Banco Chinchorro National Park, *114–115*
Banks
Campeche, 147
Cancún, 38
Caribbean coast, 120
Cozumel, 82
Isla Mujeres, 55
Mérida, 186–187
Bar La Ruina ✕, 162
Baseball, 167
Bazar Colonial ▣, *73–74*
Bazar de Artesanías Municipales (market), 159
Beaches, 4–5
Campeche State, 141, 142
Cancún, 13, 17–18

Caribbean coast, 86, 93–94, 100, 102–103, 104–105, 114
Cozumel, 59, 64–66
Isla Mujeres, 42, 46–47
Mérida/Yucatán, 151, 181
Becal, 138
Becán (Maya site), 143
Bed & Breakfast Caribo ▣, 74
Belmar ▣, 50
Better Business Bureau, *xvi*
Bicycling
Cozumel, 82
Isla Mujeres, 54
Playa del Carmen, 99
tours, xxx
Billfish tournaments, 9, 76
Bird-watching, 5
Caribbean coast, 88, 112
Isla Contoy, 42, 53–54
Yucatán State, 151
Blacky's ✕, 46
Blue Bayou ✕, 18
Boat travel. ☞ Ferry travel; Hydrofoil service
Boca Paila Fishing Lodge ✕▣, *112–113*
Boca Paila peninsula, *111–113*
Bogart's ✕, 18
Bolonchén de Rejón, 140
Bookstores
Cancún, 38
Caribbean coast, 120
Cozumel, 83
Mérida, 187
Bucanero ✕ (Cancún), 22
Bucanero ✕(Isla Mujeres), 48
Bullfights
Cancún, 33
Mérida, 167–168
Business hours, *xiv*
Bus travel, *xiii–xiv*
Campeche, 146–147
Cancún, 36, 37
Caribbean coast, 118–119
Cozumel, 82
Isla Mujeres, 55
Mérida/Yucatán State, 185, 186

C

Cabañas Ana y José ✕▣, 108
Cabañas María del Mar ▣, 50
Cabañas Paamul ✕▣, 101
Cabañas Playa Ojo de Agua ▣, 92
Cabañas Tulum ▣, 109
Caesar Park Beach & Golf Resort ▣, 25, 33
Café Caribe, 69

Cafécito ✕, 48
Cafetería Pop ✕, 162
Calakmul (Maya site), *145–146*
Calinda Viva Cancún ▣, 29
Calkiní, 138
Camcorders, *xiv*
Cameras, *xiv*
Campeche, 4, *124–148*
Cancún, 4, *12–40*
Cancún Convention Center, 15
Cancún Fair, 10
Cancún Jazz Festival, 9
Caphé-Ha ✕▣, 113
Capitán Marisco ✕, 182
Captain's Cove ✕, 21
Caribbean coast, 4, *86–122*
Caribbean Reef Club at Villa Marina ▣, 92
Caribe ▣, 164
Caribe Internacional ▣, 30
Carlos 'n Charlie's ✕(Cancún), 21
Carlos 'n Charlie's ✕(Cozumel), 68, 75
Carlos 'n Charlie's ✕(Puerto Aventuras), 101
Carnaval (Mardi Gras), 9
Car rentals, *xiv–xv*
Campeche, 147
Cancún, 38
Caribbean coast, 120
Cozumel, 83
insurance for, xv
Mérida, 187
Carriage rides, 186
Carrillo's ✕, 23
Car travel, *xix–xx*
Campeche, 147
Cancún, 36, 37
Caribbean coast, 119
Cozumel, 82
insurance for rental cars, xv
Isla Mujeres, 55
Mérida/Yucatán State, 184, 185
Casablanca ✕, 117
Casa Blanca Lodge, 113
Casa Bowen ▣, 166
Casa Cenote ✕, 108
Casa de la Cultura (Isla Mujeres), 51
Casa de las Monjas (Maya site), 173
Casa del Balam ▣, 164
Casa del Mar ▣, 73
Casa de Montejo (palace), *157–158*
Casa Mexilio ▣, 165
Casa Rolandi ✕, 21
Casa Turquesa ▣, 25
Cash machines, *xxv*
Castillo (Tulum), 107
Castillo Real (Cozumel), 61

Catedral, Campeche, *132*
Catedral, Mérida, *158*
Cave of Balancanché (Maya site), *174–175*
Cave of the Sleeping Sharks, *51–52*
Cayo Culebra, *112*
CEDAM underwater archaeology museum, *101*
Celebrity Restaurant, *20*
Celestún, *180–181*
Cemeteries, *44*
Cenote Azul, *115*
Cenote Dzitnup, *175*
Chac Mool (beach), *17*
Champotón, *142*
Chankanaab Nature Park, *61, 63*
Chankanaab Reef, *77*
Chelem, *183*
Chemuyil, *104*
Chetumal, *116–118, 119–122*
Chez Magaly ✕, *47*
Chicanná (Maya site), *144*
Chichén Itzá (Maya site), *170–174*
Chicxulub Puerto, *183*
Children, attractions for
Cozumel, *61, 63, 64*
Mérida, *158*
Children, traveling with, *xv–xvi*
Christmas events, *10*
Chumuc Mul Group (Maya site), *110*
Churches
Campeche, *132, 133*
Campeche State, *142*
Mérida, *158–159*
Yucatán State, *169*
Ciudad del Carmen, *142*
Climate, *xxxi*
Clothing for the trip, *xxvi*
Club Akumal Caribe & Villas Maya, *104*
Club de Playa ⬚, *101*
Club Grill ✕, *20*
Club Las Velas ⬚, *28–29*
Club Oasis Akumal ✕⬚, *103*
Club Oasis Puerto Aventuras ⬚, *102*
Cobá (Maya site), *101–102*
Cobá Group (Maya site), *110*
Codz-Poop (Maya temple), *179*
Colleges and universities, *160*
Colombia Reef, *77*
Colonial ⬚, *136*
Colonial customs house (Yucatán), *182*
Computers, *xiv*
Congreso del Estado building, *132*
Consulates
Cancún, *38*
Mérida, *187*

Consumer protection, *xvi*
Continental Plaza Playacar ✕⬚, *96*
Continental Plaza Puerto Aventuras ⬚, *102*
Coral reefs
Cozumel, *77–78*
Isla Contoy, *53–54*
Isla Mujeres, *44, 51*
Xcalak, *114–115*
Yucatán State, *181, 182*
Costa de Cocos (resort), *115*
Costs of the trip, *xxv*
Cozumel, *4, 58–84*
Craft shops
Campeche, *137*
Cozumel, *80–81*
Isla Mujeres, *52–53*
Mérida, *169*
Credit cards and ATMs, *xxv*
Cristalmar ⬚, *49*
Cristo de las Ampollas (statue), *158*
Croco-Cun (crocodile farm), *92–93*
Crocodile farms, *92–93*
Crossroad Pyramid (Maya site), *110*
Crown Princess Sol Caribe ⬚, *72*
Cruises, *xvi*
Cancún, *39*
Cozumel, *81*
dinner cruise, *32*
Isla Mujeres, *54*
Currency exchange, *xxv*
Customs, *xvi–xvii*

D

Da Gabi ✕, *94–95*
Dance
Cancún, *39*
Mérida, *167*
Date Group (Maya site), *173*
Day of the Dead, *10*
Day of the Immaculate Conception, *10*
Debliz ⬚, *136*
Delfin ⬚, *98*
Del Paseo ⬚, *136*
Diamond Café, *70*
Diamond Hotel & Resort, *71*
Diamond Resort ⬚, *96*
Dining, *xvii–xviii, 5.* ☞ Restaurants
Disabilities, *xviii*
Discos
Campeche City, *137*
Cancún, *32*
Cozumel, *75*
Mérida, *167*
Discounts, *xviii–xix*
Diving. ☞ Scuba diving and snorkeling
Dr. Alfredo Barrera Marin Botanical Gardens, *93*
Doctors and dentists
Campeche, *148*
Cancún, *38*

Caribbean coast, *121*
Cozumel, *83*
Dolores Alba ⬚ (Chichén Itzá), *174*
Dolores Alba ⬚ (Mérida), *166*
Dolphins, swimming with, *52*
Driving. ☞ Car travel
Duties, *xvi–xvii*
Dzibanché (Maya site), *118*
Dzibilchaltún (Maya site), *181–182*
Dzibilnocac (Maya site), *141*
Dzilam de Bravo, *184*

E

Ecotourism, *120–121, 126*
Edzná (Maya site), *139–140*
El Bocadito ✕⬚, *111*
El Capi Navegante ✕, *68–69*
El Caracol (Maya astronomical observatory), *173*
El Castillo (Maya site), *170*
El Cedral (Maya site), *61, 63*
El Centenario Zoological Park, *158*
El Día de Los Reyes (feast), *9*
Electricity, *xx–xxi*
El Faisán y El Venado ✕⬚, *114*
El Foco ✕, *70*
El Garrafón National Park, *44, 51*
El Mesón del Marqués ⬚, *175*
El Mexicano ✕, *21*
El Moro ✕, *70*
El Pescador ✕, *23*
El Playon, *142*
El Pueblito Beach Hotel, *29–30*
El Regis ⬚, *136*
El Tacolote ✕ (Cancún), *24*
El Tacolote ✕ (Playa del Carmen), *95*
El Tigre (Maya site), *146*
El Tucan Condotel ⬚, *97*
Emergencies
Campeche, *148*
Cancún, *38*
Caribbean coast, *120*
Cozumel, *83*
Isla Mujeres, *55*
Mérida, *187*
road service, *xx*
Emiliano's ✕, *117*
Equinox celebrations, *9*
Ermita de Santa Isabel (Jesuit monastery), *158*
Ethnographic museum, Valladolid, *175*
Eurohotel, *143*
Exchanging money, *xxv*
Express ✕, *162*

Ex-Templo de San José (church), *132–133*

F

Felipe Carrillo Puerto, *114*
Ferry travel, *xxi*
Cancún, *37*
Caribbean coast, *119*
Cozumel, *81*
Isla Mujeres, *54*
Festivals and seasonal events, *9–10, 31*
Fiesta Americana Cancún 🏨, *25–26*
Fiesta Americana Condesa 🏨, *26*
Fiesta Americana Coral Beach Cancún 🏨, *26*
Fiesta Americana Cozumel Reef 🏨, *72–73*
Fiesta Americana Mérida 🏨, *163*
Fiesta Inn, *73*
Fiesta of Isla Mujeres, *10*
Fiesta of Our Lord of the Blisters, *9*
Fiesta of San Román, *9*
Fiesta of the Christ of Sitilpech, *9*
Fiesta of the Virgin of the Conception, *10*
Film
Campeche, *137*
Cancún, *31*
Cozumel, *74*
Mérida, *167*
Fishing, *5*
Campeche, *137*
Cancún, *33–34*
Caribbean coast, *87, 92*
Cozumel, *59, 76*
Isla Mujeres, *43, 51*
tour operators, *xxx*
Yucatán State, *152*
Five-Story Pyramid (Maya site), *173*
Folkloric shows, *31, 167*
Forts
Campeche City, *131, 132, 133*
Campeche State, *142*
Caribbean coast, *115*
Fuerte de San Felipe, *115*
Fuerte de San Jose, *133*
Fuerte de San Luis, *142*
Fuerte de San Miguel, *133*

G

Galápago Inn, *73*
Gay and lesbian travelers, hints for, *xxi*
Glass-bottom-boat trips, *83–84*
Golf
Cancún, *33*
Mérida, *168*
Playa del Carmen, *99*
Golf cart, travel by, *55*
Gottdiener Museum, *158–159*

Government tourist offices, *xxx–xxxi*
Gran Acrópolis (Maya site), *139*
Gran Hotel, *165*
Grocery stores, *36, 53*
Group of the Thousand Columns (Maya site), *173*
Guided tours
Campeche, *147–148*
Cancún, *38–39*
Caribbean coast, *120–121*
Cozumel, *83–84*
Isla Mujeres, *55–56*
Mérida/Yucatán, *187–188*

H

Hacienda Chichén 🏨, *174*
Hacienda de la Tortuga (condominium), *103*
Hacienda El Mortero ✕, *20*
Hacienda Gomar ✕, *46*
Hacienda Katanchel 🏨, *163*
Hacienda Mundaca (estate), *44, 46*
Hacienda Uxmal 🏨, *178*
Halachó, *139*
Hammock Festival, *9*
Health and fitness clubs, *33*
Health concerns, *xxi–xxii*
Health insurance, *xxii*
Hecelchacán, *138*
Hochob (Maya site), *141*
Holiday Inn Centro Cancún 🏨, *30*
Holidays, national, *xxii*
Holy Cross fiestas, *9*
Home exchanges, *xxiv*
Hopelchén, *140*
Hormiguero (Maya site), *144*
Horseback tours, *834*
Hostels, *xxvii–xxviii*
Hotel El Conquistador, *165*
Hotel Felicidades, *181*
Hotel Gutiérrez, *183*
Hotel María del Carmen, *183*
Hotel Mucuy, *166*
Hotels, *xxiii–xxiv*
Campeche, *126, 135–136, 143, 144*
Cancún, *13, 24–31*
Caribbean coast, *87–88, 92, 96–99, 101–102, 103–104, 108–109, 111, 113, 114, 115, 117–118*
children, accommodations for, *xv*
Cozumel, *8, 71–74*
Isla Mujeres, *8, 43, 49–51*
Mérida, *152, 163–167*
Yucatán State, *173–174, 175, 178–179, 181, 183*
Hotel Zacarias, *143*
House of the Phalli (Maya site), *173*
Hunting, *5, 137*
Hyatt Cancún Caribe Villas & Resort, *26*

Hyatt Regency Cancún 🏨, *29*
Hyatt Regency Mérida 🏨, *164*
Hydrofoil service, *81*

I

Iglesia de Jesús, *158–159*
Iglesia de San Francisco, *133*
Iglesia de San Francisquito, *133*
Iglesia de San Román, *133–134*
Independence Day, *9*
Insurance, *xxii–xxiii*
International Billfish Tournament, *76*
Inter Plaza, *15*
Isla Contoy, *53–54*
Isla del Carmen, *142–143*
Isla de Pájaros, *112*
Isla de Pasión, *63*
Isla Holbox, *184–185*
Isla Mujeres, *4, 42–56*
Itinerary recommendations
Campeche, *127*
Caribbean coast, *88–89*
Mérida/Yucatán, *154–155*
Itzankanac, *142*
Izamal, *169–170*

J

Jalapeños ✕, *21–22*
Jazz festivals, *9, 31*
Jewelry shops, *80, 169*
Jogging, *33*
Juan Gamboa Guzmán Painting Museum, *158–159*

K

Kabah (Maya site), *179*
Kinich Kakmó (pyramid), *169–170*
Kohunlich (Maya site), *118*
Krystal Cancún 🏨, *29*
Kukulcán Group (Maya site), *110*

L

La Bella Epoca ✕, *161*
Labná (Maya site), *179*
La Cabaña del Pescador ✕, *66, 68*
La Casona ✕, *161–162*
La Choza ✕, *69*
La Dolce Vita ✕, *20*
La Fisheria ✕, *20*
La Flama ✕, *143*
Laguna Colombia, *61, 63*
Laguna de Bacalar, *115*
Laguna de Terminos, *142*
Laguna de Xcacel, *104–105*
Laguna Makax, *46*
Laguna Milagrosa, *117*
Laguna Rosada, *183*
La Habichuela ✕, *23*
La Lunita ✕, *103*
Language, *xxiii*

La Parrilla ✕(Cancún), 23–24
La Parrilla ✕(Playa del Carmen), 95
La Perla ✕, 135
La Pigua ✕, 135
La Placita ✕, 95
Laptops, *xiv*
Las Molcas ✕🏨, 98
Las Palapas 🏨, 98
Las Palapas ✕, 178
Las Palmeras ✕, 69
Las Pinturas Group (Maya site), 110
Lighthouses
Cozumel, 63, 64
Isla Mujeres, 46, 51
Yucatán State, 181
Limones ✕, 95
Lodging. *xxiii–xxiv.* ☞ Hotels
Lolche (market), 109
Loltún Caves, 179
Loncheria La Lomita ✕, 49
Lopez 🏨, 136
Lorenzillos ✕, 20
Los Almendros ✕(Merida), 162
Los Almendros ✕(Ticul), 179–180
Los Arrecifes 🏨, 92
Los Cocos 🏨, 118
Los Cuevones coral reef, 52
Los Manchones coral reef, 52
Los Pelícanos 🏨, 92
Luggage, *xxvi*

M

Macanxoc Group (Maya site), 110
Madagascar Reef, 181
Mail, *xxiv*
Campeche, 148
Cancún, 39
Caribbean coast, 121
Cozumel, 84
Isla Mujeres, 56
Mérida, 188
Mandinga ✕, 117
Mansión Carvajal, 134
Maracaibo Reef, 77
Marganzo ✕, 135
Margarita Cancún 🏨, 30
María del Carmen 🏨, 165
Maria del Lourdes 🏨, 30
María del Luz 🏨, 175
Maria's Kan Kin ✕, 47
Marinas, 34
Markets, 134, 159, 168
Marriott CasaMagna 🏨, 26
Mary Carmen 🏨, 74
Máscaras ✕, 95
Maya-Bric 🏨, 98
Mayaland 🏨, 173–174
Mayan Beach Resort ✕🏨, 183–184
Mayan Paradise 🏨, 96
Mayapán (Maya site), 180

Maya sites and artifacts, 5–6
Campeche State, 126, 139–140, 141, 143, 144, 145–146
Cancún, 12, 15, 17
Caribbean coast, 88, 100, 105–108, 109–111, 113–114, 118, 121
Cozumel, 61, 63, 64
guided tours, 121
Isla Mujeres, 46
Yucatán State, 153, 170–175, 176–178, 179, 181–182
Medical assistance companies, *xxii*
Medical services. ☞ Emergencies; Doctors and dentists
Meliá Cancún 🏨, 26–27
Meliá Mayan Peradisus 🏨, 71–72
Mercado de Artesanías "García Rejón," 159
Mercado Municipal, Campeche, 134
Mercado Municipal, Mérida, 159
Mérida, 4, 150–169, 185–189
Mérida Misión Park Inn Plaza, 165–166
Mesón del Bucanero 🏨, 50
Mesón San Miguel 🏨, 74
Mexico Divers (bungalows), 51
Mikado ✕, 21
Miramar ✕, 135
Mirtita's ✕, 49
Monasteries
Campeche State, 138
Mérida, 158
Yucatán State, 169
Monastery of St. Anthony of Padua, 169
Money, *xxiv–xxv*
Mopeds and motorcycles
Cancún, 37
Cozumel, 82
Isla Mujeres, 55
Morgan's ✕, 69
Motul, 184
Movies. ☞ Film
Museo Arqueólogico del Camino Real, 138
Museo Cultural Maya, 133
Museo de Armas y Barcos, 133
Museo de Arte Popular, Mérida, 159
Museo de la Ciudad, Mérida, 159
Museo de la Isla de Cozumel, 64
Museo de los Estela Dr. Roman Pina Chan, 132
Museo Graficode la Ciudad, 132

Museum of Anthropology and History, Isla del Carmen, 142
Museum of Anthropology and History, Mérida, 159
Museum of Maya Culture, 116–117
Museums. ☞ Art galleries and museums
Campeche, 131, 132, 133
Campeche State, 138, 142
Cancún, 15
Caribbean coast, 101, 116–117
Cozumel, 64
Isla Contoy, 53
Isla del Carmen, 142
Mérida, 158, 159
Yucatán State, 175, 182, 184
Music, popular
Cancún, 32
Cozumel, 75
Mérida, 167
Muyil (Maya site), 113–114

N

Na-Balam 🏨, 50
National holidays, *xxii*
National Institute of Anthropology and History, 15
Nature watching, 88
New Year's Day celebration, 9
Nicte-Ha ✕(Mérida), 163
Nicte-Ha ✕(Uxmal), 178
Nightlife
Campeche, 137
Cancún, 13–14, 31–32
Caribbean coast, 99
Cozumel, 75
Isla Mujeres, 51
Mérida, 167
Nohoch Mul Group (Maya site), 110
Nuestra Señora de las Mercedes (church), 142
Nunnery (Maya site), 177

O

Older travelers, hints for, *xxvii*
Omni Cancún 🏨, 27
100% Natural ✕, 22
Outdoor activities. ☞ Sports
Oxkintoc, 139

P

Paamul, 100–101
Packages and tours, *xxix–xxx*
Packing, *xxvi*
Palace of the Governor (Maya site), 177–178
Palace of the Masks (Maya site), 179
Palacio Cantón, 159

Palacio del Gobierno (Campeche), *134*
Palacio del Gobierno, Mérida, *159–160*
Palacio Municipal, Mérida, *160*
Palancar beach, *65*
Palancar Reef, *78*
Pancho's ✕, *162*
Pancho's Backyard ✕, *69*
Paraíso Reef, *78*
Parks, national
Caribbean coast, 114–115
Isla Mujeres, 44, 51
Yucatán state, 184
Parque Hidalgo (Mérida), *160*
Parque Natural del Flamenco Mexicano, *180–181*
Parque Principal (Campeche), *134*
Parque Santa Lucía (Mérida), *160*
Paseo El Cedral (reef), *78*
Passports, *xxvi–xxvii*
Payucán, *141*
Pelican Inn, *98*
Pepe's Grill, *68*
Pérez Island, *182*
Perico's ✕, *24*
Perla del Caribe 🏨, *50*
Peso, *xxiv–xxv*
Pharmacies
Cancún, 39
Caribbean coast, 121
Cozumel, 84
Isla Mujeres, 56
Mérida, 189
Photographers, tips for, *xiv*
Piamonte ✕, *142*
Pirámide de los Cinco Pisos (Maya site), *139*
Pirámide Inn Resort and RV Park, *174*
Pisté, *174*
Pizza Bella ✕, *163*
Pizza Rolandi ✕(Cozumel), *70*
Pizza Rolandi ✕(Isla Mujeres), *49*
Pizzeria Rolandi's ✕, *24*
Plane tours
Cancún, 38
Cozumel, 83
Plane travel, *xii–xiii*
Campeche, 147
Cancún, 36–37
Caribbean coast, 119–120
children, rules for, xv–xvi
Cozumel, 81–82
discounts, xviii–xix
luggage rules, xxvi
Mérida, 185–186
Plane wreck, scuba dive to, *78*
Playa Ballenas, *17–18*
Playa Benjamin, *142*
Playa Bonita, *141*

Playa Chen Río, *66*
Playa Cocoteros. ☞ Playa Norte
Playa Corona, *65*
Playa del Carmen, *93–100, 119–122*
Playa Delfines, *17–18*
Playa del Sol, *65*
Playa Lancheros, *47*
Playa Norte, *46–47*
Playa Oriente, *66*
Playa Paradiso, *65*
Playa Paraíso, *47*
Playa San Francisco, *65*
Playa San Juan, *65*
Playa Santa Pilar, *65*
Playa Tortugas, *17*
Plaza Carrillo's 🏨, *30*
Plaza Las Glorias 🏨, *72*
Plaza Leza ✕, *70*
Poc-Na 🏨, *50*
Pok-Ta-Pok golf course, *33*
Pórtico del Peregrino ✕, *162*
Posada Amor 🏨, *92*
Posada del Capitán Lafitte 🏨, *93*
Posada del Mar 🏨, *50, 51*
Posada Lucy 🏨, *31*
Posada Toledo 🏨, *166*
Presidente Inter-Continental Cancún 🏨, *27*
Presidente Inter-Continental Cozumel 🏨, *72*
Prima Pasta & Pizza Trattoria ✕, *70*
Príncipe 🏨, *118*
Progreso, *182–183*
Progreso 🏨, *183*
Publications
Cancún, 39
Cozumel, 84
Isla Mujeres, 56
Pueblo Maya (museum), *182*
Pueblo Maya (pseudo Maya village), *174*
Puerta de Tierra (city gate), *134*
Puerto Aventuras, *101–102*
Puerto Morelos, *91–93*
Punta Allen, *112*
Punta Bete, *93*
Punta Celerain, *65*
Punta Celerain Lighthouse, *61, 63–64*
Punta Chiqueros, *65–66*
Punta Molas, *64, 66*
Punta Molas Lighthouse, *64*
Punta Morena, *66*
Punta Norte, *47*

R
Ramada Ecovillage Resort, *144*
Ramada Inn, Campeche, *135*
Rancho Encantado ✕🏨, *115–116*
Red Eye Café, *49*
Regatta al Sol, *9*

Residencial 🏨, *166*
Restaurante del Museo, *64*
Restaurante La Peña, *51*
Restaurants, *xvii–xviii*
Campeche, 125, 135, 142–143
Cancún, 13, 18, 20–24
Caribbean coast, 86–87, 92, 94–96, 100, 101, 103, 108, 114, 117
Cozumel, 59, 64, 66, 68–70
Isla Mujeres, 43, 46, 47–49
Mérida, 151–152, 161–163
Yucatán State, 178, 182–183
Restaurant Xcaret, *100*
Río Bec (Maya site), *144–145*
Río Hondo, *117*
Río Lagartos National Park, *184*
Ritz Carlton Cancún 🏨, *27*
Rodeos, *31*
Rosa Mexicano ✕, *24*
Royal Maeva Playacar🏨, *96–97*
Royal Solaris Caribe 🏨, *29*
Ruinas del Rey (Maya site), *15, 17*
Ruins. ☞ Maya sites and artifacts
Rutilio's y Chimbo's ✕, *47*

S
Sabor ✕, *95–96*
Sacred Well (Maya site), *172*
Safety, *xxvii*
Sailboarding, *34*
San Bernardino church and convent, *175*
San Francisco Reef, *78*
San Gervasio (Maya site), *61, 64*
San Juan beach, *65*
San Miguel, *61, 64*
San Miguelito (Maya site), *17*
Santa Lucía ✕, *163*
Santa Pilar beach, *65*
Santa Rosa Wall, *78*
Santiago's Grill, *69*
Savio's ✕, *22*
Sayil (Maya site), *179*
Scuba diving and snorkeling, *6*
Cancún, 34
Caribbean coast, 87, 92–93, 99, 102, 104
Cozumel, 59, 60, 76–79
decompression sickness, 76
health concerns, xxii
Isla Contoy, 53–54
Isla Mujeres, 43, 51–52
Security, *xxvii*
Senior citizens, *xxvii*
Sergio's ✕, *117*
Seybaplaya, *141*
Shangri-La Caribe 🏨, *97*

Ship travel. ☞ Cruises; Ferry travel
Shooters Waterfront Cafe, U.S.A., 22
Shopping, *xxvii*
Campeche, 137–138
Cancún, 34–36
Cozumel, 60, 79–81
Isla Mujeres, 52–53
Mérida, 168–169:
Playa del Carmen, 99–100
Tulum, 109
Yucatán State, 153–154
Sian Ka'an (reserve) 111–113
Sian Ka'an ☒, 183
Sierra Cancún☒, 27–28
Single travelers, hints for, *xxix*
Sisal, 181
Sitilpech village, 9
Snorkeling. ☞ Scuba diving and snorkeling
Soberanis ✕, 183
Sol a Sol International Regatta, 9
Spanish-language school, 188
Splash ✕, 22
Sports
Campeche, 137
Cancún, 33–34
Caribbean coast, 87, 92, 93, 99, 102, 104
Cozumel, 75–79
Isla Mujeres, 51–52
Mérida, 167–168
Sports Page Video Bar and Restaurant, 70
Student and youth travel, *xxvii–xxviii*
Submarine cruises, 39, 83–84
Suites Elizabeth ☒, 74
Sun Palace ☒, 28

T

Tan-Kah, 105
Taxes, *xxviii*
Taxis
Campeche, 147
Cancún, 37
Caribbean coast, 120
Cozumel, 82
Isla Mujeres, 55
Mérida, 186
Teatro Peón Contreras, 160
Telchac Puerto, 183–184
Telephones, *xxviii*
Campeche, 148
Cancún, 40
Caribbean coast, 121
Cozumel, 84

Isla Mujeres, 56
Mérida, 188
Temple of the Descending God (Maya site), 107
Temple of the Frescoes (Maya site), 107
Temple of the Jaguar (Maya site), 173
Temple of the Seven Dolls (Maya site), 181–182
Temple of the Three Lintels (Maya site), 173
Temple of the Warriors (Maya site), 173
Tennis, 168
Theme trips, *xxx*
Ticul, 179–180
Timing the visit, *xxxi*
Campeche, 130
Caribbean coast, 89
Mérida/Yucatán, 156–157
Tipping, *xxviii*
Tizimín, 184
Tomb of the High Priest (Maya site), 173
Tony Rome's ✕, 69
Tormentos Reef, 78
Tortuga Marina Turtle Farm, 46
Tour operators, *xxviii–xxx*
Campeche, 148
Cancún, 40
Cozumel, 84
Isla Mujeres, 56
Mérida/Yucatán, 188
Travel agencies, *xxx*
Campeche, 148
Cancún, 40
Caribbean coast, 122
Cozumel, 84
Isla Mujeres, 56
Mérida/Yucatán, 188
Travel gear, *xxx*
Traveler's checks, *xxv*
Trinidad Galeria ☒, 167
Tropical Inn ☒, 30–31
Tulum (Maya site), 84, 105–109
Tulum (village), 105–109
Tzompantli (Maya site), 172

U

U.S. Government Travel Briefings, *xxx–xxxi*
Universidad Autonoma de Yucatán, 160
Uxmal (Maya site), 176–179

V

Valladolid, 175
Vaquerías (traditional cattle-branding feasts), 9
Velazquez ✕, 49

Villa Arqueológica Cobá ✕☒, 111
Villa Arqueológica Uxmal ☒, 177–178
Villa del Mar ✕, 49
Villa Deportiva Juvenil Cancún ☒, 30
Villa Las Anclas ☒, 73
Villa rentals, *xxiv*
Villas de las Palmas ☒, 104
Villas Tacul ☒, 28
Visas, *xxvi–xxvii*
Visitor information, *xxxi*
Campeche, 148
Cancún, 39, 40
Caribbean coast, 122
Cozumel, 84
Isla Mujeres, 56
Mérida/Yucatán, 189

W

Water sports, 6
Cancún, 14, 33–34
Caribbean coast, 92, 93
Weather information, *xxxi*
Westin Regina Resort Cancún ☒, 28
Wildlife preserves
Caribbean coast, 111–112
Cozumel, 61, 63
Isla Contoy, 53–54
Yucatán State, 180–181
Women, hints for, *xxvii*

X

Xcalak, 114–115
Xcaret (Maya site), 84, 100
Xel-Há, 84, 105
Xicalango (archaeological site), 142
Xlacah cenote, 182
Xlaches reef, 51
Xpuhá, 102
Xpujil (Maya site), 144

Y

Yalkú, 103
Yamil Lu'um (Maya site), 17
Yaxcopoil (17th-century hacienda), 180
Youth hostels, *xxvii–xxviii*
Cancún, 30
Isla Mujeres, 50
Yucab Reef, 78
Yucalpetén, 183
Yucatán State, 4, 150–189. ☞ Mérida

Z

Zaragoza Park, 142
Zazil-Ha ✕, 48
Zoos, 92–93, 158

NOTES

NOTES

NOTES

NOTES

NOTES

NOTES

NOTES

Fodor's Travel Publications

Available at bookstores everywhere, or call 1–800–533–6478, 24 hours a day.

Gold Guides

U.S.

Alaska	Florida	New Orleans	Seattle & Vancouver
Arizona	Hawai'i	New York City	The South
Boston	Las Vegas, Reno, Tahoe	Pacific North Coast	U.S. & British Virgin Islands
California		Philadelphia & the Pennsylvania Dutch Country	USA
Cape Cod, Martha's Vineyard, Nantucket	Los Angeles		Virginia & Maryland
	Maine, Vermont, New Hampshire	The Rockies	Walt Disney World, Universal Studios and Orlando
The Carolinas & Georgia	Maui & Lāna'i	San Diego	
Chicago	Miami & the Keys	San Francisco	Washington, D.C.
Colorado	New England	Santa Fe, Taos, Albuquerque	

Foreign

Australia	Europe	Montréal & Québec City	Scotland
Austria	Florence, Tuscany & Umbria	Moscow, St. Petersburg, Kiev	Singapore
The Bahamas			South Africa
Belize & Guatemala	France	The Netherlands, Belgium & Luxembourg	South America
Bermuda	Germany		Southeast Asia
Canada	Great Britain	New Zealand	Spain
Cancún, Cozumel, Yucatán Peninsula	Greece	Norway	Sweden
	Hong Kong	Nova Scotia, New Brunswick, Prince Edward Island	Switzerland
Caribbean	India		Thailand
China	Ireland		Toronto
Costa Rica	Israel	Paris	Turkey
Cuba	Italy	Portugal	Vienna & the Danube
The Czech Republic & Slovakia	Japan	Provence & the Riviera	
	London		
Eastern & Central Europe	Madrid & Barcelona	Scandinavia	
	Mexico		

Special-Interest Guides

Adventures to Imagine	Fodor's Gay Guide to the USA	Halliday's New Orleans Food Explorer	Rock & Roll Traveler USA
Alaska Ports of Call	Fodor's How to Pack	Healthy Escapes	Sunday in San Francisco
Ballpark Vacations	Great American Learning Vacations	Kodak Guide to Shooting Great Travel Pictures	Walt Disney World for Adults
Caribbean Ports of Call			
The Official Guide to America's National Parks	Great American Sports & Adventure Vacations	National Parks and Seashores of the East	Weekends in New York
Disney Like a Pro	Great American Vacations	National Parks of the West	Wendy Perrin's Secrets Every Smart Traveler Should Know
Europe Ports of Call	Great American Vacations for Travelers with Disabilities	Nights to Imagine	
Family Adventures		Rock & Roll Traveler Great Britain and Ireland	

Fodor's Special Series

Fodor's Best Bed & Breakfasts

America

California

The Mid-Atlantic

New England

The Pacific Northwest

The South

The Southwest

The Upper Great Lakes

Compass American Guides

Alaska

Arizona

Boston

Chicago

Colorado

Hawaii

Idaho

Hollywood

Las Vegas

Maine

Manhattan

Minnesota

Montana

New Mexico

New Orleans

Oregon

Pacific Northwest

San Francisco

Santa Fe

South Carolina

South Dakota

Southwest

Texas

Utah

Virginia

Washington

Wine Country

Wisconsin

Wyoming

Citypacks

Amsterdam

Atlanta

Berlin

Chicago

Florence

Hong Kong

London

Los Angeles

Montréal

New York City

Paris

Prague

Rome

San Francisco

Tokyo

Venice

Washington, D.C.

Exploring Guides

Australia

Boston & New England

Britain

California

Canada

Caribbean

China

Costa Rica

Egypt

Florence & Tuscany

Florida

France

Germany

Greek Islands

Hawaii

Ireland

Israel

Italy

Japan

London

Mexico

Moscow & St. Petersburg

New York City

Paris

Prague

Provence

Rome

San Francisco

Scotland

Singapore & Malaysia

South Africa

Spain

Thailand

Turkey

Venice

Flashmaps

Boston

New York

San Francisco

Washington, D.C.

Fodor's Gay Guides

Los Angeles & Southern California

New York City

Pacific Northwest

San Francisco and the Bay Area

South Florida

USA

Pocket Guides

Acapulco

Aruba

Atlanta

Barbados

Budapest

Jamaica

London

New York City

Paris

Prague

Puerto Rico

Rome

San Francisco

Washington, D.C.

Languages for Travelers (Cassette & Phrasebook)

French

German

Italian

Spanish

Mobil Travel Guides

America's Best Hotels & Restaurants

California and the West

Major Cities

Great Lakes

Mid-Atlantic

Northeast

Northwest and Great Plains

Southeast

Southwest and South Central

Rivages Guides

Bed and Breakfasts of Character and Charm in France

Hotels and Country Inns of Character and Charm in France

Hotels and Country Inns of Character and Charm in Italy

Hotels and Country Inns of Character and Charm in Paris

Hotels and Country Inns of Character and Charm in Portugal

Hotels and Country Inns of Character and Charm in Spain

Short Escapes

Britain

France

New England

Near New York City

Fodor's Sports

Golf Digest's Places to Play

Skiing USA

USA Today The Complete Four Sport Stadium Guide

CNN Airport Network

Your Window To The World While You're On The Road

Keep in touch when you're traveling. Before you take off, tune in to CNN Airport Network. Now available in major airports across America, CNN Airport Network provides nonstop news, sports, business, weather and lifestyle programming. Both domestic and international. All piloted by the top-flight global resources of CNN. All up-to-the-minute reporting. And just for travelers, CNN Airport Network features intriguing segments such as "Travel Facts." With an information source like Fodor's this series of fascinating travel trivia will definitely make time fly while you're waiting to board. SO KEEP YOUR WINDOW TO THE WORLD WIDE OPEN. ESPECIALLY WHEN YOU'RE ON THE ROAD. TUNE IN TO CNN AIRPORT NETWORK TODAY.

WHEREVER YOU TRAVEL, *H*ELP IS NEVER FAR AWAY.

From planning your trip to providing travel assistance along the way, American Express® Travel Service Offices are always there to help.

> ### *Cancun*

American Express Travel Service
Av. Tulum 208 Esq Agua
Supermanzana
98/84-19-99

Travel

http://www.americanexpress.com/travel

American Express Travel Service Offices are found in central locations throughout Mexico.